THE SPIRIT OF PRAISE

Edited by

Monique M. Ingalls and Amos Yong

THE
SPIRIT OF
PRAISE

Music and Worship in Global
Pentecostal-Charismatic Christianity

The Pennsylvania State University Press
University Park, Pennsylvania

Library of Congress Cataloging-in-Publication Data

The spirit of praise : music and worship in global Pentecostal-
Charismatic Christianity /
edited by Monique M. Ingalls and Amos Yong.
pages   cm
Summary: "A collection of essays exploring musical sounds
and worship practices within Pentecostal Charismatic
Christianity. Combines ethnographic case studies
with theoretical reflection informed by social science,
musicological, religious studies, and theological approaches,
resulting in a multidisciplinary analysis of a global
phenomenon"—Provided by publisher.
Includes bibliographical references and index.
ISBN 978-0-271-06662-2 (cloth : alk. paper)
ISBN 978-0-271-06663-9 (pbk. : alk. paper)
1. Music—Religious aspects—Pentecostal churches.
2. Worship.
3. Pentecostal churches.
I. Ingalls, Monique Marie, editor. II. Yong, Amos, editor.

ML3921.4.P46S65 2015
264.2—dc23
2014048713

CONTENTS

Preface | vii

Introduction: Interconnection, Interface, and Identification
in Pentecostal-Charismatic Music and Worship | 1
Monique M. Ingalls

PART I: HEALING, RENEWAL, AND REVITALIZATION

1   Musical Bodies in the Charismatic Renewal:
The Case of Catch the Fire and Soaking Prayer | 29
Peter Althouse and Michael Wilkinson

2   Salvation (Not Yet?) Materialized: Healing as Possibility and
Possible Complication for Expressing Suffering in
Pentecostal Music and Worship | 45
Andrew M. McCoy

3   Dreaming Urban Indigenous Australian Christian Worship
in the Great Southland of the Holy Spirit | 60
Tanya Riches

4   Every Creative Aspect Breaking Out! Pentecostal-Charismatic
Worship, Oro Gospel Music, and a Millennialist
Aesthetic in Papua New Guinea | 78
Michael Webb

5   Worship Music as Aesthetic Domain of Meaning and Bonding:
The Glocal Context of a Dutch Pentecostal Church | 97
Miranda Klaver

PART II: NEGOTIATING TRADITIONS IN TRANSITION

6   "This Is Not the Warm-Up Act!": How Praise and Worship Reflects
Expanding Musical Traditions and Theology in a Bapticostal
Charismatic African American Megachurch | 117
Birgitta J. Johnson

7   Singing the Lord's Song in the Spirit and with Understanding:
The Practice of Nairobi Pentecostal Church | 133
Jean Ngoya Kidula

PREFACE

This has been an enormously rewarding journey for us as coeditors. The genesis of this volume now lies amid a triangulating convergence of trajectories: Amos sensing that the theme of global renewal music and worship needed sustained and interdisciplinary consideration; Monique's scholarly research, which engaged with renewal music and worship themes, and her conference organizational work, which produced a network of enthusiastic contributors; and Amos finding Monique through what could only have been a series of providential events and their discerning a compatibility of interests, expertise, and work ethic. The result is that we have both been blessed to have navigated this path together, each learning a great deal about topics that the other knows much about. We could not have predicted, when embarking on this journey three years ago, how smoothly it would go and how remarkably complementary we would be for this interdisciplinary undertaking. We also could not have predicted how well this volume would fit into and exemplify the increasing cross-pollination of our disciplines more broadly, as religious and theological studies increasingly seek ways to integrate sound and music studies approaches, and as ethnomusicologists express a renewed and sustained interest in sacred and religious musical traditions. Illustrating this convergence of interest are the two parallel conferences from which many of the chapters in this volume arose: the 2011 American Academy of Religion's Pentecostal-Charismatic Movements Group session on music (co-organized by Amos) and the 2011 Christian Congregational Music: Local and Global Perspectives conference at Ripon College Cuddesdon, Oxford (co-organized by Monique).

We are also grateful to the contributors of this volume for their diligent and timely efforts. Patrick Alexander at The Pennsylvania State University Press was the one who initially expressed interest in publishing the book, and Kathryn Yahner at the press has been a wonderful and responsive editor. Both editors and contributors are thankful to Julie Schoelles for her thorough and constructive comments during the copyediting process. Vince Le, Enoch Charles, and Ryan Seow, Amos's graduate assistants, have helped variously in the editorial process, including with the index.

Introduction:
Interconnection, Interface, and Identification in Pentecostal-Charismatic Music and Worship

Monique M. Ingalls

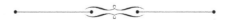

The latter half of the twentieth century witnessed the rapid growth of pentecostalism as the public face of Christianity in many parts of the world. With adherents currently estimated at five hundred million—nearly one-quarter of the world's total Christians—pentecostal growth shows no signs of abating as the twenty-first century progresses. Diverse yet recognizable expressions of corporate worship and music making are hallmark features of pentecostal spirituality across the broad reach of the movement. Music and worship practices have long served as key elements in the global reach of pentecostal Christianity, often accompanying conversions on a large scale, transforming existing institutions, and influencing churches across the spectrum of Christian belief and practice. Moving along pathways formed by mass mediation, migration, and missionization, pentecostal music and worship evidence and spur on religious globalization, as songs from influential pentecostal churches—and the record companies and media industry to which they are often intimately connected—make their way into in churches across denominational lines. "Praise and worship,"[1] a term that refers both to a segment of pentecostal church services and to the musical practices and songs used within it, has become one of the most widely diffused Christian congregational worship styles and song repertoires worldwide. These songs and their associated worship practices travel around the world to be adopted, adapted, or resisted by Christians in a variety of local communities within and outside pentecostalism.

Scholarship exploring aspects of pentecostal-charismatic worship and ritual has been steadily emerging over the last two decades (Sanders 1996; Csordas 1997; Albrecht 1999; Poloma 2003; Meyer 2009; Robbins 2009b; Lindhardt 2011), and a small but growing number of music scholars have contributed to the study of pentecostal-charismatic music making (Butler 2002, 2005, 2008; Miller and Strongman 2002; Lange 2003; Rommen 2007; Johnson 2011; Webb 2011).[2] With the aim of putting these emerging conversations in dialogue within a comparative frame, *The Spirit of Praise* brings together scholarly perspectives on pentecostal music and worship across the globe. Poised at the intersection of pentecostal-charismatic studies and music scholarship, *The Spirit of Praise* provides critical case studies of global pentecostal music and worship that shed light on such social processes as globalization and secularization, as well as the role of religion in the public sphere and in broader social and cultural change.

The book's fifteen chapters represent a multi-voiced dialogue—often in harmony but with moments of dissonance—as contributors work to define, analyze, and interpret the significance of music and worship within global pentecostalism at the beginning of the twenty-first century. The rest of this introductory chapter delineates key terms, situates the book in relation to contemporary musical and religious studies scholarship, sets out overarching themes, and provides a detailed overview of the thematic intersections and topical threads of the individual chapters.

Understanding Pentecostal-Charismatic Music and Worship: Definitions and Methods

Pentecostalism is a modality of twentieth- and twenty-first-century Christianity that has proved notoriously difficult to define (Anderson 2010). Working alongside, outside, and within older religious institutions, pentecostalism has been conceived variously as a Christian sect, a renewal movement, a set of institutions, and a theological persuasion. With antecedents in the holiness and pietistic movements of earlier centuries, the emergence of pentecostalism is generally traced to the early decades of the twentieth century. The movement has been embodied in several distinctive forms (sometimes known as "waves") throughout the twentieth century, with divergent emphases growing out of differing social conditions (Hollenweger 1997; Synan 2001; Anderson 2010). The term "Pentecostal" (or sometimes "classical Pentecostal") is often used for institutions and networks with roots in mission movements and revivals of the first half of the twentieth century, such as the Assemblies of God, the Church of God in Christ (COGIC), or West African Apostolic churches. "Charismatic" is frequently employed to describe the spread of beliefs and practices associated with pentecostal renewal within older Christian institutions and denominations, including Anglican, Catholic, and Lutheran churches. "Neo-charismatic" and "neo-pentecostal" are sometimes used interchangeably to describe independent churches and church networks arising since the 1970s, including the Vineyard, the Redeemed Christian Church of God (RCCG) founded in Nigeria, and the Universal Church of the Kingdom of God (Igreja Universal do Reino de Deus) based in Brazil. Neo-pentecostal church networks often grow out of an independent megachurch that forms networks of affiliated churches, and they overlap considerably with the post-1970s phenomenon that sociologist Donald E. Miller calls "new paradigm" churches (Miller 1997). The terms "pentecostal-charismatic" and small-*p* "pentecostal" will be used interchangeably throughout the introduction as shorthand for these diverse social formations (see Smith 2010; Yong 2005, 18–22). Because the meanings and usage of these terms vary by context, each individual chapter contributor will nuance these terms as he or she deems it necessary.

Rather than ascribing to pentecostal-charismatic Christianity certain essential traits or functions, or appealing to representative institutional frameworks, this volume follows the cultural studies approach proposed by Michael Bergunder (2010), which emphasizes pentecostalism's continuous social construction. Bergunder understands pentecostalism "neither as a nominalistic nor as an idealistic category, but as a contingent discursive network" (54)—in other words, as a social network of people who share "particular identifying doctrines and practices" that are nonetheless always "subject to transformation" (55). Following Bergunder, "pentecostal-charismatic" is used to invoke the constellation of twentieth- and twenty-first-century Christian renewal movements that are related to one another as part of a transnational social network connected by shared beliefs and practices—of which music is, of course, key. While recognizing their contingence, the music and worship practices described as "pentecostal-charismatic" share an emphasis upon the presence, work, and gifts of the Holy Spirit as manifest in glossolalia, healing, ecstatic worship practices, and prophecy.

The essays in this volume also demonstrate that, frequently, there is not a clear line of demarcation between pentecostalism and other Christian modalities. Since the latter quarter of the twentieth century, many signature emphases of pentecostalism have been woven into other noncharismatic denominations or church fellowships (Poewe 1994). As a result, pentecostal-charismatic music and worship practices often overlap significantly with those of evangelicalism, mainline Christianity, or charismatic Catholicism. Christians belonging to these groups may not use the categories "pentecostal" or "charismatic," identifying instead as "Spirit-filled," "sanctified," "evangelical," or simply "Christian." The widespread diffusion of pentecostal-charismatic practices into nonpentecostal settings creates a complex task for scholars. Rather than drawing a hard-and-fast line between pentecostalism and its Christian "Others," this volume explores how pentecostal distinctiveness is constructed discursively—and often *musically*—within local contexts.

Both "music" and "worship" are potentially contested terms because they can refer to a wide range of multimodal activities. Several recent accounts have treated pentecostal-charismatic worship practices under the rubric of "ritual" (Albrecht 1999, 2009; Robbins 2009b; Lindhardt 2011); however, we have chosen to use "worship" as an overarching term while seeking also to contribute to the conversation about pentecostal ritual. "Worship" provides more traction for our purposes, first, because it is the preferred term that pentecostals and charismatics use to describe particular kinds of devotional activities.[3] Several scholars have noted that "ritual" is a word that pentecostals—and many other Protestants—generally eschew because of its association with what they consider the "prescribed, formal, spiritually empty liturgy of mainline churches" (Lindhardt 2011, 2). While "ritual" may be a useful umbrella term for a diverse range of embodied practices, the emic analytical category "worship" focuses the range of ritual activity to be examined and brings music to the fore. "Worship" corresponds to a specific set of rituals in which participants express devotion to God and experience divine presence in the context of a community, whether physically present or imagined.

Significant for our purposes, nearly all of the devotional practices within contemporary pentecostalism considered "worship" involve music making. This volume's approach to music is informed by contemporary theoretical approaches and concerns within the diverse fields encompassed by music studies.[4] Rather than conceiving music as a fixed object or "text" with inherent or essential meanings, we approach music as a social practice centered on—but extending far beyond—the production of sound. Following Christopher Small (1998), our approach foregrounds "musicking"—that is, the broad range of activities that entail the creation, circulation, and reception of musical sound. Some chapters analyze musical style and lyrics, while others examine bodily actions during musical performance; still others focus on the pentecostal community's discourse about music making. Through these varying methods, the chapters demonstrate the ways in which musical meanings are constantly being created and negotiated through performance.

The study of Christian hymnody has often privileged written texts and notated scores in the form of hymnals or songbooks; however, contemporary pentecostal music making calls for other approaches because the means of its circulation differ. Orality persists as the dominant mode of pentecostal-charismatic musical transmission (Land 1993; Hollenweger 1997; Albrecht 1999, 2009) because it allows for the "coordinated spontaneity," informality, and collective improvisation integral to pentecostal spirituality (Lindhart 2011, 3–4). Migration and mobility ensure that worshipping bodies remain a powerful medium of transport for music and worship practices; likewise, through a "secondary orality" (Ong [1982] 1988) brought about by new electronic media technologies, audiovisual media networks increasingly comprise the main conduits along which pentecostal music, songs, and worship practices travel. Internet-based digital media players, stores, and platforms have enabled musical materials and practices to travel not only between pentecostal-charismatic communities but also increasingly among international and interdenominational networks.

Given our understandings of "music" and "worship," there are many ways to conceive the relationship between sacred sound and devotional practices within pentecostal-charismatic Christianity. This book could as easily have addressed music *in* worship or music *as* worship; however, its topic has been formulated as music *and* worship to emphasize the considerable overlap of these two activities while allowing for their disjuncture. Though acknowledging the central place music occupies within pentecostal and charismatic expressions of worship across cultural and geographical space, we reject the popular use of "worship" and "music" as synonymous. In his influential study of pentecostal ritual, Daniel Albrecht notes that "worship" within pentecostalism "can connote general adoration of God," but among many contemporary pentecostals, "worship" in the noun form refers primarily to "the first main phase of the church service," which generally features congregational music, movement, and various verbal genres, including prayer, singing, prophecy, and glossolalia (1999, 155). Following Albrecht, this volume understands music and worship as intertwined but distinct: music is an indispensable mode of expressing and framing activities of worship within pentecostalism, but it does not encompass all worship practices or experiences. Likewise, while worship may be the primary context for musical activities self-consciously labeled pentecostal or charismatic, worship does not fully encompass the Christian musical styles and genres that pentecostals listen to and perform outside corporate gatherings.

Understanding Pentecostal-Charismatic Christianity Through Praise and Worship Music

Scholars are increasingly recognizing the influence of pentecostal-charismatic styles beyond the bounds of gatherings for worship, particularly in the early and middle part of the twentieth century. Pentecostal-charismatic musical styles and musicians—particularly those associated with the Church of God in Christ (COGIC) and the Assemblies of God—contributed to the development of influential U.S. popular music styles, both secular and sacred, including gospel music, country, rock, and soul (Reed 2002; Goff 2002; Jackson 2004; Mosher 2008). Without minimizing the continued importance of the contributions of these pentecostal movements, the majority of this volume's essays center on the intersections of pentecostal music making with the sounds, institutions, and modes of dissemination associated with post-1970s popular music styles. In particular, many chapters focus on the repertoire of congregational worship songs known as "praise and worship music," or often simply "worship music."[5] Resulting from the incorporation of contemporary folk and rock styles in the late 1960s and early 1970s, worship music was first established among youth movements and charismatic renewal networks in the United States.[6] Praise and worship music, generally performed in a soft rock, pop-rock, or gospel-influenced style,[7] relies on an ensemble of vocalists and instrumentalists known as a "praise team" or "worship band." Though the number and type of instrumentalists and vocalists vary widely between settings, a worship band generally comprises one to ten vocalists accompanied by acoustic or electric guitar, bass guitar, drum set, and keyboard. The director of the ensemble, known as a "worship leader," usually serves as lead vocalist and guitarist or keyboard player. In pentecostal-charismatic worship, the worship leader is expected to facilitate an experience of divine presence through music as well as other, extramusical worship practices, such as spontaneous prayer and tongues speech.

Developing concurrently with praise and worship music's style and repertoire were a particular liturgical structure and philosophy of worship. Within

charismatic circles, "worship" came to refer to a twenty- to forty-minute segment during which a worship band leads the congregation in singing a continuous string of songs (the "worship set").[8] During this time, members of the
worshipping community express their praise and devotion through singing
combined with other characteristic pentecostal devotional practices, including hand raising, expressive prayer postures, and ecstatic utterances such as
tongues speech and prophecy (see Miller 1997; Redman 2002; Liesch 2001).
One of the primary goals of pentecostal-charismatic worship is a personal
encounter with God, and consequently pentecostal-charismatic worship is not
a directionless sing-along. Rather, it is characterized by a goal-oriented progression involving the separate but related actions of "praise" and "worship."
Pentecostal-charismatic theologians often draw from the book of Psalms and
other Old Testament passages to explain the differing orientations of praise
and worship. They may speak of the progression of worship as a mythic journey from the outer courts of the Jewish tabernacle into the Holy of Holies
(Cornwall 1983; Sorge 1987; Liesch 2001). This ritual procession begins with
"praise" at the temple gates and then moves to "worship" in the inner sanctum
of the temple, where worshippers relate individually and intimately with God.
Music plays an important role in facilitating the transition from communal
praise to intimate worship. Praise songs, sung at the beginning of the charismatic worship set, are characterized by upbeat tempos, major harmonies,
lively rhythms, and communally oriented lyrics. In contrast, worship songs
generally feature slower tempos, more poignant contrasts between major and
minor harmonies, and intimate lyrics expressing devotion, love, and desire
for God.

The style, songs, structure, and ethos of pentecostal music and worship
became increasingly prevalent in noncharismatic evangelical churches in the
United States beginning in the early 1980s and initiated a blending of evangelical and pentecostal practice that some have termed the "pentecostalization
of evangelicalism" (Spittler 1994, 112). While local stylistic treatment varies,
commercially produced praise and worship music has generally been modeled
on a handful of widespread popular music styles, perhaps most notably soft
rock, modern rock, and contemporary gospel (Smith Pollard 2008; Johnson
2011; Ingalls 2012). In the 1990s, worship music began to overlap considerably
with contemporary Christian music (CCM), listener-oriented Christian popular music produced by the commercial Christian recording industry based
in Nashville.[9] By the first decade of the 2000s, worship music was recast as a
radio-friendly commercial genre and became the most profitable product of

the commercial Christian recording and publishing industries in the United States, the U.K., Australia, and elsewhere (Ingalls, Nekola, and Mall 2013; Evans 2006; Ward 2005; and Perkins, this volume).

As a result of increasingly far-reaching product distribution networks, world tours of celebrity "worship bands," and grassroots oral and digital circulation, in the first two decades of the early twenty-first century, praise and worship music continues to permeate the worship of Christian communities worldwide. Worship music has become pentecostal-charismatic Christianity's most widespread musical influence, rivaling nineteenth-century gospel hymnody in its global reach. But worship music is more than an export from the Anglophone world. Increasingly, it has been indigenized (Riches and Webb, this volume) and is often at the center of growing regional and national Christian music centers outside English-speaking countries, including charismatic worship music networks in Seoul and Taipei (Wong 2006), the rapidly expanding gospel music industry of Brazil (Mendonça and Kerr 2007; Maraschin and Pires 2006), and the *alabanza y adoración* of Spanish-speaking Latin America (Ingalls 2014; Gladwin, this volume). As this volume shows, while praise and worship music can be considered the lingua franca of twenty-first-century Christian communities worldwide, it remains closely tied to the pentecostal and charismatic networks from which it emerged. These networks, in turn, are often constituted in part by the flow of commodities along pathways created by commercial industries and media empires.

Despite the ubiquity of this music within global Christianity and its importance to pentecostal-charismatic self-definition and identification, with a few recent exceptions (Woods and Walrath 2007; Ingalls 2011, 2012; Nekola 2009, 2011; Johnson 2008, 2011; Smith Pollard 2008, 2013), praise and worship music has rarely been the object of study in its own right. In focusing on worship music and by highlighting other pentecostal-charismatic popular music styles, this volume fills a gap in the literature as it articulates these musical styles' shifting relationships to pentecostalism. As an agent of musical and religious change, music both embodies and produces pentecostal-charismatic beliefs and practices. Further, as a quintessential example of a "portable practice" (Csordas 2009) necessary for the transnational spread of religious practice, music, like pentecostalism itself, serves as a key site for understanding religious globalization (Anderson et al. 2010; Meyer 2009). An emphasis on worship music allows authors to address several key discussions related to cultural dimensions of globalization. These concerns include exploring to what extent translocal practices promote homogeneity or hybridity; how local agents respond to capitalist industry structures; and how artists and audiences attempt to reconcile the imperatives of ministry and the commodity marketplace.

Inter- and Cross-disciplinary Approaches to Pentecostal-Charismatic Music and Worship

In considering pentecostal music and worship as overlapping but discrete, embodied activities that are frequently orally and aurally (mass) mediated, the chapters in this volume draw from methodological approaches and theoretical frameworks informed by each author's disciplinary background and relationship to pentecostal-charismatic Christianity. Theoretical models drawn from contemporary theology, cultural theory, media studies, and music studies each find a place here, as do methodological approaches including cultural history, media studies analysis, ethnographic participant observation, and theological reflection. Whether (ethno)musicological, theological, historical, or sociological, each contributor's perspectives shine light on a different aspect of this multifaceted research topic.

Contributors' relationships to pentecostalism and its music also vary considerably. Some authors (such as Perkins and Kidula) foreground their proximity to this tradition as scholar-practitioners whose accounts resemble the pentecostal genre of testimony, while others write from a more distanced perspective. Though contributors range from pentecostal believers to nonreligious social scientists, they share a common goal: to explore the varieties, roles, and meanings of music and worship practices within contemporary pentecostal-charismatic Christianity.

Seven of the volume's editors and contributors work in the disciplines of anthropology or ethnomusicology; thus, ethnographic field research—a method characterized by extended periods of observation, participation, and dialogue within a particular congregation or gathering—is a key part of the volume's approach. Several contributors who hail from theological subdisciplines employ "theological ethnography"—that is, immersion within and thick description of social groups and realities (Phillips 2012, 99) while retaining normative theological commitments. Pete Ward (2012) and Elizabeth Phillips (2012) have charted a recent "ethnographic turn" within theological studies as theologians have engaged methods and questions from social sciences. Phillips notes that this mode of theological inquiry shares much in common with activist or applied anthropology, in which a researcher self-consciously committed to particular political or ideological goals works with or on behalf of the community of study to realize them (101). Both theological ethnography and applied ethnography proceed from certain normative assumptions, while allowing them to be challenged by firsthand engagement with social actors.

Late twentieth-century epistemological shifts in the humanistic social sciences—particularly anthropology and ethnomusicology—have also opened the space for dialogue with disciplinary perspectives, such as theology, that hold to certain ideological precommitments. In particular, the recognition of the extent to which human researchers always and irrevocably cast "shadows in the field" (Barz and Cooley 2008) has thrown into question the possibility and desirability of "objectivity" for social analysis (Clifford and Marcus 1986). The position taken by many contemporary social science researchers—namely, that human researchers studying human communities can never truly be neutral, impartial observers, and that effective research always involves negotiating competing aims and goals—has thus made way for spirited engagement between perspectives less frequently brought into dialogue. The practice of making one's ideological precommitments clear up front—whether these stem from religious traditions or "secular" social science—enables a shared space for dialogue for scholars writing from a number of different subject positions. Moreover, it opens the possibility for shared insights among scholars whose aims and goals may differ widely.

In addition to addressing an academic audience, contributors working within theological studies fields write with musical practitioners and church leaders in mind. And in addition to engaging the book's intersecting themes (discussed in further detail below), many intend their essays to be aids for reflection on musical practice. Some chapters in this more applied vein include critiques or policy recommendations that stem from a core concern: What musical models lead to the growth and health of Christian communities? Prescriptive recommendations by authors include, for instance, that Australian Aboriginal pentecostal songs should serve as a model for settler communities in promoting reconciliation (Riches); that Latin American pentecostal songs must go further in addressing social justice (Gladwin); that affluent Western Christians should look to the Global South for models for songs of lament (McCoy); and that we must consider how worship songs lose part of their distinctive value for pentecostal-charismatic worship when reformatted for radio airplay (Perkins).

This combination of approaches and goals may lead to the occasional unresolved dissonance. Ultimately, however, we believe that a polyvocal approach to the topic produces scholarship that is grounded in the language and concerns of the community of study, and yet is open to further insights and critique from those outside its bounds. As such, we intend the volume's plurality of approaches across the emic–etic spectrum to signal a shared commitment to encouraging critical thinking, dialogue, and continued debate among scholars and practitioners alike.

Overarching Themes: Interconnection, Interface, Identification

As the first collection of scholarly and analytical essays focused specifically on music and worship within contemporary pentecostal-charismatic Christianity, *The Spirit of Praise* seeks to contribute to several discussions within recent musical, theological, and religious studies scholarship. These include music making in local pentecostal congregational worship (Butler 2002, 2008; Rommen 2007; Lange 2003; Webb 2011), charismatic ritual and the ritualization of everyday life (Csordas 1997; Poloma 2003; Robbins 2009b; Lindhart 2011), media and mediation (Hackett 1998; Meyer 2009), the "fit" between pentecostal Christianity and processes of globalization (Robbins 2004b, 2009a; Meyer 2009; Csordas 2009), and the contested boundaries between pentecostal worship and popular music (Reed 2002; Mosher 2008; Kalu 2010).

The three themes of interconnection, interface, and identification are interwoven throughout the fifteen chapters of this volume. Interconnection has particular resonance within studies of pentecostalism as a product and process of contemporary globality. Pentecostalism has been called a "'laboratory' for exploring the processes of globalization" (Anderson et al. 2010, 5; see also Coleman 2000 and Robbins 2004b), a hallmark of which is the intensification of both social interconnections and consciousness of the world as a whole (Appadurai 1996; Giddens 1990). Whether contributors detail an individual church case study (Kidula, Klaver, Johnson, Mall), explore a particular musician or musical group (Webb, Riches, Reagan), or take a broadly comparative approach across church networks (McCoy, Evans, Althouse and Wilkinson), each chapter of this book demonstrates the vital role of music and worship in forming interconnections between nodes in pentecostal networks. Further, chapters show how music-making practices and media not only flow along preestablished networks but also frequently aid in forming new pathways; to this end, music becomes a primary means by which pentecostal and charismatic Christians participate within what Joel Robbins has called the Christian "transnation" (Robbins 2004a, 2004b).

Contributors demonstrate the expansive reach of these networks by exploring the dynamic interconnections among forms of pentecostal-charismatic music making on five continents. The volume's emphasis on cross-cultural and transnational comparison reflects the idea that the Global South is pentecostalism's new "center of gravity" (Anderson et al. 2010, 5) in terms of population; however, it simultaneously illustrates that pentecostalism's population center is not yet coterminous with centers of influence in the marketplace of ideas and products. Eight chapters explore pentecostal music making outside North America—from Scandinavia to Sydney, Nairobi to Papua New Guinea—while the remaining seven chapters focus on diverse expressions of pentecostal worship in North America, still a global center for the creation and dissemination of worship practices and a key node in the broader pentecostal "imaginary" (Meyer 2009).

A second thematic resonance threaded through these chapters is interface, specifically the complex relationships between pentecostal music making and the various contexts—religious, political, and sociocultural—in which its creators are embedded. A combination of synchronic and diachronic approaches shows how music making serves as a central activity through which pentecostal Christians seek to resolve sometimes dissonant strains of beliefs and practices by adapting, adopting, or rejecting influences from their cultural contexts. Whether part of indigenous movements (Riches, Marshall, Webb), urban subcultures (Kidula, Mall, Oosterbaan), or congregations and corporations at the heart of commercial musical production (Perkins, Johnson, Reagan), pentecostal music serves as an interface between pentecostal believers and their wider cultural contexts—between the "church" and the "world." Music making also serves as a site of interface between competing modalities of Christian practice within local contexts. Pentecostal and charismatic communities use music and worship to absorb elements from or define themselves against other denominational or religious traditions (Johnson, Mall, Kidula, Klaver), even as pentecostal practices influence these other traditions by introducing new musical media, expressive practices, and modes of social organization within music making (Gladwin, Evans, Reagan).

Interconnection and interface are both implied within the book's third overarching theme of identification. Whether on the level of the individual, the congregation, or the large-scale movement, music making is a key activity for identity creation. Identity is not a given but rather is produced out of constant negotiation among competing options and embedded in bodily practices (Frith 1996; Stokes 1994; Rice 2010); as such, worship and music making not only reflect pentecostal identities but also provide a participatory means of constituting them. In addressing how pentecostal music making informs the negotiation and production of regional, national, generational, and racial/ethnic identities, chapters in this volume provide a new, musical take on one of the central problems in pentecostal-charismatic studies: how to describe the simultaneous sameness and variety of pentecostal music and worship. These detailed accounts of musical practice show to what extent pentecostal music and worship is, as Harvey Cox put it, a "compendium of patterns and practices from virtually every Christian tradition" (1995, 16) and yet distinctly recognizable in local contexts. Identifiable elements of pentecostal music and worship are found as much in what pentecostal congregations identify *against* as in what they identify *with*; many chapters elaborate this dialectical relationship between pentecostalism and its "Others"—whether Christian "Others" such as evangelicals, Catholics, and mainline Protestants, or the extrareligious "Others" of secular societies or traditional religions. To borrow the description Amiri Baraka ([1968] 1998) used for the relationship of music to black American identity, contributors to *The Spirit of Praise* portray pentecostal music as a "changing same"—discursively constituted yet sharing a common repertoire of sounds, gestures, and practices transmitted through embodied practice.

Chapter Overview

In exploring these intersecting themes, *The Spirit of Praise* is divided into three parts: "Healing, Renewal, and Revitalization," "Negotiating Traditions in Transition," and "Media, Culture, and the Marketplace"—each of which comprises five chapters on these topics. The five chapters in the first section address the ways in which participating in music and worship can encourage holistic restoration within physical, emotional, social, and spiritual domains. Authors approach these themes from many levels of scale: while Althouse and Wilkson and McCoy present transnational comparisons, Riches, Webb, and Klaver focus on individual churches or musicians whose influence nonetheless resounds across geographical and cultural space. In addressing music's complex role in religious and cultural revitalization, contributors draw attention to the tension between rupture and reparation inherent in charismatic renewal. While some accounts foreground the necessity of breaking with the past in order to make anew (Webb, Klaver, Marshall), others highlight the mending of broken bonds and the reclamation of a shared cultural history and identity (McCoy, Riches).

In "Musical Bodies in the Charismatic Renewal," Peter Althouse and Michael Wilkinson draw from multi-site field research on three continents to explore "soaking prayer," a ritual associated with the "Toronto Blessing," a charismatic revival that influenced churches in many parts of the world. Employing social scientific and theological perspectives, Althouse and Wilkinson examine the relationship between music, prayer, and healing at the site of the body. Their chapter convincingly demonstrates the important roles that music plays—through its sonic construction and intimate, even erotic, lyrical themes—in setting the conditions for and enabling participants to viscerally experience the love of God, both individually and together, as sound works to synchronize embodied responses.

Writing from a theological perspective, Andrew McCoy's chapter, "Salvation (Not Yet?) Materialized," explores the interface between pentecostal theologies of healing and the expression of suffering within pentecostal music and worship. Synthesizing case studies from around the world, McCoy presents an overview of common pentecostal modes of response to suffering in worship. His close commentary on these reveals the tensions in and differing ways of reconciling the pentecostal belief in the "materiality of salvation"—which includes the possibility of healing in the present—with the reality of pervasive and ongoing suffering.

Tanya Riches further examines the interrelationship between music and physical and social healing in "Dreaming Urban Indigenous Australian Christian Worship in the Great Southland of the Holy Spirit." Intended as an intervention in contemporary missiological scholarship, Riches's account of indigenous Australian pentecostal musical expression highlights the concern with healing, reconciliation, and cultural revitalization that is pervasive within the music's lyrics, styles, and social uses. These pentecostals use indigenous instruments and languages in an attempt to reintegrate their precolonial cultural past, yet they frequently engage in musical reconciliation efforts to build bridges between themselves and Australia's settler communities. Here, music is used both to heal the forced rupture of indigenous cultural traditions and to imagine a new way forward.

Within pentecostal practice, healing and renewal on both individual and corporate levels are often tied to rupture with the past (Meyer 1998; cf. Engelke 2010). Michael Webb addresses the relationship of renewal to rupture in the context of post-independence Papua New Guinea in "Every Creative Aspect Breaking Out!" In his ethnographic account of Oro gospel music, Webb highlights worship practices and the life stories of three influential pentecostal musicians in order to sketch a "millennialist aesthetic" in which current global styles, inflected with indigenous elements, come to signify the coming reign of God. Webb reveals the intertwining of political, religious, and musical transformation and strongly emphasizes the agency of indigenous pastor-musicians in cultural transformation within indigenous Papua New Guinea societies.

The connection between renewal and rupture is also explored in Miranda Klaver's ethnography of music and worship at the Living Gospel Church (LGC), an influential center of the charismatic renewal movement in the Netherlands. In "Worship Music as Aesthetic Domain of Meaning and Bonding," Klaver shows how the tropes of revival and renewal are used to reinforce the stark contrast between the music and worship of new Dutch pentecostal churches and mainline Protestant churches. Further, Klaver demonstrates two ways in which worship music serves as a transformative medium: it mediates not only divine presence but also sounds and practices from global centers of worship music production, particularly Anglophone centers in the U.K., North America, and Australia.

The five chapters in part 2, "Negotiating Traditions in Transition," rely upon oral history and ethnography within local pentecostal or charismatic congregations to demonstrate how music is used to negotiate musical, theological, and cultural shifts. The first four essays comprise detailed case studies of single congregations, while the final chapter surveys several congregations in Scandinavia and South Africa. These accounts demonstrate the musical interplay of change and continuity within extant traditions and how music enables the negotiation of a shared past by variously overlapping with, supplanting, or existing alongside practices from other religions and Christian modalities, including evangelicalism, mainline Protestantism, and (post-)missionary Christianity. In demonstrating the context-dependent interface between local pentecostal congregations and their "Others"—whether Christian or non-Christian—each of these chapters also highlights how local churches negotiate "global" elements, particularly worship songs produced in influential megachurches and commercial media industries.

Birgitta Johnson's "'This Is Not the Warm-Up Act!'" examines music's role in the transformation of an African American Missionary Baptist congregation into a "Bapticostal" megachurch. Johnson's detailed oral history of Los Angeles–based Faithful Central Bible Church from the 1980s to the present chronicles the adoption of praise and worship music and demonstrates that musical and theological transitions often go hand in hand. While some have considered praise and worship music to be a threat to black sacred music traditions, Johnson argues that adopting this music for worship has allowed African American believers both to reaffirm "key culturally informed worship aesthetics" and to reach out to an increasingly multiethnic urban society. She shows how Faithful Central Bible Church's parallel theological shift toward a pentecostal-charismatic theology of the Spirit created new possibilities for ecumenical and cross-cultural dialogue.

Johnson's exploration is followed by a case study of the Nairobi Pentecostal Church, whose worship tradition underwent a similar transformation, also beginning in the 1980s. Jean Ngoya Kidula's "Singing the Lord's Song in the Spirit and with Understanding" explores in parallel fashion how this Nairobi church's richly textured institutional history resounds within its complex, multilayered musical tradition. Weaving a narrative based on her experience as a scholar-practitioner and longtime church member, Kidula shows how the church draws on musical resources from past traditions and allows them to resonate in the contemporary context, so as to situate the church at the nexus of rural-to-urban migration, missionary and indigenous Christianities, and contemporary African evangelicalism and pentecostalism in a global context.

If the first two chapters of part 2 demonstrate continuity and change in worship practices as pentecostal churches negotiate elements from other Christian traditions, Kimberly Jenkins Marshall's "'Soaking Songs' Versus 'Medicine Man Chant'" takes the negotiation of a tradition one step further removed, exploring a dilemma posed by interreligious musical borrowing. In her exploration of a uniquely widespread Navajo-language worship song, Marshall proposes the concept of "resonance" to explain how, through performance of this song, the Diné Oodláni (Navajo Pentecostals) are able to simultaneously separate themselves from traditional religious practices seen as problematic (the medicine man chant) and retain a sense of cultural affinity with pan-Indian pentecostal Christianity. Marshall's account of Native American pentecostals' conflicted relationship with indigenous cultural traditions provides an interesting contrast to Riches's earlier chapter, which emphasizes music's use in the indigenous Australian quest for reconciliation with the past.

While Johnson's, Kidula's, and Marshall's essays explore the process of "pentecostalization," Andrew Mall's case study of a nondenominational charismatic church in downtown Nashville questions whether an easy distinction can be made between pentecostalism and other Christian modalities. In "'We Can Be Renewed,'" Mall uses ethnography with a subcultural studies frame to show how music and worship practices are shaped by and interpreted through the Anchor's institutional emphasis on resistance and renewal. Mall's account demonstrates how music is used simultaneously to tear down and to build up, and to promote social, emotional, and spiritual healing while severing relationships with established denominational authorities, all the while foregrounding both a pentecostal *and* charismatic ethos within this local congregation.

Tracing the means and rationales for local use of translocal pentecostal songs is the central aim of Mark Evans's "Hillsong Abroad." Evans employs the indigenous Australian term "songlines" to describe the way in which worship songs produced by the Australian charismatic megachurch Hillsong Church trace paths across the geographical landscape, orienting singers in space and sacred time. Drawing from personal experience within churches in Scandinavia and South Africa, Evans shows how local churches on different continents are increasingly using Hillsong's music to orient themselves within the landscape of global Christianity. Evans also considers to what extent Hillsong music can be seen as a "colonizing force" in local congregational music making. His chapter demonstrates well the contradictory effects of Hillsong's musical globalization: how this musical empire, with its far-flung distribution channels and superior production values, can be seen structuring local musical choices even as it spurs the creation of hybrid musical forms.

Following on Evans's examination of the relationship between local and global elements in pentecostal worship, the five chapters in part 3 each explore the dynamic interconnections between a variety of cultural contexts resulting from the interface between mass media and pentecostal music and worship. Using case studies of individual musicians (Reagan, Oosterbaan, Boone) and industry networks (Perkins, Gladwin), these chapters additionally explore the interface between song genres, churches, industries, and media economies that have sprung up to support and disseminate this music. As the music's creators and promoters seek to span geographical and cultural boundaries, they must deal with conflicts inherent to "selling worship" (Ward 2005), including the borrowing of secular musical styles, marketing strategies, and artist personas, while also navigating the tensions between ministry, creativity, and commerce. The authors of these chapters weigh the relative influence of ideological, ethical, and economic motivations for the mediation and marketing of pentecostal music, as well as the effects of its mediation on local contexts far and wide. These perspectives, informed by the authors' own differing relationships to industry structures, come into a productive tension in this section: some authors emphasize the pervasive influence of commercial structures in shaping the practice of charismatic worship (Perkins, Gladwin), while others put greater emphasis on the agency of local pentecostal actors in reframing and repurposing mass-mediated commercial products for their own purposes (Boone, Oosterbaan).

Ryan Gladwin's chapter, "Charismatic Music and the Pentecostalization of Latin American Evangelicalism," intended as a theological examination and critique, explores the role of music in effecting widespread social and cultural change within Latin American evangelicalism. Gladwin draws on accounts from evangelical public demonstrations in Argentina and a close examination of the musical theology of Latin American celebrity worship pastor and songwriter Marcos Witt, demonstrating that music has been an effective tool for "pentecostalization" on a mass scale. While highlighting the central role of charismatic music in the creation of a more unified "pentevangelical" public, Gladwin's account also offers a theological critique of the shortcomings of this repertoire in class divisions within Latin American societies.

Wen Reagan's "Blessed to Be a Blessing" focuses on Israel Houghton, the worship leader at Houston's Lakewood Church and a well-known recording artist on the contemporary U.S. worship music scene. Through close attention to lyrical themes, musical style, and narratives that circulate as part of Houghton's "image," Reagan theorizes why, despite its embodiment of a neo-pentecostal prosperity gospel, Houghton's music holds appeal across denominational, racial, and ethnic lines within American Christianity. Reagan shows that through the complex array of meanings embodied in musical sounds and through the narratives that circulate with it, music is uniquely able to bypass theological and cultural tensions and thus unite a disparate religious public in a shared practice.

While Reagan highlights the ways in which pentecostal emphases and values make it into commercially produced music, Dave Perkins argues that the musical and theological values unique to charismatic Christianity are frequently diluted when charismatic music is taken up in the heart of the Christian "culture industry" in Nashville. In "Music, Culture Industry, and the Shaping of Charismatic Worship," Perkins demonstrates the effect of mass production and mediation on worship music's sound, style, and ethos. Perkins's account draws from his own observations as an industry insider, worshipper, and scholar and from conversations with Nashville-based Christian music industry executives, whom Perkins depicts as complex agents whose actions continue to profoundly shape how worship music is practiced and understood in local church settings, sometimes with contradictory effects.

Will Boone's chapter, "We Can't Go Back," traces the influence of a powerful commercial structure on local worship practice—in this case, the African American gospel music industry. Boone begins his examination of commodification from the perspective of local reception, exploring in detail the unfolding of a singular moment from his field research and employing this as a lens through which to view the many cultural contradictions of using commercially produced songs in worship. Boone highlights the complex interplay between local agency and commercial structure, as local context shapes and gives meaning, while the market shapes and conditions local expression.

Working in the context of urban Rio de Janeiro, Martijn Oosterbaan similarly explores the mediation of meaning between local and translocal levels in the context of pentecostal youth revival services in the chapter "Gospel Funk." Rather than focusing on the industry structures, Oosterbaan interrogates the meaning of musical style through discourses surrounding performance in his case study of pentecostal musicians involved in *funk carioca*, a Brazilian popular music style once considered unacceptable for use in worship. Oosterbaan argues against reductionist accounts that present Brazilian popular music as homogenous and thus assume that evangelical and pentecostal Christians find all "secular" musical styles to be equally problematic. Oosterbaan instead shows performers' and audiences' agency in the "cultural reworking" of funk carioca into gospel funk on the uneven, varied terrain of Brazilian popular culture. Here, religious motivations take on new analytical importance as an impetus for cultural change.

Conclusion

We hope that this diverse range of chapters exploring the role of music and worship in healing and renewal, transforming traditions, and marketplace mediation will not only prove useful to scholars within pentecostal studies and music studies but also expand the avenues of inquiry in the interdisciplinary exploration of music and religion more broadly. By putting a range of disciplinary perspectives in dialogue, *The Spirit of Praise* contends that pentecostal-charismatic Christianity in the early twenty-first century is insep-arable from its unique practices of music and worship. Corporate worship and music making are important ways in which this broad religious network con-stitutes itself, represents and replicates its values, and transforms the sociocul-tural, religious, and economic spheres that its members inhabit. As such, music is an essential lens through which to view pentecostal-charismatic movement's growth, ethos, and identity, and a full understanding of this important Chris-tian modality requires close attention to its songs and patterns of worship.

NOTES

1. For further discussion of praise and worship music and its relationship to pentecostal-charismatic Christianity, see Ingalls (2011, 2012), Johnson (2011), Redman (2002), and Woods and Walrath (2007).

2. In addition to the sources cited here, there is a large and robust literature within African American and Africana studies that explores music within the black church in North America, conceived broadly, and its connections to black "secular" styles. See, for instance, Boyer ([1995] 2000), Spencer (1990), Reagon (1992), Hinson (2000), Reed (2002), Costen (2004), Jackson (2004), Smith Pollard (2008), and the periodical *Black Sacred Music: A Journal of Theomu-sicology*, published between 1989 and 1995. The Africana studies literature is often directed toward scholars of African American music, history, and culture, rather than engaging in a comparative study of pentecostal-charismatic communites more generally. This literature is nonetheless significant and instructive for studies of pentecostal music making, because there is considerable overlap between the shared social practices that constitute transnational pentecostal-charismatic worship and practices represented and experienced as "black" in the context of North American Christian worship. It is widely acknowledged that pentecostal expressions of worship have been heavily influenced by African diasporic practices, from the beginning of the movement to the present day. To further explore the ways in and extent to which African and African American cultural practices have shaped pentecostal belief and practice, see Booker (1988), Spencer (1990), Gerloff (1995), Hollenweger (1997, 1999), and Mills (1998).

3. For further reflection on the merit of etic versus emic analytic categories in the study of pentecostalism, see Anderson (2010).

4. Following Nicholas Cook (2008), I use the inclusive term "music studies" to refer to all branches of music scholarship, including ethnomusicology, musicology, and music analysis, out of a conviction that historical, ethnographic, and analytic methods can make an important contribution to pentecostal-charismatic studies of music making. As reflected by this volume, however, the majority of music studies research on pentecostalism in the late twentieth and early twenty-first centuries is being done within the specific subdiscipline of ethnomusicology.

5. This musical repertoire has also been called "contemporary worship music," "praise music," and "modern worship music." For further discussion of this music's changing nomen-clature in the U.S. context, see Ingalls (2012) and Ingalls, Nekola, and Mall (2013).

6. Members of "classical" pentecostal groups, such as the Assemblies of God and the Church of God, were also instrumental in the creation and promotion of this new music (see Redman 2002). Still other older pentecostal groups encountered praise and worship music from their association with these new charismatic groups and adopted it for their gatherings.

7. For more detailed discussion of changing musical styles used in evangelical and charismatic worship in the U.S. context, see Johnson (2011), Ingalls (2012), and Smith Pollard (2008, 2013).

8. Barry Liesch describes the characteristic pentecostal-charismatic worship structure as "sustained, unbroken, flowing praise" (2001, 54) and provides a helpful comparison to other Protestant liturgical structures.

9. While acknowledging the considerable overlap between praise and worship music and CCM, we have chosen to treat the two as distinct genres. Here we follow Ingalls, Nekola, and Mall (2013), who suggest that, due to significant differences in their histories, audiences, discourses, and uses, CCM and worship music should remain distinct within academic analysis. Further, the designation "CCM" is employed only selectively for Christian popular music outside the United States—for example, *musica cristiana contemporanea* in Spanish-speaking Latin America and CCM in Korea (see www.ccmpia.com). Christians in other contexts, including the Caribbean, Brazil, and West Africa, often use "gospel" as an umbrella term for Christian popular music that may or may not include worship music (see Rommen 2007, Burdick 2013, and Ingalls 2014). By contrast, the term "praise and worship" is found frequently in translation worldwide—for example, *alabanza y adoración* (Spanish); хвала и поклонение (Russian); *iyin ati adura* (Yoruba); 경배와 찬양 (*Kyŏngpaewa chanyang*; Korean, lit. "worship and praise"); *louvor e adoração* (Portuguese); and 敬拜和赞美 (*Jìng bài hé zànměi*—Chinese, lit. "worship and praise").

REFERENCES

Albrecht, Daniel E. 1999. *Rites in the Spirit: A Ritual Approach to Pentecostal/Charismatic Spirituality*. Journal of Pentecostal Theology Supplement Series 17. Sheffield, U.K.: Sheffield Academic Press.

———. 2009. "Worshiping and the Spirit: Transmuting Liturgy Pentecostally." In *The Spirit in Worship, Worship in the Spirit*, edited by Teresa Berger and Brian D. Spinks, 223–44. Collegeville, Minn.: Liturgical Press.

Anderson, Allan. 2010. "Varieties, Taxonomies, and Definitions." In *Studying Global Pentecostalism: Theories and Methods*, edited by Allan Anderson, Michael Bergunder, André Droogers, and Cornelis van der Laan, 13–29. Berkeley: University of California Press.

Anderson, Allan, Michael Bergunder, André Droogers, and Cornelis van der Laan. 2010. *Studying Global Pentecostalism: Theories and Methods*. Berkeley: University of California Press.

Appadurai, Arjun. 1996. *Modernity at Large: The Cultural Dimensions of Globalization*. Minneapolis: University of Minnesota Press.

Baraka, Amiri [LeRoi Jones]. (1968) 1998. "The Changing Same (R&B and the New Black Music)." In *Black Music*, 180–211. New York: Da Capo Press.

Barz, Gregory, and Timothy J. Cooley. 2008. *Shadows in the Field: New Perspectives for Fieldwork in Ethnomusicology*. 2nd ed. New York: Oxford University Press.

Becker, Judith. 2004. *Deep Listeners: Music, Emotion, and Trancing*. Bloomington: Indiana University Press.

Berger, Teresa, and Bryan D. Spinks, eds. 2009. *The Spirit in Worship, Worship in the Spirit*. Collegeville, Minn.: Liturgical Press.

Bergunder, Michael. 2010. "The Cultural Turn." In *Studying Global Pentecostalism: Theories and Methods*, edited by Allan Anderson, Michael Bergunder, André Droogers, and Cornelis van der Laan, 51–73. Berkeley: University of California Press.

Bohlman, Philip V., Edith L. Blumhofer, and Maria M. Chow. 2006. *Music in American Religious Experience*. New York: Oxford University Press.

Booker, Queen. 1988. "Congregational Music in a Pentecostal Church." *Black Perspective in Music* 16 (1): 30–44.

Boyer, Horace Clarence. (1995) 2000. *How Sweet the Sound: The Golden Age of Gospel*. Champaign: University of Illinois Press.

Burdick, John. 2013. *The Color of Sound: Race, Religion, and Music in Brazil*. New York: New York University Press.

Butler, Melvin L. 2002. "'Nou Kwe nan Sentespri' (We Believe in the Holy Spirit): Music, Ecstasy, and Identity in Haitian Pentecostal Worship." *Black Music Research Journal* 22 (1): 85–125.

———. 2005. "Songs of Pentecost: Experiencing Music, Transcendence, and Identity in Jamaica and Haiti." Ph.D. diss., New York University.

———. 2008. "The Weapons of Our Warfare: Music, Positionality, and Transcendence Among Haitian Pentecostals." *Caribbean Studies* 36 (2): 23–64.

Clifford, James, and George E. Marcus. 1986. *Writing Culture: The Poetics and Politics of Ethnography*. Berkeley: University of California Press.

Cohen, Judah. 2009. "Hip-Hop Judaica: The Politics of Representin' Heebster Heritage." *Popular Music* 28 (1): 1–18.

Coleman, Simon. 2000. *The Globalisation of Charismatic Christianity: Spreading the Gospel of Prosperity*. Cambridge: Cambridge University Press.

Cook, Nicholas. 2008. "We Are All (Ethno)musicologists Now." In *The New (Ethno)musicologies*, edited by Henry Stobart, 48–70. London: Scarecrow Press.

Cornwall, Judson. 1983. *Let Us Worship: The Believer's Response to God*. South Plainfield, N.J.: Bridge.

Costen, Melva Wilson. 2004. *In Spirit and in Truth: The Music of African American Worship*. Louisville: Westminster John Knox Press.

Cox, Harvey. 1995. *Fire from Heaven: The Rise of Pentecostal Spirituality and the Reshaping of Religion in the Twenty-First Century*. Reading, Mass.: Addison-Wesley.

Csordas, Thomas J. 1997. *Language, Charisma, and Creativity: The Ritual Life of a Religious Movement*. Berkeley: University of California Press.

———, ed. 2009. *Transnational Transcendence: Essays on Religion and Globalization*. Berkeley: University of California Press.

Darden, Robert. 2004. *People Get Ready! A New History of Black Gospel Music*. New York: Continuum.

Engelke, Matthew. 2010. "Past Pentecostalism: Notes on Rupture, Realignment, and Everyday Life in Pentecostal and African Independent Churches." *Africa* 80 (2): 177–99.

Evans, Mark. 2006. *Open Up the Doors: Music in the Modern Church*. London: Equinox.

Frith, Simon. 1996. "Music and Identity." In *Questions of Cultural Identity*, edited by Stuart Hall and Paul du Gay, 108–27. London: Sage.

Gerloff, Roswith I. H. 1995. "The Holy Spirit and the African Diaspora: Spiritual, Cultural, and Social Roots of Black Pentecostal Churches." *Journal of the European Pentecostal Theological Association* 14 (1): 85–100.

Giddens, Anthony. 1990. *The Consequences of Modernity*. Cambridge: Polity Press.

———. 1991. *Modernity and Self-Identity: Self and Society in the Late Modern Age*. Cambridge: Polity Press.

Goff, James R. 2002. *Close Harmony: A History of Southern Gospel*. Chapel Hill: University of North Carolina Press.

Hackett, Rosalind. 1998. "Charismatic/Pentecostal Appropriations of Media Technologies in Nigeria and Ghana." *Journal of Religion in Africa* 28 (3): 258–77.

Hannerz, Ulf. 1996. *Transnational Connections: Culture, People, Places*. London: Routledge.

Hinson, Glenn. 2000. *Fire in My Bones: Transcendence and the Holy Spirit in African American Gospel*. Philadelphia: University of Pennsylvania Press.

Hollenweger, Walter J. 1997. *Pentecostalism: Origins and Developments Worldwide*. Peabody: Hendrickson.

———. 1999. "The Black Roots." In *Pentecostals After a Century: Global Perspectives on a Movement in Transition*, edited by Allan H. Anderson and Walter J. Hollenweger, 36–43. Sheffield: Sheffield Academic Press.

Ingalls, Monique M. 2011. "Singing Heaven Down to Earth: Spiritual Journeys, Eschatological Sounds, and Community Formation in Evangelical Conference Worship." *Ethnomusicology* 55 (2): 255–79.

———. 2012. "Contemporary Worship Music." In *The Continuum Encyclopedia of Popular Music of the World*, vol. 8, *Genres: North America*, edited by David Horn, 147–52. New York: Continuum.

———. 2014. "International Gospel and Christian Popular Music." *333Sound* (blog), Bloomsbury Press, June 9. http://www.333sound.com/2014/06/09/epmow-vol-9-gospel -and-christian-popular-music/. Forthcoming in *Encyclopedia of Popular Music of the World*, vol. 12, *International Genres*, edited by John Shepherd and David Horn. New York: Bloomsbury Press.

Ingalls, Monique M., Anna E. Nekola, and Andrew Mall. 2013. "Christian Popular Music, U.S.A." In *The Canterbury Dictionary of Hymnology*, edited by J. R. Watson and Emma Hornby. Canterbury Press. http://www.hymnology.co.uk/c/christian-popular -music,-usa.

Jackson, Jerma A. 2004. *Singing in My Soul: Black Gospel Music in a Secular Age*. Chapel Hill: University of North Carolina Press.

Johnson, Birgitta J. 2008. "'Oh, for a Thousand Tongues to Sing': Music and Worship in Black Megachurches of Los Angeles, California." Ph.D. diss., University of California, Los Angeles.

———. 2011. "Back to the Heart of Worship: Praise and Worship Music in a Los Angeles African-American Megachurch." *Black Music Research Journal* 31 (1): 105–29.

Kalu, Ogbu U. 2010. "Holy Praiseco: Negotiating Sacred and Popular Music and Dance in African Pentecostalism." *Pneuma* 32 (1): 16–40.

Land, Steven J. 1993. *Pentecostal Spirituality: A Passion for the Kingdom*. Sheffield: Sheffield Academic Press.

Lange, Barbara Rose. 2003. *Holy Brotherhood: Romani Music in a Hungarian Pentecostal Church*. New York: Oxford University Press.

Liesch, Barry. 2001. *The New Worship: Straight Talk on Music in the Church*. 2nd ed. Grand Rapids, Mich.: Baker Books.

Lindhardt, Martin, ed. 2011. *Practicing the Faith: The Ritual Life of Pentecostal-Charismatic Christians*. New York: Berghahn Books.

Maraschin, Jaci Correia, and Frederico Pieper Pires. 2006. "The Lord's Song in the Brazilian Land." *Studies in World Christianity* 12 (2): 83–100.

Marti, Gerardo. 2012. *Worship Across the Racial Divide: Religious Music and the Multiracial Congregation*. New York: Oxford University Press.

McGann, Mary E. 2002. *Exploring Music as Worship and Theology: Research in Liturgical Practice*. Collegeville, Minn.: Liturgical Press.

McGuire, Meredith B. 2008. *Lived Religion: Faith and Practice in Everyday Life*. New York: Oxford University Press.

Mendonça, Joêzer de Souza, and Dorotéa Kerr. 2007. "Canção gospel: Interações entre religião, música e cultura pós-moderna" [Gospel song: Interactions between religion, music, and postmodern culture]. *Pesquisa em Debate* 6 (4): 1–12.

Meyer, Birgit. 1998. "'Make a Complete Break with the Past': Memory and Post-colonial Modernity in Ghanaian Pentecostalist Discourse." *Journal of Religion in Africa* 28 (3): 316–49.

———, ed. 2009. *Aesthetic Formations: Media, Religion, and the Senses.* New York: Palgrave Macmillan.

———. 2010. "Pentecostalism and Globalization." In *Studying Global Pentecostalism: Theories and Methods,* edited by Allan Anderson, Michael Bergunder, André Droogers, and Cornelis van der Laan, 113–32. Berkeley: University of California Press.

Miller, Donald E. 1997. *Reinventing American Protestantism: Christianity in the New Millenium.* Berkeley: University of California Press.

Miller, Mandi M., and Kenneth T. Strongman. 2002. "The Emotional Effects of Music on Religious Experience: A Study of the Pentecostal-Charismatic Style of Music and Worship." *Psychology of Music* 30 (1): 8–27.

Mills, Robert A. 1998. "Musical Prayers: Reflections on the African Roots of Pentecostal Music." *Journal of Pentecostal Theology* 6 (12): 109–26.

Mosher, Craig. 2008. "Ecstatic Sounds: The Influence of Pentecostalism on Rock and Roll." *Popular Music and Society* 31 (1): 95–112.

Muller, Carol Ann. 1999. *Rituals of Fertility and the Sacrifice of Desire: Nazarite Women's Performance in South Africa.* Chicago: University of Chicago Press.

Nekola, Anna E. 2009. "Between This World and the Next: The Musical 'Worship Wars' and Evangelical Ideology in the United States, 1960–2005." Ph.D. diss., University of Wisconsin–Madison.

———. 2011. "U.S. Evangelicals and the Redefinition of Worship Music." In *Mediating Faiths: Religion and Socio-cultural Change in the Twenty-First Century,* edited by Michael Bailey and Guy Redden, 131–43. Burlington, Vt.: Ashgate.

Ong, Walter J. (1982) 1988. *Orality and Literacy: The Technologizing of the Word.* New York: Methuen.

Phillips, Elizabeth. 2012. "Charting the 'Ethnographic Turn': Theologians and the Study of Christian Congregations." In *Perspectives on Ecclesiology and Ethnography,* edited by Pete Ward, 96–106. Grand Rapids, Mich.: Eerdmans.

Poewe, Karla, ed. 1994. *Charismatic Christianity as Global Culture.* Columbia: University of South Carolina Press.

Poloma, Margaret M. 2003. *Main Street Mystics: The Toronto Blessing and Reviving Pentecostalism.* Walnut Creek, Calif.: AltaMira Press.

Reagon, Bernice Johnson. 1992. *We'll Understand It Better By and By: Pioneering African American Gospel Composers.* Washington, D.C.: Smithsonian Institution Press.

Redman, Robb. 2002. *The Great Worship Awakening: Singing a New Song in the Postmodern Church.* San Francisco: Jossey-Bass.

Reed, Teresa L. 2002. *The Holy Profane: Religion in Black Popular Music.* Lexington: University Press of Kentucky.

Rice, Timothy. 2010. "Disciplining Ethnomusicology: A Call for a New Approach." *Ethnomusicology* 54 (2): 318–25.

Robbins, Joel. 2004a. *Becoming Sinners: Christianity and Moral Torment in a Papua New Guinea Society.* Berkeley: University of California Press.

———. 2004b. "The Globalization of Pentecostal and Charismatic Christianity." *Annual Review of Anthropology* 33:117–43.

———. 2009a. "Is the *Trans-* in *Transnational* the *Trans-* in *Transcendent*? On Alterity and the Sacred in the Age of Globalization." In *Transnational Transcendence: Essays on Religion and Globalization,* edited by Thomas J. Csordas, 55–72. Berkeley: University of California Press.

———. 2009b. "Pentecostal Networks and the Spirit of Globalization: On the Social Productivity of Ritual Forms." *Social Analysis: The International Journal of Social and
Cultural Practice* 53 (1): 55-66.

Robertson, Roland. 1992. *Globalization: Social Theory and Global Culture*. London: Sage.

Rommen, Timothy. 2006. "Protestant Vibrations? Reggae, Rastafari, and Conscious Evangelicals." *Popular Music* 25 (2): 235-63.

———. 2007. *"Mek Some Noise": Gospel Music and the Ethics of Style in Trinidad*. Berkeley:
University of California Press.

Sanders, Cheryl J. 1996. *Saints in Exile: The Holiness-Pentecostal Experience in African American Religion and Culture*. New York: Oxford University Press.

Small, Christopher. 1998. *Musicking: The Meanings of Performing and Listening*. Middletown:
Wesleyan University Press.

Smith, James K. A. 2010. *Thinking in Tongues: Pentecostal Contributions to Christian Philosophy*. Grand Rapids, Mich.: Eerdmans.

Smith Pollard, Deborah. 2008. *When the Church Becomes Your Party: Contemporary Gospel
Music*. Detroit: Wayne State University Press.

———. 2013. "'Praise Is What We Do': The Rise of Praise and Worship Music in the Black
Church in the U.S." In *Christian Congregational Music: Performance, Identity, and
Experience*, edited by Monique Ingalls, Carolyn Landau, and Tom Wagner, 33-48.
Surrey: Ashgate.

Sorge, Bob. 1987. *Exploring Worship: A Practical Guide to Praise and Worship*. Canandaigua,
N.Y.: Oasis House.

Spencer, Jon Michael. 1990. *Protest and Praise: Sacred Music of Black Religion*. Minneapolis:
Augsburg Fortress.

Spittler, Russell P. 1994. "Are Pentecostals and Charismatics Fundamentalists? A Review of
American Uses of These Categories." In *Charismatic Christianity as Global Culture*,
edited by Karla Poewe, 103-17. Columbia: University of South Carolina Press.

Stokes, Martin. 1994. "Introduction: Ethnicity, Identity, and Music." In *Ethnicity, Identity,
and Music: The Musical Construction of Place*, edited by Martin Stokes, 1-28. Oxford:
Berg.

Summit, Jeffrey A. 2000. *"The Lord's Song in a Strange Land": Music and Identity in Contemporary Jewish Worship*. New York: Oxford University Press.

Synan, Vinson. 2001. *The Century of the Holy Spirit: 100 Years of Pentecostal and Charismatic
Renewal*. Nashville: Thomas Nelson Press.

Wagner, C. Peter. 1988. *The Third Wave of the Holy Spirit*. Ann Arbor, Mich.: Servant.

Ward, Pete. 2005. *Selling Worship: How What We Sing Has Changed the Church*. Waynesboro, Ga.: Paternoster Press.

———, ed. 2012. *Perspectives on Ecclesiology and Ethnography*. Grand Rapids, Mich.:
Eerdmans.

Webb, Michael. 2011. "*Palang* Conformity and *Fulset* Freedom." *Ethnomusicology* 55 (3):
445-72.

Wong, Connie Oi-Yan. 2006. "Singing the Gospel Chinese Style: 'Praise and Worship' Music
in the Asian Pacific." Ph.D. diss., University of California, Los Angeles.

Woods, Robert H., and Brian D. Walrath. 2007. *The Message in the Music: Studying Contemporary Praise and Worship*. Nashville: Abingdon Press.

Yong, Amos. 2005. *The Spirit Poured Out on All Flesh: Pentecostalism and the Possibility of
Global Theology*. Grand Rapids, Mich.: Baker Academic.

PART I

Healing, Renewal, and Revitalization

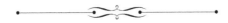

1

Musical Bodies in the Charismatic Renewal: The Case of Catch the Fire and Soaking Prayer

Peter Althouse and Michael Wilkinson

Introduction

In the mid-1990s, reports of religious fervor at a Vineyard church[1] in Toronto began to spread throughout North America and Europe, if not the world. The British media dubbed it the "Toronto Blessing" as thousands of people came to Toronto to experience the latest wave of Pentecostal-charismatic renewal. During those early years, the church became independent from the Association of Vineyard Churches following a series of questions about the role of renewal and the strange bodily behavior of its participants and renamed itself the Toronto Airport Christian Fellowship. Its meetings reached their peak in about 1997, and some scholars reported that the renewal was over (Hunt 2009; Richter 1997). However, while scholars gave the Toronto church less attention, the renewal was undergoing transformation and gaining momentum in other ways.

In the last decade, the church has extended its reach, expanding into numerous countries with new churches. In 2010, the Toronto Airport Christian Fellowship rebranded itself and its affiliations as Catch the Fire (CTF) to align with its global expansion. Numerous events are still held annually in Toronto, with thousands of people in attendance. CTF Toronto has planted new churches in Montreal, Raleigh, Houston, London, Oslo, and Reykjavik, with plans to expand in Germany, South Africa, and Australia. CTF Toronto has also developed ministry training schools for young adults, inner healing programs, prayer schools, and seminars. It has partnered with other renewal churches through a global network called Partners in Harvest. Other partnerships have developed with Randy Clarke and Global Awakening, Heidi Baker and Iris Ministries, Bill Johnson from Bethel Church in California, and Mike Bickle's International House of Prayer.

Soaking prayer is an integral part of CTF's expansion. It is an innovation in the charismatic renewal that captures numerous types of charismatic prayer, including resting in the Spirit, anointing, prayer of the heart, divine presence, waiting on God, contemplation, hearing God, intimacy, healing, prophecy, and impartation (Csordas 1994, 1997; Poloma 2003; Althouse and Wilkinson 2011; Wilkinson 2012; Wilkinson and Althouse 2014). Impartation is a practice in which leaders quietly pray for those who are soaking in prayer by lightly touching the person on the shoulder or head. Participants believe that impartation releases spiritual power from charismatic leaders and their collaborators to the recipients of prayer. Soaking prayer cultivates the experience of divine love, which in turn facilitates loving others through acts of forgiveness, reconciliation, compassion, and benevolence. Soaking prayer is practiced in the context of CTF renewal meetings where people lie on the floor with pillows and blankets and claim to receive the Father's love, while soaking prayer music plays softly in the background. Soaking prayer is also practiced individually at home, in small, intimate home groups, and in soaking centers in churches. CTF Toronto has expanded the practice of soaking prayer through conferences, schools, and weekend seminars. It has developed a structure of local soaking prayer leaders, regional soaking prayer coordinators, and national soaking prayer coordinators in Raleigh, Toronto, and cities within other strategic countries. It has also developed soaking prayer kits and teaching manuals to educate people on how to pray. Teaching on soaking prayer encourages people to play soaking prayer music CDs while they rest in a prone position and meditatively "receive from the Father."

Music plays a vital role in the ritual context of praise and worship as well. In CTF churches and conferences, contemporary pop music is played while participants engage in kinesthetic movements of swaying, hand raising, dancing, jumping, bodily jerks, and flag waving to express their emotional jubilance. Others will lie on the floor, sometimes shaking and jerking, crying, or laughing. A Christian charismatic music group usually consisting of guitars, keyboards, bass, and singers performs from the auditorium's platform. The two-stage progression of worship music begins with fast-paced music to encourage praise through bodily excitement, accelerating until it reaches a crescendo, and then quiets down in a calming manner for worship. It often includes emotional and/or bodily healing, manifestations, and signs and wonders. As the style of music and worship shifts from an energetic and expressive form to a slower and meditative one, participants are encouraged to "rest in the Father" and "soak in the Father's Love" as they position themselves in a receiving mode. CTF leaders typically encourage participants to practice "soaking prayer" during this time at renewal meetings. Music helps cultivate embodied experiences such as laughing, weeping, spontaneous bodily movements, claims of sensory experiences of taste and smell, weighted pressure on the body, and feelings of tingling in the body. Participants report "prophetic revelations," which include mental impressions or images believed to be divine communication.

Musical bodies in the charismatic renewal add to our understanding of the social and theological relationship between music, religious renewal, and embodiment. More specifically, music facilitates emotional entrainment between bodies in the context of sacred space (Clayton, Sager, and Will 2005; Collins 2004; Riis and Woodhead 2010; Robbins 2011; Smilde 2011). In this chapter, we draw on social scientific theories of embodiment and music to explain soaking prayer and the role that music plays in the production of emotional energy. We also include a discussion of the role of breathing, musical processes, and bodily interaction.

Theoretical Considerations

Our observations on the relationship between music and bodily experience in the charismatic renewal are shaped by social scientific theories on emotions, the body, and religion (see Riis and Woodhead 2010; Turner 1996; also Becker 2004; Clayton, Sager, and Will 2005). Theories of embodiment take their cue from the social sciences. For example, in *Interaction Ritual Chains* (2004), Randall Collins argues that life situations are characterized by social interactions. These interaction rituals (IRs) have the capacity to produce emotional energy (EE) in bodies through intense face-to-face situations. IR is a social mechanism in which mutually focused emotion produces a shared reality. Extending Durkheim's collective effervescence and Goffman's ritual theory, the shared reality produced by IR intensifies group solidarity and symbolism.

The IR model operates according to five qualities. First, an IR is a social activity that includes an aspect of situational co-presence. Second, human encounters may be characterized by focused interaction through the presence of people. Third, social interactions entail some pressure to maintain social solidarity, and so rituals are entraining. Fourth, rituals respect what is socially valued by promoting human interaction that leads to the establishment of sacred objects. Finally, when rituals are broken, there is a sense of unease, which may be met with a range of responses meant to exert social control or conformity to a moral code.

The basic ingredients of IR include the physical assembly of a group of people, a process involving shared action, awareness, and EE that contributes to new group symbols and identity. Collins's model of IR, therefore, is one that varies along two lines: mutual focus and emotional entrainment. According to Collins, emotional entrainment occurs in group rhythmic synchronization that produces high levels of EE. The creation of EE is prolonged through symbols that effect morality. When the IR ends, the symbols of belief lose their emotional strength and revert to mere memories that eventually become dead and meaningless. However, new symbols can be created within the group as participants assemble and give focused emotional attention to one another in ritual activity.

Collins identifies a number of outcomes that are central to IR, including group solidarity, EE, symbols that represent the group, and feelings of morality. He states, "At the center of an IR is the process in which participants develop a mutual focus of attention and become entrained in each other's bodily micro-rhythms and emotions" (2004, 47). EE is an important part of IR that requires attention. It accounts for the emotions experienced during a highly intensive IR, which is embodied by the participants. EE also has the ability to be maintained by the individuals after the ritual is over, so that it continues to motivate them to act accordingly in relation to the group and its objectives.

EE, however, is not just about a highly charged ritual that demonstrates a lot of excitement or the dramatic effects that one might associate with charismatic Christianity. EE refers to the long-term effects of IR. In other words, EE is a long-lasting effect that carries over to such an extent that participants are convinced of the experience to the point of acting upon it. EE is a strong, durable emotion that lasts over an extended period of time, not just a short-term disruption. It produces the capacity to initiate and act with resolve, in order to direct social situations. EE is therefore associated with a high level of attunement and long-term consequence.

Collins's work on IR is not specifically focused on religion, although religion is not precluded from his theory. He briefly postulates that larger religious gatherings produce the strongest effects of EE, which fade with the smaller and less collectively emotional gatherings. The dominant person in the collective becomes a sacred object and repository of stored EE that can be expressed in a charismatic manner. Thus, large revivals or renewal gatherings are important in the continuation of EE, which will sustain smaller church gatherings for a time but eventually dissipate without the larger gatherings. Nevertheless, the concepts of entrainment and attunement and their relationship to the aural symbols of music help explain the religious intensity of soaking prayer and the charismatic renewal.

Chris Shilling (2005) argues that an embodied analysis of music must include how the body is both an important source for the creative production of music and deeply attuned to musical processes. Consequently, music has the capacity to take the body "beyond" itself in ways that transcend written communication and cognitive processes, and to shape behavior, form personal identity, and consolidate group fidelity. Music can stimulate "peak experiences" and religious epiphanies, acting as a stimulant or sedative. The body is the locale for the production of music involving techniques of fingering, vocalizing, and breathing, but the body is also the locus for the reception of music and inspires behaviors such as foot tapping, finger drumming, swaying, and dancing. Shilling examines three areas: the commercialization of music that influences human behaviors in the process of production and consumption; the social interaction between people as creative agents of music and the bodily receptivity of music where people are positioned within social environments; and the commercialization of music in the West, as well as whether this diminishes the degree of creativity in music. The second area is most relevant to a discussion of the role of music in the charismatic renewal, specifically in the way that the attunement of musical processes coincides with the interaction of social bodies in a particular collective milieu.

A phenomenological approach examines the relationship between musical processes in techniques such as rhythm, beat, meter, and tone; bodily interaction; and processes of movement (or stillness). However, music is not only a social construction but also rooted in the generative powers of the body (Shilling 2005; Csordas 2002; Becker 2004). Music has the capacity to heighten or lower arousal, which can influence a whole range of behavioral activity. The use of music in ritual contexts has been shown to affect the body by increasing or releasing tension, consolidating group identity, and heightening the effects of cultural symbols. Music has therapeutic effects on the body, supporting physical, mental, social, and emotional well-being. Music has been shown to affect heart rate, blood pressure, and sleeping habits in neonatal care. It can affect respiration, muscular energy, and receptivity to stimuli in adults. Music has been used to alleviate pain and to help in the rehabilitation of the body (Shilling 2005; Clayton, Sager, and Will 2005).

Judith Becker (2004) draws on the disciplines of phenomenology, cognitive science, neuroscience, and biology to argue that religious trancing is an ecstatic or alternate state of consciousness that is sensually rich and physically exertive, heightens emotional responses, and is enveloped in musical processes. She distinguishes between trancing, meditation (which strives for stillness and silence and transcends the emotions), and deep listening (which goes below the surface sounds to unlock the layers of imagination, memory, and meaning). Both trancing and deep listening embody strong emotions. Trancing triggers autonomic arousal and powerful emotional responses, while low-key emotions such as calm, peace, soothing, or comfort may follow trancing (49–52). Musical rhythm is also embodied as rhythmic entrainment, in which bodies synchronize in their gestures, muscular energy, breathing, and brain waves (127–28). Charismatic praise and worship resembles the state of trancing described by Becker and includes ecstatic phenomena, while the prayer time throughout the service (but especially after the service) produces low-key emotions of calm, love, forgiveness, soothing, and comfort. However, our informants report phenomena such as mental images, tongue speaking, sensory experiences, and prophetic communication while practicing soaking prayer, contradicting Becker's assessment of meditation.

In *Main Street Mystics* (2003), Margaret Poloma's analysis of the early stages of the Toronto Blessing accounts for the role of music and the body in renewal. She observed the significant place of music in charismatic worship rituals, which were normally performed for an hour at the beginning of the service, and in the context of prayer, usually at the end of the service. Music facilitates "mutual tuning-in," a form of social interaction that is nonconceptual and precognitive; it is common in mysticism and Pentecostal-charismatic renewal generally. As such, music facilitates ecstatic practices in altered states of consciousness. Borrowing from David Wulff's psychological arguments, Poloma discusses four bodily issues related to music: auditory driving (the use of loud rhythmic sounds in ecstatic states); subauditory sounds (noise that is inaudible to the normal range of hearing but picked up by other sensory clues); the Pavlovian model (the way in which vigorous and prolonged movement in ecstatic states increases or decreases heart rate, breathing rate, blood chemistry, and the sense of balance); and endorphins (the chemical known to affect altered states of consciousness in trances and pain reduction). She also makes a distinction between Ionian music, which is celebrative, and Lydian music, which is contemplative—types of music observed in worship rituals and prayer, respectively.

Poloma discusses the "mystical body" to capture the relationship between bodily phenomena such as shaking, laughing, weeping, and falling down with spiritual experiences. Experience is how reality is represented to personal consciousness, and that reality then needs to be expressed or rather communicated to others in the social milieu. In ecstatic settings, the mode of communication is often precognitive, verbally inchoate, and somatic. Rituals of play, prophetic symbolism, and prophetic mime are categories used to account for unusual bodily reactions while in an ecstatic state. Likewise, claims of inner or emotional healing, which include forgiveness, pain reduction, and physical healing, are among Poloma's observations. Poloma makes a passing observation in her book that the cultivation of love is an important aspect of the ecstatic experiences of charismatics that social scientists need to take seriously, an observation that comes more to the forefront in the interactional model of "godly love" (see Poloma and Hood 2008; Poloma and Green 2010; Althouse and Wilkinson 2011; Wilkinson 2012).

Finally, the lens through which we observe our subjects is one of social interaction. Margaret Poloma, Ralph Hood Jr., Stephen Post, and Matthew T. Lee (see Lee and Yong 2012; Lee, Poloma, and Post 2013) developed a model of social interaction that attempts to account for the interactions between various social actors; it includes exemplars, collaborators, beneficiaries, and perceived interactions with the divine. Unique to the model is the attempt to capture human-divine interactions by taking seriously social actors' claims of experiencing the love of God, which may produce motivational impulses to love others along a spectrum of observable benefits or acts of benevolence. The model is referred to as "godly love" to account for the range of such interactions, from claims of experience with the divine to social interactions between exemplars, collaborators, and beneficiaries.

The model is influenced by the sociological work of Pitirim Sorokin presented in *The Ways and Power of Love* ([1954] 2002). Sorokin postulated that love is a kind of energy that motivates and energizes people to engage in altruistic activities, but he also entertained the possibility that love could have a supraconscious or divine source. He proposed that love could be observed and empirically measured in terms of its intensity, extensity, duration, purity, and adequacy. The "godly love" model takes its cue from Sorokin in order to account for religious experience and the social benefits that result. Shilling's theories mesh with Collins's notion of the attunement and entrainment of

EE in ritual chain interactions and Sorokin's idea of love energy that has the capacity to prompt people to act in loving ways toward others. These works are further supported by studies of musical entrainment and social interaction conducted by Becker and Clayton, Sager, and Will. The synchronization of bodies with one another in the production of love and EE is facilitated through the attunement of music, in which rhythms, tone, and tempo reverberate with bodily rhythms.

Observing Musical Bodies

The interface of music, worship, and soaking prayer in the charismatic renewal was observed in our two years of fieldwork, participant observation, interviews, and survey data.[2] During this time, we traveled across the United States, Canada, U.K., Australia, and New Zealand, where we carried out 25 different site observations of large renewal conferences, smaller soaking prayer schools and seminars, and intimate soaking prayer meetings in homes and churches. We conducted 126 face-to-face interviews with leaders and participants who practice soaking prayer, as well as a survey with 258 respondents. Part of our strategy in traveling to diverse sites was to capture the translocal character of the renewal that expands through numerous charismatic networks.

"Soaking prayer" is a rich term that refers to an embodied prayer ritual that captures all kinds of bodily practices and experiences. In the early stages of the renewal, people who attended the Toronto meetings would manifest somatic expressions such as laughing, weeping, jerking, or groaning. A prominent manifestation was that when people were being prayed for by the leaders or the prayer team, they would fall to the ground in a way that resembled fainting. Often they would stay on the ground and claim to experience a deep love of God. In the early stages, this practice was referred to as "carpet time," because people could be seen strewn across the floor for long periods of time. One participant referred to soaking as a time when "you got prayed with and you fell down. . . . Carpet time. That's the word. And you experienced his presence and you were gone. . . . We just, we had a prayer meeting, and then we'd have a prayer meeting after the prayer meeting just to do this, which wasn't called soaking yet, to have ministry time, and to have worship, music playing [softly]; but not to worship, but to receive" (P33).[3] Spontaneous falling, often identified as being "slain in the Spirit" by older Pentecostals or "resting in the Spirit" by charismatics, was initially called "carpet time" in the Toronto revival. However, the practice was soon regularized. Toronto Vineyard pastor John Arnott's wife, Carol, was prominent in the development of soaking prayer. The ministry teams would spend much time praying for people, into the early hours of the morning, and continue for weeks on end. Carol claims to have been feeling very tired one night and God told her to just "lie down and let me soak you." From that moment, soaking prayer developed into a ritualized practice of lying down and soaking in God's presence for an hour to three hours at a time.

Music plays an important role in the practice of soaking prayer in both the large renewal meetings and the small, intimate settings of churches and homes. The large renewal meetings have four broadly discernible segments. They begin with a time of energetic praise, when people in attendance engage in enthusiastic singing and bodily movements. Although this portion of the service is more akin to patterns of charismatic praise, participants are observed lying down at the front and sides of the auditorium in soaking prayer, and leaders occasionally refer to this segment in terms of "soaking in the Father's love." A more intimate time ensues when the music slows and people are seen intently worshipping. The message or sermon is then given by one of the leaders or exemplars. And, finally, after the service, committed participants engage in an extended time of prayer (described above). There are also transitional times for announcements, testimonies, or tithes and offerings.

Renewal meetings take on the characteristics of music festivals in that pilgrims from all over the world will step away from the routines of daily life to attend conferences and immerse themselves in a different culture in order to experience renewal (Percy 1998; Althouse and Wilkinson 2011; Dowd, Little, and Nelson 2004). Musicians play in the style of contemporary pop music and begin with songs that have an energetic and fast tempo. The musical processes produce an atmosphere of emotional arousal and dissociative states through techniques such as acoustic driving, monotony, repetition, accelerando and crescendo, suspended musical phrases, and ascending fifths (Miller and Strongman 2002). As the musicians play, the worshippers engage in excited bodily expressions. People sway, moving their feet and nodding their heads. Some charismatics can be seen moving into the aisles and to the front of the auditorium in order to dance. Others carry colorful banners or flags and wave them about as the worship continues. In one meeting, the group marched around the church, accompanied by drumming, and chanted "press in." If someone falls to the floor, a swarm of people circle around and pray for that person with loud exclamations of "more Lord," "deeper Lord," or "higher Lord." In several of the large renewal meetings, we observed people

lying around the edges of the auditorium, soaking, as the main event continued. Thus, in the large renewal meeting, "soaking" metaphorically describes
the ecstatic experiences of participants who sense divine presence and who
"receive" the "Father's love" in the energetic state of worship. In these large
events, we were aware of the collective energy that was being produced and
could feel it reverberating through our own bodies. One researcher made the
following comments in his field notes:

> As I walk into the auditorium the energy is palpable. There is a driving
> drum beat anchoring contemporary praise music. Flags are being waved.
> Streamers are being spun around by enthusiastic participants. People
> are dancing, jumping up and down; some have their hands raised up
> praying. At about 7:30 the group breaks out in a chorus of glossolalia,
> a ritual called "singing in tongues" or "singing in the Spirit." It lasts for a
> few minutes and then one of the female singers sings out a short prayer
> in sync with the music. A lull occurs in the service where the music
> quiets down and the lead singer asks the congregation, "Do we need to
> wait for that part of the service, or can we do it right now? Grasp onto
> the hand of Jesus for healing." My own emotional reaction and bodily
> experience is one of tingling and the feeling of intense energy.[4]

Throughout the entire episode, music reverberates in the background and
people synchronize to its rhythm, which in turn facilitates the bodily rhythms
of those gathered in face-to-face co-presence (cf. Collins 2004; Shilling 2005;
Becker 2004). Energetic bodily movements such as swaying and dancing
and the body's natural rhythm of breathing are attuned to the music and to
other bodies as EE is produced, expressed, and stored. However, at about the
midpoint in the service prior to the speaker's message, the music reaches a
crescendo, signaling the end of the time for praise, and the time for worship
begins. The music for the latter slows down and becomes softer as people
engage in a more intimate time, in which they claim to be in God's presence.
At this point, the service takes on a more contemplative, prayerful sense and
the emotional tenor shifts from intense excitement to inwardness and intimacy. People are no longer dancing and have slowed their bodily movements.
It is not uncommon in this segment of the service to observe people quietly
weeping or laughing, many with intense expressions observable on their faces.

Soaking prayer also occurs in small, intimate groups in local churches
and participants' homes. These meetings do not have the excitement of the

large renewal meetings but replicate and continue to cultivate their emotional intimacy. Unlike the renewal meeting, these smaller groups do not use live music but rather soaking CDs. The music can be instrumental or vocal and, depending on locale and the leaders involved, is particularized for differing contexts. Most soaking prayer music is melodic, played in major modes, and slow in tempo; it uses repetitive phrases and reprises and produces a calming, dreamy effect that allows participants to rest (or relax) in order to be in God's presence and receive from God. Soaking prayer is a meditative type of prayer, but instead of occurring in silence, it is faciliated through entrainment by the music. The production of soaking CDs has become a cottage industry in which amateur musicians and singers record music to be sold through charismatic venues and at renewal gatherings (see Ward 2005). Individuals such as Jeremy and Connie Sinnott (the worship leaders of CTF Toronto), Ruth Fazal, Kelley Warren, Julie True, Marcel Preston, and Jonathan Clarke have become popular soaking musicians. Their music is played in small prayer gatherings in partic-ipants' homes, in local churches, or privately by oneself. The music is usually limited to a few instruments. Keyboards play a central role in soaking music, though a listener can discern other instruments, such as the flute, violin, guitar, or cymbals.

Martyn Percy (1997) noted the sentimentality and sublime eroticism in the music of the Vineyard and the early years of the Toronto Blessing. The overtly romantic and erotic language of Vineyard music focuses on the relationship of the worshipper to God, in which the secret of knowing God lies in the inward movement toward intimacy, where God is experienced. Emotions and feelings are surrendered to God in order to produce inner control that counters the external forces of chaos: sickness, evil, dissipation, and impotence. The same could also be said of soaking prayer music, with lyrics such as "my heart beats as one with yours," "take the sinner by the hand," "love me every day," "when I look into your eyes I am lost in everlasting love," "longing," "desire," "surren-der," "melt my heart," "your love enwraps around my heart," "in my Father's arms," "come away my beloved," "Jesus it's your love that I receive," "may the current of your love flow in the deepest part of me," "take me deeper into your love," and so forth. Moreover, the songs are often sung as a kind of love letter to God the Father, with an emphasis on referring to God and the worshipper in the first-person singular. The romantic language is not unique to soaking music but is part and parcel of the message of the renewal. John Arnott often talks about the renewal as a great love story in which the church as the bride is being prepared for the wedding. At one renewal event, Carol Arnott began the message with a string of exclamations, saying "I love you" as a sign of relationship to her beloved. In fact, she designed a prayer discipline in which every ten minutes her watch would beep and she would take a few minutes to express her love to the Father, Jesus, and the Spirit. This was while she was delivering a sermon to a crowd of more than one thousand.

Percy is quick to note that subliminally erotic language has a theological place within the broader Christian heritage of mysticism. Visions, sensual tickling, and bodily stirrings were elements observable in mysticism. The symbolism of marriage and consummation coincided with ecstatic behavior. Idioms such as "tasting" God, "kissing" him, "heart," and being "embraced" by Christ were regularly used. Erotic spirituality was a way to embody religious experience that offered women marginalized by male-dominated clerical structures a means to reclaim authority (see Bynum 1992; Nelstrop 2009).

Finally, the practice of breathing, with its rhythms of inhalation and exhalation, the in-and-out process of physical air moving through the body, is an embodied practice related to prayer and is facilitated by the rhythms and beat of music (Percy 1997; Shilling 2005; Kearns 2005; Irigaray 2002). The vigorous bodily activity and excitement of charismatic worship produces rapid breathing, whereas the meditative practice of soaking prayer, in which one rests, slows the breathing rhythms. Breathing slowly and from the diaphragm is often associated with de-stressing and relaxation. In our observations and interviews, people reported that their bodies slowed down and their breathing became more regulated. This was our own experience, too, as we participated in the practice of soaking, noticing how our breathing changed within minutes and the muscles in our bodies started to relax. As the breathing deepened, the body relaxed, the mind slowed down, and the heart decelerated, as far as we could perceive. Exhalation would deepen and come from the diaphragm, and at times there would be sounds of contentment.

Curiously, breathing is an important practice of soaking captured in songs such as Julie True's "Breathe You In" and Kelley Warren's "Breathe on Me Breath of God." The slow tempos and repetition of certain words, as well as nonverbal sounds such as "mmmm" and "oooooo," regulate the movement of air through the body, allowing participants to slow down their breathing, relax muscular energy, and lower the heart rate. One young woman relayed a vision she experienced while soaking in prayer. As she was praying, she was being drawn deeper into the Father's love but began to get panicky and could not breathe. She said, "And then I realized how deep I was. And I couldn't breathe. I couldn't breathe. When I was—you know, lying on my back on the sofa and I was just so paralyzed. And—my chest, my chest was like, I felt my chest was breathing in and out. And I know that he was giving me the breath" (P59). Another person commented, "And so, I tend to just breathe in prayer, like I automatically pray" (P100).

The rhythms of breathing can be modified by the rhythms and beat of music. As groups of people come together for soaking prayer, bodily responses begin to synchronize through ritual interaction and produce high levels of emotional energy. Music is a vehicle through which attunement and entrainment are facilitated.

Conclusion

Charismatic renewal is especially effective in encouraging worshippers to allow their bodies to engage one another through music and prayer. The practice of soaking prayer is especially instructive, highlighting the ways in which charismatics experience attunement and embodiment while claiming to be transformed by divine love. This transformation is expressed in a love relationship, fully supported by the music, in which God as loving Father embraces the beloved, calling them to rest while enjoying his presence. In turn, the practice of soaking prayer is shared with other worshippers, who claim that these encounters with a greater love also fill them with love for others. The rhythm of worship is balanced with breathing, which is consequential for the participant in a therapeutic way as the mystical body is renewed through an experience of interactional love.

NOTES

1. The Association of Vineyard Churches is a group of charismatic churches begun by Ken Gulliksen in 1975. In 1982, John Wimber's church officially affiliated with the Vineyard. A short time later, he assumed leadership of the Vineyard churches and embarked on an aggressive church-growth agenda that resulted in numerous church plants in North America and eventually the U.K. Vineyard churches are charismatic in style, with claims of glossolalia, prophetic utterance, words of knowledge, laughter, and bodily falling while in an ecstatic state. C. Peter Wagner (1988) described this development in Pentecostal-charismatic Christianity as the "third wave" of Pentecostalism. For further reading, see Percy (1996) and Miller (1997, 2005); for a popular history, see Jackson (1999).

2. The project was supported by a grant from the Templeton Foundation and the Flame of Love Project.

3. We use the letter *P* to refer to participants throughout the chapter. Interviews were conducted with 126 participants. P91, for instance, means "participant 91."

4. The field notes were written in point form and put into narrative structure to capture the sense of what was observed.

REFERENCES

Althouse, Peter, and Michael Wilkinson. 2011. "Playing in the Father's Love: The Eschatological Implications of Charismatic Ritual and the Kingdom of God in Catch the Fire." *ARC: The Journal for the Faculty of Religious Studies, McGill University* 39:1–24.

Becker, Judith. 2004. *Deep Listeners: Music, Emotion, and Trancing.* Bloomington: Indiana University Press.

Bynum, Caroline Walker. 1992. *Fragmentation and Redemption: Essays on Gender and the Human Body in Medieval Religion.* New York: Zone Books.

Catch the Fire Ministries. 2009. "Student Manual: Soaking Prayer Center Training School."

Clayton, Martin, Rebecca Sager, and Udo Will. 2005. "In Time with the Music: The Concept of Entrainment and Its Significance for Ethnomusicology." *European Meetings in Ethnomusicology* 11:3–75.

Collins, Randall. 2004. *Interaction Ritual Chains.* Princeton: Princeton University Press.

Csordas, Thomas J. 1994. *The Sacred Self: A Cultural Phenomenology of Charismatic Healing.* Berkeley: University of California Press.

———. 1997. *Language, Charisma, and Creativity: The Ritual Life of a Religious Movement.* Berkeley: University of California Press.

———. 2002. *Body/Meaning/Healing.* New York: Palgrave Macmillan.

Dowd, Timothy J., Kathleen Little, and Jenna Nelson. 2004. "Music Festivals as Scenes: Examples from Serious Music, Womyn's Music, and Skatepunk." In *Music Scenes: Local, Translocal, and Virtual,* edited by Andy Bennett and Richard A. Peterson, 149–67. Nashville: Vanderbilt University Press.

Durkheim, Émile. 1912. *The Elementary Forms of the Religious Life.* New York: Free Press.

Foster, Richard J. 1992. *Prayer.* New York: HarperCollins.

Hunt, Stephen. 2009. "The 'Toronto Blessing'—A Lesson in Globalized Religion?" In *Canadian Pentecostalism: Transition and Transformation,* edited by Michael Wilkinson, 233–48. Montreal: McGill–Queen's University Press.

Irigaray, Luce. 2002. *Between East and West: From Singularity to Community.* New York: Columbia University Press.

Jackson, Bill. 1999. *The Quest for the Radical Middle: A History of the Vineyard.* Cape Town: Vineyard International.

Kearns, Cleo McNelly. 2005. "Irigaray's *Between East and West*: Breath, Pranayama, and the Phenomenology of Prayer." In *The Phenomenology of Prayer,* edited by Bruce Ellis Benson and Norman Wirzba, 103–18. New York: Fordham University Press.

Lee, Matthrew T., Margaret M. Poloma, and Stephen G. Post. 2013. *The Heart of Religion: Spiritual Empowerment, Benevolence, and the Experience of God's Love.* New York: Oxford University Press.

Lee, Matthew T., and Amos Yong, eds. 2012. *The Science and Theology of Godly Love.* DeKalb: Northern Illinois University Press.

Miller, Donald E. 1997. *Reinventing American Protestantism: Christianity in the New Millennium.* Berkeley: University of California Press.

———. 2005. "Routinizing Charisma: The Vineyard Christian Fellowship in the Post-Wimber Era." In *Church, Identity, and Change: Theology and Denominational Structures in Unsettled Times*, edited by David A. Roozen and James R. Nieman, 141–62. Grand Rapids, Mich.: Eerdmans.

Miller, Mandi M., and Kenneth T. Strongman. 2002. "The Emotional Effects of Music on Religious Experience: A Study of the Pentecostal-Charismatic Style of Music and Worship." *Psychology and Music* 30 (1): 8–27.

Nelstrop, Louise. 2009. *Christian Mysticism: An Introduction to Contemporary Theoretical Approaches*. With Kevin Magill and Bradley B. Onishi. Burlington, Vt.: Ashgate.

Percy, Martyn. 1996. *Words, Wonders, and Power: Understanding Contemporary Christian Fundamentalism and Revivalism*. London: SPCK.

———. 1997. "Sweet Rapture: Subliminal Eroticism in Contemporary Charismatic Worship." *Theology and Sexuality* 3 (6): 71–106.

———. 1998. "The Morphology of Pilgrimage in the 'Toronto Blessing.'" *Religion* 28 (1): 281–88.

———. 2005. "Adventure and Atrophy in a Charismatic Movement: Returning to the 'Toronto Blessing.'" *Journal of Contemporary Religion* 20 (1): 71–90.

Poloma, Margaret M. 2003. *Main Street Mystics: The Toronto Blessing and Reviving Pentecostalism*. Walnut Creek, Calif.: AltaMira Press.

Poloma, Margaret M., and G. H. Gallup. 1991. *Varieties of Prayer*. Philadelphia: Trinity Press International.

Poloma, Margaret M., and John Green. 2010. *The Assemblies of God: Godly Love and the Revitalization of American Pentecostalism*. New York: New York University Press.

Poloma, Margaret M., and Ralph W. Hood Jr. 2008. *Blood and Fire: Godly Love in a Pentecostal Emerging Church*. New York: New York University Press.

Richter, Philip. 1997. "The Toronto Blessing: Charismatic Evangelical Global Warming." In *Charismatic Christianity: Sociological Perspectives*, edited by Stephen Hunt, Malcolm Hamilton, and Tony Walker, 97–119. New York: St. Martin's Press.

Riis, Ole, and Linda Woodhead. 2010. *A Sociology of Religious Emotion*. New York: Oxford University Press.

Robbins, Joel. 2010. "Anthropology of Religion." In *Studying Global Pentecostalism: Theories and Methods*, edited by Allan Anderson, Michael Bergunder, André Droogers, and Cornelis van der Laan, 156–78. Berkeley: University of California Press.

———. 2011. "The Obvious Aspects of Pentecostalism: Ritual and Pentecostal Globalization." In *Practicing the Faith: The Ritual Life of Pentecostal-Charismatic Christians*, edited by Martin Lindhardt, 49–67. New York: Berghahn Books.

Shilling, Chris. 2005. *The Body in Culture, Technology, and Society*. London: Sage.

Smilde, David. 2011. "Public Rituals and Political Positioning: Venezuelan Evangelicals and the Chávez Government." In *Practicing the Faith: The Ritual Life of Pentecostal-Charismatic Christians*, edited by Martin Lindhardt, 306–29. New York: Berghahn Books.

Sorokin, Pitirim A. (1954) 2002. *The Ways and Power of Love*. Philadelphia: Templeton Press.

Turner, Bryan S. 1996. *The Body and Society*. London: Sage.

Wagner, C. Peter. 1988. *The Third Wave of the Holy Spirit*. Ann Arbor, Mich.: Servant.

Ward, Peter. 2005. *Selling Worship: How What We Sing Has Changed the Church*. Waynesboro, Ga.: Paternoster Press.

Wilkinson, Michael. 2012. "The Institutionalization of Religion: Impediment or Impetus for Godly Love?" In *Godly Love: Impediments and Possibilities*, edited by Matthew T. Lee and Amos Yong, 153–70. Lanham, Md.: Lexington Books.

Wilkinson, Michael, and Peter Althouse. 2012. "Apology and Forgiveness as an Expression of Love in a Charismatic Congregation." *PentecoStudies* 11 (1): 87–102.

———. 2014. *Catch the Fire: Soaking Prayer and Charismatic Renewal.* DeKalb: Northern Illinois University Press.

2

Salvation (Not Yet?) Materialized:
Healing as Possibility and Possible Complication
for Expressing Suffering in Pentecostal
Music and Worship

Andrew M. McCoy

Like many other streams of Christian tradition as of late, Pentecostal theology is showing signs of renewed interest in issues of human suffering and the expression of suffering through lament.[1] Simultaneously, this emerging scholarship tends to note the lack of suffering expressed in Pentecostal liturgical practice (Ellington 2000, 58; Hunter and Robeck 2006, xv; Mittelstadt 2008, 154)—a lack that has not always gone unnoticed by those who write and perform Pentecostal music, as it has grown increasingly influential on much Christian worship throughout the world.[2] Yet, in this chapter, I will examine how some form of expression of suffering to God often already happens in Pentecostal worship, as a result of that which Miroslav Volf (1989) describes as the "materiality of salvation." Volf observes that Pentecostal theology regularly correlates the atoning person and work of Jesus Christ with the experience of divine healing in the present, and Pentecostals consequently affirm that God responds to present suffering not only spiritually or morally but also as it is manifest physically and psychologically in the bodies and circumstances of believers. In what follows, I will demonstrate how belief in the possibility of a material experience of healing leads Pentecostals in many different parts of the world to bring pain to God through vibrant expression in worship and music. However, I will also consider how this belief can potentially complicate the liturgical expression of suffering when healing doesn't seem to happen, or happens only partially, or when suffering continues to persist. I will frame this discussion in terms of common Pentecostal modes of response to suffering through worship—confrontation with evil, confession and repentance of sin, and affirmation of faith amid suffering—each of which relates to the wider history and tradition of the Christian faith and is distinctly influenced by Pentecostal affirmation of divine healing and the materiality of salvation. I will then conclude by briefly considering how the contemporary movement of Pentecostalism between differing cultural and socioeconomic environments impacts how Pentecostals affirm the materiality of salvation, which in turn requires a more complex view of how suffering is expressed in Pentecostal music and worship.

Pentecostal Worship as Confrontation with Evil

While the spiritual reality of evil is affirmed throughout Christian Scripture and tradition, in Pentecostalism, evil spirits are regularly understood to plague the material world and perpetrate negative consequences from within human life. In places as far apart as sub-Saharan Africa (Kalu 2008, 218), El Salvador (Williams 1997), and Korea (Kim 1999), Pentecostal liturgical practice provides a common means by which evil may be confronted and the materiality of salvation made manifest.

> Especially in the global south, it is not unusual to find pentecostals blaming the demonic for the prostitution industry, the AIDS virus, medically inexplicable conditions, unemployment, political corruption, and other real-life challenges. Given these assumptions, Jesus as savior is understood not only as healer but also as deliverer, and, in some cases, as exorcist, and pentecostal evangelistic services thus include moments in the liturgy devoted to prayer for the sick as well as to rituals of deliverance and exorcism. When understood in this manner, it is clear that pentecostalism in global context preaches a much more holistic as well as this-worldly gospel: Jesus saves not only human souls in the next life but also human bodies and lives in the present age. (Yong 2010, 123)

Melvin Butler's recent studies of music in Haitian Pentecostalism offer a trenchant example of this global phenomenon. Butler compares and contrasts the practices of a group of independent Pentecostal congregations in Haiti (known as "heavenly army" churches) with organizational Pentecostal churches more influenced by the United States and argues that both Haitian groups turn to worship through music in response to difficult socioeconomic realities. Haitian nationals must navigate a history of recent military violence, systemic issues of poverty and suffering, and a complex spiritual climate tied to the influence of both native Haitian voudou and Catholicism. Worship in Haitian Pentecostalism thus functions as a means of spiritual warfare against evil—with music as a kind of spiritual weapon—which materially repositions the faithful for the reception of healing and renewal.

As a result, the concrete expression of suffering is common across the spectrum of Haitian Pentecostal worship and music practice. In the "heavenly army" worship characterizing certain independent Pentecostal churches, Butler describes the singing of *plent*, or a type of lament consisting of "slow songs [that] express a particularly somber or plaintive mood and provide congregants a means of communicating to God feelings of despair and dependency" (2002, 90). One particular example makes explicit various types of suffering common to Haitian experience:

> Here we are before you, Lord.
> We are unable, Lord.
> We have need of you, Lord.
> We are not employed, Lord.
> I am persecuted, Lord.
> Evil spirits challenge me, Lord.
> Meet their challenges, Lord.
> I've been suffering for a long time, Lord.
> I've been sick for a long time, Lord.
> You are my good doctor, Lord
> (Butler 2008, 41)

Butler finds the above to exemplify how the congregation positions itself "toward God in a lyrical and physical display of vulnerability" for the purpose of receiving spiritual rescue (41).

Expressions of suffering are also typical of worship in Haiti's more mainline or U.S.-influenced Pentecostal congregations. In the various Churches of God, a classical Pentecostal denomination from the United States that has long had a mission presence in Haiti, music "facilitates an ecstatic state of worship that encourages congregants to trust in God despite the daily hardships of poverty and sickness, which pose a constant threat for many Haitians" (Butler 2002,

101). When Haitian Pentecostals cry for deliverance, these various laments can hardly be understood as responses to *either* spiritual *or* material realities. Indeed, the spiritual and material are *intertwined* in response to the evil and suffering perceived to challenge everyday existence in Haiti.

Yet, as Butler puts it, the embodied musical practice that forms a "weapon" in the spiritual arsenal of Haitian Pentecostalism is also "a two-edged sword." Music may be a common means of Pentecostal confrontation with evil and suffering, but music also divides: "Across Haiti's political and religious landscape, individuals and groups strategically employ musical and rhetorical performances of faith to reposition themselves positively in relation to spiritual, social, and national others" (2008, 30). On the one hand, participants in the independent "heavenly army" churches described above often claim increased access to divine power through worship using traditional Haitian music, as well as related spiritual practices and beliefs. On the other hand, many organizational Pentecostal churches disapprove of this approach, considering Haitian music too closely derived from voudou and so, to some degree, *intrinsically* evil. Music in these congregations derives instead from the United States or other foreign places of influence and is combined with an emphasis on renewal and healing through personal holiness. These two Pentecostal groups consequently diverge at the very point in which both seek to respond to problems in Haiti—through worship in music. Butler describes this reality as Haiti's "paradox of Pentecostal music making—its spiritually amalgamative but socially divisive potential" (23).

Butler's research is revealing in terms of the light it sheds on the complexity of Haitian Pentecostalism in particular, but also more generally, as it demonstrates how Pentecostal worship and music create a context for expressing suffering while, at the same time, potentially further complicating that expression. Spiritual warfare *inherently* expresses suffering by naming it as an aspect of evil, and Pentecostals may do so not only as individuals or congregations at worship but also by "singing praise in the streets" (Ingalls 2012, 343–46) and effecting public demonstrations of worship in hopes to "heal the nation" and beyond (Wightman 2007, 245–53). Nevertheless, this practice can also lead to further perpetration of suffering and evil, if spiritual warfare is instrumentalized against other aspects of Christian affirmation (which might otherwise militate against the possibility of spiritual warfare spilling over into violence) or when discernment of spiritual evil as a corrupting force *invading* the material world is overtaken by the theological conclusion that aspects of the material world are *intrinsically* evil or corrupt.

Butler's concern over potential social division in Haiti is not without merit; Pentecostal worship can and has been co-opted by political forces bent on nationalistic violence or oppression (the massacre of indigenous Guatemalans by the infamous Montt regime is an oft-cited example). Kalu, for instance, describes "guerrillas for Christ" who arose from revival at a theological college in Uganda and "encouraged people not only to cut down plants used in brewing local beer, but to cut down coffee cash crops because the *abomwoyo* (people of the spirit) should have no investment in earthly things" (2008, 94–95). When faith practice hardens along this dualistic line, various physical or material realities—whether embodied practices such as music and dance, or other aspects of culture, or even entire peoples or nations—become "demonized" to the extent that they are judged to be beyond redemption. Salvation may then be understood to materialize *over and against* part of God's creation itself, resulting in worship that either flees this demonized material or becomes the battle cry to fight against the same.

Pentecostal Worship as Confession and Repentance of Sin

Alongside confrontation with evil, confession and repentance of sin are responses to suffering generally prescribed by all Christian Scripture and prevalent throughout Christian liturgical tradition. What consistently distinguishes Pentecostalism is its theological emphasis on Christ's atonement for sin as providing not only spiritual salvation but also material renewal for body, mind, and lived circumstances. In Pentecostal liturgical practice, the *experience* of confession and repentance is crucial, but unlike many other Protestant traditions, Pentecostal worship typically features no formal liturgy, such as a read or sung congregational confession followed by words of assurance spoken by a minister or worship leader. Instead, Pentecostal music, singing, and movement of the body through dance or gestures are all understood to elicit deep feeling and emotion within individuals, which may then result in the confession of sin in later parts of the service, either as testimony or when healing is offered and received. Miller and Yamamori describe the view of a former drug addict in Hong Kong: "In worship you don't simply sing about God and Jesus, you 'touch' God" (2007, 89). Emphasis on healing may lead to songs that are more introspective or observably slower (Csordas 1997, 112), but the simultaneously joyful, Jesus-adoring orientation of much Pentecostal music should not be dismissed as incongruent with the experience of sinners who wish to confess. In previous research on the U.S. Vineyard Fellowship, Miller observed that for many "it is as if the potential for joy—nurtured by the Christian perception that Jesus offers unconditional love and acceptance— allowed them to acknowledge the underside of their lives, the ugliness that they usually attempted to hide from view" (1997, 89).

The materiality of salvation and the possibility of receiving God's "touch" may potentially make the context for confession and repentance all the more joyful. But they can also create the potential for tension within Pentecostal-ism regarding to what degree Pentecostals will continue to struggle with evil and suffering once they have repented of sin and begun to worship Christ in faith. Volf notes, "The majority of Pentecostalists claim that divine healing is provided in the atonement, yet they caution that the Bible does not teach 'that every sickness will flee in the face of faith in the same way sin is overcome in every instance where the sinner repents and believes'" (1989, 458). As classical Pentecostal practice is regularly accompanied by some degree of theological differentiation between the reality of the atonement and the human experience of salvation in the present, repentance of sin is not necessarily understood to result in immediate or complete manifestation of healing. The experience of suffering can then be understood as ongoing, and its continued expression can be affirmed alongside continued healing as a regular part of the Pentecostal life of faith (Bomann 2011, 195).

But this is not always the case. Other forms of Pentecostalism approach the materiality of salvation very differently: "Grounding healing in the atone-ment . . . makes it possible for some more radical Pentecostalists to speak of its appropriation in a way parallel to the reception of justification. Since the Scrip-ture says, by 'his wounds' Christians 'were healed' (1 Pet. 2:24), healing is a fact already accomplished for every believer. Just as every person who believes will be saved (Rom. 10:9), so also every Christian who believes will be healed" (Volf 1989, 458). This "more radical" view of healing significantly impacts how the experience of suffering is theologically understood and liturgically expressed. For Pentecostals who expect health or prosperity to result *inevitably* from faith, conversion typically involves more than turning to God and away from sin and disbelief; it also requires turning away from suffering, however it is experienced in life (Sánchez-Walsh 2011, 164). Suffering's persistence tends to be construed as a lack of faith or acquiescence to evil—a kind of theology that can readily silence the ongoing expression of suffering (Bowler 2011, 98).

Still, even when health and prosperity theology takes hold in Pentecos-tal practice, it does not necessarily result in the complete disappearance of the expression of suffering from Pentecostal music and worship. The healing affirmed through an underlying belief in the materiality of salvation usually ensures that expression of suffering will remain crucial—at least *before* conversion and repentance of sin. Many African converts to Pentecostalism, for example, attend worship for the first time in order to address physical maladies that modern and traditional medicine have been unable to cure (Cox 1995, 247). R. Andrew Chesnut argues that in Brazilian Pentecostalism "the most efficacious manner of expressing one's faith" is through a vow, or *promessa*, which trades on conversion as a response to suffering: "The pentecostal convert [in Brazil] must repent, rejecting the sinful (sick) world of 'men' in favor of the righteous (healthy) world of God and his saints" (1997, 83). A strong causal link between illness and sin, godliness and health—also observed in India (Bergunder 2008, 149)—can further solidify the connection between atonement and material experiences of salvation. Yet, in order for this connection to hold, physical or socioeconomic experiences that are being confessed as sin must still be *acknowledged*. For this reason, suffering is often expressed to some degree in the worship of even the most extreme versions of "health and wealth" Pentecostalism.

A case in point is found in the evangelistic services of a Brazilian neo-Pentecostal movement known as the Universal Church of the Kingdom of God (Igreja Universal do Reino de Deus, IURD). André Corten argues that although the IURD unceasingly proclaims faith as the path to prosperity, it often does so through worship oriented to the unconverted and the difficulties of their lives. The unconverted individual who passes through an IURD worship service finds himself

> caught in the gesture of a multitude. He feels included, on an equal footing, in an activity which is no longer the pure and simple struggle for daily material survival. We call the emotion he feels "consolation." The individual is consoled by the discourse of prayer, in the form of complaint or lamentation. He no longer confronts his own problems, but his suffering is borne through the centuries by biblical psalms. He merges into this complaint of the poor who have had enough, a complaint which rises toward God. (Corten 1999, 57)

The IURD may make use of scriptural lament and complaint to help suffering individuals identify with its evangelistic vision, but this hardly means that the IURD validates worship *amid suffering*.

> In this discourse of the IURD, inspired by the theology of prosperity, poverty is lack of faith or ignorance. . . . This is exactly why, in a first stage, consolation does not entail conversion. It is the poor whom these Churches address, those who "are poor because they lack faith." These Churches must make them understand that God hates poverty. Yet in order to continue speaking to them, there is one language, that of consolation; it is a language of lamentation. Even if conversion consists of making the converts shoulder the negation of poverty, the success of the "autonomous Churches" depends on their capacity to receive this lamentation and to give it a semi-historical place. (Corten 1999, 58)

Lamentation in the worship of the IURD is "semi-historical" in the sense that the IURD expresses suffering as the reality of life *before* faith, while simultaneously rejecting all experience of suffering in the present life of the faithful. Hence the prominent display of posters proclaiming "Put an End to Suffering" at IURD places of worship (Ruuth and Rodrigues 2000, 29). Ongoing suffering can only indicate faithlessness, evil forces, or both at work in the sufferer's life. The assumption is that when one *truly* begins to worship God, suffering will cease to persist and there will be no more suffering to express.

This assumption is also a fundamental aspect of how the Word of Faith movement utilizes worship to respond to sin and suffering through "positive confession." Beckford cites the teaching of a Word of Faith church in the U.K.: "Words have been known for a long time as tools that: influence your perspective, affect your performance, determine your possession. Since words are such powerful tools, you should use your words to: build your spirit man, re-write the negatives spoken into your life, paint the picture of your desired future, lift yourself from defeat to victory" (2006, 133). Faith churches and other prosperity movements stress the linguistic activation of faith and so begin by naming physical and material realities to which the claims of faith can respond. Wen Reagan's analysis of the music of Israel Houghton in this volume observes that assuming these "blessings" in faith may also entail becoming a blessing amid the struggling of others or in response to social structures perceived as unjust. Even so, in many of these particular Pentecostal settings, it may well be the case that one will struggle to "revisit the altar again and again" and express ongoing suffering (Bowler 2011, 91). Once one has turned away from suffering by repenting of sin, liturgical space for lament may collapse into a kind of spiritual vacuum, leaving behind little means to give language to pain *as an act of faith.*

Pentecostal Worship as Affirmation of Faith amid Suffering

Encompassing both confrontation with evil and confession of sin, the most general mode by which Pentecostalism may be understood to address suffering is through affirming faith by acts of worship. Christian Scripture and tradition prescribes joyful affirmation of faith in all circumstances, including suffering, but as we have seen above, for Pentecostals this translates into much more than mere acknowledgment of spiritual or cognitive realities. Rather, faith empowers believers to experience physical and material realities that result from salvation in Christ. Because worship is understood as a means by which the materiality of salvation becomes manifest, Pentecostals often explicitly express suffering to God when seeking out divine healing in and through the context of such practices as music, dance, and fully embodied forms of prayer. However, the way in which suffering comes to liturgical expression in Pentecostalism may also complicate the ongoing expression of suffering as an act of faith. Worship as spiritual warfare brings suffering to expression in confrontation with evil but, at times, risks being consumed by the confrontation itself, thereby becoming a means for bringing violence into the material world or a means for escaping aspects of the material world experienced as intrinsically evil and beyond salvation. Pentecostalism also expresses suffering in worship through confession and repentance of sin, but there still remains the pervasive influence of Pentecostal movements that press the materiality of salvation to extremes by focusing on the experience of suffering as *already overcome* in Christ. When health and/or wealth become understood as inevitabilities of faith, the ongoing reality of suffering may become very difficult for otherwise faithful Pentecostals to express.

For much of Pentecostalism, though, worship of God *amid* suffering remains a crucial, if not *the* crucial, means of dealing with the persistence of suffering. The saving person and work of Christ may make material healing a viable possibility in the present, but much of Pentecostalism also affirms, as Land puts it, that "the passion of Christ on the cross is finished. The passion of the believer and the church in Christ is not" (1993, 202). Worship, as a place in which the ongoing problems of evil and sin are addressed, and music, as an indispensable means by which the varied realities of Pentecostal existence may come to expression, both serve to facilitate experiences of God's response to suffering, even while healing is in process or when harsh realities of everyday life remain.

Examples abound. Ramírez finds that for Latino Pentecostals who labor along the borderlands of the southwestern United States, "their music output captur[es] something of the experience of exhausted bodies dragged in from a day's work, quickly splashed with water and nourished with beans and tortillas before dashing off to the campsite or tent service to embrace other bodies in fervent and ecstatic worship" (2009, 162). Geographically nearby—but in a profoundly different context culturally, socially, and economically—Miller observes U.S. congregations of the Vineyard Fellowship where people "get in touch with deep wounds inflicted by others; other times they return to personal failures that have been rationalized and repressed. Connecting with these memories and feelings and giving them to God for healing are import-ant byproducts of worship" (1997, 88). On the other side of the world, Kim describes the ongoing release of *han* in Korean Pentecostalism, a term signify-ing the depth of suffering experienced in human existence: "Through singing so-called gospel songs (a kind of church rock music) while clapping hands, weeping in loud prayer and especially praying in tongues, they express their oppressed feelings, thus helping people experience the release of *han*" (1999, 137). In the context of both black British and African Caribbean Christianity, Beckford argues that worship enables "Black people to negotiate the existential absurdity of being Black in a White society," in part through embodied worship and sound that affirm black identity and evoke the "realised eschatology within the theology of the church hall, where the power of the future is dragged into the present so that all the joy, power and peace of the future Kingdom of God is [*sic*] experienced now" (2006, 106). Outside the church hall much of this eschatological hope goes unrealized, and, as Sanders (1999, ix) proposes in terms of the African American holiness experience, this may be best expressed as "exile" such as that testified to in Psalm 137, a biblical lament that asks, "How can we sing the Lord's song in a foreign land?" Still, Sanders, like Beckford, finds black identity eschatologically affirmed and performed through worship: "In worship, the saints replicate the 'other' world, the place where the exile can be at home" (64). Finally, a restatement of this eschatological-liturgical con-nection can be found by looking in a Southeast Asian direction to Tan-Chow, who, while critical of aspects of Pentecostalism in Singapore, remains hopeful that the best of Pentecostal worship is "a profoundly eschatological act of cel-ebration. . . . The gift of doxological joy enables the Church to sing, to dance, to serve, to suffer, to heal and to forgive while awaiting the full coming of the eschaton" (2007, 153–54).

No wonder Cox proclaims that Pentecostalism is "a global vehicle for the restoration of primal hope" (1995, 119). Yet these examples also suggest that the material characteristics of Pentecostalism's eschatologically defined existence may look very different when Pentecostal music and worship transfers across different cultures and confronts various global realities such as poverty, immigration, racial tensions, oppression, and war. Likewise, Pentecostal liturgical practice may be substantially impacted when socioeconomic conditions improve or where greater access to medical care and education prevails.

Consider what can happen when the roles of traditional Pentecostal missionary efforts to the Global South are reversed and Pentecostals from the South migrate to the Global North. Währisch-Oblau describes the fascinating case of West African Pentecostals living in Germany who have had to rethink their approach to ministry "in a situation where people are materially secure and where religion is highly privatized and spiritualized" (2011, 73). West African Pentecostals find that Germans are more likely to attend concerts of music and worship than evangelistic events that emphasize healing. Speaking of this change, two Ghanaian immigrant pastors put it this way: "Basically, the message is the same, whether Germans or Ghanaians or Americans, the message is the same. But . . . there are times you need to change the method" (72). Indeed, the message may continue to include healing, but it is offered *in private*, away from "showy" services that might make many Germans "uncomfortable" (74–75). This change in evangelistic method demonstrates how the *context* in which the materiality of salvation is affirmed and made manifest has shifted, moving away from what is familiar to Ghanaian Pentecostals in order to adapt to that which is typical of German culture and much of the contemporary Western world. Accordingly, suffering is no longer expressed to God and responded to within a communal gathering such as a healing crusade. Instead it becomes addressed in an individualized setting away from corporate worship. All the while, Pentecostal music remains an effective means of gathering all manner of people for evangelistic events of worship. As the two Ghanaian pastors note, "European, Western, German, they're going to come to a concert, and that's an open door. The place is packed!" (72).

Pentecostal Worship and Salvation *Not Yet* Materialized

The context for divine healing, and even the concept of it, may change as Pentecostals move into an upwardly mobile context, and, especially in the West, suffering may become more a matter of individual struggle and concern. But does the transfer of Pentecostalism into elevated socioeconomic conditions result in less expression of suffering through Pentecostal music and worship? Volf's comparison of liberation theology and Pentecostalism further illuminates the concern behind the question here. Volf finds the concept of the materiality of salvation to be a common aspect of worship for both liberation theology and Pentecostalism, but argues that each affirms it in different ways. Liberation theology primarily explains the salvation experience as the overthrow of systems and structures that oppress the poor, while Pentecostalism "is interested in the individual's salvation (regeneration) and hopes for societal change as a consequence of the multiplicity of personal commitments to Christ" (1989, 448). Thus, both liberation theology and Pentecostalism tend to *instrumentalize* worship in response to suffering, but they do it in different ways; whereas liberation theology understands worship as a collective action meant to challenge oppressive structures, Pentecostalism, in contrast, tends to emphasize the transforming possibilities of worship as an *individual experience*. And in the light of this Pentecostal emphasis, we might ask the previously stated question more pointedly: Will Pentecostals continue to bring suffering to God through worship even when it is not their particular experience or when their embrace of the materiality of salvation necessitates that they experience sacrificial suffering on behalf of those who do not share a similarly upwardly mobile existence?

Our above examination of the relationship between Pentecostal understandings of the materiality of salvation and various global circumstances in which Pentecostal music and worship practices are now emerging would at least suggest avoiding answers that, perhaps, reach too far, too quickly. Regarding the state of much contemporary Pentecostal faith practice in the Global North, Mittelstadt writes, "Since Pentecostal Christians expect 'the blessing of God,' suffering seems to infringe on this right to happiness, causing an increasing gap between expectations and any potential suffering connected with God and/or godliness. . . . Given this mindset, contemporary pursuit of the Spirit is often relegated to a personal, self-empowering experience, which gives further impetus to 'the blessing of God,' measured in terms of secular power and success" (2008, 165–66). While this is undoubtedly the case with much "health and wealth" Pentecostalism, the picture is more complicated amid Pentecostal worship that offers some affirmation of both the materiality of salvation and the ongoing reality of human suffering. As noted in an earlier section above, Miller's research on the Vineyard Fellowship observes that the joyful experience that arises through music and worship can allow those who are suffering to "acknowledge the underside of their lives" and connect difficult feelings and memories with the healing power of God (1997, 88–89). There is further evidence that addressing one's own suffering is not the only by-product of Pentecostal worship. In their recent examination of a socially "progressive" element within global Pentecostalism, Miller and Yamamori argue that worship is "the single most important element that empowers" the social ministries of progressive Pentecostals (2007, 221). These ministries may not be beyond critique with regard to awareness of problems in systemic social structures (213–16), but in many different parts of the world, progressive Pentecostals are significantly responding to the diseased and marginalized on the basis of how they have been "touched" by God through worship. As seen in other examples throughout the present chapter, "for Pentecostals, worship provides the opportunity to experience an alternative reality. . . . The challenge is to channel these emotions, these feelings, these desires" (221). Clearly, Pentecostals in many contexts do channel their experiences of the materiality of salvation in worship to respond to aspects of the world where salvation has not yet materialized.

But even if our examination of the connection between Pentecostal healing and music and worship reveals ongoing opportunities for suffering to be expressed and receive response, difficulties still remain. In fairness to Mittelstadt, who contrasts his concerns over Pentecostals in the Global North and those in the Global South, many of the progressive Pentecostals identified by Miller and Yamamori are "channeling" these experiences of worship into a social response to suffering in the context of the South. It may be similarly revealing to note that when Canadian worship songwriter Brian Doerksen asks, "Where are the laments? Where are the transparent songs?" (Coggins 2008), the best place to look often remains music from Pentecostal contexts in the Global South, on the one hand, and Pentecostalism in the marginalized contexts of Doerksen's own Global North, on the other. In these places, the manifest desire and need for divine healing remain very clear. As Pentecostalism struggles alongside much of historic Christianity to renew the place and use of lament in its worship, perhaps these honest expressions about present healing, so much like those in the Psalms and other parts of Scripture, can provide current examples *and* calls to action for Pentecostalism in prosperous cultures and other Christian traditions as well.

NOTES

1. Recent Pentecostal theology addresses suffering from a number of angles, including lament in the Hebrew Bible (Ellington 2008), the theme of suffering in the New Testament

(Mittelstadt 2004, 2008), the function of testimony in the Pentecostal tradition (Ellington 2000), reflections on Pentecostalism and theology of Christ's suffering and death on the cross (Kärkkäinen 2004), Christian persecution in the contemporary world (Hunter and Robeck 2006), and the overall place of suffering within the tradition of Pentecostal theology (Warrington 2012).

2. In a recent interview, well-known worship leader and songwriter Brian Doerksen wonders aloud, "Where are the laments? Where are the transparent songs?" (Coggins 2008).

REFERENCES

Beckford, Robert. 2006. *Jesus Dub: Theology, Music, and Social Change*. New York: Routledge.

Bergunder, Michael. 2008. *The South Indian Pentecostal Movement in the Twentieth Century*. Grand Rapids, Mich.: Eerdmans.

Bomann, Rebecca Pierce. 2011. "The Salve of Divine Healing: Essential Rituals for Survival Among Working-Class Pentecostals in Bogotá, Colombia." In *Global Pentecostal and Charismatic Healing*, edited by Candy Gunther Brown, 187–205. New York: Oxford University Press.

Bowler, Catherine. 2011. "Blessed Bodies: Healing Within the African American Faith Movement." In *Global Pentecostal and Charismatic Healing*, edited by Candy Gunther Brown, 81–105. New York: Oxford University Press.

Butler, Melvin L. 2002. "'Nou Kwe nan Sentespri' (We Believe in the Holy Spirit): Music, Ecstasy, and Identity in Haitian Pentecostal Worship." *Black Music Research Journal* 22 (1): 85–125.

———. 2008. "The Weapons of Our Warfare: Music, Positionality, and Transcendence Among Haitian Pentecostals." *Caribbean Studies* 36 (2): 23–64.

Chesnut, R. Andrew. 1997. *Born Again in Brazil: The Pentecostal Boom and the Pathogens of Poverty*. New Brunswick: Rutgers University Press.

Coggins, Jim. 2008. "Songs of Lament: An Interview with Brian Doerksen (Part 2)." *Canadian Christianity*, May 15. http://www.canadianchristianity.com/songs-lament -interview-brian-doerksen-part-2-3424/.

Corten, André. 1999. *Pentecostalism in Brazil: Emotion of the Poor and Theological Romanticism*. Translated by Arianne Dorval. New York: St. Martin's Press.

Cox, Harvey. 1995. *Fire from Heaven: The Rise of Pentecostal Spirituality and the Reshaping of Religion in the Twenty-First Century*. Reading, Mass.: Addison-Wesley.

Csordas, Thomas J. 1997. *Language, Charisma, and Creativity: The Ritual Life of a Religious Movement*. Berkeley: University of California Press.

Ellington, Scott A. 2000. "The Costly Loss of Testimony." *Journal of Pentecostal Theology* 16:48–59.

———. 2008. *Risking Truth: Reshaping the World Through Prayers of Lament*. Eugene, Ore.: Pickwick.

Hunter, Harold D., and Cecil M. Robeck Jr. 2006. Introduction to *The Suffering Body: Responding to the Persecution of Christians*, edited by Harold D. Hunter and Cecil M. Robeck Jr., xv–xxii. Waynesboro, Ga.: Paternoster Press.

Ingalls, Monique M. 2012. "Singing Praise in the Streets: Performing Canadian Christianity Through Public Worship in Toronto's Jesus in the City Parade." *Culture and Religion* 13 (3): 337–59.

Kalu, Ogbu. 2008. *African Pentecostalism: An Introduction*. New York: Oxford University Press.

Kärkkäinen, Veli-Matti. 2004. "Theology of the Cross: A Stumbling Block to Pentecostal/ Charismatic Spirituality?" In *The Spirit and Spirituality: Essays in Honour of Russell P. Spittler*, edited by Wonsuk Ma and Robert P. Menzies, 150–63. London: T&T Clark.

Kim, Dongsoo. 1999. "The Healing of *Han* in Korean Pentecostalism." *Journal of Pentecostal Theology* 7 (15): 123–39.

Land, Steven J. 1993. *Pentecostal Spirituality: A Passion for the Kingdom.* Journal of Pentecostal Theology Supplement Series 1. Sheffield: Sheffield Academic Press.

Miller, Donald E. 1997. *Reinventing American Protestantism: Christianity in the New Millennium.* Berkeley: University of California Press.

Miller, Donald E., and Tetsunao Yamamori. 2007. *Global Pentecostalism: The New Face of Christian Social Engagement.* Berkeley: University of California Press.

Mittelstadt, Martin William. 2004. *The Spirit and Suffering in Luke–Acts: Implications for a Pentecostal Pneumatology.* Journal of Pentecostal Theology Supplement Series 26. London: T&T Clark.

———. 2008. "Spirit and Suffering in Contemporary Pentecostalism: The Lukan Epic Continues." In *Defining Issues in Pentecostalism: Classical and Emergent*, edited by Steven M. Studebaker, 144–73. Eugene, Ore.: Pickwick.

Ramírez, Daniel. 2009. "Alabaré a Mi Señor: Culture and Ideology in Latino Protestant Hymnody." In *Los Evangélicos: Portraits of Latino Protestantism in the United States*, edited by Juan F. Martínez and Lindy Scott, 149–70. Eugene, Ore.: Wipf and Stock.

Ruuth, Anders, and Donizete Rodrigues. 2000. "A Kingdom of Heaven in Expansion—Until When? Some Reflections About the Universal Church of the Kingdom of God in Brazil." In *The Religious Phenomenon: An Inter-disciplinary Approach*, edited by Donizete Rodrigues and Pablo del Río, 29–42. Madrid: Fundación Infancia y Aprendizaje.

Sánchez-Walsh, Arlene. 2011. "Santidad, Salvación, Sanidad, Liberación: The Word of Faith Movement Among Twenty-First-Century Latina/o Pentecostals." In *Global Pentecostal and Charismatic Healing*, edited by Candy Gunther Brown, 151–68. New York: Oxford University Press.

Sanders, Cheryl J. 1999. *Saints in Exile: The Holiness-Pentecostal Experience in African American Religion and Culture.* New York: Oxford University Press.

Tan-Chow, May Ling. 2007. *Pentecostal Theology for the Twenty-First Century: Engaging with Multi-faith Singapore.* London: Ashgate.

Volf, Miroslav. 1989. "The Materiality of Salvation: An Investigation in the Soteriologies of Liberation and Pentecostal Theologies." *Journal of Ecumenical Studies* 26 (3): 447–67.

Währisch-Oblau, Claudia. 2011. "Material Salvation: Healing, Deliverance, and 'Breakthrough' in African Migrant Churches in Germany." In *Global Pentecostal and Charismatic Healing*, edited by Candy Gunther Brown, 61–80. New York: Oxford University Press.

Warrington, Keith. 2012. "Suffering." In *Handbook of Pentecostal Christianity*, edited by Adam Stewart, 201–4. DeKalb: Northern Illinois University Press.

Wightman, Jill M. 2007. "Healing the Nation: Pentecostal Identity and Social Change in Bolivia." In *Conversion of a Continent: Contemporary Religious Change in Latin America*, edited by Timothy J. Steigenga and Edward L. Cleary, 239–55. New Brunswick: Rutgers University Press.

Williams, P. J. 1997. "The Sound of Tambourines: The Politics of Pentecostal Growth in El Salvador." In *Power, Politics, and Pentecostals in Latin America*, edited by Edward L. Cleary and Hannah W. Stewart-Gambino, 179–200. Boulder, Colo.: Westview Press.

Yong, Amos. 2010. *In the Days of Caesar: Pentecostalism and Political Theology.* Grand Rapids, Mich.: Eerdmans.

3

Dreaming Urban Indigenous Australian Christian Worship in the Great Southland of the Holy Spirit

Tanya Riches

Contemporary worship music publisher Hillsong Church from Sydney's northwest suburbs is Australia's most famous Christian music exporter, having produced many gold-certified albums and received industry accolades (Riches and Wagner 2012). Known for its adaption of American industrial models—for example, annual CD releases and conferences—it promotes church resources for similarly highly energetic, technologically focused services (Hawn 2006, 16; Riches 2010b; Ingalls 2008, 118). Hillsong's globalized music product now reflects its expansion beyond Sydney to numerous international campuses, and its identity as a transnational church thus challenges notions that it produces specifically *Australian* music (see Evans, this volume).

In contrast, another significant Pentecostal expression—relatively invisible on the international stage—has been arising in Australia among its Indigenous peoples.[1] These worship musicians do not utilize the resources of large publishing houses, often traveling long distances as solo artists or bands for evangelistic concerts in rural communities. Marketing is largely word of mouth or through low-budget video clips, and products are self-distributed, but in limited supply in the usual Christian bookstores and distribution channels. Considered primarily evangelistic but rarely commercial, much of this music is digitized and available through music-sharing websites such as Spotify. CCLI's Australian Web resource SongSelect omits most Indigenous artists' songs,[2] and thus they are best known locally rather than nationally. Many nonindigenous Australian Christians are unaware of the contribution of these worship musicians, although they draw directly from Australia's geographical landscape and cultural heritage. This chapter contends that scholars should examine

Aboriginal Pentecostal music more closely because music is of central importance to these Christians, who construct their religious identity in relationship
to and in dialogue with dominant (nonindigenous) Australian culture, and
because it shows the contribution of Indigenous Australians toward reconciliation with this dominant culture.

Peter Dunbar-Hall and Chris Gibson state, "Aboriginal people have consumed and performed folk music, gospel and choral music for at least a century, and country music for over fifty years. At what point these musical her-
itages take on meaning as 'traditional' is unclear" (2004, 17). Despite these
years of Aboriginal Pentecostal music making, scholars have largely ignored
songs within the Christian tradition, perhaps in part because of Christianity's
previous collusion with colonization. This chapter does not seek to minimize
the painful effects of Australia's damaging mission history upon the lives of
Indigenous Australians, but challenges continuing scholarly disregard for
Indigenous Christianity and its music.

Defining Australian Pentecostalism

Noel Loos claims that Christianity is now woven into the fabric of indigeneity
(2007, 2). Australian census data claims that while 1 percent of Indigenous
Australian peoples hold to traditional religions (6 percent in rural areas), over
73 percent identify as Christian (Bouma 2006, 31; Australian Bureau of Statistics 2006). Of this number, one-third identify as Catholic and one-third
as Anglican, with the remainder including adherents of the Uniting Church
denomination and Pentecostals (Australian Bureau of Statistics 2006).[3] Malcolm Calley (1955) first noted Pentecostalism among the Bandjalang in rural
New South Wales in 1955, although Akiko Ono (2011) considers its identity markers (for example, Spirit baptism) to have been minimized as tribal
religion. Bouma distinguishes Australian movements from their American
counterparts but declares, "Focus on Spirit baptism, glossolalia, and healing
is definitional for contemporary Pentecostalism" (2001, 89). Within his nonindigenous Australian Pentecostal ecclesiology, Shane Clifton cites appeal to
experience, narrative testimony, and a culture of change as other defining
markers (2005, 110; see also Hutchinson and Wolffe 2012). Adding to these
themes, I suggest that the immanent presence of the Spirit and supernatural
empowerment for evangelism are important within Australian Pentecostal
music (Riches 2010b, 58). Furthermore, a contention of this chapter is that the

greatest contribution of Indigenous Pentecostalism and its music to Australian Pentecostalism as a whole is its emphasis on holistic reconciliation—between God, the people, and the land of Australia—made possible through a theology of the power of the Spirit.

Methodology

In order to address silences within scholarly accounts of Indigenous Christian music making, this chapter highlights Pentecostal themes in Indigenous Australian Christianity from a missiological frame, seeking specifically to redress a lack of written material acknowledging the contribution of Indigenous Australian worship musicians. As a review, it is not exhaustive, nor does it suggest broad uniformity across Indigenous Australian worship, which utilizes a range of genres and styles. As a nonindigenous Pentecostal songwriter and worship leader, my own engagement with this community occurred when I moved into Sydney's Redfern area in 2001 to conduct the Hillsong City Campus choir. Indigenous Christianity eventually became the topic of my Ph.D. research. My Indigenous contacts recommended the music of notable Indigenous worship leader Robyn Green, and I conducted a content analysis of three of her albums in order to illustrate her contribution to Pentecostalism, as presented below. Additionally, Pastor David Armstrong, an Indigenous colleague at the Australian Christian Churches denominational Bible college Alphacrucis, invited me to visit the Mount Druitt Indigenous Choir, the core ministry of Initiative Church in Sydney's western suburbs. Participant observation was conducted over a period of four weeks in summer 2012, as I attended weekly rehearsals, Sunday services, and two performances—a fundraiser in Mount Druitt Square and a celebration hosted by Christian City Church, Prospect. I also contributed to the musical life of the community, teaching warm-ups and breathing exercises.[4]

Music in the Mission and Post-mission History of Australia

The undiscovered Southern land had long ignited the European imagination. When Portuguese navigator Pedro de Quirós reported having found the continent, his announcement of the "Great Southland of the Holy Spirit" (Australia del Espiritu Santo) implied a concomitant missional interest in its peoples (Hardiman 2009, 9). Hardiman notes the continued influence of this phrase on the Pentecostal imagination, particularly through the song "This Is the Great Southland" by Geoff Bullock, sung as a prophetic declaration in many churches nationally during Australia Day services.

Prior to colonization, Australia was home to more than two hundred Indigenous nations, its intricate social system conducted primarily via overland walking tracks (Trudgen 2000, 25). Music was crucial to this life, with two- and four-line lyrical verses committing geographical information to memory in a functional musical mapping of the land (Dunbar-Hall and Gibson 2004, 21). Individuals were initiated into a repertoire accompanied by the clapping of sticks, boomerangs, or hands (Maddern 1988, 595; Gibson and Dunbar-Hall 2000, 73; Treloyn 2003) and, in the northern nations, the iconic didjeridu (Moyle 1981).[5] Sporadic contact with Dutch ships on Australia's west coast and annual trading with Macassan sea slug traders on the northern coastline occurred until English adventurer James Cook formally drove a European flag into the soil in the 1770s (Trudgen 2000; Banner 2005). By this time, entrenched mythological thinking about Aborigines motivated the declaration of Australia as Terra Nullius, or uninhabited land. Early records reveal clashes of Indigenous value systems and knowledge with English property ownership law as the foundation of civilization—and Australia's nomadic nations were deemed barely human, being "in the genuine state of nature" (Banner 2005).

During colonization, Indigenous Australians suffered greatly, as settlers, pastoralists, and government agents contributed to the atrocity that Noel Loos controversially terms "the Aboriginal Holocaust" (2007, 41). In collusion with White Australia policies, missionaries participated in the Europeanization of Aboriginal culture, language, and music (Breen 1989, 4). But most damaging was the church's role in "the Stolen Generation" and the forcible removal of Aboriginal "half-caste" children to missions by government officials, exposed in the report *Bringing Them Home* (Wilson 1997). This blight upon the witness of the church led many to question Christianity's relevance to Indigenous Australian peoples. Gary Bouma states, "Again we had hoped for better and expected more. The violation of trust was bad enough, particularly for those directly victimised. But for others, for the whole society, it was a violation of hope. One of the sources of hope had in fact undermined hope" (2006, 20).

Prime Minister Rudd's government apology to Indigenous Australian people in 2008 acknowledged the role of the missions in assimilation policies and cultural loss suffered by families placed in these often-impoverished and harsh disciplinary institutions (Rudd 2008). Nevertheless, as David Hollinsworth notes, "Not all examples of the abandonment of cultural practices were due to suppression or interference by non-Aborigines. . . . Conversion to Christianity was then, as it is now, often a conscious choice by an individual or a family rather than imposed from outside" (1992, 144).

In the 1970s, self-determination policy sought to remove missionaries and empower Indigenous leadership. Whereas traditional religion encompassed every aspect of life, following conversion Indigenous Christians grappled with a secularized European faith that missiologist Paul Hiebert describes as "the excluded middle" (1982, 36). The Elcho Island charismatic revival, or the "Adjustment Movement," was an attempt to reconcile missionary teaching with the anthropological push for reclamation of culture within a former Methodist mission site. Christian crosses were erected upon the *madayin*, or sacred sites (McIntosh 1997, 281). Indigenous leaders such as Terry Djiniyini Gondarra wove traditional rites, sacred objects, and the Ten Commandments into an influential Aboriginal theology (Magowan 2003, 296), and David Burramurra declared that "*Walitha 'walitha* was one and the same as the Christian God" (McIntosh 1997, 278). Wesleyan hymnbooks were replaced with "translocal" charismatic choruses, promoting reconciliation through "brotherhood," "love," and "friendship" (Magowan 2007, 469). Following the revival, Indigenous evangelists and musicians carried this indigenized Pentecostal Christianity throughout Australia, emphasizing continuity between the Spirit's involvement in Australia before and after missionaries. One such early Indigenous gospel band, Soft Sands, was highly influential in the composition of popular song in Arnhem Land (Dunbar-Hall and Gibson 2004; Corn 2005, 64).

However, famous ethnomusicologist Bruno Nettl recounts traveling to Australia in search of Indigenous repertoire, where gathered representatives shared a rendition of "The Old Rugged Cross." He concludes, "I could find no difference between this performance and what I expected of white Australians" (2005, 426). Due to the belief that Christianity replaced Aboriginal culture, indigeneity and Christianity are largely still presented as conflicting forces within the academic literature (Schwarz 2010; Tippett 2006). Thus, scholars have long discounted the Christian spirituality contained in Indigenous cultural expression. Yet Fiona Magowan's emphasis on the deep intentionality of song selection by her Indigenous teacher (2001, 91) and the notable omission of the geographical origins of the Indigenous singers in Nettl's accounts suggest that their attempts to illustrate the absorption of gospel tunes into Indigenous repertoire(s) may have been minimized. The integration, translation, and innovation within Christian hymnody in Oceania has only recently been acknowledged by scholars such as Amy Stillman (1993).[6] While Christianity has played a significant, though sometimes problematic, role in the history of Indigenous Australian peoples, Indigenous evangelists and musicians have played and do play a meaningful role within Australian Christianity, as seen in their innovative use of music as an expression of urban Indigenous Christianity.

Embodying Pentecostal Music History: Robyn Green

Of Australia's Indigenous Pentecostal worship leaders, Robyn Green[7] is often considered the most influential. Formerly from Darwin, Northern Territory, Green's itinerant worship ministry is based in Tingoora, Queensland. Since 1986, she has released seven independently recorded and distributed albums; however, her online promotion consists of a simple website (www.robyngreen .com.au) with limited biographical information and links to online sales. Credited with ministering in Darwin's prisons, Green has also participated in notable worship events such as the BBC's *Songs of Praise* episode recorded in the iconic Sydney Opera House (Rhodes 2000).

In order to understand Robyn Green's passion for music and worship, it is important to examine her musical roots. Green's father was evangelist Peter Morgan, born within the Mullinbulla nation in 1923 near Gordonvale, North Queensland. Removed from his family by the government, he was sent to Palm Island at four years old. He never again saw his mother and was reunited with his father only in adulthood. Yet he was known to be "full of love and forgiveness." Converting to Christianity in 1949, he met and married his wife, Eva, in the Atherton Tablelands. Peter recorded a cassette of country gospel songs, with Eva's accompaniment on piano, entitled *It's in My Heart*, distributed by Australian Heart Ministries. He was considered to "[know] the power of 'Nadji'"—the traditional name for God in the Northern Territory (Australian Prayer Network 2004). The Morgan family moved to Darwin with their daughters in 1966, planting churches within the Pentecostal denomination Assemblies of God (now Australian Christian Churches, or ACC), as well as Darwin Full Gospel Church and Faith Centre Darwin (now known as C3 Church Darwin).

The Morgan family often traveled from church to church, and it was on these tours that Robyn Green's singing and songwriting talent was made clear. Her first album, *He Is the Answer*, is a country/gospel fusion utilizing country vocal inflections and instrumentation. Songs such as "I'm a Believer," "He Is the Answer," and "He Is the Reason" reveal the album's primarily evangelistic emphasis. Many of Green's songs directly address the Spirit. From her 2003 album *Shine On,* the song "Reign on Me" features a saloon-style honky-tonk piano under a country rock band. The humorous lyric likening a move of the Holy Spirit to a downpour is accentuated by the piano's comic sound:

> Reign on me, don't forget
> Cover me 'til I'm soaking wet
> All I'm asking, Holy Spirit reign on me

"Pour Out Your Spirit," the first track on the 2000 album *Sweet Surrender,* is a piano-led contemporary Christian ballad. After the band vamps on the final chorus, Green begins to ad-lib:

> Pour out Your Spirit, Oh God
> Revive us, Lord
> Australia needs You, Lord

An electric guitar note is sustained, and a didjeridu begins to play behind the vocals. In this way, the song draws sonic continuity between Australia's present and history, emphasizing the role of the Spirit in bringing both reconciliation between indigenous and nonindigenous people and healing to the land.

Healing is an important part of Green's story, featuring in her music and narrative of her calling as a musician. In a video testimony, in a simple spoken style, she faces the camera with an iconic Australian gum tree behind her and attests to the miraculous power of God in her own physical healing: "When I was eleven years of age I lost my sight and I was paralyzed from the waist down. I was a very sick girl. I had acute nephritis. . . . And it was during the night, I remember praying to the Lord and just saying, 'God, just heal me, if you heal me I'll sing for you.'" Green describes a vision of a visitation from Jesus Christ, explaining that she has kept her promise by singing for the Lord. She outlines recent miracles during ministry trips to Groote Eylandt and Vanuatu. Then she prays for her viewers, asking the Holy Spirit to directly touch those who have needs, saying, "God is the Healer. You know, ever since he healed me I know that he can do anything, He can do the impossible. So whatever your need is, whatever you need . . . just reach out and believe" ("Robyn Green Healed from Blindness" 2011).

Restoration is another important theme in Green's music. From her latest album, *I Will Arise* (2008), the song "On Eagle's Wings" begins with the ambient, laid-back sounds of an electric guitar playing in lounge style, followed by a groove with a bass and a very "present" lead vocal. Multilayered backing vocals emerge under the chorus. The verses describe human oppression through metaphors of being lost and being bound by chains and heavy weights, while in the chorus Green sings,

> He promised we'd mount up
> On eagles' wings
> Fly like the wind
> We'll see victory
> Up over the clouds where we're meant to be
> On eagles' wings

Here, the biblical imagery of Isaiah 60 could be interpreted with Indigenous significance, connecting to the Australian wedge-tailed eagle, as well as evoking black history within the United States. A restoration of strength and clarity of vision are here associated with physical and emotional healing.

However, Green's choice of performance venues makes clear that the healing about which she sings extends beyond Indigenous Australian communities; the rifts between Indigenous and settler communities can also be healed in the transformative context of Christian worship. Throughout her career, Green has been involved in several important cross-cultural endeavors, including the BBC's *Songs of Praise* episode, televised during the 2000 Olympics (Rhodes 2000). This musical performance is symbolic, reminiscent of the healing themes prevalent in Green's music, and it emphasizes what Fiona Magowan refers to as "performative dialogue" between Aboriginal and white Australian Christian communities (2000, 310).

During the introductory segment, two contemporary Indigenous dancers stand in the center of the stage, shrouded in smoke, while moving to the sounds of Pentecostal didjeridu artist Adrian Ross. Green's haunting voice cuts across this music, embodying the voice of Indigenous Australians in the well-known song "I Am Australian":

> I came from the Dreamtime, from the dusty red soil plains
> I am the ancient heart, the keeper of the flame
> I stood upon the rocky shores and watched the tall ships come
> For forty thousand years I've been the First Australian

Country gospel artist Steve Grace sings the settler verses of this anthemic song, which outline the story of Australia's nonindigenous migrant inhabitants:

I came upon the prison ship bound down by iron chains
I cleared the land, endured the lash and waited for the rains.
I'm a settler, I'm a farmer's wife on a dry and barren run
A convict then a free man, I became Australian

The duet weaves the two narratives, Indigenous and nonindigenous Australian, together into a chorus of unity. As the dancers continue moving to the beat using both traditional and contemporary shapes, the video pans to a young, predominantly white Australian choir joining in from the choir loft above the stage. The image is one of reconciliation on various levels, ethnic and generational.

Dance is often considered a means of Aboriginal resistance against a "homogenized identity" imposed by Australia's dominant culture (Hollinsworth 1992, 147). Magowan terms this "poetic politics" and writes that "the symbolic power of dance lies in its ability to conceal as much as it reveals to performers and audience. Consequently, performative dialogue is a chess game of coming to know the nature of embodied sentiment between groups" (2000, 310). Within this Pentecostal worship service, however, the use of this nonreligious song as the opening chorus is an intentional declaration by Aboriginal Australians: they demonstrate the continuous line of the Spirit's presence in their land between Dreamtime and Christian spirituality, colonial and now Pentecostal.

The contribution of traveling music evangelists such as Green cannot be overestimated in regard to Pentecostal expansion into indigenous communities. Green serves as a forerunner and present-day representative of a generation of indigenous musicians and singers who are drawing contemporary worship songs into urban Christian Aboriginality and sounding the promise of healing and reconciliation within Australian Christianity more broadly.

Dreaming of Our Future: Mount Druitt Indigenous Choir

However, the influence of Indigenous Pentecostal expression on Australian Christian music making is not limited to the Northern Territory or to one generation of Indigenous musicians. Thirty-five kilometers from Sydney's center, the suburb of Mount Druitt is bounded by the M2, M4, and M7 freeways.

Named after military officer and Australian settler George Druitt, the area was farmland, but housing developments have recently claimed its open grassy spaces. It hosts "the largest urban Aboriginal and Torres Strait Islander population in NSW with 7,055 people [and] 2.6% of the area's population" (Blacktown City Council 2012). Mount Druitt is also considered a socioeconomically disadvantaged community (Australian Bureau of Statistics 2011). Although boasting the new Westfield shopping center, local residents cite concerns about safety after dark, gangs, and substance abuse. The Indigenous population in this area is predominantly young, with many single-parent family units (Blacktown City Council 2007, 6, 33). Hope regarding the youth and a sense of uncertainty about the future for teens simultaneously persist in this suburb. The following field narrative draws from visits to this community and showcases the ways in which Pentecostal music is used as a bridge between Aboriginal ethnic groups, as a vehicle for teaching new generations the value of the Indigenous cultural heritage, and as a way of reconciling Indigenous and Christian identities.

In July of 2012, my husband and I returned to Sydney from Los Angeles to visit family and renew visas. Having interacted previously with Pastor David Armstrong via email, we were invited to visit his choir ministry in Mount Druitt. An ACC pastor of mixed Indigenous and white Australian heritage, David is originally from Rockhampton, Queensland. With his wife, Angela, he pioneered this musical project and missional outreach among Indigenous children of the Mount Druitt area during the Christmas season of 2010. The choir consists predominantly of children under ten years old, who attend rehearsals, performances, and weekend services. Angela Armstrong writes most of the music for the choir, and three of their four children are musically involved.

We arrived about fifteen minutes late, due to a misdirected drive past Whalan's shops, where fire-damaged and vandalized roller doors betrayed the area's reputation. I reminded myself that for locals, it's just home. Angela met us on the front lawn of "Aunty's" house, where three adults sat on the front porch, one smoking.[8] Around ten kids played on the front lawn, waiting for choir rehearsal. They varied from about three to sixteen years old, all running around together and tossing a rugby football. Angela sent a worried text to Pastor David, who was picking up the last five children so that they could begin rehearsal.

While we waited, Angela talked to me about the philosophy of the choir. She explained that it was "calming" for the kids to rehearse outdoors, even in Sydney's chilly weather. She outlined how local elders had encouraged them to choose to sing in Dharug, the language of the Mount Druitt land, although some consider it a dead language. Angela was honest about struggles to accommodate cultural differences among Sydney's diverse urban Aboriginal community, a diaspora drawing from a large geographical area. A number of conflicts had caused the choir to now host two weekly rehearsals to allow cultural "avoidance" norms to be observed with appropriate members of kin.

By the time Pastor David returned, he had seven children (two extras had turned up unexpectedly), and Angela had largely talked me through the choir's schedule. The children laid a rug on the grass and procured an electric piano. Then two didjeridus were carried over and held by some young boys. During my time with the choir, it was stated repeatedly that girls are not allowed to touch this traditional instrument, and Pastor David asked me not to touch it while with the community. However, clapsticks were handed out to everybody.

David loudly announced that my husband and I were special visitors from Los Angeles in America. The mothers stared at us as though we had walked out of a Hollywood sitcom, while the children acted impressed. Angela looked at me and asked, "What would you like to do with the choir today?" She smiled politely. But, as I led impromptu choir vocal exercises with the children, I worried that the announcement about having traveled from such a faraway place would give us an aura that we did not want to perpetuate, as Australians.

When we finished our exercises, I asked the children to sing a song. They selected "Dreaming,"[9] which was poignant, as it consists of both a welcome in the Dharug language and a statement in English about indigenous leadership moving from healing to leading:

> Gi Walawa Nalawala
> Gi Walawa Nalawala
> Gi Walawa Nalawala in Jesus
>
> Warami Wellamabamiyui
> Warami Wellamabamiyui
>
> Dreaming of our past
> Dreaming of our present
> Dreaming of our future

Angela later translated the Dharug lines as "Please stop here and rest (in Jesus)" and "It's good to see you wherever you have come from." The children sang proudly and confidently.

FIG. 3.1 The Mount Druitt Indigenous Choir rehearsing. Photo by Mount Druitt Indigenous Choir.

The choir has performed over forty times, at indigenous events including Sorry Day 2012 and NAIDOC (National Aborigines and Indigenous Day Observance Committee) Week and at private functions for Aboriginal and Torres Strait elders and the governor-general of Australia (see figs. 3.1 and 3.2).[10] In local performances, the choir sings original songs such as "Dreaming" and "Nalabiyuni," a song about Australia's wildlife; the children use appropriate gestures for seabird, kangaroo, and emu. They also adapt contemporary Christian songs from Hillsong and Bethel Live.[11]

David notes that the children do not object to Christian content in songs, and he believes that this is because Indigenous children are socialized to be attuned to the spiritual world: "I take a group of aboriginal kids to a park. Immediately they will start talking about the spirits or ghosts in that area. . . . The spirit world is more real to them than the physical or material world."[12] Thus, many of the songs sung by the choir explicitly attend to the role of the Spirit, as Armstrong believes that there is a great need to address the invisible world within the bounds of Christianity. During practice, when they spoke about troubles or fear, the immanent presence of the Spirit was emphasized.

FIG. 3.2 The Mount Druitt Indigenous Choir performing. Photo by Mount Druitt Indigenous Choir.

Each prayer concludes with the children joyfully shouting "In the name of Jesus" three times in unison. Through indigenous instrumentation and language, as well as traditional cultural values within the music (for example, welcoming the stranger), the Armstrongs model an indigenous Christian spirituality, thus reconciling both Aboriginal and Christian identities through music. The Mount Druitt Indigenous Choir is the fulfillment of the Armstrongs' desire to use music as a bridge to bring the local community together and link that community to Aboriginal groups elsewhere. It also facilitates successful dialogue with nonindigenous Australian Christian groups.

Conclusion

Common "inalienable qualities," defined by Minette Mans as "qualities that are so closely aligned with identity that they cannot / may not be transferrable" (2007, 240), can be noted within Indigenous Australian Pentecostal music. The didjeridu is representative of Aboriginality within the urban environment in both the recordings of Robyn Green and the repertoire of the Mount Druitt Indigenous Choir. Moreover, lyrical themes including Spirit baptism and divine healing emphasize the Holy Spirit's presence and the continuity between pre-colonial Indigenous identity and contemporary Christianity. Although these Indigenous Pentecostals do not often refer to glossolalia in their repertoire, the theme of supernatural empowerment for evangelism is clearly evident. Important to the music and performance of Indigenous Pentecostalism is holistic reconciliation—between God, the people, and the land of Australia—through the power of the Spirit. Pentecostal influence has long existed within the Indigenous musical repertoire, and Indigenous worship musicians have also contributed to the expansion of Pentecostal Christianity. For many, these artists and bands powerfully embody the sound of the nation's worship.

While the Aboriginal Pentecostal musical repertoire is less visible than its nonindigenous Pentecostal counterpart, their emphasis on healing and reconciliation may be having a broader effect. Influential songwriter Geoff Bullock, in a video of his performance of "The Great Southland" at Gospel Live in Manly, announced, "Our role . . . is to find a way of bringing grace to the Aboriginal nation, and healing and restoration, and whatever else we can do—all that must come after simply saying sorry" ("Geoff Bullock—Great South Land" 2010). For many, his song has now become a song of unity and prayer for reconciliation between Indigenous and nonindigenous Australians:

> This is the Great Southland of the Holy Spirit,
> A land of red dust plains and summer rains
> And to this Great Southland we will see a flood
> To this Great Southland His Spirit comes
> (Bullock 1993)

Thus, the desire for reconciliation, birthed within the Indigenous Australian Christian community, is still a sung national prayer today. Perhaps in listening to the Christian spirituality in the music of Australia's Indigenous peoples, we can best understand the power of the Spirit for reconciliation—in its spiritual, physical, and emotional dimensions. These powerful songs embody the fervent prayers of Aboriginal Australian Christians—and, increasingly, their nonindigenous neighbors—that, through repentance and restoration, the land might be healed.

NOTES

1. Indigenous Australians consist of Aboriginal and Torres Strait Islander groupings constituting about 2.2 percent of the national population (Australian Bureau of Statistics 2006). Most Indigenous Australian people prefer their national terms—for example, Eora nation. The term "Aborigine" or its plural, "Aborigines," although used within the literature, is often considered pejorative within Australia. The Australian government has a tripartite system of genetic relationship, personal identification, and community acceptance for definition of indigenous status.

2. Christian Copyright Licensing International (CCLI) administers the SongSelect database through its online site http://www.ccli.com. This popular fee-based website provides access to lyrics, charts, and music sheets for contemporary Christian songs. None of leading Indigenous gospel singer Robyn Green's songs could be found on SongSelect.

3. While specific statistics for Indigenous Australian Christianity are not readily available, the literature and my fieldwork suggest that Pentecostalism may account for a significant portion of these Indigenous Christians, perhaps up to 10 percent of this population, compared to 1–2 percent of the general population. Moreover, the Elcho Island revivals heavily influenced Uniting, Anglican, and Catholic denominations, particularly in regard to musical worship. Thus, statistics alone cannot illustrate the significance of indigenous Pentecostal communities.

4. During this time, I traveled to Tweed Heads, Queensland, and spoke with seventeen Indigenous Bible college students at Ganggalah College, in addition to Pastors Will and Sandra Dumas, who were recently appointed Indigenous Ministry leaders for the ACC denomination. The conversations do not feature in this chapter, but I am indebted to the information that the students and staff shared with me, as well as their assistance in obtaining Robyn Green's albums.

5. The didjeridu (or didgeridoo) is a traditional Aboriginal wind instrument consisting of a hollowed-out piece of wood, played using circular breathing.

6. In the North American context, Luke Lassiter (2001) similarly notes the unique musical contribution of Native American Christians, including the Kiowa.

7. Green stated in an interview that her next release will be recorded under her married name, Robyn Beezley.

8. "Aunty" (or "Uncle") is an endearing and respectful term for an Indigenous Australian elder or community leader.

9. "Dreaming" is an unpublished song that Angela Armstrong wrote in 2011.

10. The governor-general is appointed by the Queen as her representative and respected as the highest formal authority in the Australian state.

11. One of the children's favorite songs during my time with them was "Deep Cries Out" by Bethel; they sang along loudly and created actions to go with the lyrics.

12. Email correspondence with David Armstrong, September 29, 2011.

REFERENCES

Australian Bureau of Statistics. 2006. "Population Characteristics, Aboriginal and Torres Strait Islander Australians." Commonwealth of Australia, Canberra. http://www.abs .gov.au.
———. 2011. "Socio-economic Indexes for Areas." Commonwealth of Australia, Canberra. http://www.abs.gov.au.
Australian Prayer Network. 2004. "A Tribute to Pastor Peter Morgan (18/3/1923–15/8/2004)." http://www.ausprayernet.org.au.

Banner, Stuart. 2005. "Why Terra Nullius? Anthropology and Property Law in Early Australia." *Law and History Review* 23 (1): 95–132.
Blacktown City Council. 2007. *Blacktown City Council Social Plan*. Blacktown City, N.S.W.:
Blacktown City Council. http://www.blacktown.nsw.gov.au.
———. 2012. "Statistics: Demographic Overview." http://www.blacktown.nsw.gov.au.
Bouma, Gary. 2001. "Globalisation and Localisation: Pentecostals and Anglicans in Austra-
lia and the United States." In *The End of Religions? Religion in an Age of Globalisation*,
edited by Carole M. Cusack and Peter Oldmeadow, 83–92. Sydney: University of
Sydney Press.
———. 2006. *Australian Soul: Religion and Spirituality in the Twenty-First Century*. Cam-
bridge: Cambridge University Press.
Breen, Marcus, ed. 1989. *Our Place, Our Music*. Canberra: Aboriginal Studies Press.
Bullock, Geoff. 1993. *The Great Southland*. Castle Hill, N.S.W: Word Music. Cassette tape.
Calley, Malcolm. 1955. "Aboriginal Pentecostalism: A Study of Changes in Religion, North
Coast, NSW." M.A. thesis, University of Sydney.
Catholic Australia. 2010. "Indigenous Catholics in the 2006 Census." http://www
.catholicaustralia.com.au.
Clifton, Shane. 2005. "An Analysis of the Developing Ecclesiology of the Assemblies of God
in Australia." Ph.D. diss., Australian Catholic University, Strathfield.
Corn, Aaron. 2005. "Ancestral Precedent as Creative Inspiration: The Influence of Soft Sands
on Popular Song Composition in Arnhem Land." In *The Power of Knowledge, the Res-
onance of Tradition: Electronic Publication of Papers from the AIATSIS Conference, Sep-
tember 2001*, edited by Graeme Ward and Adrian Muckle, 31–68. Canberra: AIATSIS.
Dunbar-Hall, Peter, and Chris Gibson. 2004. *Deadly Sounds, Deadly Places: Contemporary
Aboriginal Music in Australia*. Sydney: UNSW Press.
Evans, Mark. 2006. *Open Up the Doors: Music in the Modern Church*. London: Equinox.
"Geoff Bullock—Great South Land—Live at Gospel Live 2010/6." 2010. YouTube video, 4:19.
From a performance at GospelLive. Posted by GospelLiveAustralia, July 11. http://
www.youtube.com/watch?v=WHk_7O_s8Ak.
Gibson, Chris, and Peter Dunbar-Hall. 2000. "Nitmiluk: Place and Empowerment in Aus-
tralian Aboriginal Popular Music." *Ethnomusicology* 44 (1): 39–64.
Green, Robyn. 2000. "Pour Out Your Spirit." On *Sweet Surrender*. Darwin: Turnaround
Music. Compact disc.
———. 2003. "Reign on Me." On *Shine On*. Darwin: Independent. Compact disc.
———. 2008. "On Eagle's Wings." On *I Will Arise*. Newcastle: The 316 Label. Compact disc.
Hardiman, Ron. 2009. "Celebrating Australia Day: Unwrapping 'The Great Southland of the
Holy Spirit.'" *Pastoral Liturgy* 39 (1): 9–12.
Hawn, C. Michael. 2006. "Congregational Singing from Down Under: Experiencing Hill-
song's 'Shout to the Lord.'" *The Hymn* 57 (2): 15–24.
Hiebert, Paul. 1982. "The Flaw of the Excluded Middle." *Missiology* 10 (1): 35–47.
Hollinsworth, David. 1992. "Discourses on Aboriginality and the Politics of Identity in
Urban Australia." *Oceania* 63 (2): 137–55.
Hutchinson, Mark, and John Wolffe. 2012. "'The Actual Arithmetic': A Survey of Contem-
porary Global Evangelicalism." In *A Short History of Global Evangelicalism*, 209–38.
Cambridge: Cambridge University Press.
Ingalls, Monique Marie. 2008. "Awesome in This Place: Sound, Space, and Identity in
Contemporary North American Evangelical Worship." Ph.D. diss., University of
Pennsylvania.
Lassiter, Luke Eric. 2001. "'From Here On, I Will Be Praying to You': Indian Churches,
Kiowa Hymns, and Native American Christianity in Southwestern Oklahoma."
Ethnomusicology 45 (2): 338–52.

Loos, Noel. 2007. *White Christ, Black Cross: The Emergence of a Black Church.* Canberra: Aboriginal Studies Press.

Maddern, Eric. 1988. "'We Have Survived': Aboriginal Music Today." *Musical Times* 129 (1749): 595–97.

Magowan, Fiona. 2000. "Dancing with a Difference: Reconfiguring the Poetic Politics of Aboriginal Ritual as National Spectacle." *Australian Journal of Anthropology* 11 (3): 308–21.

———. 2001. "Shadows of Song: Exploring Research and Performance Strategies in Yolngu Women's Crying-Songs." *Oceania* 72 (2): 89–104.

———. 2003. "'It Is God Who Speaks in the Thunder . . .' Mediating Ontologies of Faith and Fear in Aboriginal Christianity." *Journal of Religious History* 27 (3): 293–310.

———. 2007. "Globalisation and Indigenous Christianity: Translocal Sentiments in Australian Aboriginal Christian Songs." *Identities* 14 (4): 459–83.

Mans, Minette. 2007. "Tourism and Cultural Identity: Conservation or Commodification?" In *Music and Identity: Transformation and Negotiation*, edited by Eric Akrofi, Maria Smit, and Stig-Magnus Thorsén, 235–55. Stellenbosch: Sun Press.

McIntosh, Ian. 1997. "Anthropology, Self-Determination, and Aboriginal Belief in the Christian God." *Oceania* 67 (4): 273–88.

McIntyre, Elisha. 2007. "Brand of Choice: Why Hillsong Is Winning Sales and Souls." *Journal for the Academic Study of Religion* 20 (2): 175–94.

Moyle, Alice. 1981. "The Australian Didjeridu: A Late Musical Intrusion." *World Archaeology* 12 (3): 321–31.

Muirhead, James. 1996. *Indigenous Deaths in Custody, 1989–1996.* Report prepared by the Office of the Aboriginal and Torres Strait Islander Social Justice Commissioner. Sydney: Aboriginal and Torres Strait Islander Social Justice Commission.

Nettl, Bruno. 2005. *The Study of Ethnomusicology: Thirty-One Issues and Concepts.* 2nd ed. Champaign: University of Illinois Press.

Ono, Akiko. 2011. "Who Owns the 'De-Aboriginalised' Past? Ethnography Meets Photography: A Case Study of Bundjalung Pentecostalism." In *Ethnography and the Production of Anthropological Knowledge: Essays in Honour of Nicolas Peterson*, edited by Yasmine Musharbash and Marcus Barber, 51–68. Canberra: Australian National University Electronic Press.

Rhodes, Pam. 2000. *Songs of Praise: From the Sydney Opera House.* London: BBC Worldwide. VHS.

Riches, Tanya. 2010a. "The Evolving Theological Emphasis of Hillsong Worship (1996–2007)." *Australiasian Pentecostal Studies* 13:87–132.

———. 2010b. "Shout to the Lord: Music and Change at Hillsong, 1996–2007." M.A. thesis, Australian Catholic University.

Riches, Tanya, and Tom Wagner. 2012. "The Evolution of Hillsong Music: From Australian Pentecostal Congregation into Global Brand." *Australian Journal of Communication* 39 (1): 17–36.

"Robyn Green Healed from Blindness—Inspirational Videos." 2011. GodTube video, 4:16. Posted by aussietestimonies. http://www.godtube.com/watch/?v=7GWYYWNX.

Rudd, Kevin. 2008. "Apology to Australia's Indigenous Peoples." Parliament of Australia, House of Representatives, February 13. Available from http://www.australia.gov.au/about-australia/our-country/our-people/apology-to-australias-indigenous-peoples.

Schwarz, Carolyn. 2010. "Sick Again, Well Again: Sorcery, Christianity, and Kinship in Northern Aboriginal Australia." *Anthropological Forum* 20 (1): 61–80.

Stillman, Amy Ku'uleialoha. 1993. "Prelude to a Comparative Investigation of Protestant Hymnody in Polynesia." *Yearbook for Traditional Music* 25:89–99.

Tippett, Alan. 2006. "Formal Transformation and Faith Distortion." *Global Missiology* 4 (3): 97–118.
Treloyn, Sally. 2003. "Scotty Martin's *Jadmi Junba*: A Song Series from the Kimberley Region of Northwest Australia." *Oceania* 73 (3): 208–20.
Trudgen, Richard. 2000. *Why Warriors Lie Down and Die.* Darwin: Aboriginal Resource and Development Services.
Wilson, Ronald, ed. 1997. *Bringing Them Home.* Report prepared by the National Inquiry into the Separation of Aboriginal and Torres Strait Islander Children from Their Families. Edited by Ronald Wilson. Sydney: Human Rights and Equal Opportunity Commission.
Woodley, Bruce, and Dobe Newton. 1987. "I Am Australian." North Ryde, N.S.W.: Warner/ Chappell Music Australia.

4

Every Creative Aspect Breaking Out!
Pentecostal-Charismatic Worship, Oro Gospel Music,
and a Millennialist Aesthetic in Papua New Guinea

Michael Webb

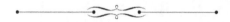

In Port Moresby in April 2010, while undertaking research on Christian musical expressions in Papua New Guinea (hereafter PNG),[1] I was invited one
midweek evening to the training center of Covenant Ministries International,
an isolated, open-walled venue at Eight Mile, on the city outskirts, to attend
an event billed as Breakthrough Praise. Here, I was told with pride, I would
experience "high praise." As I was to learn, this is a local term for an extended
form of song-based Christian worship involving shouting, cheering, speaking in tongues, jumping, and club-style dancing by teenage girls (fig. 4.1).
The entire two-hour-long song sequence—which followed forty minutes of
microphone-led and often-hectic prayer and tongues—was sung in English
and set in the same key. An expert gospel rock band was absorbed in shaping
and responding to the mood; its musicians spontaneously wove contrapuntal
lines into and around the sound stream, while punctuating it with rhythmic
accents and cymbal splashes. Around eighty people of all ages and from at
least several PNG ethnic groups were in attendance, and from the start their

I am indebted to Pastor Tony Ando, Pastor Peter Bogembo, Pastor Daniel Meakoro, Pastor Oswald Tamanabae, Digby Ho Leong, Edric Ogomeni, and Iara Eliakim for their time,
patience, humor, and friendship. In Lae, thanks to Angela Panap of Joseph Kingal Ministries,
Pastor Ernest Menemo of City Tabernacle Church–CRC, and Kich Bernard of Our Saviour
Lutheran. I am particularly grateful to Don Niles of the Institute of Papua New Guinea Studies
for advice and encouragement over thirty years. Fieldwork was funded by the New Frontiers
grant scheme of the Sydney Conservatorium of Music, University of Sydney. Photographs,
song-text transcription, and all translations are mine.

FIG. 4.1 "High praise" freestyle dancing at the SOS Breakthrough Praise night in Port Moresby, April 2010. Pastor Daniel Meakoro is on the microphone in the top left-hand corner. Photo by the author.

singing was a harmonious cloud of contained exuberance. It began with the gently rocking sounds of the locally composed theology-laden worship classic "Abounding Grace":

We are born because we're called
We are running because we're chosen
We are serving for we were ordained
Living our lives predestined by grace, amazing grace
Until we see the coming of our King.

Amazing grace open my eyes
Abounding grace unveiling your ways
Till your glory manifests in us
Men on earth will see your face.[2]

Over the song's eight-minute rendition, backing vocalists offered impro-vised solo interjections and responses, and the worship leader and song's co-composer, Pastor Daniel Meakoro, flanked by fellow pastors Oswald Tamanabae and Peter Bogembo, measured out tuneful exhortations: "Jesus, we worship you! Jump into the river—jump into the river of worship! Send a proclamation across this nation!"

Breakthrough Praise was part of a weeklong series of workshops entitled SOS, or School of Strategies, culminating in a public outdoor Praise Extrav-aganza, all conceived to equip participants with skills in media technology useful in Christian outreach. Here, it appeared, was a gathering of local Pentecostal Christians rehearsing their liturgy (and evangelism "strategies") in accordance with their understanding of transnational models and meth-ods. The SOS was organized and run by Bogembo, Meakoro, and Tamanabae, a trio of PNG's veteran elite musicians, all Pentecostal pastors who had been pioneers in popularizing local gospel and worship music. Those in attendance were drawn from small Port Moresby Pentecostal "fellowships" affiliated with Covenant Ministries International, including those established and led by Pas-tors Meakoro and Tamanabae—Brook by the Wayside and House of Bread, respectively.[3]

Given the technical and stylistic versatility of the musicians, the extensive use of English-language global praise "hits," and the incorporation of freestyle disco dancing, "high praise" appeared to be a sophisticated urban variant of the Pentecostal (and Pentecostal-like) worship[4] I had previously encountered on the north side of PNG.[5] This liturgical form or set of practices, which I refer to more generally as Pentecostal-charismatic worship (hereafter P-CW), is a postmissionary-era phenomenon in PNG that has become widespread and influential over the past several decades.[6] Anthropologist Courtney Hand-man, for example, recently noted a "Pentecostal norm" of worship conventions becoming ever more common in the country (2010, 231n3).

Significantly, in a nation renowned for radical linguistic and cultural diver-sity, as well as a fragmented religious landscape resulting from a variegated history of evangelization, P-CW practices began forming in the mid-1970s, during the immediate post-independence era, and have become a widely shared indigenous form of participatory music making.[7] In this chapter, I consider P-CW practices as representing a transformational shift within the urban and rural musical culture of PNG. First, I employ various sources, including my own fieldwork, to construct an overview of manifestations of the new liturgical form.[8] Then, by way of a case study of the three organizers of the SOS, gospel musicians whom I refer to as the Oro "brothers" after their province of origin, I explore the Pentecostal revival–inspired transmission of instruments and song repertory between villages and urban centers, which led to the founding of P-CW.[9] These three "brothers"—and a fourth, Tony Ando—were important as brokers of both commercial gospel and grassroots-level worship music.[10] Finally, I discuss ways in which their music is imbued with what I term a "spatiotemporal millennialist aesthetic"—that is, how, in terms of musical form and style, they believe that their songs and "high praise" or P-CW performance prepare individuals and the PNG nation, as part of the Christian transnation, for God's future blessing.

Pentecostal-Charismatic Worship: A New Liturgy

P-CW is a liturgical form that in PNG involves "ecstatic singing and dancing, vigorous backchannels of 'amen' and 'hallelujah,' lots of hand clapping and hand raising, and group prayers" (Handman 2010, 230). Two broad types of P-CW are practiced in the country—one at church services, the other at crusades (table 4.1). Each is shaped according to its key purpose, which, in the case of the former, is worship, broadly construed, while the latter is dedicated to public witness and outreach. In worship services, the P-CW segment is prefaced with an extended time of prayer, led by a specially designated individual from a microphone, which builds in fervency as the congregation joins in—a practice known as *bung beten* (Tok Pisin [TP], collective prayer). The prayer time is generally shortened for crusades and tends not to involve the audience in *bung beten*, and the person praying is also the worship leader. Preaching follows in both forms, and healing and (or) an "altar call" involving confession of sin and (or) a decision to follow Christ bring the event to a close.

The church service version of P-CW tends to involve committed congregants intensely focused in purpose; hence, as already mentioned, the attendant atmosphere can be fervent. Services are usually held in a structurally open building of the kind designed for public meetings in a tropical climate. Since these are partially or completely open sided, the sound of worship spills out into the environment, itself a form of witness (see Farhadian 2007).

"Crusade," Handman notes, is a "local term roughly equivalent to a tent revival" (2010, 239n9). All over PNG, Pentecostal groups constantly mount crusades, outdoors and mostly at night, erecting stages in public parks and open areas in cities, towns, and villages.[11] Since crusade P-CW invites wide and

TABLE 4.1 Comparison of the place of Pentecostal-charismatic worship (singing, dancing, and praying with instrument backing) in generalized crusade and church service. The crusade format is more fixed; in the church service format, announcements, offertory, and perhaps other short segments are inserted at various points.

Crusade (ca. 2 hr, 30 min.)

Solo-led prayer, with instrument backing	Singing and dancing	Preaching		Healing / altar call, with instrument backing	Closing song
10–15 min.	30–40 min.	40 min.		30–40 min.	5–10 min.

Church service (ca. 2 hr, 30 min.)

Ecstatic prayer or *bung beten*, with instrument backing	Singing and dancing	Preaching	Transition: solo song or instrumental music	Altar call, with instrument backing	Closing song
15–25 min.	30–50 min.	40–50 min.	5 min.	10–15 min. OR Testimony time (no instruments) 25 min.	5–10 min.

often spontaneous communal participation, the event can become a kind of all-purpose public celebration. Those who attend are often affiliated with other denominations or church groups. Children, youth, and women, in particular, join in by singing, jumping, and waving palm fronds or branches of cordyline plants.[12]

P-CW is led by at least one singer on a microphone and ideally is driven and accompanied by a *fulset* (PNG English, full set)—that is, a rock band setup with some combination of acoustic guitar with pickup, electric rhythm / lead guitar, bass guitar, keyboard, and drum kit—as well as guitar amplifiers, a multichannel mixer, and public address system. Spoken exhortations of encouragement to congregants by the worship leader are an important feature of P-CW. These are intermingled with snatches of prayer asking the Holy Spirit to descend and bless not only the local place and people gathered but also the wider sphere and often the whole nation.[13]

For P-CW leaders, dress in the colors of the national flag—red, black, gold, and white—is fast becoming the standard formal attire at crusades and Pentecostal churches in urban centers. Women leaders wear a long home-sewn version of the *meri blaus* (TP, women's blouse, a long loose-fitting dress introduced by missionaries) and men a polo shirt in these colors. In a YouTube video of a recent "Holy Spirit Crusade" held at Kimbe in West New Britain Province, men and women, locals and visiting guests, are seen wearing the national colors (see "Kimbe Holy Spirit Crusade" 2012, from 1:06), and the various indoor and outdoor venues are extensively decorated with red, black, and gold bunting. Wearing the national colors is an indication that Pentecostals in PNG identify as a community at the national rather than primarily the local level, as well as an index of "participation in the Christian transnation" (Robbins 2004, 176).

P-CW songs are either very local in origin or from around the country or overseas. They are sung in indigenous languages, Tok Pisin, and English, depending on geographical location and context. Songs are sequenced so as to progressively build emotional intensity. Angela Panap, a Pentecostal worship leader with the Joseph Kingal Miracle Centre in Lae, explains that P-CW songs are ordered with the aim of taking participants to *wanpela kain poin, na level, na mak* (TP, a particular point, and level, and mark). When this mark is attained, "everyone is so alert to receive the Word. But if we don't hit that mark in praise and in worship you'll see the people are tired" (October 7, 2008). In an effort to reach an emotional high point, crusade P-CW sometimes threatens to descend into disorder, and I have witnessed a pastor sternly warning a crowd to cool down after the music team has worked single-mindedly to foster exuberance.

P-CW involves various kinds of dance. During the 1998 Assemblies of God Jubilee celebrations at Maprik in northwestern PNG, many of those in attendance at the outdoor daytime event waved palm branches as they moved counterclockwise in a large circle, while singing to fulset-accompanied songs such as the early praise "hit" "Holi Spirit kukim" (TP, Holy Spirit burning) (see "Revival Celebrations" 2012). This crusade-type gathering took on the general appearance of a *singsing* (TP, traditional dance festival). Crusade P-CW dancing I observed in Lae in 2008 was less organized, with participants jumping up and down in a crowd-like mass in front of the stage platform, waving palm branches. The aforementioned "Holy Spirit Crusade" at Kimbe in 2012 featured a formal opening ceremony that included dancing by a group of women dressed in the colors of the national flag, over which some wore *bilas* (TP, from the English "flash," meaning dance accoutrements, decorations). They performed two distinctively traditional-style dances to fulset-accompanied singing. The first was a welcome procession with dance movements; the second involved around thirty women and traditional-style choreography ("Kimbe Holy Spirit Crusade" 2012, 1:06–2:18). In contrast, dancing in church service P-CW tends to be more contained but also more individualistic, although it can be exuberant, as was the case at the SOS Breakthrough Praise event (see fig. 4.1).

New Era, New Sounds, in Village and City

A general mood of optimism surrounded the 1975 declaration of political independence in PNG. Independence in the political sphere to some extent coincided with a handover of the nation's churches to indigenous leaders. All over the country, people composed and sang songs of unity, in both *tok ples* (TP, local indigenous language) and Tok Pisin, and the subsequent, related rise of a national music industry stimulated a great interest in mastery of the rock band as an ensemble. Probably not coincidentally, around this time intense Christian revival activity broke out in various parts of the country. Anthropologist Joel Robbins suggests that this was an era of Melanesian "great awakening," as communities were "swept by waves of healing, prophecy, visions, tongue speaking, and other ecstatic phenomena" interpreted locally as "outpourings of the gifts of the Holy Spirit" (2004, 122). Indigenous theologian and musician

Andrew Midian interpreted the revival as "the young people's cry for religious independence" (1999, 47).

"Instruments create consequences everywhere," ethnomusicologist Mark Slobin observes, and this was certainly the case surrounding the 1970s PNG revivals (2010, 17). Through the revival, the guitar became pivotal to the foundation of P-CW in two ways (see Strathern and Ahrens 1986, 20). First, it sparked the creation of the *kores* (TP, chorus)—that is, indigenous praise and worship songs (Midian 1999, xxxiii–xxxiv). This explosion of local songs was largely a rural phenomenon. Second, with the drum kit and later the keyboard, the guitar was central to fulset worship taking hold in the PNG church. These instrumental skills were largely disseminated from the cities of Port Moresby, Lae, and Rabaul.

In 2012–13, the PNG P-CW musician Robin Kawaipa teamed up with the Australian-based transnational Pentecostal church Hillsong under the name OneBell to produce a polished album of praise and worship songs sung in Tok Pisin, entitled *Kisim i go*.[14] This collaboration resulted from Kawaipa's study at Hillsong College in Sydney.[15] While one might be inclined to assume that such global musical connections are relatively recent, in reality they date back some thirty years, as the case of the Oro musicians makes clear.

The Oro "brothers" (fig. 4.2)—Peter Bogembo (b. 1968), Daniel Meakoro (b. 1966), and Oswald Tamanabae (b. 1965)—were peers with a background in the Anglican Church whose families originated from different villages within the Binandere language area of Oro (Northern) Province.[16] The revival that broke out in their province was spearheaded by an Australian Pentecostal organization called the Christian Revival Crusade (CRC), which had established the Bethel Centre as its base in Port Moresby in 1972 (Gallagher 2011, 197–99). As Gallagher reports, Oswald's parents (Grace and Thomas) were instrumental in persuading other members of their family to become committed members of the Bethel Centre congregation. It was through members of the Tamanabae family worshipping there that in 1976 "revival ignited and spread like fire across Oro Province" after some of them returned to evangelize villages in their home district of Ioma (202). This revival had a profound impact throughout Binandere and later other villages, including on members of Bogembo's and Meakoro's family, resulting in what Robbins terms "second-stage conversion."[17]

As youths during the time of the revival, the brothers were excited by musical changes in the wind. Bogembo recalls, "Before we were used to hearing hymns, and suddenly they're singing songs like [Hank Williams's] 'I Saw the

FIG. 4.2 The Oro brothers (and mentor) at Boroko, April 2010. Left to right: Oswald Tamanabae, Daniel Meakoro, mentor Iara Eliakim, Peter Bogembo. Photo by the author.

Light' and [the "country-fied" hymn] 'At the Cross.' When they put music into [added instruments to] those type of songs—they had a bit of rhythm—it became totally new, a new sound! And it caught the attention of all the young ones, especially the younger generation" (April 20, 2010). Gallagher explains that such English songs, used by CRC team members in their "missionary outreach patrols,"[18] gave way to songs of praise and worship in indigenous languages (2011, 276–77). Until the revival, "language songs" had been considered the domain of the secular, guitar-based string band idiom, but at that time it occurred to youth that the string band could be adapted to Christian ends. According to Richmond Tamanabae, Oswald's uncle, as a result of the revival, "language songs became very, very popular and powerful" (quoted on 277). Digby Ho Leong, a close friend and musical associate of the Oro brothers, explains that revival-prompted, Spirit-inspired song composition became the norm in villages around the country: "Every so many years revival breaks in and then everybody is renewed. . . . It starts in one place and spreads throughout the nation. . . . When everybody catches on, that's where all the new songs come in, because everybody gets different impartations and different revelations, and they write about them. . . . They just sing about them and express what they feel inside" (January 15, 2008). Midian, an ordained minister of the United Church who was deeply moved through his encounters with a Pentecostal revival in northeastern New Britain in the 1980s, confirms this, noting that "many young indigenous Christians are writing gospel songs . . . indigenous in sound . . . [which] have gained popularity with Christians throughout the nation" (1999, xxxi).

Meakoro recalls that while the brothers were involved in this string band changeover, they always had an ear open for what they considered more dynamic sounds: "We were enjoying the local[19] and watching the trends—country music and rock music that was playing on the radio. They [that is, country and rock] were a lot more appealing." He continued, "We wanted the beat, we wanted the drums. . . . And then, this revival was coming and we couldn't sing hymns, because we needed something that was more upbeat, more up tempo, that could gain a bit of rhythm . . . that people could dance with and jump with—or, you know, flow with" (October 18, 2012).

Moving around between their home province and the cities of Lae and Port Moresby during their later teens, they discovered that *laiv ben* (TP, live band) or amplified gospel country rock was beginning to be used in several churches in the cities. "We were trying to pattern after" two groups in particular, explained Meakoro: a "country"-style Christian band called the Jesus Experience based at the Foursquare Gospel Church in Lae, where Meakoro undertook some of his secondary schooling, and the Bethel Singers, a band formed at the CRC's Bethel Centre at Tokarara in Port Moresby, where Oswald Tamanabae began as a drummer. These groups were among the first church worship bands in PNG comprising local musicians. The sounds and idea of Christian popular music "just rubbed on us as we were growing," Tamanabae remembers. "The first time I heard the Jesus Experience [on cassette]," Bogembo concurs, "it was like, 'Wow! Christians can sing like this?' I said, 'So Christian music does sound like this too?' It was a new [concept]!" (April 20, 2010).

Meakoro refers to himself and Tamanabae as "dropouts" (October 18, 2012) and explains that at first the brothers had no clear direction, only an urge to be creative. Despite feeling that they were church "captives" due to their families' deep involvement, it was the eventual personal "discovery" of God that brought purpose to their innovation: "At the early stage we were captured with the church, the Faith, and everything in there. Because this passion was strong and we were creating, you know, we were actually really initiating a new trend. . . . Then we discovered God for ourselves, and I think that's where the trend of music—the trends and the desires, the passion, and even the worship aspect of it started taking another trend. But the creative aspect of it continued, you know" (April 20, 2010).

Meakoro and Tamanabae were encouraged to gain proficiency on rock band instruments by "our big fathers" (October 18, 2012), Richmond Tamanabae and Pastor Peter Igarobae, respected family elders who served as their spiritual guardians. Motivated to make a musical impact on their own local area in those early years, they remember being stretched for resources:

MEAKORO: We didn't lose our passion for music—we were developing that, really literally from scratch. We didn't have amps, so we have stories that we laugh about.

BOGEMBO: We were using loud-hailers to amplify the guitars . . .

MEAKORO: We had to hang cymbals on a kind of clothesline . . .

BOGEMBO: And on one trip up to Kokoda, we didn't have a mic stand, so we had to put a forked stick in [the ground] and hang the mic down . . .

TAMANABAE: And wherever the wind blew we had to follow. [*laughter*] (April 20, 2010)

Such were the challenges involved in establishing "live band" or fulset worship in the remote, rural areas of PNG.

Understanding this era as their "season" collectively (discussed further below), in retrospect the brothers see themselves as agents of a spiritual change— or, as Bogembo put it, an "awakening"—that was "breaking out" at the time:

MEAKORO: Every creative aspect, it was breaking out, if you like! The trend of [break] dancing, the trend of music, anything to do with performing arts, we were tapping into that.

BOGEMBO: We could even write scripts of drama—dramatizing Bible stories— we were actually writing the script and getting young guys, and just train them and they would go out and they would make the Bible stories so alive!

MEAKORO: And choreographing. It was our season, you know, those days.

TAMANABAE: That's right. And we used that as a tool of evangelism, in a way in which we could capture the young people . . .

BOGEMBO: To share the Gospel.

TAMANABAE: And really, I think that was one of the ways in which we created an opening for the young people to start filling up the churches. (April 20, 2010)

The revival prompted the three of them to experiment in these early years with a "diversity of ritual modalities" previously unknown to the PNG church (Yong 2010, 206). "Once we got the hang of it," Meakoro relates, "we started getting into creativity and . . . we just took off" (October 18, 2012).

In 1986, an opportunity arose for Meakoro and Tamanabae to travel overseas with the Pentecostal organization Youth with a Mission (YWAM), and the timing—in those early years after independence—proved to be critical. While Tamanabae undertook evangelism training in South Carolina, Meakoro spent over three years based in Hong Kong, learning ballet, jazz dance, and break dancing. Through dance, he evangelized in the red-light districts and gay bars of Amsterdam, Haarlem, Paris, and Copenhagen. In the late 1970s, the Oro brothers had become aware of contemporary Christian music (CCM) and were particularly drawn to the songs and sounds of Andraé Crouch, Keith Green, Dallas Holm, the Imperials, and Petra. While abroad, they became ever more attracted to such music and the emerging interracial nature of CCM of the era. Being among PNG's first overseas missionaries themselves, and encouraged by YWAM's progressive, ethnically inclusive policies, Meakoro and Tamanabae learned firsthand that their new nation of PNG was part of a Christian transnation.

Upon Meakoro's return to PNG in 1988, the Oro brothers formed the gospel group Higher Vision with a number of other Spirit-revived brothers, most of them also from Oro Province. This was the first of a number of widely popular PNG gospel bands they founded over the following decade, which led to their becoming major recording artists within the PNG popular music industry. Around the same time, they began a tradition of traveling at the end of each year from the different corners of the country where they were studying or working to Popondetta, the capital of their home province, where they would hold a public "Jesus march." As Bogembo put it, "Those are moments [when] what we used to desire, we'd take it [live, amplified gospel music] out onto the streets and in the town and just explode it!" He continued, "At the time, when we brought that new sound, it's like suddenly our people in the province started hearing, like, 'Hey, a new sound—this is a new sound!'" By this time, they were writing original gospel songs in earnest and touring around parts of the country performing (April 20, 2010).

The Oro brothers began to branch out: Higher Vision soon became Tamanabae's band, Meakoro started Voice in the Wind in the early 1990s, and several years later Bogembo formed P2-UIF with a number of PNG session musicians.[20] All of the bands contained a core of Oro "clan" members;

hence, this was a kind of dynasty of PNG Pentecostal music makers. As Bogembo phrased it, the bands were "all coming out of the same matrix, the same womb"—that is, a common cultural background, faith "encounter" (their term), and creative impulse (April 20, 2010).

A Millennialist Aesthetic

I now turn to a discussion of the Oro brothers' music performance aesthetic as it relates to the Pentecostal expressions of their faith in the PNG context. I term this a "spatiotemporal millennialist aesthetic" since, taken together, their music style, song repertories, and embodied communal performance practices can be understood as enfolding an apocalyptic sense of space and time that anticipates the coming reign of God. That is, although not overtly articulated as such, their oeuvre is informed by a sense of the PNG nation playing a contributing role to the larger transnational Christian community, which itself foreshadows the imminently arriving kingdom of God. Further, it represents a predilection for current and new global styles over older local ones, and by driving the experience of "high praise," it initiates a new, future "season" of spiritual blessing.

Over the years, the Oro brothers have paid close attention to the cultural meanings of musical sounds. Indeed, for some years, they encountered intense opposition to their musical innovations from Anglican church leaders. They have been impressed by performances in PNG by Island Breeze, a YWAM peripatetic performance group that "channels the power of cultural music and dance as a visual way to share the message of Christ" (Youth with a Mission Perth 2012). Wrestling with how to understand PNG traditional music from a biblical perspective, they have consciously employed indigenous musical elements in some of their recordings. Fascinatingly, Meakoro sees the brothers' music making as being parallel in vision to that of the high-profile and decidedly "secular" PNG transethnic fusion ensemble Sanguma:[21]

> While we were in these pioneering stages in the gospel scenery, we were also influenced by our own [national] creative arts band, Sanguma, [which] had this kind of a vision also—they wanted to display PNG and its culture. So, they studied music and then they went deeper into the cultural aspect of it, spirits and all. We were around about the same time, but were in a very sensitive spot, as well. [*chuckles*] We were influenced

by them, but at the same time we had a culture in the church to try and enforce, you know, with our music. But I think somewhere along the line, we didn't cross the line, but we tapped into that [cultural] dimension because we are also Papua New Guineans. (April 20, 2010)

Here, Meakoro emphasizes that they shared with Sanguma a vision to musically represent the PNG nation and its culture. In Robbins's terms, the Oro brothers and many other Pentecostals in PNG firmly believe that "the modern world is properly a world of nations" (2004, 170).

As I have shown, in the early post-independence revival years, P-CW song repertories arose as a response to local revival experience, although they circulated around the nation orally (a situation that continues). In the latter 1990s, following the practice in the Christian transnation beyond PNG and influenced by the worldwide success of Australian Hillsong Church songwriters Geoff Bullock and later Darlene Zschech, as well as Ron Kenoly from the United States, various members of the Oro brothers' groups began composing and recording songs for use in corporate worship. P2-UIF later achieved a first in PNG with the inclusion of lyrics on a gospel cassette so that the songs could be used in worship, and with Tony Ando and several others, Meakoro formed the studio worship band Covenant Praise. As Tamanabae explains, the songs on their recordings followed a three-language format, indicating an intention to reach local as well as national and perhaps global worshippers: "When we started coming into the early '90s, I think our songs, our arrangements, started changing. We started incorporating a little bit of the English version, our language—*tok ples* [TP, indigenous language]—and pidgin. And that actually emerged into the church scenery in the revival that hit in 1997" (April 20, 2010). Further, keeping in mind Meakoro's comparison with Sanguma, as the Oro brothers were consciously composing Christian music for consumption across the nation, they occasionally infused a song arrangement with a local rhythmic feel. For example, Meakoro referred to the underlying rhythm of the Covenant Praise song "Sigarap" (TP, Desire or Passion) as "Sepik beat" (October 9, 2008; see Covenant Praise 2000).[22]

Recording engineer Digby Ho Leong confirms Tamanabae's linking of these new songs with the 1997 revival and notes with enthusiasm how the songs began to find a place in the repertories of the Christian transnation: "When the revival was on . . . we wrote how many—twelve or thirteen songs—and we recorded them, and it spread like wildfire around the country. [The songs] even got down to Alice Springs [in Central Australia], and they translated them into

English. And Tony's [Tony Ando's] songs have been sung in Malaysia!" (January 15, 2008). More recently, Meakoro has begun employing his songwriting "trademark," in which he composes lyrics mostly in English but "slip[s] in a phrase or two of pidgin" in the hope that someday songs in a PNG language will enter the transnational worship canon (October 9, 2008).

Indigenous musical elements and languages notwithstanding, ultimately the way the Oro brothers have chosen to represent their vision of the nation is not by composing string band–style songs, nor by incorporating indigenous instruments or other musical elements, as in the approach taken by Sanguma. Rather, they adopt the sounds and style elements of Western pop, gospel, and, more recently, popular worship music. Clearly, they have always seen themselves as innovators, as brokers of new sounds and styles. This emphasis on musical currentness corresponds with their sense that Christians need to be "up to date" with God, alert to a change of "season."

In temporal terms, the Oro brothers are guided by their understanding of the biblical notion of "season," a Pentecostal usage derived from Jeremiah 8:7 that appears to be related to dispensationalist thinking.[23] Meakoro explains that their music assists in moral transformation because it is biblically inspired and is future—and hence purpose—oriented: "I like to see my songs that I'm writing as basically going to help someone find Life. . . . So I like to have a source that is Life, that is good, that is wholesome, that has got the future, you know, in perspective—that has got purpose." He continues, "On the other side is the 'now,' the *season* that we are tapping into. And while you have a source you are connecting to, one of the things that has helped me so that I stay current, I stay 'in the now' and I'm relevant with what I'm saying. I'm updating [that is, renewing] my material, I'm updating [renewing] my life; I'm helping others update the church—by tapping into the season" (October 9, 2008). This season is one in which God may choose to "manifest his glory" among his people in a new way, as "Abounding Grace," the opening song of Breakthrough Praise and Ando and Meakoro's best-known worship song, puts it.[24]

In Robbins's study of the Urapmin, a group of 390 people who live in the remote West Sepik Province of PNG, most of whom are Pentecostal Christians, he documents a "redemption ritual" they call "Spirit disko" (2004, 281–88). This bears some resemblance to "high praise" and P-CW more generally, although it is held separately from worship and outreach services. In any case, as Robbins explains, "it is through this institution that the Urapmin most fully elaborate their vision of collective salvation" (305). Interestingly, the 2010 SOS, with its musical Breakthrough Praise night and Praise Extravaganza model, coincided with a decision among the small Oro Pentecostal ministry groups living in Port Moresby, and the many musicians who had been members over the years of one or another of the Oro gospel groups, to "merge." As Meakoro put it, "[We] are more concerned about the corporate destiny than our own individual streams. Because we are feeling it's like the corporate destiny of the church, the corporate destiny of the nation—more for a corporate pursuit" (April 20, 2010). There was a sense that it was time to turn away from the individualism that had come to characterize their musical pursuits for several decades and to prepare for a new "season" with a new strategy. Tamanabae summed up their several decades of gospel music making with a teleological reflection: "All this time we've been saying, 'Let's just keep building; let's keep preparing it. We don't know what's going to happen but something's going to open up for us. We never know—it may come in its full timing!'" (April 20, 2010).

Conclusion

In this chapter, I have examined aspects of the liturgy of P-CW as it has come to be practiced across PNG over the last two decades and outlined the historical circumstances that saw it emerge as a new form of shared sacred Christian ceremony incorporating elements of popular, traditional, and national culture. Through a case study of the Oro brothers, who in their youth were inspired by a Pentecostal revival in their province and who went on to both innovate in the field of gospel music and creatively enliven worship locally and nationally, I have attempted to uncover the processes involved in establishing the liturgical form. Finally, I have proposed that the Oro brothers operate within the framework of a spatiotemporal millennialist aesthetic. This is encapsulated in the logo screen printed on the back of T-shirts worn at the SOS Breakthrough Praise event:

PNG
Praise Extravaganza
United for Purpose
<u>Destiny is Dawning</u>

"PNG" and "United for Purpose" indicate a relating to space as nation. "Praise Extravaganza" conveys participation in "extravagant" performance and the entering into musical and sacred time. And "Destiny is Dawning" announces an imminent future age of blessing and fulfillment. Considering the three strands of the logo together and the work the Oro brothers have done to shake up and transform worship nationally, we might better understand their belief that through "high praise" their merged congregations, and the PNG nation more broadly, can experience moral transformation in readiness for "the coming of our King."[25]

NOTES

1. Papua New Guinea is an independent state with a population of around seven million. Located north of Australia in the southwestern Pacific Islands subregion generally designated Melanesia, it is one of the most linguistically and culturally diverse regions of the world, where well over one thousand distinct languages are spoken.

2. The text of "Abounding Grace," by Tony Ando and Daniel Meakoro, is reproduced with the composers' permission. Breakthrough Praise was held on April 10, 2010, in Port Moresby, PNG. A field recording of an excerpt of this session, with additional analytical notes, can be found on the author's website, http://www.melanesianmusicresearch.com, under Libraries: Sound Recordings: Papua New Guinea. Also uploaded there are excerpts from field recordings of Pentecostal-charismatic worship accompanied by a *fulset* (electric rock band) from an outdoor public evangelistic crusade in Lae, on the northern side of PNG.

3. These groups are also affiliated with the Malaysia-based I.S.A.A.C. network. See http://www.jonathan-david.org.

4. According to Allan Anderson, those participating in Pentecostal and charismatic worship are given an opportunity to "pray simultaneously, to dance and sing during the 'praise and worship,' to exercise the gifts of the Spirit, to respond to the 'altar call,' and to call out their approval of the preaching with expletives like 'Amen!' and 'Hallelujah!' and with applause and laughter" (2004, 9).

5. Webb's (2011) detailed discussion of Pentecostal-charismatic worship as practiced in and around the city of Lae provides contextual information relevant to the present study.

6. The postmissionary "era" in PNG more or less coincides with political independence in 1975 and the earliest phase of decolonization, and it signals the beginning of a time of financial and institutional independence for local Protestant (including Pentecostal) churches (see Howell 2008, 23).

7. While P-CW is commonly associated with Pentecostalists, it has been adapted for use by many different denominations, both Catholic and Protestant.

8. I draw on the following interviews in this chapter: Digby Ho Leong and Edric Ogomeni, January 15, 2008, Port Moresby, PNG (1 hr., 14 min.); Angela Panap, October 7, 2008, Lae, PNG (43 min.); Daniel Meakoro, October 9, 2008, Port Moresby, PNG (1hr., 20 min.); Peter Bogembo, Daniel Meakoro, and Oswald Tamanabae (group interview), April 20, 2010, Port Moresby, PNG (1 hr., 21 min.); Daniel Meakoro (Skype conversation), October 18, 2012 (15 min.). In the text, I reference these by date. In quoting from interviews, I have omitted minor repetitions.

9. In interview and conversation, the three referred to one another as brothers, an overlap of a Christian usage, shared history, and provincial origin.

10. Tony Ando was unavailable at the time I conducted the interviews on which this case study is based. I subsequently met and interviewed him in February 2013, although this data is not drawn upon in the chapter.

11. For one example, in 2008 the well-resourced Pentecostal organization Joseph Kingal Ministries of Lae launched Flame of Touch, a "national spiritual strategic plan" to evangelize each of the nation's eighty-nine electorates over twenty years, with five major crusades per year (Aihi 2008).

12. The *Cordyline fruticosa*, a plant native to many parts of the Pacific Islands, has sacred connotations. Its leaves are often worn in dance performance.

13. Consult field recordings of P-CW on the author's website, http://www .melanesianmusicresearch.com.

14. OneBell (from *wanbel*; TP, of the same conviction); *Kisim i go* (TP, Take it out).

15. In a YouTube video performance of the OneBell song "Yu yet yu Namba Wan" (TP, You alone are Lord), Kawaipa plays guitar and sings a duet with Australian Hillsong musician Raymond Badham ("Ray Badham" 2012). Interestingly, in terms of musical glocalization, both the PNG and Australian musicians sing in Tok Pisin, and it is Badham, the Australian, who provides a lead guitar introduction and coda comprising a genericized string band guitar motif. Both Badham and Kawaipa reproduce the *ailan reggae* (PNG English, island reggae) guitar strum and overall "feel" common in PNG studio-produced pop music from the early 1990s.

16. The Oro "brothers" form the core of a larger group of influential musicians that includes Oswald's brothers Steve and Brian, Tony Ando, and Edric Ogomeni, as well as John Uware, who comes from the Orokaiva region.

17. According to Robbins, "second-stage conversion" occurs "when Christian meanings have come to shape people's world to such an extent that those meanings themselves, rather than ones drawn from traditional culture, begin to provide the motive for conversion" (2004, 215).

18. The term used by Port Moresby–based CRC members for their evangelistic excursions into the provinces (see Gallagher 2011, 202).

19. In PNG, *lokal* (TP, local) is a synonym for *stringben* (TP, string band). Meakoro's usage of the word is interesting—an unintended pun, perhaps?

20. The group's alphanumeric name derives from the registration code of an aircraft owned by the CRC that crashed in rugged terrain in PNG in 1992, resulting in the death of the pastor pilot and passengers. For the band, P2 came to stand for "Two Partners" and UIF for "United in Fellowship."

21. See Crowdy (2004) for a history of this ensemble.

22. This is a studio-created approximation of a rhythmic "feel" derived from a string band strumming style from the Sepik River region, created by juxtaposing the melody in triple meter against the quadruple metrical structure set up by drums.

23. For an explanation of dispensationalist theology and an account of its impact on a PNG society, see Robbins (2004, 158–68).

24. In the dispensationalist system, the current church age is marked by the dispensation of grace.

25. From the text of "Abounding Grace."

REFERENCES

Aihi, D. 2008. "20-Year Crusade Plan Launched." *The National,* June 12.
Anderson, Allan. 2004. *An Introduction to Pentecostalism: Global Charismatic Christianity.* Cambridge: Cambridge University Press.
Covenant Praise. 2000. *Spirit of the Word.* Port Moresby: Chin H. Meen. Cassette tape.

Crowdy, Denis. 2004. "From Black Magic Woman to Black Magic Men: The Music of San-guma." Ph.D. diss., Macquarie University.
Farhadian, Charles. 2007. "Worship as Mission: The Personal and Social Ends of Papuan Worship in the Glory Hut." In *Christian Worship Worldwide: Expanding Horizons, Deepening Practices*, edited by Charles Farhadian, 171–95. Grand Rapids, Mich.: Eerdmans.
Gallagher, Sarita. 2011. "Abrahamic Blessing Motif as Reflected in the Papua New Guinean Christian Revival Crusade Movement: Blesim bilong Papa God." Ph.D. diss., Fuller Theological Seminary.
Handman, Courtney Jill. 2010. "Schism and Christianity: Bible Translation and the Social Organization of Denominationalism in the Waria Valley, Papua New Guinea." Ph.D. diss., University of Chicago.
Howell, Brian. 2008. *Christianity in the Local Context: Southern Baptists in the Philippines.* New York: Palgrave Macmillan.
"The Kimbe Holy Spirit Crusade." 2012. YouTube video, 5:00. Posted by Fred Evans, September 19. http://www.youtube.com/watch?v=o_JqMIJKcPQ.
Midian, Andrew. 1999. *The Value of Indigenous Music in the Life and Ministry of the Church: The United Church in the Duke of York Islands.* Port Moresby: Institute of Papua New Guinea Studies.
"Ray Badham, Robin Kawaipa, and Hillsong College Team@ PNG EncounterFirst 2012 Conference." 2012. YouTube video, 2:26. Posted by Robin Kawaipa, June 12. http://www.youtube.com/watch?v=vImcxvBn7mM.
"Revival Celebrations in Papua New Guinea." 2012. YouTube video, 3:34. Posted by Fred Evans, August 28. http://www.youtube.com/watch?v=oEqTz63kcTo.
Robbins, Joel. 2004. *Becoming Sinners: Christianity and Moral Torment in a Papua New Guinea Society.* Berkeley: University of California Press.
Slobin, Mark. 2010. *Folk Music: A Very Short Introduction.* New York: Oxford University Press.
Strathern, Andrew, and Theodoor Ahrens. 1986. "Experiencing the Christian Faith in Papua New Guinea." *Melanesian Journal of Theology* 2 (1): 8–21.
Webb, Michael. 2011. "*Palang* Conformity and *Fulset* Freedom." *Ethnomusicology* 55 (3): 445–72.
Yong, Amos. 2010. *In the Days of Caesar: Pentecostalism and Political Theology.* Grand Rapids, Mich.: Eerdmans.
Youth with a Mission Perth. 2012. "Island Breeze." http://www.ywamperth.org.au/missions/island-breeze/.

5

Worship Music as Aesthetic
Domain of Meaning and Bonding:
The Glocal Context of a Dutch Pentecostal Church

Miranda Klaver

Newcomers in evangelical/pentecostal churches in the Netherlands stress the importance of worship music and singing in their relationship with God. The contemporary style of singing and musical performance of worship music create a sensory environment that stands in great contrast to the worship style in Dutch traditional Protestant mainline churches. In this chapter, worship music is approached as a practice of mediating divine presence and as a social process that transforms how believers understand their place within the world, allowing them to question how the world is ordered in terms of relationships between people and between an individual and God. Furthermore, I argue that the transnational character of evangelical/pentecostal worship music creates a potential deinstitutionalizing force, enabling worshippers to identify with a revivalist global community.

Experiencing God Through Worship Music

The impact of music and singing turned out to be a far more important issue than I expected in my research on the meaning of conversion for newcomers in evangelical/pentecostal (hereafter e/p) churches in the Netherlands.[1] When converts spoke about intense religious experiences, they often recalled the time of praise and worship during the church service. Since most of the new visitors and recent converts had previous experiences in mainline Protestant churches, for them the contrast in musical style and genre between mainline churches and e/p churches was obvious: not only was the organ replaced by a full band, but the performative style and repertoire of songs exhibited a rupture with former church traditions. For those with no church background, the contemporary style and performance of the music often came as a total surprise, contrasting sharply with their preconceived ideas about church services and Christianity in general.

The ways in which music was brought up in the narratives of new believers indicates that music and singing can serve as important media for experiencing the divine. This raises the general question of how experiences of music and singing, due to their sensational appeal, invoke the presence of God and can be persuasive as a revitalizing force in the lives of former members of mainline churches and new believers. In order to answer these questions, I will discuss the contextual arrangement of music and singing in a Dutch e/p church. By investigating aesthetic forms and discourses of worship music, I will demonstrate how worshippers have access to distinct semiotic domains of meaning that enable them to both situate themselves within narratives and embody them at the same time.

I will start with a brief overview of the rise of e/p worship music in the Netherlands. Following a theoretical discussion on music as aesthetic form and the distinctive features of my approach to worship music, I will present ethnographic accounts of music and singing in an e/p church in the Amsterdam area, based on a year of ethnographic research in 2006–7.[2] I will demonstrate how this church uses mass-mediated products and practices from the global Christian marketplace to create a musical world of its own, with a particular configuration of words, music, and performance. In the local context of this Dutch pentecostal church, globally circulating pentecostal styles of worship are incorporated, including both musical and performative styles. This underscores the dynamic relationship between the global and the local, often described as the process of "glocalization" (Robertson 1995). I will close this chapter with a discussion of the importance of aesthetics as one of the main modes of bonding in e/p communities.

Dutch Protestantism and the Creation of "Glocal" Worship Music

Characteristic of Dutch Protestantism is the strong division between mainline Protestant churches and e/p churches. The differences include baptism practices (for example, infant baptism by sprinkling versus adult baptism by immersion), liturgy (psalms and hymns according to the church order versus contemporary worship music), and church leadership (professional clergy versus lay pastors) (Klaver 2008, 2011a). While e/p churches operated outside or at the margins of the established mainline Protestant churches until the 1950s, their song repertoire had been of great importance for mainline Protestant lay spirituality since the early part of the twentieth century. The influence of e/p songs—an early form of glocalization within Dutch Protestantism—began with the hymnal of Johannes de Heer, published in 1905.[3] De Heer, inspired by the revival in Wales, translated an extensive number of English-language revival songs, such as those composed by Ira David Sankey (1840–1908) and drawn from the Salvation Army repertoire. Initially, his hymnal was used in evangelistic tent meetings and conferences, and over time it became the main hymnal used in e/p churches (Klaver 2011b, 189).

In the 1930s and 1940s, these songs became popular among lay Protestants through radio broadcasts. They were often sung in the private sphere of the home and in extra-liturgical settings such as youth associations and camp meetings. In spite of the wide acceptance of these songs, various Protestant churches were able to uphold their liturgical traditions and church orders free from e/p influences, as the songs were not integrated into the hymnal repertoire of Dutch mainline churches (Elsman 1995, 141).

As church membership declined after World War II, the mainline Protestant hymnal culture was challenged in different ways. Through the rise of new media such as radio, television, and records, new popular musical styles became accessible to the masses. In the wake of these developments, a new repertoire of Christian music was introduced by American evangelistic organizations such as Youth for Christ (Roeland 2009, 38). Characteristic features of the new Christian music included easily accessible tunes and contemporary language and style, which made the pieces more suitable for accompaniment by a guitar or praise band than an organ. With the growth of e/p churches in the Netherlands in the 1970s, the evangelistic organization Opwekking (translated as "Revival") has, since 1972, initiated the spread of new worship songs through the annual release of recently written, but mostly translated, English worship songs (Smelik 2006, 174).[4] From early on, the selection of new worship songs has been determined by a team of independent e/p revivalist preachers, worship leaders, and musicians, part of the Opwekking network. As a result, the Opwekking songs—currently numbering more than seven hundred—display the development of the Dutch e/p movement, as well as that within the English-speaking world, since most of the songs have been selected from abroad.[5] In the early 1970s, worship songs by Scripture in Song (David and Dale Garratt, New Zealand) and Maranatha Music were introduced; in the 1980s and 1990s, many songs by Thank You Music, Integrity Music, and Mercy Publishers / Vineyard were distributed. More recently, Hillsong Publishing and worshiptogether.com have been the major sources for new worship songs.

The new songs introduced by Opwekking differed from the songs of Johannes de Heer by virtue of their interconnectedness with the rise of popular youth culture in the 1960s, introducing a countercultural subculture with the new idiom of pop music. According to Koenig, in the 1970s, the tradition of evangelical revival songs was transformed into the genre of contemporary "worship music"—a synthesis of popular music and the charismatic/pentecostal experience. This alteration in style brought about a change in e/p liturgy: so-called praise and worship time has become a defining feature of e/p worship services (Koenig 2008).

From early on, the Opwekking songs were well accepted by and integrated into Dutch e/p churches, and gradually Opwekking became fully glocalized, serving as the main worship song repertoire of the Dutch e/p movement at large. A recent development, observed since the mid-1990s, is the selective adoption of the Opwekking repertoire in some mainline Protestant churches during Sunday morning services. Although sometimes in seeming conflict with the formal church liturgy, these contemporary worship songs are often included in an attempt to meet the needs of e/p-oriented church members and the younger generation. The cautious acceptance of Opwekking songs serves as an important indicator of processes of evangelicalization within the mainline Protestant churches (Klaver and Versteeg 2007).

The introduction of contemporary worship music not only changed the musical repertoire within e/p churches but also brought about a shift in performative style. This includes, broadly speaking, the use of musical instruments and idioms that resemble contemporary styles of popular music, and, more importantly, the e/p view of worship and music as mediating practice. The narratives of newcomers in e/p churches reveal the importance of music and singing as constitutive practices for religious experience and the construction of meaning. This underscores the necessity that scholars pay attention to all that happens in worship, in addition to what is being said (Chaves 2004, 11). I will therefore approach music and singing from a phenomenological perspective, considering the ways in which people sing, make music, perform music, and select the songs they wish to sing. In the following section, I will discuss my main theoretical framework with regard to music and singing.

Worship Music as Aesthetic Form

What happens during a time of worship and how participants give meaning to music and singing are complex questions to answer. Since one of the key features of e/p worship lies in its sensational appeal, I will approach music and singing as a semiotic practice that functions within perceptible experience by virtue of its material properties. Following recent works that emphasize the "materiality" of religion—that is, the value attributed to bodies, things, texts, and gestures (Keane 2007; Meyer and Houtman 2012)—I regard music as part of a larger semiotic domain of meaning, encompassing doctrines and ideas that not only are expressed in material forms but also generate new meanings by the constitutive power of social practices. This perspective on worship music as a formative semiotic practice leads me to the following issues at play in the process of meaning making.

First, the interpretation and experience of worship music as a semiotic practice draw attention to the material qualities of sound and rhythm and therefore to bodily sensations that are experienced through embodied processes of learning and socialization. As Classen (1993), Howes (2003), and others have observed, the senses are socially and historically organized and influenced by the period of time in which people live. In this respect, the larger sociocultural development of the sensorium, as well as the contextual nature of sensory experience, is at play in the sound formation of the body. With regard to worship music, this prompts me to focus on the ways in which the body is mobilized through music and singing. In contrast to mainline Protestant churches, e/p churches create a distinct religious sensory environment through the integration of a contemporary musical idiom and the use of electronic media.

The importance of the social formation of the body and the senses leads me to the second issue: music is intrinsically connected to performance (Frith 1998; Small 1998). As one cannot disassociate music from enactment and performance, processes of meaning making will be determined by all those involved in the act of making music. Small captures the performative aspects of music as action in the use of a verb rather than a noun by introducing the concept of "musicking." He states that "the act of musicking establishes in the place where it is happening a set of relationships, and it is in those relationships that the meaning of the act lies" (1998, 13). In musicking, these social and relational aspects are not merely evoked and imagined as expressions of longing and desire, but experienced as real: we experience the world as it is, and through the experience, we learn about the world as it should be. This understanding of music as enactment implies that music—as embodied performance—encourages the formation of identities. As such, instances of collective sensual arousal are crucial to social bonding and community building (Durkheim [1912] 1995).

A third issue with regard to worship music is the question of how one is to approach songs. Though music and words are inseparable in worship music, songs require separate analysis of lyrics and musical setting. In his study on congregational singing, Adnams (2008) focuses on the different ways in which lyrics are appropriated by individual worshippers, showing how the singing of hymns—as opposed to contemporary worship songs—presupposes a different relation to texts. Different types of songs posit a particular intentionality on the part of the singer. Adnams states that "song is the inseparable experience of music and word and in this marriage, many things happen to words when they are sung" (116). In fact, the meaning of words can even turn negative if texts are perceived as inauthentic or unbiblical. From a different angle, Sample (1998) shows how the meaning of words is affected by the use of electronic culture in popular music, suggesting that meaning emerges as an outcome of the convergence of different sensorial experiences. Versteeg convincingly demonstrates, based on extensive ethnographic research in a Dutch Vineyard church, the relation between worship music and the ideology of the pop musical form (2010, 232). He reveals the congruence between romantic ideology as found in pop songs and the charismatic Vineyard discourse as, in Frith's terms, "formulas of love" (1998, 161). Therefore, the meaning of worship is not primarily found in the text of the lyrics but produced in the performance and musical style.

These three dimensions of the semiotic domain of music—namely, the body, performance, and the relation between words and music—lead me to focus simultaneously on the intersections between the different dimensions. In doing so, I consider the fact that the meaning and relevance of lyrics are contextually arranged in relation to the other performative features. In the following ethnographic account, I regard the experience of music and singing as being embedded within a number of narratives that dialogue with the worshipper. This constellation goes beyond the lyrics; the worshipper is physically surrounded by particular sounds that have the potential to bridge different domains of meaning. Moreover, as the worshipper is presented with a particular order of songs, certain song elements are stressed through repetition. The worship is thus performed within a specific configuration of musicians, vocalists, and audience members, in addition to a wide range of material expressions (or media). All of these different aspects have the potential to evoke emotions, moods, and memories and are involved in the dialogical process of meaning making through worship music.

The Living Gospel Church

The Living Gospel Church (hereafter LGC) was founded in the 1980s by members of a charismatic Bible study group that split off from a local Dutch Reformed church. On average, around seven hundred congregants now attend the Sunday morning service. The church owns and is housed in a former school building that has been transformed into a multifunctional church complex, including a large auditorium with a stage and extensive multimedia equipment.

From the beginning, the church has exhibited an international outlook on the world, shown in its receptive attitude toward international renewal movements. In the mid-1990s, the LGC attracted national attention, as it was known as the place to experience the "Toronto Blessing" in the Netherlands.[6] The church's location close to the national airport, family relations across the Atlantic, and many transnational business relations have fostered transnational connections among traveling pastors, revivalist preachers, Christian bands, and the LGC. In fact, the LGC has been recognized nationally for its use of contemporary worship music, as one of the first Dutch Christian worship bands was formed in this church in the 1980s.

The Sunday worship service at the LGC has the character of a spontaneous celebration and exhibits an informal liturgy. The band usually consists of four male instrumentalists—a drummer, bassist, and two guitarists (electric and acoustic)—and two or three female vocalists in addition to the worship leader. The worship leader takes center stage, while the vocalists stand on the left side of the stage. The drum is positioned on the right, and the guitarists stand behind the worship leader. The lyrics of the songs are projected in Dutch and English on a large screen centered above the stage.

The sound of the worship service is dominated by the drums, bass, and guitars. Generally, the volume of the music is rather loud; as the room fills with sound, little sonic space is left for the congregation itself. The worshippers are drowned out by the band, and consequently it is difficult to hear oneself singing. The band performs according to the aesthetic rules of pop music, in terms of volume, performance, and audience reaction, creating a complete and powerful soundscape (Adnams 2008, 225). Here, the mixing of popular music and contemporary worship practices becomes tenuous; the musicians' performance assumes certain expectations of the relationship between stage and audience. Volume plays an important role in managing this power dynamic and bridging the gap between stage and audience.

The upbeat opening song acts as a call to worship. It invites and encourages the audience members to forget their mundane sorrows and situations and directs them to focus on God who is good, faithful, and worthy of all praise. The structure of the worship time consists of a successive progression of songs and musical styles according to the so-called tabernacle model (Cornwall 1983), based on the metaphoric movement of worshippers entering the temple in Jerusalem from the outer courts, moving into the inner courts, and eventually meeting God in the center of the temple, the holy place. This particular worship scheme offers the audience a structure for experience. In e/p worship music, a stylistic difference between praise and worship is recognized by worship leaders and the worshippers themselves: "Praise tends to be emotional while worship is devotional, and [praise] is often loudly exuberant while worship is more apt to be quietly exultant" (Cornwall 1983, 151). Whereas praise songs are "about God"—who he is and what he has done—worship songs are sung to God as a direct response from the heart of the worshipper. In practice, however, this distinction is not always clear, because the usual correspondence between the lyrics and musical style is not always upheld. The overall purpose of worship is to experience an immediate and intimate encounter with God—"to be in his presence." As Tim, the LGC's worship leader, explains, "Leading worship is like taking a group of people on a journey. We want to bring them to the place where we can be together with God, so that your heart is connected to the heart of God."[7]

The expectation that worship leads to an experience of divine encounter involves a high level of participation from the worshippers. Their "successful" response is reflected in the performance of the worship leader. According to Tim, as a worship leader, "you are aware of what God wants to do and at the same time observe whether the audience comes along or not." He fulfills a central role onstage and communicates with the audience members as he frequently encourages them to praise God with their voices by singing wholeheartedly and enthusiastically. At the same time, the worship leader communicates with God by praising him during short interludes between songs and during the singing and by voicing short prayers such as "Fill us, Lord" and

"More, more of you." The worship leader also directs the worship team in how to perform songs at particular moments during the service. With finger and hand gestures, he occasionally signals for the team to repeat the entire chorus or a certain line of a song. According to Tim, these improvisations depend on spontaneous divine inspiration, which is achieved through attuning one's inner ear to the voice of the Spirit during the time of worship. However, in practice, the worship leader adjusts his songs to enhance a certain response from the audience, based on a normative understanding of progressive bodily engagement of the congregation throughout the service. First, during the time of praise, the *ordinary body* is transformed into an *exuberant body,* as observed in bodily movements such as clapping, the raising of hands, jumping, swaying, and dancing with happy, smiling faces. This is followed by the time of worship, when the outwardly focused, enthusiastic body is gradually transformed into the inwardly focused *devoted body,* expressed in postures such as closed eyes, outstretched arms and hands, kneeling, or even lying prostrate on the floor.

During the worship service, bodily movements serve as powerful indices for identifying the presence of God. Intriguingly, while Tim explains that the worshippers reflect what God is doing during worship, he himself mobilizes them in such a way that their visible bodily movements lead to the interpretation that "God is moving the audience." The interplay of listening to the inner voice of the Spirit and, at the same time, watching the audience to see what God is doing is primarily based on the expectation of particular bodily responses from the congregation.

Authoritative Worship Styles

The question arises of how authoritative models of bodily responses are generated and informed. While live performances of national and international worship bands at conferences and concerts offer performative models of worship, the technological development of the Internet provides an additional venue for authoritative worship styles. As I was searching on the Internet for the composer of the song "This Is How We Overcome," I came across a YouTube video of its performance by the megachurch Hillsong in Sydney.[8] I was struck by how similar the bodily gestures exhibited in the Australian church were to those in the LGC: the turning of the body in a full circle while raising the right arm and pointing a forefinger in the air when singing the words "you have turned," as well as the rhythmic jumping and moving of both outstretched arms with the palms of the hands turned outward at the phrase "this is how we overcome." The reason for this marked similarity was confirmed in my conversation with the LGC's worship leader. According to Tim, in his preparation for the worship services and in his selection of new songs, worship DVDs, in particular the Hillsong productions, serve as important media for inspiration. Mimicking the bodily expression seen on these DVDs may not be a conscious process. Rather, since viewing such a DVD involves the intersection of listening to music and watching a particular form of bodily expression, an interconnection between sound and image is created. Furthermore, the image of the "mega," enhanced by the way in which Hillsong invites the viewer to be part of a huge audience, evokes e/p images of revival and embodies a seemingly tangible presence of God (Goh 2008). In the past, the imitation of sound has often been made possible by the distribution of cassettes and later CDs. However, exceeding time-bound and space-bound live performances, the technological emergence of DVDs and the Internet has made both e/p music and prescribed bodily performances available on demand; they are globally enhanced, mediated, and shared. This global flow and circulation of worship music and practices demonstrates the critical role of media in the globalization of religions (Csordas 2009, 6).

Thus, it is clear that the worship leader's task—next to leading the worship team—is to bring about a transformation in the audience in terms of atmosphere and emotional engagement, resulting in the pre-scripted charismatic form of bodily expression that the audience recognizes and experiences as an authentic encounter with God. Paradoxically, a particular, globally spread aesthetic form becomes authoritative as an index for the presence of God and serves as the authentication of the desired experience.

Sing a New Song

So far, I have focused my attention on the performative aspects of worship, but I will now turn to an investigation of songs and lyrics.[9] The Sunday services at LGC display not only a large variety of songs but also a high turnover of new songs. In addition to the latest releases from Opwekking, other resources are readily tapped; these include the latest songs released by Hillsong Church in Sydney and new songs written by international Christian music artists and worship leaders such as Chris Tomlin, Tim Hughes, and the band Delirious? Obviously, in the selection of songs, there is a fascination with the new that is intrinsically bound to the revivalist identity of the church. The longing for a time of refreshing and special anointing is reflected in "Touching Heaven, Changing Earth," [10] a song that was included in one out of three services on average during my year of field research:

> We will seek your face almighty God
> Turn and pray for you to heal our land
> Father let revival start with me
> Then every heart will know your kingdom comes,
> Send revival, send revival, send revival to us

As part of my research, I conducted an analysis of themes in LGC's songs, and I found that the foremost theme of a number of these songs is that of revival. This theme strongly reflects the identity of the church, as it has been a center for national revival. These revival songs portray God as the coming king who will descend from heaven and bring revival, a depiction connected to eschatological notions of the dawning of the kingdom of God, as described in the song "God Is Great":[11]

> All creation gives you praise
> You alone are truly great
> You alone are God who reigns for eternity
> God is great and his praise fills the earth, fills the heavens
> And your name will be praised through all the world

The image of God as king, as ruler of the earth, and as creator of the universe was a recurrent theme in the LGC's songs, stressing the powerful transcendence of God. The up-tempo musical idiom of these songs and the energetic, vigorous, and loud musical interpretation of the band created a soft rock sound and encouraged an atmosphere of joyous and positive celebration.

A second theme in a number of songs emphasizes individual transformation and conversion. Here, Jesus is addressed as the redeemer of the believer's soul. The new life found in him is celebrated in festive songs with phrases such as "you turned my mourning into dancing" ("Touching Heaven, Changing Earth") and "I know he rescued my soul" ("My Redeemer Lives").[12] More contemplative songs stress the crucifixion, suffering, and death of Jesus as the price paid for the sins of humankind.

More difficult to categorize is a third type of song that emphasizes the special name of Jesus in lyrics such as these:[13]

> The name of Jesus
> We exalt the name of Jesus
> There is power, there is power in the name of Jesus
> There is hope, there is hope in the name of Jesus
> The name of Jesus

The narrative structure of these songs is rather meager, consisting of short phrases that are repeated over and over again. Eventually, through the practice of repetition, these fragments force a wedge between the intention of the singer and the uttered musical phrase itself, as the powerful cadence establishes a sense of flow. As these songs are sung, the words become almost independent from the music. As performative utterances (Austin 1962), they take on an aura of objective and transformative power. From the perspective of the worshippers, the proclamation of particular words is related to the church's specific understanding of "spiritual warfare" and the effect of spoken words in the spiritual world. This category of songs, which employ powerful words and emphasize the name of Jesus, seems to point in particular to the understanding that words have a quality independent of the intention of the singer.

During the worship service, these three categories of songs are, in practice, not necessarily patterned according to theme; rather, they are mixed according to successive rhythms, from the fastest to the slowest. However, a fourth category of songs, which concerns the intimate relationship between the worshipper and God, is most often found at the end of the worship service. While in the other songs the worshipper addresses God as "he" or "you" (for example, "Lord You Are Good"),[14] these songs switch to the "I" perspective of the worshipper and metaphorically speak of the love relationship between God and the individual. The emphasis on intimacy and love is, at the same time, connected to the holiness of God. While holiness might imply a sense of hierarchy and induce reflection on the unworthy state of humanity, the desire to be in the presence of God and the assurance of his acceptance through grace seem to overcome this tension. It is in these songs—for example, "Draw Me Close to You"[15] and "Jesus Lover of My Soul"[16]—that the romantic ideology of the pop idiom and the worship song merge in an experience of intimacy, warmth, and closeness with the sacred.

Worship Music: Aesthetic Domain of Meaning and Bonding

Worship in the LGC church exhibits a double focus: it stresses the importance of being in the presence of God and also reflects a strong desire for change and renewal. If worship and singing are together regarded as an enactment of relationship (Small 1998), the relation between music and identity construction comes to the forefront. Music enables worshippers to position themselves within imaginative narratives (Sample 1998, 101). They begin to ask, "Who am I?," "Who am I in relation to those around me?," and "Who am I in relation to God and in relation to the world?" The act of singing facilitates reflection on one's life while simultaneously making the enactment of one's life possible.

On an individual level, participants say that they easily connect to the contemporary style of worship music because it greatly resembles popular music in everyday life. This contrasts with the musical style of the mainline Protestant tradition. Furthermore, the structural ordering of e/p worship embodies the importance of the recurrent transformation of the individual. Guided by the worship leader, each worshipper is expected to move toward the presence of God, which potentially leads to a divine encounter by means of active and expressive bodily participation. The importance of sound and movement, together with the rock style of the band, tends to suppress the song text, as hearing one's own voice while singing becomes difficult at times and the singing of the vocalists blends into the band's overall sound.

While the themes of the songs do not necessarily display cohesion, the LGC's model of worship reflects a progressive journey into the presence of God. The congregation is directed from a more disengaged appeal to God as "he," through a more personal address to God as "you," to an eventual subjective turn to the "I" perspective of the worshipper, signaling a migration of the sacred from transcendence to immanence. As this progression is accompanied by changes in musical style, from celebratory and upbeat tempos to softer and mellower sounds, the words and the music blend together, enforcing a particular mood and sentiment among the audience.

Worshippers recall the encounter with the sacred as an immediate and unmediated experience. However, processes of mediation are always at play in the domain of religion (Meyer 2009; Meyer and Houtman 2012), because the sacred requires some media forms in order to be experienced and understood by believers. As this account of the worship service illustrates, the encounter with the sacred is mediated by the interplay of musical style, performance, and words, mobilizing the body in a sensory regime, submitting the body to successive phases of engagement, and surrounding the body with lyrics that underscore the transformation of not only the worshipper but also the sacred.

The revivalist theme and worship practices at the LGC emphasize the desired identity of the church while providing insight into its relation to the past. In the aftermath of the revivalist period (in this case instigated by the Toronto Blessing), the church has faced difficulties in establishing its identity. Its fascination with the new reflects a previous attempt to deal with tensions between the desired state of the church and its contemporary context. The continuous introduction of new songs underscores the deprecation of traditions and the past and reveals a global orientation, expressed by being in touch with new centers of revival through the field of music. Noteworthy is the association of the new with the presence of God, which draws attention to the extraordinary and, by contrast, runs the risk of desacralizing the mundane and everyday experiences of life. Paradoxically, the use of popular musical sounds and performative style in worship creates the possibility of sacralizing the everyday life. Noteworthy in this respect is the role of new media, which enforces a transnational mode of expression that is accessible and normative across e/p branches of Christianity on a global scale.

The importance of worship music and singing for believers reveals that suitable aesthetic forms are powerful means of creating commitments and modes of bonding. Embodied participation during the time of worship is not just an expression of commitment but, at the same time, operates as a mode of binding, as the act itself generates commitment and convictions. In addition to its emotive character, this form of community making is based on shared sensorial sensibilities between people rather than formal ties of church membership or other "official," observable forms of commitment. This mode of bonding not only involves the actual community of worshippers but also has the potential to evoke a sense of community within a larger imagined and relational network. Similar to Maffesoli's (1996) understanding of community, which is based on the sharing of aesthetic styles, worship music creates an imagined community (B. Anderson 1983) that is stretched over churches, conference sites, and retreats—and has a global outreach. The concept of "aesthetic community" has been introduced by Bauman (2001) to describe the fluid and event-like character of new forms of communities closely linked through entertainment; Bauman believes, however, that these communities are doomed to disappoint due to their lack of binding power (71). In contrast to what Bauman suggests, the instantaneousness and fluidity of the worship experience can be fruitfully applied to a new understanding of community as comprising powerful modes of binding evoked across local and even national boundaries. The intertwinement of narratives—rooted in the Christian tradition—and aesthetics has the power to move individuals beyond their own horizons and merge them into a larger world of faith. Therefore, the aesthetics of the e/p worship style operates as an important identity marker in the global e/p movement and, as a sensational form, "governs a sensory engagement of humans with the divine and each other and generates particular sensibilities" (Meyer 2009, 13).

NOTES

1. My Ph.D. research (Klaver 2011b) was conducted in two independent Dutch churches: an evangelical church influenced by the seeker church movement, which was initiated by Willow Creek Community Church in Chicago (Sargeant 2000), and a neo-pentecostal or charismatic church loosely aligned with transnational revivalist networks. Both churches represent contemporary evangelicalism as Shibley describes it: they are world affirming and employ new organizational forms (1998, 72). Shibley divides these churches into noncharismatic evangelical churches and evangelical/pentecostal churches, based on a different understanding of the presence of the Holy Spirit. In the Dutch context, the connotation and content of the term "evangelical" is limited in comparison to the English-speaking world. In general, "evangelical" is used to denote movements and churches outside of the Catholic and Protestant mainline churches. From this perspective, Dutch pentecostal churches, established since 1907, are considered to be part of Dutch evangelicalism. However, the rise of the charismatic renewal movement in the 1970s, influenced by the pentecostal experience but within the boundaries of mainline churches, points to the difficulties in definitions. Since the 1980s, the term "charismatic" has often been used by newer or neo-pentecostal churches to distinguish themselves from denominational pentecostal churches such as the Assemblies of God (cf. A. Anderson 2004, 158). Since the 1990s, there has been an observable spread of the Pentecostal understanding of the power and gifts of the Holy Spirit in the Dutch evangelical movement, including evangelical churches. Thus, I use the term "evangelical/pentecostal" because a clear theological distinction can no longer be made when discussing contemporary worship music.

2. From September 2006 to July 2007, I attended most of the church meetings and participated in courses and small groups. In addition to informal meetings and social gatherings, I conducted twenty-five life-history interviews. Since the research was conducted in Dutch, the quotations used in this chapter have been translated into English.

3. Barbara Lange has remarked upon a parallel instance of glocalization of nineteenth-century gospel hymns among Romani pentecostals in Hungary. For further discussion, see Lange (2003, 131–48).

4. The introduction of new songs takes place at the annual Opwekking Pentecost Conference, a three-day Christian festival. This conference started in 1974 and attracted more than sixty thousand visitors from mainline, evangelical, and pentecostal churches in 2014.

5. New worship songs composed by Dutch songwriters have increasingly numbered among Opwekking's selections.

6. The Toronto Blessing was a sensational and controversial charismatic revival movement. See Poloma (2003) and A. Anderson (2004, 162–65).

7. Quotations from Tim are based on personal conversation.

8. "This Is How We Overcome," by Reuben Morgan, ©Integrity's Hosanna! Music 1998. See "This Is How We Overcome Hillsong" (2009).

9. I made an inventory and categorized the songs sung during fifteen Sunday services. On average, eight songs were sung per service, and sixty-two different songs were counted.

10. "Touching Heaven, Changing Earth," by Reuben Morgan, ©Integrity's Hosanna! Music 1997.

11. "God Is Great," by Marty Sampson and Hillsong Publishing, ©Integrity Media Inc. 2001.

12. "My Redeemer Lives," by Reuben Morgan and Hillsong Publishing, ©Integrity Media Inc. 1998.

13. My translation from Dutch to English. The song "De naam van Jesus" is sung in Dutch, but the church does not know the author. I have not been able to identify the author or publisher of the song (I also searched for an English version).

14. "Lord You Are Good," by Israel Houghton, ©Integrity's Praise! Music 2001.

15. "Draw Me Close to You," by Kelly Carpenter, ©Mercy/Vineyard Publishing 1994.

16. "Jesus Lover of My Soul," by Daniel Grul, John Ezzy, and Steve McPherson, ©Hillsong Publishing 1992.

REFERENCES

Adnams, Gordon A. 2008. "The Experience of Congregational Singing: An Ethno-phenomenological Approach." Ph.D. diss., University of Alberta.

Anderson, Allan. 2004. *An Introduction to Pentecostalism: Global Charismatic Christianity*. Cambridge: Cambridge University Press.

Anderson, Benedict. 1983. *Imagined Community*. New York: Verso.

Austin, J. L. 1962. *How to Do Things with Words*. Oxford: Clarendon Press.

Bauman, Zygmund. 2001. *Community: Seeking Safety in an Insecure World*. Malden, Mass.: Blackwell.

Chaves, Mark. 2004. *Congregations in America*. Cambridge: Harvard University Press.

Classen, Constance. 1993. *Worlds of Sense: Exploring the Senses in History and Across Cultures*. New York: Routledge.

Cornwall, Judson. 1983. *Let Us Worship: The Believer's Response to God*. South Plainfield, N.J.: Bridge.

Csordas, Thomas J. 2009. "Introduction: Modalities of Transnational Transcendence." In *Transnational Transcendence: Essays on Religion and Globalization*, edited by Thomas J. Csordas, 1–29. Berkeley: University of California Press.

Durkheim, Émile. (1912) 1995. *The Elementary Forms of Religious Life*. New York: Free Press.

Elsman, Domus. 1995. *Johannes de Heer: Evangelist in het Licht van de Wederkomst*. Zoetermeer: Boekencentrum.

Frith, Simon. 1998. *Performing Rites: On the Value of Popular Music*. Cambridge: Harvard University Press.

Goh, Robbie B. H. 2008. "Hillsong and Megachurch Practice: Semiotics, Spatial Logic, and the Embodiment of Contemporary Evangelical Protestantism." *Material Religion: The Journal of Objects, Art, and Belief* 4 (3): 284–304.

Howes, David. 2003. *Sensual Relations: Engaging the Senses in Culture and Social Theory*. Ann Arbor: University of Michigan Press.

Keane, Webb. 2007. *Christian Moderns: Freedom and Fetish in the Mission Encounter*. Berkeley: University of California Press.

Klaver, Miranda. 2008. "De Evangelicale Beweging." In *Handboek Religie in Nederland*, edited by M. ten Borg et al., 146–59. Zoetermeer: Meinema.

———. 2011a. "From Sprinkling to Immersion: Conversion and Baptism in Dutch Evangelicalism." *Ethnos* 76 (4): 469–88.

———. 2011b. *This Is My Desire: A Semiotic Perspective on Conversion in an Evangelical Seeker Church and a Pentecostal Church in the Netherlands*. Amsterdam: Amsterdam University Press / Pallas Publications.

Klaver, Miranda, and Peter Versteeg. 2007. "Evangelicalisering als Proces van Religieuze Verandering." *Praktische Theologie: Nederlands Tijdschrift voor Pastorale Wetenschappen* 34 (2): 169–84.

Koenig, Sarah. 2008. "This Is My Daily Bread: Toward a Sacramental Theology of Evangelical Praise and Worship." *Worship* 82 (2): 141–61.

Lange, Barbara Rose. 2003. *Holy Brotherhood: Romani Music in a Hungarian Pentecostal Church*. New York: Oxford University Press.

Maffesoli, Michel. 1996. *The Contemplation of the World: Figures of Community Style*. Minneapolis: University of Minnesota Press.

Meyer, Birgit. 2009. "Introduction: From Imagined Communities to Aesthetic Formations: Religious Mediations, Sensational Forms, and Styles of Bonding." In *Aesthetic Formations: Media, Religion, and the Senses*, edited by Birgit Meyer, 1–30. New York: Palgrave Macmillan.

Meyer, Birgit, and Dick Houtman. 2012. "Introduction: Material Religion—How Things Matter." In *Things: Religion and the Question of Materiality*, edited by Dick Houtman and Birgit Meyer, 1–23. New York: Fordham University Press.

Poloma, Margaret M. 2003. *Main Street Mystics: The Toronto Blessing and Reviving Pentecostalism*. Walnut Creek, Calif.: AltaMira Press.

Robertson, Roland. 1995. "Glocalization: Time–Space and Homogeneity–Heterogeneity." In *Global Modernities*, edited by Mike Featherstone, Scott Lash, and Roland Robertson, 25–44. London: Sage.

Roeland, Johan. 2009. *Selfation: Dutch Evangelical Youth Between Subjectivization and Subjection*. Amsterdam: Amsterdam University Press / Pallas Publications.

Sample, Tex. 1998. *The Spectacle of Worship in a Wired World: Electronic Culture and the Gathered People of God*. Nashville: Abingdon Press.

Sargeant, Kimon H. 2000. *Seeker Churches: Promoting Traditional Religion in a Nontraditional Way*. New Brunswick: Rutgers University Press.

Shibley, Mark A. 1998. "Contemporary Evangelicals: Born-Again and World Affirming." *Annals of the American Academy of Political and Social Science* 558:67–87.

Small, Christopher. 1998. *Musicking: The Meanings of Performing and Listening*. Middletown: Wesleyan University Press.

Smelik, Jan. 2006. "Opwekkingsliederen ter Discussie." *De Reformatie* 82 (8–9): 174–75, 189–92.

"This Is How We Overcome Hillsong." 2009. YouTube video, 1:50. Posted by Sebastian Fernandes, June 6. http://www.youtube.com/watch?v=FkVbjf4RsRc.

Versteeg, Peter G. A. 2010. *The Ethnography of a Dutch Pentecostal Church: Vineyard Utrecht and the International Charismatic Movement*. Lewiston, N.Y.: Edwin Mellen Press.

PART II

Negotiating Traditions in Transition

6

"This Is Not the Warm-Up Act!"
How Praise and Worship Reflects Expanding
Musical Traditions and Theology in a Bapticostal
Charismatic African American Megachurch

Birgitta J. Johnson

In my ethnographic research of music in African American congregations in Los Angeles, I have seen praise and worship music employed in several ways.[1] Some churches view this subgenre as a way to draw young and middle-aged believers back to the church, add variety to weekly church music repertoire, keep up with commercial trends in black gospel music, quickly increase stagnant church attendance and membership, maintain or attract younger musicians, and/or revitalize participation in congregational singing in church services. In one particular case, however, the use of praise and worship music has gone beyond the typical enhancement of a church's musical repertoire. In a 2006 sermon on worship settings in the Old Testament, Kenneth C. Ulmer, pastor of the Faithful Central Bible Church, declared, "What we do at the beginning of service every week . . . is not the warm-up act."[2] He was referring to the approximately twenty minutes of congregational singing and prayer that initiate weekly services. On that particular morning, the praise and worship period had lasted over thirty minutes, and Ulmer would continue preaching about the role of praise, worship, and song in the lives of believers for an additional forty minutes.

The popularization of praise and worship music in African American churches and its adaptation for gospel music audiences have sometimes been a source of tension for traditionalists and preservationist scholars. However, the rise of praise and worship in African American Christian worship has also reflected a reaffirmation of key culturally informed worship aesthetics, as well as a desire to appeal to the growing diversity within today's congregations, especially in large urban megachurches (Johnson 2011, 108). In order to explore some issues raised by the adoption of praise and worship music in more depth, this chapter gives a brief ethnographic and historical account of Faithful Central Bible Church in Inglewood, California, and will be divided into two parts. The first section, "A Spirit-Filled Music Tradition Meets Spirit-Filled Life Theology," examines the theological journey and transformation of Faithful Central and its head pastor from its founding as a Missionary Baptist church in 1936 to its migration and growth in the latter half of the twentieth century, and outlines the ways in which musical preferences and decisions on local levels often foreshadow and mirror emerging theological perspectives in African American Christian settings. The second, shorter section, "Team Ministry and Cross-cultural Opportunities for Unity in Worship," will describe weekly worship at Faithful Central and how a team approach to preaching and music ministry has allowed the church to loosen hierarchical relationships between the pulpit and the platform. This approach has also further opened venues for musical and ministerial fellowships with multiracial and ethnic congregations around the city.

In order to examine closely the intertwined trajectories of musical change, doctrinal shifts, and church growth, this chapter will draw from interviews with church members and ministry workers, participant observations of weekly services, and Christian-centered media publications. It shows how Faithful Central's adaptation of praise and worship music over the last thirty years has reflected and paralleled its theological transition from a Missionary Baptist church to a self-described "Bapticostal charismatic nondenominational church." While near-simultaneous changes in theological perspective and in musical repertoire have meant drastic losses in membership for some churches, Faithful Central's inclusion of Pentecostal and charismatic doctrine and approaches to weekly worship services partially fueled its exponential growth from a church of two hundred members in 1982 to a church of more than ten thousand members by 1999. Musical decisions as well as broadening theological perspectives have also provided Faithful Central with opportunities to engage in musical and ecumenical worship in cross-cultural settings. With its "team ministry" approach to preaching and music, this congregation has expanded beyond local influence in Inglewood and reached across racial and ethnic enclaves of southern California.

A Spirit-Filled Music Tradition Meets Spirit-Filled Life Theology

The rise of neo-Pentecostalism within African American denominational churches over the last thirty years has been an infrequently examined factor contributing to church growth and the emergence of megachurches in the United States. This is particularly seen among churches from black Baptist denominational fellowships.[3] Alongside changes in its approach to music styles and liturgical format, a parallel shift in theological frames of reference occurred at Faithful Central. But while changes in theology would ordinarily stunt church growth or even divide a church, it set this traditionally Baptist church on fire—for the Holy Ghost.[4]

In its forty-six-year history prior to Ulmer's appointment in 1982, Faithful Central had been a Missionary Baptist church. It began in a storefront on South Central Avenue with a dozen members and grew into a church of approximately two hundred people who worshipped in a sanctuary on Hoover Street, adjacent to downtown Los Angeles, under the leadership of two pastors, Dr. A. C. Capers and Dr. W. L. Robinson. After Robinson's sudden death, Kenneth Ulmer, an East Saint Louis native, well-known music minister and organist, and talented but newly ordained preacher, was invited to serve as Faithful Central's new pastor.[5] Ulmer's ministerial development and study were particularly inspired in 1982 when he met Benjamin F. Reid of the First Church of God, a holiness church in Inglewood. Reid was the first black man he'd ever met who had an "earned doctorate," and in a 2012 interview Ulmer recalled that after meeting Reid he developed "this almost unquenchable thirst for education. . . . It was not egotistical. I wanted to be as prepared as I could be" (Anderson 2012, 3). He continued graduate studies at Pepperdine University, Hebrew Union College, and the University of Judaism and in 1986 earned a Ph.D. from Grace Graduate School of Theology in Long Beach, California (now the West Coast campus of Grace Theological Seminary in Indiana). Reid also introduced the Baptist-raised Ulmer to Spirit-filled life theology and further teachings on gifts of the Spirit. Among these gifts, speaking in tongues troubled Ulmer, as he had been raised to find it suspect as a Baptist and trained to discount it at a conservative,[6] highly dispensationalist seminary (Ulmer 1995, xii–xiii). However, during his ministerial preparation and education, Ulmer continued to study and pray on the matter and other doctrines of Pentecostal and charismatic movements, and he admitted that he gradually went through a "great theological metamorphosis" during the 1980s and into the 1990s, during which he went from engaging in conservative evangelical "intellectual elitism" to being a respected and sought-after voice among Baptists embracing Pentecostal and charismatic theology (Ulmer 1995).

During the mid-1980s, the church's leadership began addressing the role of music in worship more explicitly and reviving full congregational participation in weekly musical worship that went beyond responsorial behaviors (for example, clapping along, standing, and reactively exhorting the choir). Ulmer combined two warring choirs and placed Barbara Allen (née Hale), a highly trained musician raised in Faithful Central, over the choir and the music department. Ulmer's sermons frequently included biblical references to the relationship between worship and music making in the lives of believers, as well as homiletic exegesis of biblical Hebrew and Greek terminology paired with black colloquial speech and culturally shared anecdotes. The choir's participation in the order of service and the role of the congregation in musical worship were also modified. Instead of two or three of the church's deacons or elders opening the service with devotional songs or lined hymns, as was typical in many traditional black Baptist churches, Ulmer and Allen began to open Sunday services with congregational singing led by the choir. Songs included popular hymns and gospel songs that could be sung by the whole church. Familiar songs were sometimes arranged or connected to form medleys. The choir also sang two selections later in the service, as was customary in Baptist churches, but at that time it was unusual to start a church service with a choir singing sacred music that did not consist of the typical traditional hymn or church anthem selected from the hymnal (Ulmer 2006). Some choir members recall that the choir opened Sunday services in those days very much like modern praise teams of the twenty-first century (Byous 2005; Elmore 2006).

As with the changes to weekly liturgical practices, the period between 1986 and 1988 marks a significant frame of reference in the theological journey of Faithful Central and set the stage for its progressive doctrinal shift and physical growth from an average-sized Missionary Baptist church to a very large neo-Pentecostal, charismatic megachurch by 1994. In 1986, Ulmer started preaching and teaching on "fullness of life in the Spirit" at Faithful Central while finishing his doctorate at Grace Graduate School. In 2012, he reminisced about those times: "Our church still had a Baptist sign out front, but inside we were embracing charismatic and Pentecostal theology" (Anderson 2012, 4).[7]

Through interviews conducted with church members and an examination of Faithful Central's movements from the 1980s onward, it became clear that growth spurts and theological shifts in the church were often foreshadowed

or closely accompanied by changes and developments in its musical repertoire and order of worship practices. Teachings on the Holy Spirit's role in the
lives of believers and power in everyday life continued as Faithful Central's
music department expanded, from one choir to four and a dance ministry.
In addition to offering workshops, classes, and concerts on sacred styles such
as spirituals, anthems, hymnody, and devotional music, hosted by black music
scholars and composers including Wyatt Tee Walker, Margaret Pleasant Dou-
roux, and Diane White, some members of the music department were exploring what would become the biggest trend in contemporary gospel for church
use—praise and worship music.

Originating in the 1970s in Anglo-American, mostly charismatic Christian churches, contemporary congregational songs, or praise and worship
music, draw from popular music styles including rock, folk, adult contemporary, R&B, and jazz (Ingalls 2011, 276–77). The main characteristics that
distinguish praise and worship music from more ambiguous subgenres—such
as "inspirational music" and sacred music that also draws from secular pop
music styles, as in the case of contemporary gospel—is that it is primarily
driven by and concerned with participatory group singing and lyrical content
that is explicitly God- and Christ-centered (Johnson 2008, 252). Some writers
describe it as music sung directly to God by believers (Cusic 2002, 383; Price
2004). Influenced by the development of praise and worship music at West
Angeles Church of God in Christ (COGIC) and particularly its use of a praise
team, Faithful Central experimented with using a worship leader / praise team
to commence Wednesday night services with prayer and communal praise
and worship through song in 1988 (Elmore 2006). Led by Berkeley, California, native Aladrian Elmore, the praise team blended the congregational gospel songs already popular at Faithful Central with gospel-flavored praise and
worship songs being developed at West Angeles COGIC and popular songs
from the contemporary Christian music genre (CCM) during the opening
devotional period of church services.[8]

Like West Angeles, Faithful Central's musicians and praise team leaders
became adept at modifying the harmonic progressions and rhythmic sensibilities of popular CCM-style praise and worship music. Since many church
choirs of the 1980s referred to gospel recordings for new song content, choir
directors were constantly looking for commercial albums that offered more
than slick musical production and vocal pyrotechnics. One way to address this
problem and tap into a wealth of vertical worship lyrical content in CCM was
to modify praise and worship songs that were popular and highly participatory

(for example, songs that include or can be modified to include high rates of call and response and unison singing) for African American congregations (Elmore 2006). Songs such as "How Majestic Is Your Name" by Michael W. Smith, "Awesome God" by Rich Mullins, and "Lord, I Lift Your Name on High" by Rick Founds were among several CCM songs that were "gospelized" for use at Faithful Central and a growing number of black churches in Los Angeles. By 1989, the praise team led the beginning of every Sunday and midweek service with twenty to thirty minutes of congregational singing and prayer. Unlike some churches that were initially resistant to the use of praise teams and even the music of praise and worship during the 1990s, the transition into augmenting the musical duties at Faithful Central with a praise team of six to nine singers was relatively smooth. The church's band, which included a piano / electric keyboard, organ, electric bass, rhythm guitar, and drums, accompanied all its vocal ensembles.

In addition to the rising notoriety of Faithful Central's music department and its popularization of a more communal, singing-centric worship style for Sunday services, Ulmer's thematic preaching and candid approach to contemporary issues facing congregants attracted many people to the church. Blending a teaching style centered on analytical exegesis of contemporary and traditional theological streams of thought with the storytelling and performed preaching style of the black Baptist tradition, sermon series such as "You Can Make It" and "How to Live Holy in a Hollywood World" drew educated, working-class and middle- to upper-middle-class single young adults, young families, and baby boomers to Faithful Central (Johnson 2011, 116). They were the "excited attendees" whom church growth scholar Scott Thumma (2006) refers to as key to the exponential growth that occurs in megachurches: they actively invited friends, family, and coworkers to church, and many of these invitees eventually joined and enthusiastically invited their family and peers, continuing the cycle of sustained growth and consistent weekly attendance. Rooms at the rear of the church, outside the main sanctuary, were used as overflow space until the Hoover Street church could no longer contain the congregation.

From 1989 to 2000, Faithful Central was a church on the move physically but also in terms of denominational affiliation, publicly acknowledging its shift toward neo-Pentecostalism and charismatic beliefs. During that period, weekly services were held in a 1,700-seat high school auditorium, a conference center near the airport, a converted two-story office building, and a 2,500-seat converted warehouse space. In each facility, multiple services were still required, and Ulmer usually preached each one of them.

Faithful Central's affiliation with the Missionary Baptist Church ended in 1994, when it became one of the thirteen founding congregations of the Full Gospel Baptist Church Fellowship (FGBCF) organized by Paul Morton, pastor of Greater St. Stephen Full Gospel Baptist Church in New Orleans, Louisiana. In the years preceding the organization of the fellowship, Morton was among several Baptist preachers who introduced black Baptists to teachings from the Pentecostal tradition. The beliefs and behaviors of Pentecostals that had historically been viewed as strange, primitive, and/or cultish by Baptist and Methodist groups during the first half of the twentieth century were, by the 1960s, being studied, explored, and consciously embraced by a growing number of Baptists in particular (Gaines 2003; Ulmer 2006). The FGBCF was influential in officially recognizing the thousands of traditional black Baptists moving toward more Pentecostal and charismatic beliefs and styles of worship, and it provided formal support for these churches under one organizational banner. However, many Baptist churches associated with the FGBCF were dismissed from their national conventions or socially ostracized on local church levels (Byous 2005). The latter was especially noticed by members of Faithful Central's music ministry, as regular choir engagements they had at other Baptist churches in the city disappeared overnight.

With a congregation of approximately four thousand, Faithful Central was one of the largest churches to join the FGBCF, and Kenneth Ulmer was appointed as the fellowship's bishop of Christian education. In 1994, he authored *A New Thing*, chronicling the fellowship's early history and theological beliefs. *A New Thing* also sought to answer questions raised about what the FGBCF represented to the black Baptist tradition and why members of the fellowship didn't just affiliate with or join Pentecostal denominations and sever ties with their Baptist roots. In the book, Ulmer identifies the FGBCF as a part of what C. Peter Wagner calls "Third Wave" churches. Recognized as a contemporary move of the Holy Spirit among traditional evangelicals who previously did not identify with Pentecostals or charismatics, the "area of freedom" common among Third Wave churches concerns the recognition of spiritual gifts but not the privileging of one gift over another. Echoing Wagner and attempting to destabilize several areas of polarization among both Pentecostals/charismatics and evangelical/conservative non-Pentecostal theological traditions, Ulmer further explains, "As a Third Wave aggregation of congregations, the Full Gospel Baptist Church Fellowship is a conglomerate of churches in which both the person who does speak in tongues and the one who does not have that gift, dwell together in a context of mutual affirmation without an air of superiority or inferiority based on the possession or absence of a given gift" (Ulmer 1995, 18). This area of freedom and acceptance of post–Azusa Street Pentecostal and charismatic modes of theological belief and practice has contributed greatly to the growth of some churches within the FGBCF.

The influence of music and music ministry was also an identifying aspect of the FGBCF. The recording of a commercially released live album at the fellowship's second national meeting in the New Orleans Superdome signaled that, while young, the FGBCF was an organization and movement on the rise and music was central to carrying out its mission. Members of Faithful Central's music ministry participated in the recording of the Full Gospel Baptist Church Fellowship Mass Choir's first two gospel albums, *A New Thing: Experience the Fullness* and *Bow Down and Worship Him*. The first album was released in 1996 by Los Angeles–based Gospocentric Records, and it featured a 1,500-voice mass choir composed of musicians and singers from churches in the fellowship. *A New Thing* featured one of the biggest gospel hits of the 1990s, "Shabach," and launched the gospel music career of Byron Cage, dubbed "the Prince of Praise" after the single's pervasive success. Eight of the fellowship's founding pastors provided sermonettes or spoken-word interludes between songs on the twenty-one-track album, which also featured gospel music stars such as Daryl Coley, Kirk Franklin, and BeBe Winans, as well as top producers Rickey Grundy, Buster and Shavoni, and Jeffrey LaValley.

Not only did the first two albums produced by FGBCF help promote neo-Pentecostalism, but they also reflected the increasing stylistic shift in gospel music back toward songs that encouraged congregational singing in church worship settings. By the end of the 1980s, gospel was the dominant musical expression of most black churches, but while the artistry of modern and contemporary gospel was masterful and very popular, the average layperson's ability to sing the gospel songs had diminished for various reasons. Highly rehearsed choirs began to take over many of the congregational singing duties in numerous African American urban churches. Outside of hymnody, the performance of older traditional gospel and devotional songs, and songs for ritual sacraments, music within many black congregations became a spectator's activity, with congregants watching choirs and reacting, but not able to fully participate until several repetitions of a chorus or vamp allowed for group involvement.

Paralleling the movement toward highly participatory, vertically oriented praise and worship music occurring under the large stylistic tent of CCM in Anglo-American Protestant churches, songs such as "Shabach," "Bow Down and Worship Him," "He Is Here," and "Yet Praise Him" from FGBCF albums offered a black gospel interpretation of praise and worship—one that favored large vocal groups and choirs instead of the small ensemble, "praise team," or "worship band" typical of most CCM-produced praise and worship music. In the midst of a shrinking global music industry, the massive and award-winning popularity of these two album projects, produced by a newly formed denominational fellowship and distributed by an independent gospel music record company, was an early sign that gospel-influenced praise and worship music would be one of the biggest growth areas in the gospel and Christian music industries going into the twenty-first century. With founding churches in New Orleans, Atlanta, Los Angeles, Memphis, Houston, Miami, Shreveport, Chicago, and Flint, the sound of the FGBCF could be carried to all parts of the country through fellowship-affiliated churches.

Though the phrase "praise and worship" was still relatively unknown in gospel music circles at the time, youth and young adult choirs were able to introduce praise and worship styles into their churches' musical repertoires. By applying the vertical worship–themed lyricism of praise and worship music to vocal arrangements for choirs and congregational singing, the FGBCF albums illustrated the continued appreciation for participatory communal singing in African American churches. In reconnecting with the preferred aesthetic of highly participatory group singing, recordings by the FGBCF allowed the performance of praise and worship to vacillate between smaller vocal groups and larger choirs during the 1990s, before the direct lines of influence from the globally marketed CCM repertoire made their way into the gospel music industry and African American churches outside of Pentecostal and charismatic circles.

However, Faithful Central's time in the FGBCF was brief; by 1996, the church had left the fellowship, and it became a self-described independent, nondenominational "Bapticostal" charismatic church. Regardless of the affiliation changes, longtime members of Faithful Central insist that there was no change in Kenneth Ulmer's sermon content, his style of delivery, or the church's general beliefs (McDonald 2005; Byous 2005). Whereas difficulty often arises when black Methodist or COGIC congregations deviate from the doctrines and liturgical/ritual protocols of the presiding denomination, Baptist churches, even under denominational banners, tend to emphasize local church authority and are less bureaucratic in ensuring that each congregation maintains a set of rigidly established practices (Lincoln and Mamiya 1990, 41–42). Sonya Byous, a member of Faithful Central for over thirty years, reflected on Ulmer's approach to biblical doctrine during the changes in affiliation at Faithful Central:

> Whereas our name was Missionary Baptist, I don't think our practices were so much Missionary Baptist. You know, the Bishop broke the Word. That's his gift (well at least one of them). I can read a scripture; [but] he's going to see five hundred things that I did not see. And that's a gift and so he [was] not teaching us [anything different] or [he] didn't start teaching us differently than he had been teaching because he was rightly dividing the Word. What the Word said is what we got. . . . Nothing really different happened. . . . It never happened with any of the changes. It was just all about affiliation. (Byous 2005)

The affiliation changes and nondenominational status did not hinder Faithful Central's growth, and in 1998 a warehouse was purchased and converted into a 2,500-seat sanctuary space named the Tabernacle." Even with the larger converted space, Ulmer was still preaching four times per Sunday. "Missionary Baptist" was officially dropped from the church's moniker, and it became known as the Faithful Central Bible Church and the parent church of the Macedonia International Bible Fellowship at the close of the century.

In 2000, Faithful Central purchased the 17,500-seat Great Western Forum for $22.5 million. A few community and business interests applauded the purchase of the Forum by an owner who would not demolish the property and thereby cripple the local economy of Inglewood. Having held multiple services since the late 1980s, church leaders realized that the congregation was much larger than they had initially quantified when nearly eleven thousand people attended the New Year's Eve Watch Night service held in the Forum in 1998. Faithful Central became the first church to purchase a sporting arena and the largest house of worship in the United States.

Faithful Central held its main Sunday morning worship services and special events in the Forum from January 2001 to summer 2008. By the time the church moved into the Forum in 2001, its weekly pattern of worship and approach to music in worship had been firmly established. Faithful Central's weekly order of worship maintained its mix of Baptist, Pentecostal, and charismatic influences, usually taking a very malleable approach to liturgical procedures and processes (Johnson 2011, 122–24). Unfortunately, the national economic crisis of 2008 forced the church to move its weekly services back to the Tabernacle building; however, the same preaching and musical worship that had filled half the Forum continued to anchor the congregation when it returned to having services in the Tabernacle full-time in 2009.

Team Ministry and Cross-cultural Opportunities for Unity in Worship

Faithful Central's approach to music in worship and the role of congregational singing in its weekly worship services have pushed participatory, vertically oriented praise and worship music to the forefront of its "local liturgy."[9] Though the church was recognized in the local community for its choirs' excellence in a variety of black sacred music styles, between December 2005 and September 2006, praise and worship music made up 52 percent of the music occurring during church services.[10] The opening praise and worship period is one of the biggest focal points of weekly services, because praise and worship and congregational singing are purposefully used to create an overall atmosphere of vertical worship, praise, and reverence that is intended to last the entire church service, and they allow congregants to have individual and focused "time with God in a corporate setting" at the very beginning of the church service (Elmore 2006). The church's worship leaders, Jimmy Fisher and Kurt Lykes, prayerfully select songs for this period that are easy for the laity to learn quickly and sing and that prompt congregants to exhort one another to take part in the service. During my observation of worship services between 2003 and 2010, there were even times when the praise and worship period lasted the entire church service; the delivery of the sermon was altered to capture the spiritual and worshipful essence of the moment, or the sermon was completely set aside for communal singing, prayer, worship, and reflection. Praise and worship songs are also used throughout the service for other ritual and sacramental moments, such as communion, the altar call, and the invitation to discipleship. Songs from local influences in southern California and the broader CCM and black gospel music industry charts, as well as songs composed by the church's own worship leaders, are in regular rotation for Sunday and midweek services.

Occasionally, Ulmer directs the congregation in the singing of praise and worship music, gospel music, and/or hymns during times of high praise and worship. The church's musical director, praise team leaders, and choir directors are always poised and efficient in making shifts in repertoire or liturgical order at a moment's notice or a signal from Ulmer, if the flow of worship or the Spirit calls for a change in mode, mood, or heightened focus (Johnson 2011, 123–24). When asked about the verbal and nonverbal aspects of his communication with the worship leaders, choir directors, band, and even ushers during these and other impromptu moments, Ulmer described the relationship between himself and the others as a "team ministry" (Ulmer 2006). In this team approach, there is an acute realization of a unity of preaching and music, with equal respect given to the preached Word and the Word in song (Johnson 2011, 126; "Zion Rejoice" 2005).

Periodically, in a sermonic context, Ulmer discusses the role of music in church worship as well as in the daily lives of believers. As the church grew over the years, welcoming many members who were new to its approach to opening worship and devotion, Ulmer would matter-of-factly note, "What we do at the beginning of service every week . . . is not the warm-up act." Dispelling the assumption that the opening musical period is just like any other routine church ritual or merely the result of a church tapping into a popular music trend, the role of praise and worship—the approach to worship through song—has been thoroughly communicated over the years as worship leaders exhort and guide congregants in song and during sermons or sermon series preached by Ulmer.

Not only are music and corporate worship in biblical settings often described in Ulmer's sermons, but his theological and musical education and oratorical gifts impact his homiletic approach.[11] It is not uncommon for Ulmer to request in advance that the praise team or choir sing a specific song at the conclusion of his sermons. While this is a common and traditional practice among preachers within the black church tradition, Ulmer's requests usually involve not only the performance of a song immediately *following* a sermon but the interpolation of a song *while* he is closing a sermon, creating a call and response between himself and the choir or praise team. This ultimately ends in a musical and cognitive call and response between his preached word and the entire congregation, who sing parts of a song that emphasize the main premise of the sermon or affirm its pragmatic application. It is typical for Ulmer to draw on vamps and choruses of praise and worship songs, gospel music, and even hymns during these moments, thus encouraging a specific mindset or spiritual focus for congregants *after* they leave a church service. More so than short-term memory or even notes jotted down in notebooks or on iPads, music in this context is portable and encourages the retention of the spiritual, emotional, inspirational, and factual elements of a sermon. Music and impromptu responsorial singing summarize the sermon in an easily learned and performable medium that can be repeated or recreated at any time during the week by the average congregant in his or her daily personal devotion or meditation.

Faithful Central's extensive use of praise and worship songs and worship-oriented gospel music also connects it with other churches, ministries, and fellowship groups that share similar repertoires, approaches to congregational singing, and conceptualizations of "music as worship and theology"—not just "music in worship," which is often bound by culture, denomination, and/or nationality (McGann 2002, 11; Ulmer 1986, 32). Similar to the ways in which shared repertoires of Protestant hymnody connected churches and inspired mission-centric revival movements across racial, denominational, and geographic boundaries during the 1960s, the musical subgenre of praise and worship and worship-oriented congregational singing have grown to provide a twenty-first-century heir apparent facilitated by digital media in many Christian liturgical and globally minded ecumenical circles. Since its thorough integration of praise and worship–centered CCM and contemporary gospel music into weekly services by the 2000s, Faithful Central has held joint services, shared worship leaders and choirs, and hosted worship concerts with Anglo-American, Latino American, and multiethnic congregations of different sizes, denominations, and economic class strata around Los Angeles on numerous occasions. Thus, congregational music and a more widely shared subgenre have become additional resources in Faithful Central's efforts to build connections across the aisles of race, class, and nationality in the city.[12]

Conclusion

While Faithful Central's membership numbers have stabilized over the last half decade, it remains firmly rooted in its blend of Baptist, neo-Pentecostal, and charismatic beliefs. Playing on the theme of the arena it purchased in 2000, the church colloquially refers to itself as the "House of Champions," and through the power and indwelling of the Holy Spirit and the grace and mercy of God, it seeks to "build champions for divine deployment" not only within the church but also outside church walls in the city, throughout the country, and around the world. As Faithful Central has evolved from a Missionary Baptist church born in the early twentieth century into a "Spirit-led extension of Christ's body"[13] by the century's end, it has held onto a rich and similarly evolving tradition of African American Christian music and has led the way in the adaptation and expansion of praise and worship music performed within African American Christian congregational worship contexts. In exploring and adapting a sacred music subgenre with origins in Jesus music and the CCM movement of the 1970s and 1980s, Faithful Central actually affirms a vibrant aspect of its cultural identity. The use of praise and worship as a tool of congregational worship as well as religious instruction and exhortation has returned aspects of its weekly musical worship to the highly participatory worship and song traditions of the first black churches in America, particularly those practices from the nineteenth century.

What distinguishes this recent and widely occurring reaffirmation of African American congregational and sacred music from previous eras (for example, soul gospel or neotraditional gospel), however, is that the use of the subgenre stylistically and as a theologically realized approach to liturgical and congregational worship practices dually aligns Faithful Central with a broader Christian identity and connects it to other believers of different ethnicities and nationalities—not only in the diverse metropolis of Los Angeles but also abroad. Its congregants are among millions of believers who now share a common repertoire and similar Pentecostal and charismatic modes of worship, not bound by denominational affiliation. They also share a willingness to move beyond the warm-up act, mutually seeking out opportunities for fellowship in service and song across ethnic, racial, class, and geographic borders.

NOTES

1. Between 2003 and 2010, I conducted ethnographic fieldwork in three African American megachurches in Los Angeles, California. During the fieldwork project, I also visited small and average-sized congregations in the city, in addition to two other megachurch congregations in Gardena and Hollywood, California. See Johnson (2008) for further cultural-historical information and ethnographic data related to the details of this chapter.

2. From the 10 A.M. service of Faithful Central Bible Church at the Forum in Inglewood, California, on January 1, 2006.

3. I use the phrase "denominational fellowships" because, among black Baptists, a church can be a member of more than one Baptist denominational group at a time. In contrast to black Methodists, Pentecostals, and holiness denominations, this distinction allows for more overlap among groups such as the National Baptist Convention U.S.A. Inc., the National Baptist Convention of America Inc., the Progressive National Baptist Convention Inc., and the more recent formation that grew out of the first two fellowships—the National Missionary Baptist Convention of America.

4. The Holy Spirit is often referred to as the Holy Ghost in black Pentecostal settings and music. In this chapter, the two names will be used interchangeably.

5. Ulmer was a graduate of the University of Illinois with a dual degree in broadcasting and music (1969). He had formerly served as organist for the singing preacher Cleophus Robinson and, after moving to Los Angeles in 1970, succeeded Thurston Frazier as minister of music at Mount Moriah Baptist Church, a key gospel center in the city (see DjeDje 1993).

6. In 1995, Ulmer distinguished between his use of terms such as "conservative," "evangelical," "Pentecostal," and "charismatic," acknowledging that (at the time) Pentecostals and charismatics were considered by many to be evangelicals. At the time—and to some extent today, particularly among African American Christian denominational aggregations—his references to "conservative" and "evangelical" referred to those conservative evangelicals "who have traditionally rejected Pentecostal and Charismatic doctrine" (Ulmer 1995, xii).

7. Though Ulmer himself would not experience speaking in tongues until years later, he still studied and preached about it, along with other spiritual gifts and the character of the Holy Spirit, to the growing congregation.

8. The songs that Elmore and the current pastor of worship, Jimmy Fisher, were learning at evening services at West Angeles in particular would eventually become the pioneering albums in urban praise and worship—*Saints in Praise*, volumes 1 and 2, released in 1991 and 1992, respectively.

9. Liturgical studies scholar Mary McGann uses the term "local liturgy" to describe a church's locally maintained musical repertoire, which in essence is "a matrix of the church's understanding of its ritual life" and is influenced by factors such as denominational affiliation, theological beliefs, age of congregants, class, and ethnic/racial demographics. See McGann (2002, 16) and Johnson (2013, 260) for further ethnographic descriptions.

10. In the other two African American megachurches observed during my ethnographic research, praise and worship accounted for approximately 10 percent of the music genres incoporated into church services (Johnson 2013, 261–63).

11. Ulmer has studied ecumenical liturgy and worship at Cambridge's Magdalene College and Oxford's Wadham College. In 1999, he earned his doctor of ministry degree from United Theological Seminary in Dayton, Ohio.

12. Faithful Central has had four joint services with the predominantly Anglo-American Bel Air Presbyterian Church (twice in Inglewood, twice in Bel Air). After being the musical guests during special services, the Latino Christian vocal group GB5 (Gutierrez Brothers) served as the praise team supporting Jimmy Fisher in Faithful Central's first totally bilingual Sunday service in May 2012. Faithful Central's worship teams also hosted two free worship concerts; 2010's concert included worship teams and bands from City of Refuge in Gardena (Apostolic), the multiracial Spirit Food Center in Woodland Hills (nondenominational), and the predominantly Latino Parkcrest Christian Church in Lakewood (evangelical satellite).

13. Information taken from the "About Us" section of the church website: https://www.faithfulcentral.com/about-us/basics/.

REFERENCES

Anderson, Troy. 2012. "Professor in the Pulpit." *Charisma Magazine*, June 1. http://www.charismamag.com/life/education/15248-professor-in-the-pulpit.
Byous, Sonya. 2005. Interview with the author. Los Angeles, July 6.
Cusic, Don. 2002. *The Sound of Light: A History of Gospel and Christian Music*. Milwaukee: Hal Leonard.

DjeDje, Jacqueline Cogdell. 1993. "Los Angeles Composers of African American Gospel Music: The First Generations." *American Music* 11 (4): 412–57.

Elmore, Aladrian. 2006. Phone interview with the author. August 22.

Gaines, Adrienne. 2003. "Revive Us, Precious Lord." *Charisma Magazine*, April 30. http://www.charismamag.com/site-archives/146-covers/cover-story/891-revive-us-precious-lord.

Ingalls, Monique. 2011. "Singing Heaven Down to Earth: Spiritual Journeys, Eschatological Sounds, and Community Formation in Evangelical Conference Worship." *Ethnomusicology* 55 (2): 255–79.

Johnson, Birgitta J. 2008. "'Oh, for a Thousand Tongues to Sing': Music and Worship in Black Megachurches of Los Angeles, California." Ph.D. diss., University of California, Los Angeles.

———. 2011. "Back to the Heart of Worship: Praise and Worship Music in a Los Angeles African American Megachurch." *Black Music Research Journal* 31 (1): 105–29.

———. 2013. "Old School Worship: Celebrating Traditional Music Through Re-enactment." In *Resiliency and Distinction: Beliefs, Endurance, and Creativity in the Musical Arts of Continental and Diasporic Africa; A Festschrift in Honor of Jacqueline Cogdell DjeDje*, edited by Kimasi L. Browne and Jean N. Kidula, 257–87. Point Richmond, Calif.: MRI Press.

Lincoln, C. Eric, and Lawrence H. Mamiya. 1990. *The Black Church in the African American Experience*. Durham: Duke University Press.

McDonald, Kenrick "ICE." 2005. Interview with the author. Inglewood, Calif., June 6.

McGann, Mary E. 2002. *Exploring Music as Worship and Theology: Research in Liturgical Practice*. Collegeville, Minn.: Liturgical Press.

Price, Deborah. 2004. "Praise and Worship: A Primer." *Billboard*, April 24, 36.

Thumma, Scott. 2006. "Outreach Lessons from the Fastest Growing Megachurches." PowerPoint presentation for the National Outreach Conference in San Diego, November. http://www.hirr.hartsem.edu/megachurch/MegachurchOutreach&Growth.ppt.

Ulmer, Kenneth C. 1986. "Theology in the Music of the Black Church in America as an Element of Church Growth." Ph.D. diss., Grace Graduate School.

———. 1995. *A New Thing: A Theological and Personal Look at the Full Gospel Baptist Church Fellowship*. Tulsa, Okla.: Vincom.

———. 2006. Interview with the author. Inglewood, Calif., August 30.

Wagner, C. Peter. 1988. *The Third Wave of the Holy Spirit*. Ann Arbor, Mich.: Servant.

"Zion Rejoice—Live from Faithful Central." 2005. GospelCity.com, September 13. http://www.gospelcity.com/news/headlines/1052.

7

Singing the Lord's Song in the Spirit and with Understanding: The Practice of Nairobi Pentecostal Church

Jean Ngoya Kidula

Introduction

Pentecostalism in Africa has received much scholarly attention in the last decade. These scholars, drawn mostly from religious studies, come from different continents. Part of this attention is due to the perceived migration of the Christian center from the West or North to the South, as Africa is often referred to in terms of economic and political shifts (Jenkins 2002; Kacowicz 2007). Much of the discussion on Pentecostal Christianity in Africa centers on understandings regarding "the Spirit" or supernatural and extraordinary acts. This discourse recognizes how African churches have embraced the Spirit in ways that mainline, evangelical, and other churches in the West have not nor seem to continue to actively pursue, as was the case until the 1980s. Thus, regardless of whether they fit the general classic definitions of Pentecostals or charismatics, the majority of churches in Africa that invoke the supernatural or use terms that suggest a work of the Spirit are labeled Pentecostal or charismatic. A large number of Christian groups in Africa are subsumed under this label (Droz 2001; Gifford 2009; Mwaura 2008; Parsitau 2007).

These scholars further recognize that significant numbers of Africa's Pentecostal and charismatic groups learn their theology orally. Music's potency in indoctrination and memorializing is well acknowledged in both stereotypical readings of Africa and in Pentecostal circles. That the "Pentecostal movement has been distinguished for the important role it gives to music in all aspects of the lives of its adherents" (Alford 2002, 912) makes for an unprecedented symbiotic transfer with regard to the performance and practice of matters of the Spirit. Yet it is not only in singing that Pentecostalism makes for a wedding of church life and the other lived experiences of the African worshipper, for musicking is more than just song.[1] Pentecostals are known for diverse articulacy, including clapping, dancing, spontaneous interjections during sermons or in response to a testimony (which might include a song in the Spirit or singing with understanding), and ecstatic passing out during fervent worship. These behaviors are well documented in continental and diasporic African musicking. In Pentecostal and charismatic gatherings, it is not just special artists who perform; any and all participants are technically licensed to musick. Thus, there is room for the specialists, but there is opportunity for everyone else. This has generally been a characteristic of much communal African musicking as well.

It is not my intention in this chapter to compare Pentecostal song performance with musicking in an African ethos. I propose, however, that the Pentecostal approach to and beliefs about musicking have resonated with practices in many African culture groups. This became evident in the trends in charismatic and Pentecostal renewal movements that crystallized in the West beginning in the late 1960s but that included seminal African participation. It may be that African involvement and the reverberation of musicking drawn from an indigenous ethos conflated in an explosion of "Spirit" churches in urban spaces in different African countries. The repertoire in these churches includes hymns of missionary and local inception in colonial and local languages along with gospel songs and choruses, as well as contemporary songs of foreign and indigenous origin. Before the turn of the twenty-first century, it was customary to use hymnals and songbooks published internationally and locally. Today, lyrics are posted on overhead projectors in churches that find this practice valuable. Thus, one can find the same "praise song" in a Catholic assembly and in an Anglican, Pentecostal, or nondenominational congregation. It is an overwhelming endeavor to seek to differentiate the repertoire of the Pentecostal and the charismatic from that of Catholics, high Protestant churches, evangelical movements, or other traditions. Their practice speaks beyond denominational lines to the impact of globalization.

A summary of the manifestations of Pentecostal and charismatic musicking in Africa in a short chapter would hardly do justice to the wide and complex trajectory of its expressions. I will therefore focus on a church that I believe is at the crossroads of the Pentecostal and charismatic movement in

Kenya—the Nairobi Pentecostal Church (NPC). I was involved in NPC's music and worship programs as a singer, choral director, organist, and pianist. I also organized music and other events for children, youth, and adults between 1982 and 2003. My discussion will examine NPC's practice of singing with understanding (known songs from oral and written sources) and singing in the Spirit (songs "received" in a moment of visitation by the Spirit from known or unknown sources, in known or unknown "tongues"). I begin with a description of two services at NPC that were billed as "music" services but inevitably morphed into Pentecostal gatherings, in order to emphasize the centrality of music in Pentecostal-style worship. The historical section that follows provides insight into the multiple variables in the global Christian world and Kenya's postcolonial society that fed the diverse repertoire embraced by NPC and similar multicultural urban churches in Nairobi. I thereafter locate NPC within the broader sphere of Pentecostalism to reiterate the movement's outstanding musical legacy in the twentieth century.

The Service of Music

In August 1992, Dennis White, then senior pastor of NPC, asked me to prepare an evening song service. The service would be underscored by "choir" songs he felt the church members valued, which had been integrated into congregational lore. While these songs were not raised for the congregation during Sunday services, it was common knowledge that members sang them in small group fellowships and other gatherings and that parts of the songs were often invoked in prayer meetings as well as in youth and children's services. Together with the choir members, we (the choir committee and I) made a list of songs peppered with known and "favorite" church hymns and choruses, added one or two completely new numbers, and presented the set to the pastor. Pastor White had declared that he would not preach at the service; rather, he wanted the songs to speak to the people. On the day of the event, the choir sat onstage, as was our habit. We had decided that we would only stand to "perform" the completely new songs. However, as soon as we started a known choir song, some members of the congregation stood up and began to sing along or even pray aloud. The choir members immediately responded by standing, and soon everyone would be up, singing from the lyric sheets that we had printed out.

It was not long before Pastor White began to exhort, encourage, challenge, and evangelize the audience. What had begun as a song service turned into a meeting that included prayers, altar calls, the laying on of hands for healing of physical or other needs, and a celebration of praise. I was initially told that the service would last an hour. Two and a half hours later, we dismissed the congregation because it was getting late for Nairobi, where people commuted by bus and sometimes lived in neighborhoods that were dangerous after dark. The service began at 5:30 P.M. and officially lasted until 8 P.M. I left after 9:30 P.M. because the pastor always stayed until the last person who needed ministry left. Although the choir was dismissed, I stayed and played the piano, as I could get home safely later than the other instrumentalists. While I played, various pastors, elders, deacons, and other "prayer warriors" assisted those who came to the altar. My songs were not preplanned; sometimes I began a song and the pastor picked it up. Other times, the pastor began a song and I picked it up. The song service therefore became no different musically from the main services we held at the church. Singing was not just for the sake of song. It transcended the joy of singing and entertainment. Singing and music set the mood for many different service activities, enhanced the efficacy of the service items, calmed or excited the people, spoke or affirmed the Word and witness of the people, and closed out or signaled the closure of the cooperative moment.

The previous year (1991), Pastor White had asked me to prepare an evening Christmas carol service on December 22. This service was in addition to the annual Christmas program that the choir put on every second Sunday in December. The pastor was motivated to hold the carol service for at least one reason: unlike in previous decades, Nairobians no longer left the city en masse for their "countryside" ancestral homes during the Christmas season; most of them remained in Nairobi. For some, that decision was financially based. For others, who spent most of the year in the city, the villages did not have as strong a pull as in previous decades. It also appeared that the city was the only home some people knew. It was for these people's sake that the pastor proposed a Christmas carol service. The last time I could recall having a carol service was fourteen years earlier, when I was in high school. Our teachers prepared us for a month in advance through hymn and choir practice for the final service of the school year. This preparation ensured that all the students were conversant with the pieces that we collectively performed, regardless of our Christian or non-Christian backgrounds.

Putting together the repertoire for the NPC service proved to be less difficult than I had anticipated. While some carols were regularly aired on radio and television throughout the season, we proposed a few more obscure songs that were either very old or very modern. Once we decided on a set, I began to play the songs during the preservice music on Sundays, rehearsed the choir, and exhorted the church members to practice the songs elsewhere in order to familiarize their families and colleagues with the tunes. The carol service in the almost four-thousand-seat church was filled to capacity. The congregants participated as if they were familiar with every song. While classic songs were sung enthusiastically, for the lesser-known pieces, the pastor, at his discretion, reiterated some stanzas, adding spiritual, theological, and experiential layers that promoted more zealous engagement with the songs. Sometimes whole stanzas were repeated. Other times the refrain was underlined and repeated over and over again, spilling into a worship session. During these worship sessions, songs other than carols were sung. This was a Pentecostal service, replete with the musical gestures that were idiomatic of such gatherings. It was nothing like the high school Presbyterian carol services in which I had participated. As with the service in August, we continued playing after the congregation was dismissed. And Pastor White informed the church that we would henceforth hold a carol service every Christmas season. A new tradition was being birthed; that tradition was rooted in a music service.

These vignettes not only provide a window onto the musicking associated with Pentecostal-style Christianity in Kenya, but they also afford a framework for examining contemporary practices in congregational song among the diverse denominations grouped under the rubric of Pentecostal or charismatic churches in Africa.

Nairobi Pentecostal Church in the Pentecostal Christian-scape of Kenya

NPC is part of a larger complex known as Christ Is the Answer Ministries (CITAM). In essence, CITAM was launched out of NPC. NPC is affiliated with the Pentecostal Assemblies of God (PAG), a denomination started by Pentecostal missionaries from Canada and the United States in the late 1910s. The missionaries were required by the Kenyan government to be affiliated with a larger body. Thus, they applied to and were accepted by the Pentecostal Assemblies of Canada (PAOC) in 1924. The PAOC's work in Kenya was originally conducted under the Pentecostal Assemblies of East Africa, but in the 1960s, with the dawn of African independence, this work was renamed the Pentecostal Assemblies of God. PAG mostly operated in rural Western Kenya

(Kasiera 1981). As Kenyans from this area relocated to cities, they set up branch churches affiliated with this denomination. NPC, however, did not begin that way. The de facto church that had been set up to service PAG denominational adherents in Nairobi was located in a suburb known as Bahati, where many of those who relocated from rural Western Kenya lived. NPC's beginnings and establishment in Nairobi catered, for the most part, to people in the city who came from other parts of Kenya, a middle- and upper-lower-class African population that was rapidly becoming urbanized, and more elite English-speaking congregants of African and other origin. It was separate and independent from PAG, although the missionaries who served the church were granted Kenyan work permits through PAG. Thus, although it was a PAG affiliate, NPC was not one of PAG's assemblies (Mugambi 2009).

There was originally one NPC location on Valley Road, near the center of Nairobi. During Dennis White's tenure as senior pastor (1987–97, though he stayed on staff until 2003), new branches were opened in the city, named, for example, Nairobi Pentecostal Church Woodley (West) and Nairobi Pentecostal Church Karen (South) for the area of Nairobi in which they were located or the neighborhood in which their buildings were situated. However, in the last ten years, new branches have been established in other towns, the first in Kisumu, northwest of Nairobi. This branch was named Kisumu Pentecostal Church, in part because it took over the congregation of an affiliate PAG church of the same name. NPC as an organization was renamed CITAM in 2003 to facilitate expansion outside Nairobi.

CITAM is not only a collection of churches; since its early days as NPC, it has housed recording studios for music and radio programs as well as a kindergarten on its premises. As it has expanded, it now hosts a radio wave, HOPE FM, and a television station. In addition, CITAM runs grade and high schools and a children's home originally built to rehabilitate street children. CITAM sends missionaries to other parts of Kenya and, to date, has established assemblies in Malawi, Rwanda, and the United States. It is, however, well documented that NPC, the church, is the motherboard of CITAM.

NPC was envisaged by its founding missionary, John McBride, in 1953 as an English-speaking church. From the church's beginnings, contrary to most Western Christian denominations' agreement to each target a specific ethnic/language group and section of a country, he sought to bridge the racial and ethnic divide that was part of the social and political organization of Kenya. The McBrides recognized that Nairobi was multicultural. The lingua franca for the growing African elite was English. Targeting this population, the McBrides began a house church. They then collaborated with other missionaries and African pastors to set up evangelistic crusades in the city from 1955, which led them, over time, to rent halls where the budding congregation eventually grew into a sizable group. Eventually, the current Valley Road premise was acquired. A building was set up and occupied by the pastor, then Reverend Richard Bombay, in 1959. The first sanctuary was dedicated in 1960 (Mugambi 2009).

From its inception, NPC embraced the classical Pentecostal doctrines, the most distinctive of which was the baptism in the Holy Spirit as a third work of grace after repentance and sanctification. The initial evidence of the baptism was speaking in tongues. From the documentation of this experience in other parts of the world, Pentecostals were recognized for spontaneous song in known and unknown tongues and for activities such as clapping, dancing, and being slain in the Spirit, with music (vocal, instrumental, textual, or other forms) undergirding these expressions. According to various reports by PAG missionaries, including those involved in NPC, music was vital to the worship life of the congregation (PAOC archives, *Pentecostal Testimony*).[2] The music at NPC not only reflected missionaries' backgrounds; rather, it was as current as contemporary music in the Americas and Europe, because new missionaries first landed in Nairobi and usually attended NPC when they were in the city. As seen in church records and my own experience, NPC was frequented not only by Pentecostals but also by missionaries from other agencies, including Methodists, Baptists, and others of charismatic and evangelical persuasion.

However, by the mid-1970s, NPC was not the only church with a "Pentecostal" flavor in Nairobi; "Spirit" churches of indigenous African origin also had a home in the city. Most of these were birthed in rural spaces and spread into the city as their members relocated there. Some, such as the African Israeli Church Nineveh (AICN) and Akorino (also known as Aroti and Watu wa Mungu), had been operating since the 1930s. AICN had broken off from PAG, while Akorino was of indigenous Kenyan origin. AICN's behavior was similar to that of PAG, but for the most part, Akorino was considered a sect (Barrett 1973; Kalu 2007; Kalu and Low 2008; Garrard 2002). Thus, while both denominations manifested behavior associated with the larger Pentecostal world—such as lively and spontaneous songs of the Spirit, dancing, shouting, the raising of hands during congregational and spirit singing, prophetic words, supernatural healing, passing out in ecstasy—their theology was questioned by mainline and missionary churches, and their objectives were usually cast in political rather than religious language. Additionally, these churches had a rural ethos, appealed to particular ethnic groups, and did not generally attract the emerging urban elite.

In a parallel development, some members of mainline Anglican and Presbyterian churches embraced doctrines of sanctification and holiness that preceded and informed the Pentecostal explosion at the beginning of the twentieth century. These revivals were introduced to Kenya from Uganda and Rwanda through a movement whose participants were known as Valokole. This group attracted youth who had relocated to the city and whose parents belonged to mainline churches. The church had by then become the space where youth were socialized in modern, urban, independent Kenya. In the late 1960s, some Valokole youth were absorbed into parachurch organizations created by their denominations, such as the Trinity Fellowship, which fell under the auspices of the Anglican Church. Other youth were excommunicated from mainline high churches for manifesting Pentecostal behaviors such as exuberant singing, clapping, loud praying, or even praying/singing in the Spirit. Some of these "rebels" joined NPC and other emergent Pentecostal groups, such as the newly established Assemblies of God branches that set up shop in Kenya in the late 1960s.

Other youth formed new churches, the most popular being the Deliverance Church, led by the charismatic Joe Kayo, and the Redeemed Gospel Church, led by Arthur Kitonga. Students in high school and at university attended their gatherings, since the groups held evangelistic campaigns in the city on weekends and hosted revival camps during school holidays. Such meetings were promoted by ecumenical organizations such as the Christian Union (CU), established to evangelize and disciple high school students from the late 1950s, and the Fellowship of Christian Unions (FOCUS), an extension of CU in universities as well as an affiliate of the international Intervarsity Christian Fellowship. The meetings were vibrant spaces where new doctrines such as Pentecostalism could be introduced to institutions of learning that admitted students who had first been introduced to other variants of Christianity in their villages. The inclusive message of Pentecostalism, which recognized the power of God as being vested in any willing individual who was filled with the Spirit—not just ordained pastors—was not lost on youth eager to be on the front line in a country experiencing the early years of self-rule. The music introduced to and enjoyed by these youth was as diverse as the denominations they represented. It became fodder for youth groups in the students' churches back in their own villages and in other towns.

Beyond the locally established urban churches, foreign nondenominational organizations conducted Christian work in Kenya in the 1970s. They included Protestant and evangelical bodies such as the Navigators, Life Ministry (Campus Crusade for Christ), Youth with a Mission, Youth for Christ, DIGUNA (Die Gute Nachricht für Afrika), and Young Christians, an organization that sought to unite the youth of different Catholic orders. In addition to the various historical and modern musical developments that informed workers in these organizations, contemporary trends from religious social movements such as the Jesus People, the emerging commercial product known as CCM (contemporary Christian music), renewal developments that propelled music publishing houses such as Maranatha! Music, and the Catholic charismatic renewal that led to the fame of groups such as the Medical Mission Sisters became part of the soundscape of youth in Kenyan schools, colleges, universities, and churches.

Meanwhile, independent assemblies that originated in Africa were at the forefront of incorporating Kiswahili and other African-language songs into their services. Some songs were created under the guidance and promotion of mission churches, while others were spontaneous songs born in the Spirit or compositions in indigenous styles that resembled Spirit songs in form and performance style. It is no wonder that any discussion about Pentecostalism and charismatics in Africa is difficult to contain within the parameters that might more easily be applied to happenings in Europe or the Americas during the same period. It is also difficult to consolidate the musical behavior of churches in contemporary urban Africa by identifying specific music with a specific Christian denomination or theological/doctrinal persuasion. At the same time, this diversity makes for a rich palette from which to select musical materials.

Since the Reformation, hymnals have been great indices of theological and musical trends. An excellent example of the diversity in Nairobi is found in two hymnals published in the 1980s: *Victory Songbook* (1986) and *Voices Aflame: Songs from East Africa* (Purgason 1988). It is unclear who put together *Victory Songbook*. However, from my musical exposure in high school and at university, my participation in different ecumenical meetings organized by CU, FOCUS, Trinity Fellowship, Navigators, Youth for Christ, and international charismatic fellowships in Nairobi, and my involvement in NPC, I recognized most of the songs in the book. In the preface, the compilers explain that the compilation's "500 lovely *hymns* and *choruses* represent a wide range of Christian praise, adoration, worship, testimony, and response to God [that] is ideal for the home, youth groups, evangelistic meetings and churches of all

141

denominations" (*Victory Songbook* 1986). The hymnal's repertoire is in English and Kiswahili, with songs ranging from classic Lutheran standards such as "A Safe Stronghold" to the popular late 1970s chorus "Bind Us Together, Lord," as well as Kiswahili songs and choruses, including a translation of "Damu ya Yesu" ("Oh, the Blood of Jesus"), well-known Kenyan compositions such as the chorus "Moto umewaka" (A flame is lit—a fire is being burned), and the testimony song "Kuna kitu moyoni mwangu kinanitesa lazima nikiseme" (There is something in my heart that is so burning me up, I have to speak it forth). These songs were part of the core repertoire in gatherings at schools, universities, and colleges, church services and home fellowships, and any other place that prioritized Christianity, including national radio and television broadcasts. In practice, these were the songs of young Christendom in Kenya.

Voices Aflame features many of the same songs. It also contains songs in Luganda, the dominant language of Uganda. This inclusion is explained in part by the desire to recognize other East African countries and in part by contributors to the volume from Uganda. All of the songs include chord symbols. This hymnal, however, appears to target evangelical groups such as Baptists, African Inland Church members, and Anglicans who had embraced the Valokole tradition. Judging from the credits, it was probably a project of Daystar University, with contributors from the named evangelical groups.

Pentecostal Musicking and NPC

By the mid-1970s, NPC was one of the foremost entities in Nairobi now grouped by scholars of religion as Pentecostal or charismatic in doctrine and/ or behavior (Parsitau and Mwaura 2010). Such scholars refer to the members of these bodies as "urban Pentecostals," without clarifying what makes them Pentecostal in classic or other ways, apart from an emphasis on supernatural (spiritual) forces. NPC holds a historical position as a classical Pentecostal church and was a basic referent for Pentecostal and charismatic gatherings in Nairobi. Music undergirds the church life of NPC and the larger CITAM body, and Pentecostal gatherings have traditionally been identified and distinguished by the prevalence and diversity of music. Their songs are meant for both individual and congregational worship. D. L. Alford, in his entry on music in *The New International Dictionary of Pentecostal and Charismatic Movements*, states that "music occupies a vital place in the religious experience of typical Pentecostal-charismatic believers, expressing a wide range of

economic, political, and social values, styles of worship and musical tastes"
(2002, 912).

However, regardless of assigned cultural stereotypes, Pentecostals and charismatics have historically been documented as doing much more than singing.
For instance, Joseph Guthrie (1992, 81) quotes George Jackson's report on the
behavior of a white Church of God congregation in the 1930s: "The songs'
function as a rhythmic tom-tom like noise for inducing the desired ecstasy
became apparent. From that time on, oh, there was no let up. The Spirit moved
some to dance; others to speak in the unknown tongue, to jerk, or to fall in a
dead trance. . . . After half an hour of this, the singing came to an end. Also
the instrument strummers, worn out, dropped out one by one, leaving only
a piano player and a tambourine whacker." Further, Pentecostals have traditionally been known for their diverse styles, to the extent that it was usually
difficult to maintain the divide created by mainline churches between sacred
and secular sounds. As Goss notes, "Previous to the 1900s, and up until Pentecostal singing appeared, there was usually a distinct difference in the public
mind between 'worldly' and 'sacred' music. But it was impossible for people
freshly filled with the Holy Ghost to express their abounding joy in the slow,
cold reserved styles typical of 'sacred' music" (quoted in Guthrie 1992, 84).
Thus, Pentecostals did more than sing; they were known for incorporating the
most contemporary styles into their musicking. In essence, the music in any
given service revealed the diversity in historical and contemporary repertoires,
as well as in what was considered stylistically sacred or recognized as secular
in form and performance practice at the time.

John McBride and other pastors at NPC, particularly Mervin Thomas, Roy
Upton, and Dennis White, maintained the various manifestations of Pentecostal musicking. Included in the worship services were hymns of various
liturgical, evangelical, and Pentecostal traditions of the past, as well as gospel
songs, Sunday school hymns, choruses, and other music from revivals over
the years. However, there were always contemporary trends, often initially
presented as "specials." As a choir director, I knew that the "specials" would
subsequently be absorbed into the music and worship life of the church. One
choral director and worship leader from Sweden who visited NPC in 1989
commented on the choir's rendition of Handel's "Hallelujah" chorus without
piano accompaniment. On the day she visited the church, the pastor, in an
inspired moment, asked the choir to sing the piece. Since the pianist was away,
we performed it a cappella. Our guest was equally astounded when the congregation sang along with the appropriate "European" ethos, only to turn around

when prompted and sing Kiswahili pieces in a different timbre and style, accompanied by hand clapping and other action, as if it was the most normal thing. I did not know it then, but what occurred regularly in the church—the shifting between ordered, rehearsed choral, solo, and small ensemble numbers, congregational hymns and gospel songs from the hymnal, choruses raised from the pulpit, songs from contemporary global and local repertoires, and spontaneous, unrehearsed congregational singing in the Spirit—was typical of classical Pentecostals. NPC was certainly conceived and regarded as a classical Pentecostal church. However, it was not the only assembly in Nairobi with such diversity of song. It was simply the most famous and the most populous of the Pentecostal and charismatic churches until the end of the twentieth century.

Our first performance of Handel's "Hallelujah" chorus was part of a Christmas production. We showcased it in the "Singing Christmas Tree," a tradition begun by the pastors at NPC in the late 1970s as part of their evangelistic endeavors. Missionaries introduced us to cantatas by evangelical songwriter John W. Peterson, and in 1984 we tacked Handel's "Hallelujah" chorus onto Peterson's *Born a King*. The response was electric. After the first show, the church filled up. When word got out that a Pentecostal church choir was singing the "Hallelujah" chorus, which was usually the preserve of the Nairobi Chorus and the Anglican elite, more people came to every subsequent performance. This was how the congregation began to appropriate the piece.

Subsequent annual productions of the "Singing Christmas Tree" received national coverage after the president of the country saw it and requested that it be nationally televised during the Christmas season in the mid-1980s. We also learned to involve the audience. It grew to more than three thousand people a night as a result of being included in the singing of familiar carols or songs in indigenous Kenyan languages. In addition, there was the possibility of being seen on television. Thus, NPC was well-known countrywide for its Christmas music productions, which became a model for other churches. However, this reputation was preceded by radio broadcasts, including live Sunday evening services when it was NPC's turn, as per its agreement with other denominations during the late 1960s. NPC also hosted radio music programs such as *Songs for You*, featuring the latest international Christian songs, on Sunday afternoons. It was known for its congregational singing, which seemed to be more exuberant than what other "mission" churches offered, and it included songs in Kiswahili—rare in other established multilingual churches attended by the rising elite. I would go so far as to say that NPC became a model for how to sing the Lord's song, demonstrating that there were diverse tongues and ways to sing this song in the Spirit and with understanding.

Retrospect

During my intense musical involvement at NPC (1983–2003), music was embedded in every gathering. The song sources were diverse—from standard hymnals, to orally transmitted choruses, to someone "receiving a song" and sharing it with the congregation, from which time it became part of church lore. Other resources included visiting musicians and recordings from North America, Britain, and the Scandinavian countries. Additionally, East African songs were introduced through visits and recordings by special groups, choirs, and individuals, subsequently becoming a part of church church. Church members also brought songs into the church, sharing them during prayer meetings or requesting that the choir or worship leader introduce them to the congregation. Thus, song was not the domain of a special and trained few; it belonged to the assembly, and it was up to the assembly to disperse it in the wider community.

Congregational musicking may have been rooted in ecclesiastical use. It may have been intended for musical worship, to teach doctrine and reinforce theology, or to prepare, exhort, and inspire the congregants. However, I found that people liked to musick. Often, they joined the choir simply to learn to sing. And they learned as much from other choir members in the pews as from the leader. There was a strong belief that the musicking that so touched people, when done with the right motives, pleased God, who in turn responded to this offering.

My training in school as a musician prepared me to invest the most time in the interested or gifted child, in order to promote excellence of artistry in that individual. However, my ethnic group imparted the idea that everyone should musick. Song was but one dimension. In Pentecostal congregational song, as a leader—whether of the choir or from the piano or guitar—it was indeed my mandate to enable everyone to musick. Singing in the Spirit from certain classical Pentecostal understandings may mean certain things. I interpret it also to mean that the singers embody the spirit of the song—in text, tune, or other expression. Singing with understanding can be understood as meaning not only comprehension of the textbut also that people understand the essence of the musicking, get lost in it, appropriate it, make it their own, and are embodied in it. This is some of what I learned from musicking at Nairobi Pentecostal Church.

NOTES

1. Christopher Small (1998, 9) proposed that "music" should be both a noun and a verb. As a verb, "to musick" is "to take part, in any capacity, in a musical performance," whether by performing, listening, practicing, rehearsing, or dancing. The term has since been expanded as ethnomusicologists found that, in most of the world, music is defined beyond sound and silence to include what might be perceived as other disciplines, such as fine arts, drama and theater, other verbal arts outside of song, and many more expressions that feed into the complex of the process of music. Hence the broad acceptance of the term "musicking."

2. Reports appeared in the journal *Pentecostal Testimony*, which may be accessed in the PAOC Archives, Mississauga, Ontario.

REFERENCES

Alford, D. L. 2002. "Music, Pentecostal and Charismatic." In *The New International Dictionary of Pentecostal and Charismatic Movements,* edited by Stanley M. Burgess, 911–20. Grand Rapids, Mich.: Zondervan.

Barrett, David. 1973. *Kenya Churches Handbook: The Development of Kenyan Christianity.* Kisumu: Evangel Press.

Burgess, Stanley M., ed. 2002. *The New International Dictionary of Pentecostal and Charismatic Movements.* Grand Rapids, Mich.: Zondervan.

Droz, Yvan. 2001. "The Local Roots of the Kenyan Pentecostal Revival: Conversion, Healing, Social and Political Mobility." *Les Cahiers de l'IFRA* 20:23–44.

Garrard, D. J. 2002. "Kenya." In *The New International Dictionary of Pentecostal and Charismatic Movements,* edited by Stanley M. Burgess, 150–55. Grand Rapids, Mich.: Zondervan.

Gifford, Paul. 2009. *Christianity, Politics, and Public Life in Kenya.* New York: Columbia University Press.

Guthrie, Joseph Randall. 1992. "Pentecostal Hymnody: Historical, Theological, and Musical Influences." D.M.A. diss., Southwestern Baptist Theological Seminary.

Jenkins, Philip. 2002. "The Next Christianity." *Atlantic Monthly* 290 (October): 53–68.

Kacowicz, Arie M. 2007. "Globalization, Poverty, and the North-South Divide." *International Studies Review* 9 (4): 565–80.

Kalu, Ogbu U. 2007. "Pentecostalism and Mission in Africa, 1970–2000." *Mission Studies: The Journal of the International Association for Mission Studies* 24 (1): 9–45.

———. 2010. "Holy Praiseco: Negotiating Sacred and Popular Music and Dance in African Pentecostalism." *Pneuma* 32 (1): 16–40.

Kalu, Ogbu U., and Alain M. Low, eds. 2008. *Interpreting Contemporary Christianity: Global Processes and Local Identities.* Grand Rapids, Mich.: Eerdmans.

Kasiera, Ezekiel. 1981. "Development of Pentecostal Christianity in Western Kenya: With Particular Reference to Maragoli, Nyang'ori, and Tiriki, 1909–1942." Ph.D. diss., University of Aberdeen.

Kayo, Joe. n.d. "The Apostle." Joe Kayo Ministries International. http://www.joekayoministries .com/index.php/the-apostle.

Massarelli, Lewis Gary. 1998. "A Study of the Music of the Pentecostal Assemblies of Canada and How It Changes at Times of Renewal." M.A. thesis, California State University, Dominguez Hills.

Mugambi, Justus. 2009. *Five Decades of God's Faithfulness: The Amazing Story of Christ Is the Answer Ministries*. Nairobi: Evangel Press.

Mwaura, Philomena Njeri. 2008. "The Role of Charismatic Christianity in Reshaping the Religious Scene in Africa: The Case of Kenya." In *Christianity in Africa and the African Diaspora*, edited by Afeosemime U. Adogame, Roswith Gerloff, and Klaus Hock, 180–92. New York: Continuum.

Parsitau, Damaris Seleina. 2007. "From the Periphery to the Centre: The Pentecostalisation of Mainline Christianity in Kenya." *Missionalia* 35 (3): 83–111.

Parsitau, Damaris Seleina, and Philomena Njeri Mwaura. 2010. "God in the City: Pentecostalism as an Urban Phenomenon in Kenya." *Studia Historiae Ecclesiasticae* 36 (2): 95–112.

Pew Forum on Religion and Public Life. 2010. "Historical Overview of Pentecostalism in Kenya." August 5. http://www.pewforum.org/Christian/Evangelical-Protestant -Churches/Historical-Overview-of-Pentecostalism-in-Kenya.aspx.

Purgason, Ed, comp. 1988. *Voices Aflame: Songs from East Africa*. Nairobi: Step Magazine, Evangel Publishing House.

Small, Christopher. 1998. *Musicking: The Meanings of Performing and Listening*. Middletown: Wesleyan University Press.

Victory Songbook. 1986. Nairobi: Victory Publications, the Outreach Wing of Reginah Professional Designers.

8

"Soaking Songs" Versus "Medicine Man Chant": Musical Resonance Among Diné Oodláni (Navajo Believers)

Kimberly Jenkins Marshall

The song "Háálá Ayóo Diyin" should not exist. In spite of the fact that music plays a central role in the worship and manifestation of spiritual gifts among the Diné Oodláni (Navajo Believers), "Háálá Ayóo Diyin" stands alone as the only widely known and actively performed nonderivative Navajo-language Christian song. However, the uniqueness of "Háálá Ayóo Diyin" stands in direct contrast to a linguistic situation among Navajo neo-Pentecostals that largely favors Navajo-language expressive culture: prayers, sermons, and testimonies are all commonly delivered in Navajo. The fact that Oodláni music is nearly always composed and performed in English suggests that tangible barriers exist to musical composition in the Navajo language.

In what follows, I explore the ways in which neo-Pentecostal theology and Navajo language ideology combine to create barriers to new composition of Christian music in the Navajo language. Then, through close examination of an ethnographically grounded example of music with original Navajo text,

For their helpful comments on this essay, I thank the WRKD faculty writing group at the University of Oklahoma. Thanks also to Charlotte Frisbie, Ruth Stone, Anya Royce, Richard Bauman, and Jason Jackson for comments on an earlier version of the essay. Mistakes are still mine. Ronald Maldonado of the Navajo Nation Office of Historic Preservation has been consistently helpful in guiding me through the acquisition of proper permissions and reporting. I am grateful for the financial support of the Liebmann Fellowship Foundation, the Skomp Fund of the Indiana University Department of Anthropology, and the University of Oklahoma College of Arts and Sciences. As always, I am especially indebted to the members and leadership of Pastor Wallace's church. *Ahéhee'*.

"Háálá Ayóo Diyin," I argue that the key to the success of this song is its ability to capitalize on what I call *resonance*. This theoretical concept, rooted in the physics of acoustical resonance, recognizes that two concepts may be amplified by their connections, without standing in for each other. In the case of Oodlání music composition, resonance is a sufficiently flexible concept to explain how a balance can be struck between continuity and discontinuity in a context that self-consciously eschews "traditional" religion. As demonstrated by "Háálá Ayóo Diyin," the theory of resonance recognizes the emotional force of continuity in expressive forms while still taking seriously the projects of "rupture" (Robbins 2003) in which Oodlání understand themselves to be engaged.

The Oodlání

The exclusive practice of neo-Pentecostal Christianity is on the rise among Navajos living on the Navajo Nation in northeastern Arizona and northwestern New Mexico.[1] This rise reflects emerging trends throughout Native North America (Dombrowski 2001; Laugrand and Oosten 2010; Tarango 2011; Westman 2010) and globally (Jenkins 2002; Anderson 2004). Despite what Maureen Schwarz has called "a cultural heritage [that] preconditioned the Navajo to practice medical and religious pluralism" (2008, 27),[2] the exclusive practice of Christianity is now claimed by about 30 percent of Navajos, with Pentecostalism the most practiced form of exclusive Christianity (Milne 2011, 527).[3] At current population estimates (Donovan 2011), this percentage represents upward of twenty-seven thousand Navajos affiliated with the neo-Pentecostal (Oodlání)[4] movement.

The rapid growth of this movement can easily be connected to its unregulated structure and large-scale Navajo enfranchisement: Oodlání churches are led by Navajo pastors, called and authenticated by the Holy Spirit alone, who found independent, Navajo-run churches in which preaching and worshipping are predominantly in Navajo. It is also related to increasingly frequent cultural traumas after 1950 (Aberle 1982, 224) and a change in missionary approach to favor charismatic tent evangelists (Dolaghan and Scates 1978; Marshall 2011). Theologically, Oodlání follow the lead of these tent evangelists, viewing the Bible as the literal Word of God and acceptance of Jesus as personal savior as the only way to avoid eternal damnation in hell. They preach abstinence from "worldly" things such as alcohol, drugs, adultery, and even country-western dancing. They are also charismatic in that they believe in "gifts of the Spirit," including infilling by the Holy Spirit, Spirit-filled singing and dancing, speaking in tongues, and faith healing.

In spite of the fact that Oodláni are led by Navajo pastors and evangelists, a hallmark of this movement is its opposition to the traditional Navajo ceremonial system, *Diné binahaghá*—literally "moving about ceremonially" but typically glossed as "traditional religion" (Frisbie 1987, xxiii).[5] This opposition is not framed as the dismissal of traditional religion as "superstitious nonsense" but instead as a reinterpretation of the very efficacy of that system. This is an example of what José Casanova has called "uprooted local culture engaged in spiritual warfare with its own roots" (2001, 437). Navajo traditional religion includes both the negative presence of witchcraft (Kluckhohn 1967) and the positive presence of ceremonials aimed at the restoration of balance and beauty (*hózhǫ́*) in individual bodies and the world at large (Reichard 1944; Witherspoon 1977; Frisbie 1992). All of these practices are linked together by Oodláni as "traditional religion" and reinterpreted within the Pentecostal framework of divine warfare between Jesus and the devil (and his host of demons), which is manifest in the trials of the everyday lives of believers.[6] Thus, as in other areas of global Pentecostalism, Oodláni accept local ontologies (spirits, witchcraft, and so forth) but do not seek to "forge any continuity with them" (Robbins 2003, 223). While Oodláni value their Navajo identity, they strongly preach keeping the realms of traditional religion and Christianity carefully separated.

Musical practice among Oodláni reflects this theology of exclusivity, utilizing musical modes that do not evoke the music of traditionalism. Hymns from western European sources are translated into Navajo and widely available through the Navajo-language hymnbook, first published in 1979. While the western European four-part harmonies of the hymns certainly don't evoke connections with Navajo traditional religion, they are also not terribly popular in the contemporary Oodláni movement, as they primarily carry historical connotations of a denominational past. Instead, Oodláni use praise music— music that encourages maximum participation through simple lyrics, easy-to-follow melodies, and extensive use of repetition. Because praise music is a genre derived from Anglo-American and African American sources, the language of praise music is typically English. A good handful of praise songs have been translated into the Navajo language, and it is not uncommon to hear bilingual switching between verses of commonly performed praise songs. The Navajo texts of these songs are always derivative and secondary, however, and as praise songs increase in tempo and tighten in repetition in order to manifest the central rite of spiritual gifts in this community, the Navajo lyrics are dropped.

Issues of New Composition

The lack of Navajo musical innovation and ownership is in direct contrast to the broader Navajo Pentecostal expressive context, which is characterized by Navajo language use: sermons, prayers, and testimonies are all frequently given in the Navajo language. The near absence of any new Navajo-language musical composition in Oodlání worship contexts, then, suggests that tangible barriers to Navajo-language musical composition exist. These barriers are intimately connected to the role of song in Navajo traditional religion, the practice of which Oodlání assiduously avoid.

One of the primary barriers to new song composition in the Navajo language for Oodlání is the close connections between the realms of songs, words (especially Navajo words), and prayer within the traditional ceremonial contexts. In short, Navajos have traditionally held ceremonies (also called chants, ways, or sings, depending on the translation of the Navajo enclitic "-jí")[7] whenever there is a need felt for one, most commonly by an individual and often in response to a concern about health. Once the proper ceremony has been determined, a hataałii, or singer (also called a "medicine man"), is hired to perform the ceremony, or sing. Sings last between one and nine nights and are communal gatherings that take place in a ceremonial hogan, a traditional Navajo dwelling (Gill 1981, 58–59). The singer and the patient, more accurately named "the one sung over," are the focus of this sing, but everyone who attends the ceremony benefits from what is done there (Reichard 1950, xxxvii).

Within these contexts, songs constitute a major part of the ritual activities that aim to restore harmony and balance (hózhǫ́) (Witherspoon 1977, 155), restating and reemphasizing things already stated in prayer. In part, songs have the power to restore hózhǫ́ during ceremonies because speech and song (or chant) are seen as closely related within the traditional Navajo worldview, and both can be used in intensified form as prayer. In fact, the noun for "song" in the Navajo language has what Gladys Reichard called "a complicated series of corresponding verb-stems, referring, however, not to singing or song but to holiness, reverence, prayer, and, in the passive voice, to sorcery" (1950, 297–98). For Navajo Pentecostals, who equate traditional religion with the devil, this association between sung Navajo words and traditional forms of prayer is problematic.

As an example of the charged nature of the associations between Navajo language, song, and traditional Navajo religion, take the musical compositions of Ben Stoner. Stoner has been a missionary at the Brethren of Christ mission in Bloomfield, New Mexico, for over forty-five years and is widely recognized as one of the handful of Anglos not raised among Navajos who has ever gained fluency in the Navajo language. Disturbed by the lack of "Navajo hymnody," Stoner has for years been working on a project that would "set Scripture to music" by cuing off of the melodic aspects of the Navajo language (in this case Navajo-language biblical passages). When read aloud, Navajo vowels can be short or long, high tone or low tone, and rising or falling. Stoner's project is to "musicalize" these aspects, using a quarter note for a long vowel and an eighth note for a short vowel, raising or lowering the pitch of the chant for the high- or low-tone vowels, and slurring the pitch up or down for rising or falling vowel tones. By Stoner's own admission, the result sounds "much like a traditional chant" (Baldridge 2000, 68).

Despite efforts by Stoner and some Navajo gospel musicians (such as Daniel Smiley, Andrew Begay, and Julie Redhouse) to popularize this type of music, which they claim will help build a "true Navajo church" (Baldridge 2000, 94), the emotional associations of traditional Navajo chant and the theological associations of traditional religion as still containing the efficacious power of demons are too strong for the majority of Oodláni. From radio hosts to pastors to lay participants, there seems to be a near-universal Oodláni condemnation of this type of musical blending (Baldridge 2000; Marshall 2011).[8]

Thus, one of the barriers to new composition in the Navajo language for Oodláni is the difficulty of setting the Navajo language to music in a way that doesn't sound like "medicine man chant." However, the problematic associations for Oodláni go even further. It is not simply a matter, for them, of staying away from what they left behind. It is also that the Navajo language continues, for many Oodláni, to have performative force, particularly when set to song.

Performative Song

The major barrier to new Navajo-language composition for Oodláni, I argue, is the performative force traditionally ascribed to that language. Using J. L. Austin's classic framework, certain phrases in English have performative force: saying "I name this ship" in the context of a christening ceremony is the actual act of naming, not a reference to that naming (Austin 1970, 235). In the Navajo ceremonial context, the performative force of language is the central mechanism by which the rituals are understood to have efficacy. But this very performative force inherent in the language creates problems when it is imported into new contexts, such as Navajo Pentecostalism.

The use of performative language as a central part of traditional Navajo rituals reflects a distinctive Navajo language ideology. Language ideology is the collection of feelings and beliefs about language related to rationalizations about "perceived language structure and use" (Silverstein 1979, 193). Navajo language ideology is distinctive from Euro-American language ideology (but similar to other Native American language ideologies) in that it privileges the performative nature of language. Euro-American language ideology regards language as primarily "reflectionist"—that is, the primary function of language is in providing names for things. Many Native Americans, on the other hand, possess language ideologies that "view language and speech more 'performatively'—as a more powerful and creative force that 'makes' the natural and social worlds they inhabit" (Field and Kroskrity 2009, 10).

Navajo language, and particularly Navajo language within ritual contexts, has been widely documented to emphasize its performative function (Reichard 1944; Witherspoon 1977; Gill 1987; Field and Blackhorse 2002). The performative nature of Navajo ritual language is linked to Navajo mythology, philosophy, and cosmology. According to the creation myths, the world was created out of the thoughts of the Holy People but did not come into being until these thoughts were spoken and sung (Witherspoon 1977, 47). In this view of creation, transformative acts proceed from knowledge, "organized in thought, patterned in language, and realized in speech." And from this perspective, Witherspoon makes the claim that for Navajos "language is not a mirror of reality; reality is a mirror of language" (34). A theology that places the burden for creation on the directed and enacted thought of the Holy People does not just apply to events in the Navajo past, however. Navajo ceremonies (sings) consistently revisit this act of creation through the reenactment of the mythology as a fundamental part of the curing ceremony. The words are spoken again, restoring the world to the state of balance and harmony with which it first came into being (25). The ceremonial prayers also actively transform the world by addressing the deities with kin terms and declaring the binding relationship of reciprocity and mutual help that these kinships oblige (Gill 1987, 122). In all of these ways, Navajo ceremonial language relies on the performative power of the Navajo language.

The performative potential of the Navajo language is the key to understanding why it is so difficult to use Navajo in newly composed Oodlání song. Linguist David Samuels has noted a similar situation in the closely related Apache context. According to Samuels, Apache schoolchildren are taught Apache translations of European songs, such as "Old MacDonald Had a Farm," rather than traditional Apache children's songs, because sung Apache often "run[s] the risk of being coded as medicine man talk" (2006, 551). In Samuels's example, translation rendered the Apache version of "Old MacDonald" almost nonsensical but was preferred to a newly composed Apache children's song, because the latter "included the text *ha'íaayú la' gozhóó*[,] 'where the sun rises is beautiful,' and some parents said that it sounded like a prayer to the sun" (536). A parallel situation exists in Navajo schools, where Deborah House has found that Navajo Christians are supportive of Navajo-language education, but only if "the instruction program has no religious or sacred content" (2002, 74).[9] These examples show that in Southern Athabaskan contexts, songs can carry connotations of "medicine man chant," and these connotations are incredibly problematic for Navajo Pentecostals, who self-consciously eschew traditionalism.

The referential (naming) and performative (acting) aspects of language thus come into contention in this context. While Stoner and Baldridge argue that Navajo words become meaningless when set to a Western tonal harmony that does not preserve linguistically necessary high and low tones (Baldridge 2000, 67),[10] Oodlání themselves are much more concerned with the traditional connotations of the newly composed Christian "chant." Given a language ideology that hears performative power in traditional chants, paired with a theology that equates that power with the forces of evil, bringing anything that sounds like "medicine man chant" into the church isn't just irrelevant; it is potentially very dangerous.

"Háálá Ayóo Diyin"

The unique success of "Háálá Ayóo Diyin" as the only widely accepted Oodlání song with original Navajo lyrics suggests ways in which Navajo language can be set to song without evoking "medicine man chant." Its popularity lies in its ability to capitalize on what I call *resonance*.

"Háálá Ayóo Diyin" was composed by a family group called the Kinlichini Singers. This traveling group was formed in the 1980s and sponsored by the Southern Baptist denominational mission. It comprised the children of two sisters, cousins who would be classed, in Navajo kinship reckoning, as brothers and sisters. Ranging in age from teenagers to young adults at the time, the Kinlichini Singers traveled around the Navajo nation in a large bus (provided by the Baptist denomination) covered in psychedelic paintings and the words

"American Indian Gospel Movement." They journeyed to remote areas and conducted revivals, setting up a generator and getting out their guitars.

"Háálá Ayóo Diyin" arose out of the creative energy of this group as its members traveled, rehearsed, and played together. Although there is some contention about who composed which parts of the song, it would not exist at all without the combined energies of Raymond Begay (now an elected representative to the state legislature), his brother Russel Begay, his sister Alice Norton, and his "cousin-sister" Julia Redhouse.

Structurally, "Háálá Ayóo Diyin" includes extensive use of repetition and what Raymond Begay describes as "short phrase beats" (1-2, 1-2) characteristic of Navajo "social song and dance" (2008). Although it is composed linearly, its highly repetitive structure allows for a certain degree of flexibility in performance. During my research, I heard this song performed a number of ways, from a simple chorus-bridge-chorus form to a more complex mix of chorus, bridge, and nonlinear verse choices. This type of free, nonlinear repetition allows "Háálá Ayóo Diyin" to be performed as a praise song, with an emergent form based on the interaction between the resources of the performer and the interest of the audience (Bauman 1975).

The song is lyrically noncomplex, emphasizing a few main ideas. Although Navajo lyrics and English translation are provided below, this is not a bilingual song. This is a song composed and exclusively performed in Navajo. The English translation is given here for English readers, but it is an artificial creation, not an ethnographic reality.

Chorus

Háálá Ayóo Diyin	Oh how holy
Doo lá dó' nizhóní da	And amazingly beautiful
Háálá . . . Háálá Ayóo Diyin	How very, very holy

Jesus Ayóo Diyin	Jesus, very holy
doo lá dó' nizhóní da	And amazingly beautiful
Háálá . . . Háálá Ayóo Diyin	How very, very holy

Verse 1

Jesus yisdá shííłtxį	Jesus saved me
doo lá dó' nizhóní da	How very beautiful
Háálá . . . háálá Ayóo Diyin	How very, very holy

Jesus ná shííłdzíí'	Jesus healed me
doo lá dó' nizhóní da	How very beautiful
Háálá . . . háálá Ayóo Diyin	How very, very holy

Chorus

Verse 2

Jesus ayóo shik'is	Jesus is my best friend
t'áá íyisí shik'is	Without a doubt, my friend
Háálá . . . háálá Ayóo Diyin	How very, very holy

Jesus baa hashniih	Jesus I praise
t'áábí baa hashniih	He, himself, I praise
Háálá . . . háálá Ayóo Diyin	How very, very holy

Chorus

Bridge

hiiná, hiiná dooleeł	He is alive, he is alive
hiiná, hiiná dooleeł	He is alive, he is alive
. . . . Lá	. . . . because of it

Verse 3

Jesus Nánádááh	Jesus will return
doo lá dó' nizhóní da	How very beautiful
Háálá . . . háálá Ayóo Diyin	How very, very holy
[Repeat]	

Chorus

Verse 4

Jesus ayóo'ó shó'ní	Jesus loves me so much
doo lá dó' nizhóní da	How very beautiful
Háálá . . . háálá Ayóo Diyin	How very, very holy
[Repeat]	

Chorus

"Háálá Ayóo Diyin" and Resonance

The key to understanding the success of "Háálá Ayóo Diyin" lies in our ability to see how it *resonates*. The concept of resonance I am using is a musical one, an acoustical principle that explains how certain vibrations amplify other vibrations, but without assuming identical frequencies. Resonating chambers (such as the hollow body of a guitar or violin) amplify the sound of a plucked or bowed string. The resonant frequencies of a wine glass and the voice of an opera singer are the physical properties that explain her ability to shatter the object. And brass instruments produce sound based on the alignment between the harmonic overtone series (a mathematical arrangement of related sound waves) and the vibrations of the column of air inside the horn. When these "resonant peaks" are achieved, the instrument produces a clear, well-focused, rich, and amplified sound (Myers 1997, 21). The sense of something new amplifying something else is key to both the formal and informal concept of resonance.

Taking music as a metaphor for culture and imagining that all expressive practices hum with meaning, I argue that sometimes new practices are adopted because they *resonate* with existing practices, without necessarily taking on the meaning of those existing practices. A similar concept is David Smilde's "imaginative rationality," which explains culture change by arguing that we interpret meaning of new domains through reference to "a relatively better known domain" (2007, 215). The similarity between the two domains is important, but it should not be mistaken for "replacement."

Resonance helps explain the meaning shifts that are happening specifically within expressive culture (music, oratory, ritual, and so forth) in situations of culture change. The aesthetic practices of expressive culture are a realm in which the sense of something being "similar but different" gains a powerful expression. In situations of culture change as dramatic as Pentecostal conversion, the "feeling for form" that Michael Owen Jones (1987) identifies as one of the hallmarks of aesthetics can remain the same while the meanings can change very greatly.

"Háálá Ayóo Diyin" resonates with traditional Navajo expressive culture in two important ways. First is its use of incremental repetition. A well-known hallmark of complex oral literature such as traditional Navajo ceremonials, incremental repetition aids with the memorization of long texts by altering the verses only slightly at each iteration. Raymond Begay (2008) calls this a "soaking quality," like the gentle soaking rain Navajos call "female rain." The "soaking quality" of incremental repetition can be seen in a well-known Navajo daily prayer:

> With beauty before me, I walk.
> With beauty behind me, I walk.
> With beauty above me, I walk.
> With beauty below me, I walk.
> From the East beauty has been restored.
> From the South beauty has been restored.
> From the West beauty has been restored.
> From the North beauty has been restored.
> From the zenith of the sky beauty has been restored.
> From the nadir of the earth beauty has been restored.
> All around me beauty has been restored.
> (Witherspoon 1977, 153–54)

In this text, the repetation of the formula "With beauty _____, I walk" is incrementally altered with the four modifying phrases: "before me," "behind me," "above me," "below me." This pattern of incremental repetition is used extensively in the text of Navajo ceremonials, as has been documented by Wyman (1975), Haile (1938), and Matthews (1995). In "Háálá Ayóo Diyin," incremental repetition appears in the slight alteration of the first line of each verse, with the second and third lines remaining nearly identical. The slight alteration of the first line is a repetition of the many things that Jesus "does" for the faithful. Therefore "Jesus _____" is altered at each repetition with the modifying phrases *ayóo diyin* (is so holy), *yisdá shííłtxį́* (saved me), *ná shííłdzíí'* (healed me), *ayóo shik'is* (is my best friend), *Nánádááh* (will return), and *ayóo shó'ni* (loves me).

Like a traditional prayer, "Háálá Ayóo Diyin," with its incremental repetition, has a soaking quality, a connection that Begay (2008) has explicitly pointed out. The parallel structure of "Háálá Ayóo Diyin" and traditional Navajo prayer does not represent simple cultural continuity, however, because the meanings expressed by the two songs are very different. Incremental repetition is used in "Háálá Ayóo Diyin" to express the very Christian ideas of salvation, healing, and blessings through Christ, as well as the Rapture, rather than beauty and harmony. This song emphasizes concepts at the very core of Navajo Pentecostal Christianity. The key idea behind resonance is that although the aesthetics of the form remain the same, the meanings have changed and, in the case of Pentecostal Christianity, changed dramatically.

The other major way in which "Háálá Ayóo Diyin" represents a point of resonance is through its "Native feel." Begay (2008) claims that the "melody" for this song was taken from a Cree chant by Jimmy Anderson that he heard while at college in California. Furthermore, the melody for the bridge (*hiiná*) was taken from a song by Red Bone, a Native American popular music group from the 1970s. These musical influences give "Háálá Ayóo Diyin" a non-Western feeling that resonates with Navajo converts; it feels somewhat more familiar than the songs derived from Western vertical harmony. The appeal of the "Native feel" in "Háálá Ayóo Diyin," however, is that it is generically "Native," not specifically Navajo. Thus, the danger of new composition in Navajo (that is, sounding like "medicine man chant") is mitigated by using the musical traditions of other tribes and Native pop culture. In incorporating pan-Indian musical influences, "Háálá Ayóo Diyin" succeeds where other new composition in Oodlání contexts fails. The Native influences are similar enough to resonate but different enough to allow for the attachment of new meanings. These two points of resonance provide the familiarity that "Háálá Ayóo Diyin" needed to become popular, while maintaining a safe distance from Navajo traditional religion—the ingredients necessary for the success of this Navajo Christian musical composition.

Conclusion

The success of "Háálá Ayóo Diyin" is unique because this song alone has been able to capitalize on the productivity of resonance. The Navajo language is a common medium of creative expression among Diné Oodlání. However, creative use of this language has largely not translated to musical composition, primarily due to important theological barriers constructed by Oodlání between Christianity and traditional religion.

"Háálá Ayóo Diyin" has been successful because its emotional force has been amplified by related Navajo musical practices. In this sense, resonance is a way of understanding the aspects of continuity that are nearly always a facet of culture change. Resonance, however, speaks to change as much as continuity. Regardless of how strong the bridge formed by expressive culture is, the destination is a different realm. The paradoxical nature of "Háálá Ayóo Diyin" lies in the fact that far from attempting to forge cultural continuity through the expressive use of the Navajo language, this song emphasizes dramatic cultural change.

NOTES

1. Research for this chapter was conducted under Navajo Nation ethnographic research permit #Co614-E, and prepublication approval was obtained from the Navajo Nation Office of Historic Preservation. This chapter draws on fieldwork I have conducted with a Navajo-led neo-Pentecostal church in northwestern New Mexico since 2006. Given Christianity's contentious and colonial history within Native American communities, I will clarify that I am not a missionary but an ethnographer, and I describe a movement that is led not by Anglos or outsiders but by a small but vocal minority of Navajos. My research is descriptive, not prescriptive, and I am exploring the musical contestation that exists, not recommending musical best practices for the service of Christian mission.

2. Arguments for the inherently pluralistic nature of Navajo religion have also been made by Aberle and Stewart (1957), Blanchard (1977), and Frisbie (1987, 1992).

3. Milne's demographic data was gathered during a random-sample and Navajo Nation-wide survey about Navajo attitudes toward renewed uranium mining in 2000. Milne reports that of the 30 percent of respondents reporting exclusive practice of Christianity, Pentecostalism was the most popular form, followed by Mormonism and Catholicism, and that these three accounted for almost 90 percent of the Christian total (2011, 527).

4. Neo-Pentecostalism is a global religious movement that practices charismatic manifestations of faith (for example, speaking in tongues) but that, unlike historical Pentecostalism, operates without central organization or denominational affiliation. It has been the driving theology behind the spreading Oodláni movement, in which believers align themselves with independent Navajo pastors, not denominations.

5. The opposition by Oodláni pastors to Navajo traditional religion is well documented in my own work (Marshall 2011) and the work of others (Frisbie 1987, 206; Lewton and Bydone 2000, 488; Schwarz 2008, 262), in direct contrast to the claims of Pavlik that, with Navajo pastors, "the usually antitraditionalism message of the Fundamentalist movement is often toned down or eliminated" (1997, 50).

6. Milne (2011) has pointed out the artificiality of this Navajo Pentecostal construction of "tradition."

7. The enclitic "-jí" is typically attached to the Navajo word for the ceremony's purpose (Frisbie 1992, 461).

8. In fact, Baldridge's main goal seems to be providing biblical justification to counter these Navajo objections to Stoner's project.

9. Samuels is quite concerned that eliminating the performative aspects of the Apache language in order to please Christian parents reduces the Apache language to a referential system of words "to identify objects." This robs the language of its power and, he argues, will have disastrous consequences for language revitalization efforts (2006, 551).

10. Interestingly, many of my informants have directly contradicted the claims of Baldridge and Stoner, claiming that they can understand the Navajo words in hymns even without the high and low tones.

REFERENCES

Aberle, David. 1982. "The Future of Navajo Religion." In *Navajo Religion and Culture: Selected Views*, edited by David M. Brugge and Charlotte J. Frisbie, 219–31. Museum of New Mexico Papers in Anthropology 17. Santa Fe: Museum of New Mexico.

Aberle, David, and Omer Stewart. 1957. *Navaho and Ute Peyotism: A Chronological and Distributional Study.* Boulder: University of Colorado Press.

Anderson, Allan. 2004. *An Introduction to Pentecostalism: Global Charismatic Christianity.* Cambridge: Cambridge University Press.

Austin, J. L. 1970. *Philosophical Papers.* 2nd ed. Oxford: Oxford University Press.

Baldridge, Terry. 2000. "Navajo Christian Worship and Music: The Struggle for Cultural Relevance." M.A. thesis, Crown College.

Bauman, Richard. 1975. "Verbal Art as Performance." *American Anthropologist* 77 (2): 290–311.

Begay, Raymond. 2008. Interview with the author. July 3.

Blanchard, Kendall A. 1977. *The Economics of Sainthood: Religious Change Among the Rimrock Navajos.* Cranbury, N.J.: Associated University Presses.

Casanova, José. 2001. "Religion, the New Millennium, and Globalization." *Sociology of Religion* 62 (4): 415–41.

Dolaghan, Thomas, and David Scates. 1978. *The Navajos Are Coming to Jesus.* Pasadena: William Carey Library.

Dombrowski, Kirk. 2001. *Against Culture: Development, Politics, and Religion in Indian Alaska.* Fourth World Rising. Lincoln: University of Nebraska Press.

Donovan, Bill. 2011. "Census: Navajo Enrollment Tops 300,000." *Navajo Times,* 7 July.

Field, Margaret, and Taft Blackhorse Jr. 2002. "The Dual Role of Metonymy in Navajo Prayer." *Anthropological Linguistics* 44 (3): 217–30.

Field, Margaret C., and Paul V. Kroskrity. 2009. "Introduction: Revealing Native American Language Ideologies." In *Native American Language Ideologies: Beliefs, Practices, and Struggles in Indian Country,* edited by Paul V. Kroskrity and Margaret C. Field, 3–30. Tucson: University of Arizona Press.

Frisbie, Charlotte J. 1987. *Navajo Medicine Bundles or Jish: Acquisition, Transmission, and Disposition in the Past and Present.* Albuquerque: University of New Mexico Press.

———. 1992. "Temporal Change in Navajo Religion: 1868–1990." *Journal of the Southwest* 34 (4): 457–514.

Gill, Sam D. 1981. *Sacred Words: A Study of Navajo Religion and Prayer.* Westport, Conn.: Greenwood Press.

———. 1987. *Native American Religious Action: A Performance Approach to Religion.* Columbia: University of South Carolina Press.

Haile, Berard. 1938. *Origin Legends of the Navajo Enemy Way.* Yale University Publications in Anthropology 17. New Haven: Yale University Press.

House, Deborah. 2002. *Language Shift Among the Navajos: Identity Politics and Cultural Continuity.* Tucson: University of Arizona Press.

Jenkins, Philip. 2002. *The Next Christendom: The Coming of Global Christianity.* New York: Oxford University Press.

Jones, Michael Owen. 1987. *Exploring Folk Art.* Logan: Utah State University Press.

Kluckhohn, Clyde. 1967. *Navaho Witchcraft.* Boston: Beacon Press.

Laugrand, Frédéric B., and Jarich G. Oosten. 2010. *Inuit Shamanism and Christianity: Transitions and Transformations in the Twentieth Century.* Montreal: McGill–Queen's University Press.

Lewton, Elizabeth L., and Victoria Bydone. 2000. "Identity and Healing in Three Navajo Religious Traditions: Są́ah Naagháí Bik'eh Hózhǫ́." *Medical Anthropology Quarterly* 14 (4): 476–97.

Marshall, Kimberly. 2011. "Performing Conversion Among the Diné Oodlání (Navajo Believers)." Ph.D. diss., Indiana University.

Matthews, Washington. 1995. *The Night Chant.* Salt Lake City: University of Utah Press.

Milne, Derek. 2011. "Diyin God Bizaad: Tradition, Change, and Pentecostal Christianity Among the Navajo." Ph.D. diss., University of California, Los Angeles.

Myers, Arnold. 1997. "How Brass Instruments Work." In *The Cambridge Companion to Brass Instruments*, edited by Trevor Herbert and John Wallace, 19–23. Cambridge: Cambridge University Press.

Pavlik, Steve. 1997. "Navajo Christianity: Historical Origins and Modern Trends." *Wicazo Sa Review* 12 (2): 43–58.

Reichard, Gladys. 1944. *Prayer: The Compulsive Word*. New York: J. J. Augustin.

———. 1950. *Navaho Religion: A Study of Symbolism*. Bollingen Series. New York: Pantheon Books.

Robbins, Joel. 2003. "On the Paradoxes of Global Pentecostalism and the Perils of Continuity Thinking." *Religion* 33 (3): 221–31.

Samuels, David. 2006. "Bible Translation and Medicine Man Talk: Missionaries, Indexicality, and the 'Language Expert' on the San Carlos Apache Reservation." *Language in Society* 35 (4): 529–57.

Schwarz, Maureen Trudelle. 2008. *"I Choose Life": Contemporary Medical and Religious Practices in the Navajo World*. Norman: University of Oklahoma Press.

Silverstein, Michael. 1979. "Language Structure and Linguistic Ideology." In *The Elements: A Parasession on Linguistic Units and Levels*, 193–247. Chicago: Chicago Linguistic Society.

Smilde, David. 2007. *Reason to Believe: Cultural Agency in Latin American Evangelicalism*. Anthropology of Christianity 3. Berkeley: University of California Press.

Tarango, Angela. 2011. "Jesus as the Great Physician: Pentecostal Native North Americans Within the Assemblies of God and New Understandings of Pentecostal Healing." In *Global Pentecostal and Charismatic Healing*, edited by Candy Brown, 107–28. New York: Oxford University Press.

Westman, Clinton. 2010. "Pentecostalism Among Canadian Aboriginal People: A Political Movement?" In *A Liberating Spirit: Pentecostals and Social Action in North America*, edited by Michael Wilkinson and Steven Studebaker, 85–110. Eugene, Ore.: Pickwick.

Witherspoon, Gary. 1977. *Language and Art in the Navajo Universe*. Ann Arbor: University of Michigan Press.

Wyman, Leland. 1975. *The Mountainway of the Navajo*. Tucson: University of Arizona Press.

9

"We Can Be Renewed":
Resistance and Worship
at the Anchor Fellowship

Andrew Mall

The Anchor Fellowship is a nondenominational church in downtown Nashville, Tennessee. Its members practice and promote a theology that is explicitly inclusive, valuing the spiritual gifts, needs, and potential for ministry of all Christians, regardless of their backgrounds, professions, or subcultural affiliations. Worship and live music are integral components of the Anchor's services, in which aesthetics of charismatic praxis and rock club concerts often overlap. The Anchor was formerly a Vineyard church, and many of its priorities reflect members' previous church experiences as well as their participation in underground music subcultures. Dick Hebdige (1979) links subcultures to an ideology of resistance, which is present in the Anchor's origin story; its congregants were united in their disenfranchisement from mainstream churches and in their resistance to dominant ideas about church growth, congregational participation, and interchurch accountability. In its blending of evangelical and charismatic theologies and practices, the Anchor joins other Third Wave and neocharismatic congregations that resist dominant Protestant typologies in which Pentecostal-charismatic renewal and conservative evangelicalism are often separated.[1] This case study of renewal-oriented worship, theology, and ministry at the Anchor Fellowship thus highlights and further nuances the increasingly blurred boundaries between the charismatic and evangelical worlds in the United States.

The Anchor Fellowship Today

On a typical Sunday morning at 10:30 A.M., the Anchor Fellowship is as loud as a rock concert. The worship band is better than good: they sound well rehearsed, professional, balanced, and confident, and their music more than fills the 150-year-old sanctuary. The guitars and keyboard outline the chord changes, layering nicely in different registers; the vocalists trade melody and harmony easily; and the rhythm section maintains a steady beat and propels the band through dynamic shifts.[2] The band transitions easily from song to song almost without pause, vamping when the worship leader prays to invite God's presence into the church. The leader might repeat a chorus or extend a verse to heighten the congregation's engagement with the Holy Spirit, and the band members easily follow her cues. As a first-time visitor in late 2009, I was impressed by the music; the Anchor's congregants, however, almost take the band's musical proficiency for granted. The band is *always* this good. Church-goers do not attend the Anchor to marvel at the music; rather, they come to worship and encounter God in a community of believers. Worshippers are charismatic: some stand and sing, faces turned upward and arms outstretched, bodily embracing the Holy Spirit; others sit and observe in quiet contemplation; still others kneel and pray; and all are caught up in an experiential spirituality that is simultaneously private and public, intimate and communal.

The Anchor Fellowship's website quotes a passage attributed to Saint Francis of Assisi, founder of Catholicism's Franciscan order. It reads, "We have been called to heal wounds, to unite what has fallen apart, and to bring home those who have lost their way."[3] As the Anchor's unofficial mission statement, this quotation indicates that the church's pastors and congregation take seriously their ministry to Christians who have been peripheralized or made to feel unwelcome in other churches. The Anchor originated as an informal meeting of subcultural Christians dissatisfied with and disengaged from previous church experiences.[4] Members come from a variety of denominational backgrounds; many have never felt comfortable in traditional churches, while others have felt rejected by former churches. Church leaders encourage individuals to participate in the church's ministries—for example, by welcoming new members to the worship team, empowering new leaders without requiring formal seminary training, and affiliating with like-minded congregations through the Anchor Mission U.S.A. network. That churchgoers here experience spiritual moments in a corporate worship environment at all reflects the Anchor's history of resistance, ideology of inclusion, and theology of renewal.

At the Anchor, ideology and theology are co-constitutive and born from these histories; resistance and renewal are part of this church's heritage and can be seen in both its congregation's worship practices and its pastors' theological orientation toward pursuing God's calling regardless of any hurdles they might face.

Although the Anchor may feel to some like a refuge for countercultural and subcultural Christians, its pastors and members nonetheless closely follow biblical doctrine. The church's statement of faith, available on its website, is based on the Nicene Creed and contains elements common to most Christian churches: belief in the sovereign Christian God, the Holy Trinity, the resurrected Christ, and the divinely inspired, inerrant Bible. Additional elements link the Anchor to a history of charismatic renewal: belief in the active and transformative presence of the Holy Spirit, the importance of spiritual gifts and miracles, and the strength of God's grace, which enables believers to rise above their ability in order to accomplish God's will. The Anchor's statement of faith lays the foundation for some of its ministries and programs. Members are given the opportunity to learn about the faith cooperatively through the Alpha Course, a nondenominational exploration of the basics of Christianity, originally developed in an English charismatic Anglican church, that takes place over several weeks. The Anchor School of Ministry offers in-depth, full-time discipleship training in a ten-week term. I attended a formal prayer training at the Anchor, where we practiced calling on the Holy Spirit and listening to God's voice; it is mandatory for congregants who want to serve on the church's lay ministry team.[5]

The preamble to the Anchor's statement of faith is perhaps its most unique part: it recognizes the diversity of the theological and denominational backgrounds of church members, and it emphasizes the unity found in their common salvation.[6] Over time, the Anchor's diversity has grown; the congregation includes Christians of different ages, backgrounds, and theological orientations. According to former associate pastor George Brooks, many churchgoers "have come from much more conservative churches, or much less charismatic churches, however you want to call it. We have Baptists, we have Pentecostals, we have Church of Christ people . . . people from totally different theological backgrounds, all coming together because something real [spiritually] is happening despite us."[7] While this diversity clearly reflects the Anchor's inclusive theology, at a macro level it also indicates that boundaries around charismatic worship praxis—subverted here in favor of "something real"—are contested continually in local congregations, church networks and denominations, and the scholarly literature at large (see, for example, Nathan and Wilson 1995; Miller 1997; Sweeney 2005; Versteeg 2010; Luhrmann 2012).

The Anchor's staff learned their positions organically: while founding pastor Joshua Stump, current lead pastor Brian Ban, and current worship leader and associate pastor David Lim all have substantial postsecondary education, none has completed a college degree or attended seminary for pastoral training. They have all learned to pastor and disciple their congregants on the job, following God's calling and will. Indeed, Pastor Ban finds the idea that a degree or certification alone might qualify someone for pastorship laughable. Instead, the Anchor's pastors believe that anyone can be called to ministry, regardless of his or her personal background or training. Renewing disenfranchised Christians, respecting their diverse theological backgrounds, training and empowering them to hear God's voice and minister—all of these practices both reflect and produce ideals and goals of a participatory Christian faith among the Anchor's congregation. Privileging divine accountability over human qualifications is another feature of the Anchor's experiential spirituality, and it further illustrates the ways in which resistance, renewal, and worship have evolved both ethically and stylistically.

From Vineyard Congregation to Anchor Mission U.S.A.

While the Anchor Fellowship's theology and worship practices clearly align it with the Association of Vineyard Churches, its former denominational home, church leaders and members grew increasingly frustrated with Vineyard bureaucracy and eventually unaffiliated only a few years after the church officially joined the Vineyard in 2006. Vineyard U.S.A. originally emerged as a coherent network of thirty-two churches that separated from the Calvary Chapel movement in 1982 (Miller 1997, 46–50; Burgess 2002, 1177; Versteeg 2010, chap. 2). In contrast to the "mildly charismatic and completely evangelical" Calvary, Vineyard "favored a freer use of special, supernatural gifts in worship and evangelism" (Sweeney 2005, 151). Under the leadership of John Wimber, Vineyard churches emphasized worship, experiential spirituality, kingdom theology, and church planting; within fifteen years, the movement grew to comprise more than eight hundred churches (Jackson 1999, 340). Pastor Ban characterized the early Vineyard movement as one in which "individual communities were coming together, pursuing the Lord, and it didn't matter what qualifications you had. . . . There was no formal guidelines, necessarily, for

what the church was supposed to look like."[8] Contemporary worship music—
Vineyard pastor Bill Jackson describes prioritizing "culture-current music" and
"a common mission to rock 'n' roll culture" (1999, 105, 107)—remains important at many Vineyard churches, featuring often in ethnographic accounts (see,
for example, Labanow 2009; Monteith 2010; Versteeg 2010; Luhrmann 2012).

The Anchor's affiliation with Vineyard seemed like a good match. Many of
the Anchor's founding members and pastors had attended Vineyard churches,
including Stump, Ban, former worship leader Ben Crist, and former associate
pastor Christy Brooks.[9] The Anchor has much in common with other Vineyard
churches, especially in its strong focus on worship music, experiential spirituality, and congregational ministry time at the end of the service. The Anchor's
pastors benefitted from the community and fellowship with other Vineyard
congregations throughout the southeastern United States. This formal network
helped newcomers to Nashville find the Anchor; for example, members of
Ban's previous church, Trinity Vineyard in Atlanta, encouraged him to join
the Anchor when his family first moved to Nashville in August 2006. Additionally, Anchor pastors valued the Vineyard's regional conferences, where
church leaders gathered to meet and share resources and expertise. Finally, the
Anchor's affiliation with the Vineyard provided a visible system of accountability for the church, demonstrating that the congregation's beliefs and faith
practices had been approved by an outside authority.

Despite these benefits, Pastor Stump and the Anchor's staff had become
uncomfortable with the Vineyard affiliation as early as 2007. Although these
pastors had witnessed significant growth, emotional healing, and spiritual
renewal throughout their church's early years—which they saw as proof
that God was working through them and had ordained them to lead their
congregants—they felt that other area Vineyard pastors were condescending
toward them. As Ban put it, "We were seen [by other pastors] as a glorified
youth group . . . as radical and rebellious." This tension was most apparent
when other Vineyard pastors counseled the Anchor's staff. For example, Stump
quit his job to pastor the Anchor full-time only a few years after its founding
against the advice of other Vineyard pastors: according to George Brooks,
other pastors warned that "it takes at least ten years before [your church] can
be self-supporting." Despite these challenges, the Anchor's staff resolved to
maintain the Vineyard affiliation at the time. As Ban explained, they "never
felt comfortable with leaving because we were angry, or because we weren't
getting what we wanted"—a mature perspective that contrasts greatly with the
Anchor's resistant "glorified youth group" identity.

Stump and others began to feel God calling them to start new churches that would serve a similar purpose to the Anchor: ministering to the needs of Christians who "were falling in the cracks and didn't have a place," according to Ban. The Anchor's pastors and congregation networked with other peripheralized Christians and ministries around the country, often meeting them at Christian music festivals, such as Cornerstone in Illinois.[10] According to Brooks, they found "a huge cultural cross-section within the underground music scene that has rejected church but desires a relationship with God, desires a community. So what we want to do is show them, say, 'Hey, look, we were in the same place. We hated church, we didn't want to have anything to do with Christians or religion, but God has called us to be part of the church, and he's called the church to be healthy and wholesome, so here's how we're going to model it. Come and help us do this.'" The Anchor's pastors wanted to use their own experiences to encourage and advise others with similar backgrounds and visions. They discovered, however, that planting churches through their Vineyard affiliation was very difficult—"near impossible" and hindered by miles of red tape, according to Brooks—despite the denomination's focus on church planting, missions, and evangelism (Jackson 1999, 107, 340). Ban noted that one nonnegotiable requirement was two years' worth of formal training in the Vineyard's program for new pastors. While this requirement may be well intentioned and justified from the perspective of Vineyard's church-planting overseers, it posed a huge hurdle for the Anchor's staff: none had completed formal pastoral training themselves, and they were not comfortable requiring training of new pastors for their church plants. Rather, they heard God calling them "to create a place for people to use each other for a resource," said Ban, "and begin to find qualification in the Lord rather than on what you have or don't have on a piece of paper, and [we] began to encourage and release people to do church plants."

These tensions ultimately led the Anchor's congregation to leave Vineyard in late 2009 and form Anchor Mission U.S.A., a network of existing churches, new church plants, and missions with a similar theology and calling as the Anchor. Ban explained this as a positive move: "We really feel like the Lord gave us vision for a movement that he was calling us to, rather than exiting Vineyard because of a dislike." The way in which Ban frames this decision leaves little room for argument from those who believe and trust in God's will; the Anchor's separation from Vineyard in order to pursue God's calling to plant new churches was a defensible position that placed the church on the forefront of renewal, far more so than simple dissatisfaction with its perceived juvenile status within and resistance to the Vineyard church network. As of June 2014, Anchor Mission officially includes fifteen churches at locations in Chicago, New Orleans, Warsaw, and elsewhere. According to its website, Anchor Mission self-identifies as a "post-denominational organization"; much like the early years of the Vineyard movement, it has no ecumenical or pastoral hierarchy, instead operating cooperatively.[11] The Anchor Fellowship's staff provide moral support, encouragement, and the benefit of experience in pastoring peripheralized Christians and bringing them into community with one another.

Worship at the Anchor

Every Anchor Mission church prioritizes worship as a foundational method of connecting with God, though they all sound slightly different: the worship leaders and pastors have a lot of freedom in designing their worship services to be relevant for their congregations (see fig. 9.1). Ban explained that worship styles, common patterns of resistance, and fashions are ultimately not sustainable affinities; rather, "the only thing that binds us together is our pursuit of the Lord." At the original Anchor Fellowship in Nashville, worship constitutes a focused period of this pursuit in which the congregation is united emotionally, physically, and spiritually.

Sunday, September 12, 2010, 5:30 P.M. This evening's six-member worship band is arranged in an arc on the stage, facing the congregation but with no single musician providing a focal point. David Lim leads worship on electric guitar, standing stage left. Although I've already attended several services at the Anchor, I'm still surprised by the sheer volume of the band when it starts playing—I feel like I'm in a rock club. The sound engineer has mixed Lim's baritone vocals only slightly higher than the instruments; although the songs' lyrics and melodies are of primary importance, the accompanying music is a close second. The congregation stands and sings, many reading the song lyrics projected onto the bare wall above the stage; some raise their arms above their heads, hands facing outward, bodily praising God and inviting him in. The music is incredibly loud, and though I can see other congregants' lips moving, I can't hear them singing along—I can barely hear myself singing.

The church's interior is rather small and has a utilitarian aesthetic: bare brick walls, scarred wood floors, a couple hundred folding chairs, and a plywood stage. Bare lightbulbs are strung from the ceiling, where the wooden rafters are visible. This contrasts with the professional PA system in the front

FIG. 9.1 A rehearsal of the Anchor's worship band. Photo by the author. Used courtesy of the Anchor Fellowship, Nashville.

and sound console in the rear of the sanctuary, both of which are huge and look expensive. While singing, I glance around and smile and nod hello to some pastors and church members I know. Many are college students, and most have moved to Nashville from elsewhere; I see current and former members of alternative Christian rock bands, at least a few employees of the nearby United Record Pressing vinyl record manufacturing plant, and the guys with whom I attended a (secular) heavy metal show last night. Subcultural style abounds: ripped denim, T-shirts, long hair, tattoos, piercings, and thrift store chic are common.

After about forty-five minutes of worship music, senior pastor Joshua Stump carries a podium to the stage and starts preaching from Mark 1:29–34.[12] He is troubled by the current discourse on "hipster Christianity" sparked by Brett McCracken's recent book, cover article for this month's issue of *Christianity Today*, and *Wall Street Journal* opinion piece (2010a, 2010b, 2010c). At issue is the presumption that hipster Christians' faith is fashionable and has little substance. Stump sounds like he agrees: he argues that many young Christians are more attracted to the culture of Christianity than they are to the responsibilities of their faith. He exhorts the congregation to pursue an "authentic faith," arguing that one cannot be committed to the Christian lifestyle without practicing Christian love.

Pastor Stump seamlessly transitions from his sermon into the Anchor's weekly ministry time. He asks us to consider whether our faith is authentic and intentional, actively informing our daily lives, or whether it is only routinized, a facade without deeper significance. He calls for every present member of the lay ministry team to come forward and pray for the congregation as the worship band returns to the stage and resumes playing. As I look around me, I see raw emotion on many faces; some members are clearly grappling with the challenge that Stump has presented. The music rises and falls in volume and intensity, simultaneously driving and reflecting the congregation's energy. We are united in a corporate religious experience; the atmosphere is affecting and thick with emotion. The ministry team spreads throughout the congregation to pray for individuals. Titus, whom I met at Alpha Class on Thursday, comes over, places his hands on my shoulders, and prays for me to receive God's grace. The band finally decrescendos one final time, fading away into an expectant silence. Stump then directs the congregation to form a large circle around the periphery of the sanctuary. We join hands and sing an a capella doxology to close the service.[13]

As described above, Sunday churchgoers at the Anchor experience worship viscerally. The sermons frequently address issues that churchgoers face in their daily lives from a biblical perspective and can result in uncomfortable moments if congregants feel directly confronted. Corporate prayer and ministry time is literally hands-on, either on an individual basis (as when Titus prayed over me) or as a group, when (for example) the congregation lays hands on and prays over churchgoers who are moving away. The Anchor's building—one of the oldest church buildings in Tennessee, originally built in the middle of the nineteenth century for a Primitive Baptist congregation—is not well insulated and can get uncomfortably hot. The walls might perspire, and the floor may shake. Live worship music at the Anchor is as loud as at a rock concert and similarly physical; close to the stage, one can feel the speakers push the air. When the band crescendos, accelerates, modulates to a higher key, or simply starts playing a familiar and well-loved song, congregants respond both physically and emotionally. Most congregants sing along, constructing and perpetuating corporate unity through worship music. Many experience the Holy Spirit's presence in this affective environment.

Worship is a fundamental part of religious life at the Anchor. It brings individuals together in shared experience, providing a communal environment in which they can open themselves to spiritual encounters. Congregants affirm and reaffirm their faith both individually and collectively during worship services. They invite the Holy Spirit into the building and learn how to recognize God's presence (cf. Luhrmann 2012). Sermons and pastoral teaching contribute to this continual educational process and help unite churchgoers in their collective spiritual experience. As Ban explained to me in an interview, "Through worship, we can come into, we can encounter the Lord, and we can find healing, and we can be rebuilt, and we can experience who we were meant to be." This perspective on worship—that its purpose is to allow individuals to encounter the Lord, receive healing (both literally and metaphorically), and be rebuilt—shapes and is shaped by the Anchor's institutional history of resistance and renewal.

When I asked Lim about the church's reputation almost two years after the service described above, he told me, "I feel like the reputation of the church has changed positively over the last few years. For a while we were [known as] the emo church, then we were the hipster church. Hopefully, now, that's changing again. . . . We just want to be known as a church where the Lord is there, where people go and are accepted, however, that are also healed of their wounds."[14] Healing—one of the gifts of the Spirit—is a common discursive frame at the Anchor, where members have come from broken families, experienced addiction and divorce, been ostracized by their previous churches, or become disenfranchised from mainstream evangelicalism because of the culture wars with secular popular culture (Romanowski 1996; Nekola 2009). These backgrounds have shaped the Anchor's perspective on worship, as described above by Pastor Ban. Individuals who find healing have often been hurt; those who desire to be rebuilt may feel as if they have been destroyed; those who search for meaningful lives may feel adrift and purposeless. Communing with God and other Christians through worship at the Anchor heals and renews and has done so since the church's inception.

The Organization of Worship at the Anchor

Joshua Stump founded the Anchor Fellowship in 2003 as an unaffiliated home group. Early on, the Anchor was a space of resistance, a refuge for Christians who were dissatisfied with their former churches. Brooks told me that it "was just born out of rebellion, which is not a good thing. . . . I think all of us were very broken, very hurt, we had so many issues." Many of those early attendees had been professionally involved in the music industries. According to Brooks, the Anchor attracted "musicians and artists that would pretty much refer to themselves as Christians but don't really want to, that kind of vibe, and are happy to call the Anchor their home, because . . . it's not a very 'church' place." In other words, the Anchor doesn't look, sound, or feel like a traditional church. As a result, it has always attracted Christians who find traditional church worship practices, politics, and institutional hierarchies to be irrelevant—people whom Ban described as being "pissed and done with church."

The Anchor's first worship leader, Ben Crist, moved to Nashville to attend Belmont University and joined the Anchor while still in college. He wrote songs that reflected this ambivalence, brokenness, and hurt, addressing the quotidian confusion he experienced as a Christian. For example, in "We Can Be Renewed," he observes that "pain comes quietly to Earth" and claims that "we're infected with the hurt," the passive voice construction here suggesting that we experience hurt through no fault of our own.[15] The song's refrain—"What of the dreams I shared with you? Here's hoping that we can be renewed"—posits renewal as an uncertain process, instead of the assured promise heard more commonly in praise and worship songs. In an earlier song, "Hear Our Prayers," Crist addresses God directly, asking him to "take our burdens, calm our fears."[16] The song is written in the first-person plural—the pronouns "our" and "we" appear throughout—and functions as a collective lament when the congregation sings it together. The chorus makes this explicit: "God will you make us a people that love you? . . . God see our tears that we're struggling to see through."

In his lyrics, Crist often acknowledges that life can be painful for Christians and that God's plan for one's life can be difficult to perceive and follow. Churchgoers who had already experienced confusion and pain in their own lives found these songs very meaningful and evocative. Lim inherited this tradition of emotionally and spiritually powerful worship songs from Crist when he joined the Anchor's staff as head worship leader in 2006. Lim brought to the Anchor experience leading worship and an emphasis on professional-quality performance and production values, developed during his time working as a guitar technician for Christian performing artists Newsboys. Under Lim's leadership, the worship team produces a musically immersive experience and performs in an anthemic rock-based musical style that sounds similar to that of popular modern worship artists such as David Crowder or Chris Tomlin. Each worship leader is free to pick and choose songs from the Anchor's repertoire with little guidance from Lim. While this repertoire includes many CCLI-licensed songs, such as Michael W. Smith's "Let It Rain," currently about half of the songs are originals, written by Lim or Crist, or by their friends in the Christian bands Ascend the Hill, the Ember Days, or Great Awakening.[17] During rehearsals—which double as soundchecks that start two hours before each service—the leader will explain the arrangement she wants, quickly discuss parts with each musician, and identify areas where the band could vamp, extend a verse, or repeat a chorus, depending on how the Spirit directs them. Lim might provide some guidance, especially if asked, but in general he trusts the leaders and musicians on his team to prepare a worship service that satisfies both the congregation's technical expectations and its spiritual needs.

The intimacy of worship is a common theme among the Anchor's staff.[18] Lim's goal for worship is "just to be direct[ly] focused on the Lord and genuine in what we're singing. . . . I try to really encourage all my leaders and the band to lead worship by asking the Lord what he's doing and what he's saying, and roll with that, because you can't fail." He and his team pursue this goal by leaving their arrangements relatively open-ended, allowing the leader to listen to the Holy Spirit's direction and extend the song in order to prolong, heighten, or otherwise emphasize the congregation's spiritual experience. While playing, the leader will often direct the band and lyric projectionist by preemptively reciting a lyric right before shifting to the next section of the song.[19] Lim and his team gather together regularly for discipleship and worship training in which he emphasizes the spiritual foundation of leading worship. They open rehearsals with a prayer, they address their songs to God, and Lim leads each service's band through a discussion of the importance of God's presence and a prayer immediately before the service begins.

One of the Anchor's main challenges is growth and progress, as opposed to stagnation and repetition. Ban explained the Anchor's focus on worship as something that has to evolve continually if it is to remain honest and effective: "The Lord has given us worship as an avenue to connect with him, and to enter into his presence. . . . [If] you're just going through the motions or you're just trying to create a model, or a mode, [then] you can get stuck in that, not really listen and follow the Lord. . . . Having a mode and a model is easy, it's predictable, and we like that." If a specific song becomes ritualized due to its popularity with the congregation, then any spiritual connection with God through that song also becomes ritualized and, thus, inauthentic. Experiential spirituality is intended to be new, provocative, and transformative. The repetition of ritual performance subverts spirituality as a process, despite its clear meaning and significance to worship participants (see Turner and Bruner 1986; Turner 1995). Lim recognizes this as a danger and does his best to avoid it:

> No one wants to change. They find a song that they think works, and then you go with it. After a while, as good of a song as that may be—and many songs are—they lose meaning to people. It [becomes] an automatic response. . . . The intensity has to come from engaging with the Holy Spirit and communing with the Lord. It can't come from this musical moment, where we built the song so big or so dynamically or whatever that it makes you feel a certain way. That's the easy thing to get caught up in: the band does this big swell and now everyone's in it. But, can you experience this same thing in the softer moments? Well, of course. Really, at that point it's theology: Is the Lord there more during these things or less during the quieter moments? Well, we have to say no. Is the Spirit working more during the big moments? No, of course not. . . . I really don't want to plan a song that I think will just be a big song. Because, at that point, I'm doing it because I want to manipulate.

Lim's approach to resisting this danger has been to retire some popular songs and to evolve away slightly from the anthemic style that defined the Anchor's worship music for several years. "The irony," Lim told me, "is that people do want to be manipulated as much as they say they don't." Refocusing and renewing the worship experience has thus been a trial for Lim and Ban, as they are teaching their congregation how to be open to the Holy Spirit through worship in all of its manifestations and not just in the obvious, "big" moments. Some churchgoers have not reacted well and left the church because they felt that they no longer experienced an intense spiritual presence during worship at the Anchor. Others have stayed, and still more have been drawn to the church, learning to value its approach to worship, experiential spirituality, and the Christian faith without expectations born from past experiences.

The Anchor's staff is almost defiantly proud of redefining worship, subverting existing norms of pastoral accountability, eschewing formal seminary training and hierarchical interchurch relationships, and chafing under the authority of the Vineyard movement. That said, they no longer prioritize rebellion or resistance for its own sake. Indeed, a goal of Anchor Mission

U.S.A. has been to facilitate community building and interchurch support at an institutional level and thus avoid the challenges that unaffiliated, nondenominational churches face. Ban told me that for the Anchor Fellowship "to stand alone and be alone [as an unaffiliated congregation] . . . is very difficult, and it's not something that we necessarily see as a biblical model." As the Anchor Fellowship's worship services constitute resistance and renewal at the local level every Sunday, so does Anchor Mission U.S.A. at the institutional level, simultaneously resisting existing denominational hierarchies and renewing like-minded congregations. Instead of observing the boundaries that have traditionally separated Pentecostal and charismatic praxis from evangelicalism, the Anchor finds value in both the emotional and the intellectual approaches to the Christian faith. As it resists and conflates these divisive typologies, the Anchor participates in a larger project of renewing Protestantism by subverting them. Ultimately, however, theologies, ideologies, and practices at the Anchor are squarely centered in making intimate spiritual experiences available to all: Brooks told me that when outsiders ask him, "Who's your spiritual authority? Who do you guys answer to?," he replies, "Well, we answer to God."

NOTES

1. Sweeney writes that Vineyard has been instrumental in popularizing among mainline and nondenominational evangelicals a worship style—which he describes as "California-style charismatic liturgy"—that fuses charismatic praxis and evangelical theology (2005, 149–51). Versteeg explicitly links Vineyard to the Third Wave movement, which followed Pentecostalism and charismatic renewal and brought Spirit-filled praxis to existing congregations without uprooting their theologies (2010, 63). Nathan and Wilson, two Vineyard pastors, describe a similar synthesis among contemporary congregations, in which charismatic renewal empowers the ministries and theologies of traditional evangelical churches (1995, 34). See Burgess (2002) for brief discussions of the Third Wave and neocharismatic movements.

2. The Anchor worship band's anthemic rock style is best described as modern worship, which, Ingalls notes, emerged in the mid-1990s and is heavily influenced by contemporary British bands such as Coldplay, Radiohead, and U2 (2008, 140).

3. See http://www.theanchorfellowship.com.

4. Although Balmer uses the term "subculture" to describe conservative evangelicals broadly (1989, xii), my usage throughout this chapter follows Hebdige's (1979) definition and description of a subculture as a group that resists and redefines the dominant norms of mainstream culture through music, fashion, and other elements of style.

5. Prayer training, both formal and informal, is necessary for newcomers to experiential spirituality to learn how to recognize God's voice in their own heads and separate his thoughts from their own. See Luhrmann (2012) on developing and learning prayer as a skilled practice.

6. See http://www.theanchorfellowship.com/who-we-are/.

7. All quotations attributed to George Brooks are taken from an interview conducted by the author on March 7, 2010.

8. All quotations attributed to Brian Ban are taken from an interview conducted by the author on May 26, 2012.

9. Christy Brooks is George Brooks's wife and the founder of Anchor Mission–affiliated Morning After Ministries, a women-centered outreach.

10. For further discussion of the importance of festival gatherings to the Christian periphery, see Mall (2012).

11. See http://anchormissionusa.com/~anchorm/manifesto.php.

12. In this passage, Christ heals many sick individuals brought to him by townspeople who are attracted to his healing powers.

13. The Anchor closes many services with the doxology that I learned attending a Southern Baptist church during my childhood—Thomas Ken's hymn "Praise God, from Whom All Blessings Flow" (1674).

14. All quotations attributed to David Lim are taken from an interview conducted by the author on May 26, 2012.

15. Ben Crist's band, the Glorious Unseen, later signed with BEC Recordings, affiliated with the Christian label Tooth & Nail Records. "We Can Be Renewed" appears on the Glorious Unseen's album *The Hope That Lies in You* (BEC Recordings 44099, 2009).

16. "Hear Our Prayers" appears on the Glorious Unseen's album *Tonight the Stars Speak* (BEC Recordings 81136, 2007).

17. Many churches license copyrighted worship songs through Christian Copyright Licensing International (CCLI). All three of these bands, as well as Lim's project We Are Creation, record for Nashville-based Come&Live!, a nonprofit record label founded by Anchor member (and former Tooth & Nail A&R director) Chad Johnson.

18. According to Versteeg, the intimacy of worship is a broad priority throughout the Vineyard (2010, 220).

19. In practice, this sounds very similar to the "lining out" tradition of leading a congregation through a hymn without using a lyric sheet or other notation (Titon 2006).

REFERENCES

Balmer, Randall Herbert. 1989. *Mine Eyes Have Seen the Glory: A Journey into the Evangelical Subculture in America*. New York: Oxford University Press.

Burgess, Stanley M., ed. 2002. *The New International Dictionary of Pentecostal and Charismatic Movements*. Grand Rapids, Mich.: Zondervan.

Hebdige, Dick. 1979. *Subculture: The Meaning of Style*. London: Methuen.

Ingalls, Monique Marie. 2008. "Awesome in This Place: Sound, Space, and Identity in Contemporary North American Evangelical Worship." Ph.D. diss., University of Pennsylvania.

Jackson, Bill. 1999. *The Quest for the Radical Middle: A History of the Vineyard*. Cape Town: Vineyard International.

Labanow, Cory E. 2009. *Evangelicalism and the Emerging Church: A Congregational Study of a Vineyard Church*. Burlington, Vt.: Ashgate.

Luhrmann, Tanya M. 2012. *When God Talks Back: Understanding the American Evangelical Relationship with God*. New York: Alfred A. Knopf.

Mall, Andrew. 2012. "'The Stars Are Underground': Undergrounds, Mainstreams, and Christian Popular Music." Ph.D. diss., University of Chicago.

McCracken, Brett. 2010a. *Hipster Christianity: When Church and Cool Collide*. Grand Rapids, Mich.: Baker Books.

———. 2010b. "Hipster Faith." *Christianity Today*, September.

———. 2010c. "The Perils of 'Wannabe Cool' Christianity." *Wall Street Journal*, August 13.

Miller, Donald E. 1997. *Reinventing American Protestantism: Christianity in the New Millennium*. Berkeley: University of California Press.

Monteith, Andrew. 2010. "The Light and the Night: An Ethnographic Examination of Spiritual Warfare." M.A. thesis, Memorial University of Newfoundland.

Nathan, Rich, and Ken Wilson, eds. 1995. *Empowered Evangelicals: Bringing Together the Best of the Evangelical and Charismatic Worlds*. Ann Arbor, Mich.: Vine Books.

Nekola, Anna E. 2009. "Between This World and the Next: The Musical 'Worship Wars' and Evangelical Ideology in the United States, 1960–2005." Ph.D. diss., University of Wisconsin–Madison.

Romanowski, William D. 1996. *Pop Culture Wars: Religion and the Role of Entertainment in American Life*. Downers Grove, Ill.: InterVarsity Press.

Sweeney, Douglas A. 2005. *The American Evangelical Story: A History of the Movement*. Grand Rapids, Mich.: Baker Academic.

Titon, Jeff Todd. 2006. "'Tuned Up with the Grace of God': Music and Experience Among Old Regular Baptists." In *Music in American Religious Experience*, edited by Philip V. Bohlman, Edith L. Blumhofer, and Maria M. Chow, 311–34. New York: Oxford University Press.

Turner, Victor. 1995. *The Ritual Process: Structure and Anti-structure*. New York: Aldine de Gruyter.

Turner, Victor, and Edward M. Bruner, eds. 1986. *The Anthropology of Experience*. Urbana: University of Illinois Press.

Versteeg, Peter G. A. 2010. *The Ethnography of a Dutch Pentecostal Church: Vineyard Utrecht and the International Charismatic Movement*. Lewiston, N.Y.: Edwin Mellen Press.

10

Hillsong Abroad: Tracing the Songlines of Contemporary Pentecostal Music

Mark Evans

Christian music has long been a migrational and often colonizing force (Zahn 1996). Historically, the arrival of church music in foreign lands and/or indigenous communities through proselytization has sometimes proven problematic due to homogenizing forces associated with the music's adoption. This was particularly true of the missional hymnody that flowed from the U.K. and Europe into the Pacific region (Webb 2005; Love and Kaeppler 1998). This migratory force of contemporary church music (what I call "congregational song") is now felt to an unprecedented degree through the use of mass media (Bossius 2011), the involvement of the global music industry, and the emergence of Pentecostal megachurches. As a result, contemporary congregational song has the power to inculcate Christian ideologies and inform practices of musical consumption worldwide.

This chapter is particularly focused on the way in which Australian Christian music—namely, that produced by Hillsong Church in Sydney—has crossed geographical and theological borders around the world. After briefly considering its emergence and diffusion in Australian settings, the chapter goes on to trace the songlines[1] of Hillsong music within different churches and denominations in parts of Scandinavia and in particular Zulu churches in Durban, South Africa. It considers the ways in which the music has been adopted, adapted, and received in these churches. The chapter argues that Hillsong music, and music from the other global Christian "brands," is no longer strictly about message; its music portrays notions of religious freedom but essentially projects a cultural and religious identity. Various consequences of this musical globalization are considered, including its effect on local musical creativity. This chapter will also analyze the musical performance of Hillsong music around the world, seeking to ascertain the musical and lyrical alterations necessary for this vibrant migratory practice to have developed.

The effects of the music's migration are considered through a variety of methodological frameworks. The primary method involved participant observation (see Shelemay 1997, 197) of Finnish and Swedish churches over a five-month period (February–June 2009).[2] While preference was given to Hillsong-branded churches, and Pentecostal churches in general, a broad sweep of denominational churches was conducted in order to ascertain the level of penetration that Hillsong music had achieved. This participant observation was reinforced through detailed ethnographic interviews with various other participants, those involved in producing the music internationally, and those in Australia responsible for ensuring its transcultural appeal. In South Africa, two participant-observation research visits were undertaken, in 2008 and 2011, to Zulu churches in and around Durban.[3] Again, interviews and informal conversations were held with congregation members and music team members. Furthermore, traditional analytical methodologies drawn from a variety of disciplines, including theology, popular music studies, musicology, performance studies, and historiography, have been used. Such interdisciplinarity is useful in contextualizing the construction and reception of contemporary congregational music.

Hillsong Church: The Evolution of a Global Megachurch

Hillsong Church, a world-renowned center for contemporary worship songwriting and production, is part of the growing international Pentecostal movement. As I have noted elsewhere, "The growth in contemporary forms of congregational song can be directly linked to the proliferation and increased influence of Pentecostal churches worldwide. Pentecostal churches are by far the dominant producers of contemporary congregational music, and often have the larger congregation sizes and matrixes of ideologically aligned networks to support flourishing production centres" (Evans 2006, 87).

Hillsong Church began its life in August 1983 as the Hills Christian Life Centre, located in Castle Hill, part of Sydney's developing northwest suburban district. It was an outreach of Christian Life Centre Sydney (an affiliated member of the Assemblies of God denomination). Hills CLC initially met in a local high school with a congregation of seventy. Today, Hillsong Church (renamed to reinforce its musical identity) is Australia's largest church, with a congregation currently in excess of twenty-three thousand people on any given Sunday (Wagner 2014). Along with the addition of Australian churches in Brisbane and Melbourne, Hillsong has recently expanded its "brand" internationally to include churches in London, Paris, New York, Cape Town, Kiev, Moscow, Konstanz, Amsterdam, Copenhagen, and Stockholm.

Sociologist Marion Maddox states that this process of international "reproduction" is a feature of the new megachurch. In discussing megachurches such as Hillsong, Christian City Church (which claims 230 churches worldwide), and Bill Hybels's Willow Creek Association, she notes that "despite the differences of language and surrounding national cultures, [churches within these groups] exhibit remarkable uniformity of liturgy and presentation." She goes on to observe that "megachurches . . . do not merely passively absorb or reflect aspects of their social context, but are both deliberate appropriators of and vital contributors to it" (2012, 152). One of the most pronounced of these contributions is music, with megachurches often utilizing their own music in their churches worldwide, particularly when they have a strong music production and publishing arm.

In keeping with secular business models, megachurches work hard to establish and maintain their brand. Hillsong Church is a case in point, developing "a highly sophisticated and responsive method of branding that communicates its theological emphasis, corporate identity, and target audience" (Riches and Wagner 2012, 18). While not the only contributor, music is often a vital part of the branding strategy of megachurches, and this is certainly true in the case of Hillsong: "Hillsong's music 'product' is one (if not *the*) main driver of its growth—a glocalized offering adopted by Christian churches all over the world. Like McDonald's, Hillsong focuses on the consistency of its product, and achieves it by standardizing production and delivery. . . . It offers a global musical product mix that is positioned through extra-musical communication and adapted by its worshippers through the frame of the brand in the local contexts in which it is offered and received" (Wagner 2014, 4). The following section maps out how Hillsong's musical brand has been constructed.

Branding a Local Pentecostal Church Globally

A significant and signature part of Hillsong Church, especially since 1992, has been its music production and publishing arm, Hillsong Music Australia

(HMA). Hillsong Church (as Hills CLC) recorded its first album of congregational song, *Spirit and Truth*, in 1988, but the first to be marketed outside Australia was *Show Your Glory* in 1991. In 1992, the church released its first live[4] congregational album, *The Power of Your Love*, the title track of which still features on CCLI's top twenty-five congregational song lists around the world, including those in South Africa.[5] Since then, Hillsong has released one congregational album every year, in addition to numerous other albums and resources. It claims annual worldwide sales in excess of two million albums and represents one of the dominant Christian music producers worldwide.[6]

Most commentators attribute the success of HMA to former worship pastor Darlene Zschech, its face and voice since 1995 and the architect of spin-off projects such as Hillsong United. As the *Sydney Morning Herald* put it, "Darlene Zschech [is] the understated brain and voice behind Hillsong music. . . . [She] has created a brand in inspiration that is taking the Christian world by storm. Whether or not you like the genre, it's hard not to conclude that Zschech and Hillsong United are Australia's most successful music publishing export, with hundreds of thousands singing their songs every weekend around the world" (Cameron 2011). Zschech's international smash hit "Shout to the Lord"—a song that remains influential around the world and may well become the "Amazing Grace" of the future due to its recognition and prevalent use in Pentecostal and mainstream churches (Evans 2006, 120–21)—was chosen by the producers of the U.S. television blockbuster *American Idol Gives Back* to conclude their program in 2008. It became the "world's most downloaded song in the world's biggest music market on that day" (Cameron 2011).

Hillsong music is currently distributed to more than eighty-seven countries worldwide. HMA distributes directly to Christian retail stores and in recent times has had a strong presence in secular music retail stores as well. One of the most powerful outlets for Hillsong music abroad has been online stores—for instance, iTunes,[7] Amazon, and CDON.com, which is extremely influential in Scandinavian countries. This online distribution, combined with ready access to worship services, seminars, new songs, and concerts via YouTube and social media, has quickly spread the Hillsong brand[8] from its suburban Australian roots. This confirms Thomas Bossius's assertion that "[contemporary Anglophone] worship culture can . . . be said to be a media-dense culture" (2011, 53).

The global spread of Hillsong music has been a deliberate strategy of the church, one that it has sought to work into the nature of the music itself, most notably through familiar lyrics that can be understood in churches around the world, but also by creating a "Hillsong sound" that seeks to communicate a bright, contemporary, victorious Christianity. The essence of this sound has long revolved around the production aesthetics of the albums. Hillsong releases tightly produced, polished albums that are more reminiscent of the brightness and perfection often associated with Nashville production than rock and pop from Australia. Live congregational albums are meticulously overdubbed to create perfect performance and arrangement. Part of the "victorious" nature of the sound can be attributed to its density of texture. Congregational albums feature standard pop instrumentation, but often with multiple keyboard players, multiple guitarists, and a brass section. Lead vocalists are backed by a team of backing vocalists as well as a full choir. As a result, Hillsong music is marked by a "wall of sound" aesthetic, particularly in the climactic sections, which listeners find rousing and anthemic.

In attempting to explain Hillsong's transnational orientation, head of Hillsong Music Publishing Steve McPherson notes, "I do believe we initially set out to write music for our congregation but as time went on and we saw the impact our songs were having across all denominations, we became more and more aware of the responsibility and the privilege to be speaking into the broader church, and I believe our songwriting changed accordingly. Our focus went from being purely local to global."[9] The initial migration McPherson speaks of here was one from a local Pentecostal church in Sydney to numerous denominations and churches throughout Australia. Notably, many churches that would not necessary adhere to the theology of Hillsong Church were nonetheless content to sing its music. This speaks to the generalist theological foundation of the music (discussed below), which allowed it to be used in a wide range of evangelical churches, from traditional mainstream churches to smaller breakaway denominations and groups. The momentum this created allowed Hillsong to quickly dominate an emerging market and influence congregational song trends throughout the country. Hillsong clearly saw the economic benefits of its "resources" being utilized in the global church. If the music it created could cross stringent denominational boundaries in Australia, then there was no reason not to orient the music toward a broader, global Christian church. There was also a branding benefit, as the church (and the fullness of its vision and ethos) was now globally recognized via its congregational song. The change in songwriting that McPherson refers to accords with a movement toward less locally defined sounds and lyrics. Gone, for example, are songs such as "Great Southland" and others that signaled any sense of Australian-ness, replaced with songs that would sit comfortably within various denominations and churches around the world (see Evans 2006). The following sections trace how and why Hillsong music flows into various contexts by using case studies drawn from Scandinavian and South African churches.

Case Study 1: Hillsong in Scandinavia

Walking around the streets of Trondheim, Norway, in 2005, I was struck by a large poster in the front of a pharmacist shop advertising the latest Hillsong congregational album. That music from a local Sydney church that I knew well was being promoted in a pharmacy (itself a bit odd) in the back streets of a city on the other side of the world was intriguing. From then on, I began questioning how the songlines of contemporary congregational music were formed and shaped. In 2009, I was fortunate to be offered a visiting research fellowship at the University of Turku in Finland. This fellowship allowed me to investigate how Hillsong music had penetrated Scandinavia, with a partic- ular focus on Finland. Over five months of research, I visited all of the major denominational churches in the city of Turku, as well as those in Helsinki that advertised contemporary worship services on their websites. I was also able to visit Hillsong Stockholm soon after its launch.

Hillsong music has been popular in Scandinavian countries for several years. In Sweden, two Hillsong tracks feature in the Christian Copyright Licensing International (CCLI) report's period 408 chart for Sweden (Zschech's "Shout to the Lord" at number one and Reuben Morgan's "You Are Holy" at number seventeen). Popular in Sweden and Norway initially, Hillsong music has also found a place among some Finnish Christians (further discussion on that below). In part, the spread of Hillsong music in the region was directly related to its physical presence on tour, as a staff member from Turku United Methodist Church, Sarah Tiainen, indicated: "One of the main worship leaders from Hillsong [Reuben Morgan] came to a European conference at Uppsala [Sweden] a few years ago and that really helped to spread the music. He was a huge hit."[10] Hillsong "tours" its annual conferences internationally, taking its key music personnel along (for example, Darlene Zschech,[11] Reuben Morgan, and Marty Sampson). Hillsong United, the youth-oriented worship band, also tours the globe extensively, sometimes performing the same songs as those found on congregational releases. This international exposure often occurs in conjunction with key Pentecostal and/or evangelical figures (for example, Joyce Meyer, with whom Zschech works extensively) and helps establish and promote the Hillsong brand and expose its music to expanding Christian networks. The Word of Life conference to which Tiainen referred was for church leaders throughout Scandinavia (and Europe more widely), who were then able to take music that had influenced them at the conference back to their own congregations.

Through five months of participant-observation research, it became apparent that Hillsong music is most popular with Swedes, Swedish-speaking Finns, and charismatic churches in Scandinavia. These groups have had longer exposure to global Pentecostal music, as evidenced by the history of CCLI reports for Sweden, and thus more time to adopt music from Hillsong as their dominant music repertoire. There is some Hillsong music present in the Lutheran Church, although this tends to be truer for regional areas rather than major cities. The main demographic for the music is the twenty-to-thirty-five age group, which fits neatly with those who first heard Hillsong when the music became known in Scandinavia. The congregational albums and Hillsong United releases are equally popular, with Tiainen observing that "people like it because it is a brand." She qualified this by noting that Finnish Christians like to feel part of the "global Christian culture" and Hillsong represented that for them.

The most obvious incarnation of Hillsong in Scandinavia was the launch of Hillsong Stockholm in early 2009. Formerly known as Passion Church, the church renamed itself Hillsong Stockholm and adopted all of the branding insignias of its Australian parent church. When I attended the church in February 2009, only weeks after its Hillsong "debut," the similarities to the parent church were striking, to the point that, apart from the mixing of Swedish and English, there was little discernible difference. All but one of the songs sung were Hillsong compositions from the latest album release, and all were sung in English. As music team member John[12] told me, this was not uncommon: "About 90 percent, probably, of the songs we sing are from Hillsong." But John did not interpret this as musical imperialism: "We sung all these songs anyway, so [it] wasn't a big change for us to become a Hillsong church. We basically were the same." Thus, the cultural change was minimized because the church had been singing Hillsong's music and using similar liturgical structures for a long time prior. Given this shared cultural repertoire, it was an ideal candidate to become officially related to the Australian church. The songs at Hillsong Stockholm are usually sung in their original English, that being the preference of the senior church pastors, although John noted that sometimes someone will translate one into Swedish and "that is really good." That being said, he did feel that it "would be great if we sang more songs in Swedish." The issue of translation frequently accompanies Hillsong's migration and will be discussed further below.

In Turku United Methodist Church, Hillsong music has been prominent since the 2000s. This church represents a particular case study; although located in Turku, Finland, it caters specifically to Swedish-speaking Finns and conducts services in this language. Translation into English is available at every service, as the church also caters to many international students from the University of Turku, the majority of whom speak neither Swedish nor Finnish. Tiainen recalled that she first heard Hillsong "in late 1990s at confirmation camp. 'Shout to the Lord' was the first song we did, and it became an instant hit. We first sung it in English but someone soon translated it into Swedish." Presently, the church sings a selection of Hillsong tracks—both popular hits from the mid- to late 1990s and more recent compositions. The songs are normally sung in their original English, although Swedish translations are becoming more common. The church also regularly uses major hits from North American and U.K. songwriters, as well as popular Swedish hymns.

As evidence that standard denominational tags do not always apply, the Pentecostal church in Turku, Turun Helluntaiseurakunta, featured no music at all from Hillsong or the "standard" international Pentecostal repertoire when I visited in March 2009. More typical were songs associated with various praise collections from the 1980s (*Ring of Praise, Mission Praise, Scripture in Song,* and so forth), such as the well-known "As the Deer" (Martin Nystrom, 1984), and hymns sung in Finnish. In interviews, congregation members revealed that they were aware of Hillsong and other global Pentecostal music and very partial to it; however, they did not feel that they had the resources to be able to perform it. For instance, musical worship times most often consisted of a single song leader singing to backing tracks provided by an iPod—with each song individually queued up as required. The lack of a music team was viewed as an impediment to introducing music from Hillsong and similar churches.

A visit to the Helsinki Vineyard Church[13] in April 2009 revealed that the migratory element of contemporary congregational song is not exclusive to Hillsong but extends to other church "brands." Finland is a small country with a population of just over five million. Although roughly 80 percent of Finns identify as Christian, in reality this is a fairly secularized society, with low rates of church attendance[14]—evidence of what Marcus Moberg considers the "increasing privatization of Finnish religiosity" (2011, 50). Yet, within this country, there are two strong musical influences from megachurch brands, and a third if one includes the many songs produced by Soul Survivor, a youth conference in the U.K., that I heard performed in Finnish churches over a five-month period. At the Sunday Vineyard service I attended, all of the songs were sung in English, with the exception of one that was sung in Finnish and then repeated in English. The worship leader of the church was from the U.K., and as such there was a reliance not only on Vineyard songs but also on songs from Soul Survivor. The songs performed during the service were "Joy" by Jon Ellis (1997), "Everlasting God" by Chris Tomlin (2006), "Come and Fill Me Up" by Brian Doerksen (Vineyard, 1990), and "Surrender" by Marc James (Vineyard, 2000), which featured the partial Finnish translation. These case studies in Scandinavia show that the internationalization of several powerful brands—especially that of Hillsong—is one important aspect of the songlines of contemporary congregational music.

Case Study 2: Hillsong Meets Zulu Durban

In South Africa, Hillsong music has been popular for over a decade. The current CCLI top twenty-five[15] worship songs for the country include four Hillsong tracks, including Zschech's "Shout to the Lord" at number one. As interviewee Thanda Mthembu reported of KwaMashu Christian Centre, a predominantly Zulu church in Durban, "We sing several [Hillsong songs in services]; the famous chorus that most churches sing is 'Lord I Give You My Heart.'"[16] Here, Mthembu recognizes Reuben Morgan's song, which features at number eighteen on the CCLI chart for South Africa. What is notable about the four Hillsong tracks on this chart is that they all come from the mid-1990s (including Zschech's number one, which was released in 1995). Reasons for this relatively slow incorporation include the distance created by church members' comparatively lower socioeconomic position and a lack of established distribution pathways. Akin to the testimony of Scandinavian congregation members, the Durban-based music team members with whom I spoke indicated that most Hillsong music is brought into Zulu churches (such as KwaMashu Christian Centre and His Glory Worship Tabernacle) via individuals who acquire CDs or sheet music personally. Given that this can be a relatively rare event, as congregants are unable to keep up to date with the regular Hillsong releases due to economic constraints and a lack of availability, it is understandable that there is often a time lag in when the music reaches the church. That all of the popular Hillsong tracks in South Africa came from one particular period in the mid-1990s indicates that, at that time at least, someone had a knowledge of Hillsong and the means to bring its music into Zulu churches.[17]

Recent data provided by CCLI suggests that South African churches may have moved away from Hillsong tracks, focusing more on releases from Vineyard and Soul Survivor. This general sense was confirmed at services of His Glory Worship Tabernacle that I attended in June 2011, where no Hillsong music was sung at all. Music team members reported that it was rare to sing Hillsong material, their preference being to improvise songs based on the day's theme and type up the words live, on projector, as the song evolved. Hillsong United toured South Africa in February/March 2013, five years after its previous tour there. During that earlier tour, it even recorded a live track in Johannesburg ("Look to You") for its worldwide compilation *The I Heart Revolution: With Hearts as One*, which was released on March 8, 2008. Whether the general movement away from Hillsong music in South Africa continues in the wake of the launch of Hillsong Cape Town and the recent Hillsong United tour remains to be seen.

As I learned from conversations with congregation members in Durban, there is a sense in which all the music from "elsewhere" is grouped together in their minds, irrespective of any brand association. All of the songs imported from Australia, the United States, and the U.K. are sung in their original English, which Mthembu pointed out is important "because there are people in church who can't sing African songs only, but English songs accommodate everybody in the church." This speaks to a desire to accommodate what is essentially a minority English-speaking segment. So, in one sense, the music has a very functional role. But it is also seen as having a strong sense of meaning and purpose. Steve McPherson, head of Hillsong Music Publishing, views meaning as a crucial element in Hillsong's success: "There's no question that our songs have a lyrical flavour that is uniquely 'Hillsong' but we do try to keep our songs based in scripture and sound theology, so that alone is a huge factor in why we see our songs cross over cultural and denominational boundaries." This lyrical solidity is independent of any uniquely Australian flavor. As McPherson notes, "There is a rawness, and a light-heartedness, that is uniquely Australian, but it is subtle to the listener." Though clearly hard to qualify, it could be argued that overseas listeners hear this lightheartedness as energetic and vibrant—words often used to describe Hillsong music by overseas interviewees.

One of the most popular uses of Hillsong music in Durban actually occurs outside the church. As Mthembu reported, "Almost all the Christian people

I know play Hillsong music in their cars, houses, offices, laptops, and in the camp [township]." Interviewees revealed that the use of congregational song as an accompaniment to daily life activities is a common feature of Christianity in South Africa. However, despite the music's frequent function as a lifestyle product, McPherson maintains that this is not the primary purpose of Hillsong's music: "We have always and will always see the main purpose of our product, or as we prefer to call them 'resources,' as being exactly that, resources for the church. However there is no doubt that people purchase our resources for other reasons, whether that be for personal devotional listening, inspiration or purely for the love of the music." Acknowledging again that music enters the international settings studied via personal introduction and prompting, I would contend that this personal saturation outside the church is vital for the music to ultimately migrate *into* the church, its intended destination. Not only must the music reach foreign shores, but it must also be integrated into the lives of active Christians who have the ability and means to bring the music into the church (or at least to the attention of the musical personnel). This personal engagement with Hillsong music has prompted the church to film and release a documentary that details the role of its music in the lives of people around the world, particularly those living in the developing world. McPherson commented, "We are thrilled when we hear of how our music is touching the lives of people in far reaching places of the earth. It was part of the motivation behind the iHeart Revolution documentary [which] follows the Hillsong United team around the world to places such as Brazil, Rwanda, Columbia, and others, focusing on the believers in these areas, looking at how they are impacting their world, and also giving a glimpse of what the impact of these songs are on these people." While notionally separate from the main congregational album releases, the role and influence of Hillsong United, particularly on Christian churches in the developing world, deserves future research and analysis of its own.

Global Flows: A Cost to Local Songwriting/Creativity?

One possible consequence of the global migration of popular Christian congregational song is the disappearance of the local within congregational song. I have noted elsewhere the need for contemporary congregational song to differentiate between the universal and the idiosyncratic. If we take the universal to be represented by Hillsong and other megachurches, then the idiosyncratic becomes the individual nuances of denominations, churches, revivals, missions, and the like (Evans 2006, 162). In Finnish churches, for example, local elements might most obviously be represented lyrically, in references to landscape, seasonal change, or individual church teaching. In Turku United Methodist Church, there was consistent biblical teaching on the family of God and Christian unity, a powerful message given that many congregants were far from home and family. There are also possibilities for localizing musical style, perhaps by integrating popular genres or instrumentation native to the area. Finland is one of the world's most ardent consumers of hard rock and metal music in all its subgenres. Thus, music with heavier, denser, guitar-based arrangements often resonated more with some demographics of the church who listened to heavy metal music for recreation.

For reasons such as these, local songs specific to congregations, churches, or missions remain important. This importance was a point keenly addressed by those interviewed for this study. Tiainen noted, "I would love to see people influenced by what God is doing here, by writing their own songs, and creating an environment to praise God or sing our agony. I think both are needed." And Hillsong Stockholm team member John reported, "Some of us are writing songs, and others in Sweden too, but we are not very good at bringing our songs into the house [of worship]." By this, John acknowledged the disparity, most likely in quality, between locally written songs and those carefully crafted and produced by HMA. It becomes almost impossible for local songwriters to bring their own songs into the "house"—the live congregational gathering—because their music is not regarded as "equal" to the imported music. In part, this is a problem of experience and ability, but it also sounds a warning that unequal resources may be hard to overcome. Many of the key congregational song producers around the world distribute and market their product on such a scale that smaller independent releases often go unnoticed. Unlike the secular music industry, where smaller markets are encouraging independent talents through industry awards programs, private gig sales, and digital delivery systems (see Evans and Crowdy 2005), congregational song runs the risk of alienating emergent artists to the point that the genre itself suffers. What would be beneficial is an engagement with the local as different and valuable, rather than local churches only attempting to replicate the sound imported under the banner of Hillsong. John Lindenbaum makes a similar argument in relation to contemporary Christian music (CCM) in the United States, where, over the years, the city of Nashville has become akin to a megachurch with its own prescribed "sound": "The most stylistically and lyrically inventive forms of CCM tend to originate outside Nashville, while much Nashville-produced CCM ascribes to tried-and-true song structures, simple almost-clichéd lyrics, and radio-friendly studio polish" (2009, 288).

It is fair to assume that this issue of local songwriters struggling to have their music played is not restricted to Scandinavian churches. Rather, it is a logical consequence of the globalizing forces of contemporary congregational song producers and the various megachurches that drive them. From a primary data survey of Pentecostal churches in Australia, Daniel Robinson has found that 97.6 percent of them perform Hillsong music in their services (2011, 116). This correlates to figures from the United States that reveal the similarly heavy influence of music from the Association of Vineyard Churches, as "it is estimated that . . . eighty percent of all white Protestant churches . . . include Vineyard songs in their public worship" (Basden 2004, 143). A similar phenomenon has occurred in Canada, where "many Pentecostal churches now view [Toronto's] Airport Vineyard–style worship as the only legitimate worship. . . . Their focus of energy is to replicate it in their churches" (Careless 1999). Perhaps this influence would be less problematic if the Airport Vineyard Church was constructing corporate worship tools designed to specifically reach the Canadian psyche. However, although it is the largest producer of congregational music in Canada, much of its music is simply Vineyard music from below the border that has been recorded in Toronto or given an international gloss to serve Vineyard churches the world over. It is this music that migrates into Scandinavian settings, only to be further internationalized in its presentation.

It does not have to be a one-way flow, however, and research has shown that local and global music cultures can coexist. Even in churches dominated by the immigration of music from the megachurches, local song production can flourish. Despite 97.6 percent of Pentecostal Australian churches surveyed using Hillsong music, Robinson also found that 66 percent of those churches included music written by members of their own worship teams (2011, 116). The development of local music production in the face of global music flows is something to which future research should pay attention.

Global Flows: Issues of Translation

Another recurring theme to come out of the research was the issue of translation. For many Scandinavian churches in particular, this was an ever-present struggle. Two factors complicate translation: the melodic contour of the song and the language into which one is seeking to translate it. Translations can either help a song work powerfully in a local setting or destroy the original power of the song. As Tiainen noted, whether translation works "depends on the song. If it's a good translation, then it is like, 'wow,' and it speaks to the heart of the congregation. But a bad translation can ruin the song, and then you should use the original." For Tiainen, translation is ineffective when the words do not fit the melody or are inappropriate in meaning. The former challenge is particularly pertinent to the Finnish language, in which even simple words can be polysyllabic: "It is so hard to translate into Finnish. You often need to alter the melodies to do it." Thus, translation becomes a path to local ownership, though at some expense. Lap Yin So (2011) has spoken of similar frustrations that plague the Chinese church in Hong Kong. He reported that congregants prefer to sing in English, for they feel that the language allows for greater emotional meaning to be conveyed. It also avoids the grammatical complexity inherent in the Chinese language and the pronunciation problems that arise when Mandarin songs are sung in Cantonese.

In all such examples, additions and alterations must be made to the musical properties of the songs to enable the language to work within them. In a sense, there is a degree of musical composition, or at least arrangement, that must take place. Similarly, the act of choosing an appropriate replacement for an English word, or even the attempt to create a similar sentiment overall, involves a degree of artistic choice. Hillsong itself is keenly aware of the problems, benefits, and possible creative ambiguities that arise as a result of translation. McPherson explained, "People like to worship God in their native tongue and so to truly resource the body of Christ, globally with songs, we cannot be limited to English alone. We plan to put more and more focus into this area in the coming years, with more non-English recordings and other resources." However, while initially framing its translation efforts as a benevolent gift to the world, McPherson went on to discuss Hillsong's desire to exert control over the final product: "We are actively involved in the translations of our songs, and if not involved directly, we have engaged sub-publishers and/or translators who work under our strict guidelines to approve and create translations on our behalf. Translations are extremely important to us." While protecting its brand and theological position is no doubt in Hillsong's corporate interest, it is doubtful that Hillsong will be able to stem the tide of local translations as its product continues to spread to churches throughout the world. The history of congregational song importation contains examples of local cultures adapting music to local customs and translating original lyrics into vernacular tongues (Love and Kaeppler 1998). Such examples abound throughout the Pacific Islands, where English and German hymnody was introduced and quickly manipulated to suit local custom and tradition (see Dowley 2011). Despite Hillsong's initiatives in this area, the fact remains that much translation takes place at a local, informal level. Songs are often brought into the church by individuals who own CD recordings. Translations are made from these when a church or individual team member decides that vernacular translations are achievable. Consequently, there is often local variation between translations of the same song. It might be that the (re)localization of the global is the next key step for the expansion and health of the global Christian church.

Conclusions

In tracing the songlines of contemporary congregational song, we discover several important facets of this migration. The first is the speed and reach with which music from Pentecostal megachurches, no matter where they are located, is able to traverse the globe. This is largely due to mass media, social media, and the ideology of Pentecostal megachurches, which emphasize the importance of actively contributing their own music to the cultures in which they plant themselves. We see that in order for music from megachurches such as Hillsong to achieve the widest reach, songs must necessarily be stripped of identifiers that would mark them as belonging to a particular geographical location or denomination (Wagner 2014). As with other historical migrations of church music, some churches adapt the music, out of either necessity (via translation) or artistic choice. This should not be a surprise; Christians have been adopting and adapting dominant congregational song cultures for their own benefit for centuries. It makes sense that Pentecostal music is the latest vehicle for that expression, given its reach, exposure, and popularity around the world.

Moreover, Pentecostal Christians are using the music they receive from the megachurch brands to connect and unify themselves with other elements of the church. As Tiainen noted, "I think Hillsong has blessed us a lot and inspired young people to think about church music. There is this global church going around the world so global culture means that Hillsong works around the world." The advance of a global Pentecostalism is a powerful identifier. As Butler has found in his work among Haitian churchgoers, "Pentecostals are seen as connected to a more extensive, worldwide community of Christian believers" (2008, 55).

This chapter's analysis of global songlines reveals the potential for future congregational song. The ability of megachurches to disseminate their music internationally and of local churches to then add their own nuances might lead to the genuine development of the local within the global. New musical expressions of faith may arise as a result. Feeding these musical expressions back into the megachurches could expand musical and theological horizons enormously. As Gordon Lynch reminds us, the global reach of formerly localized worship scenes "creates cultural conditions in which certain alternative religious identities and ideologies can be transmitted across national boundaries to create the possibility of new, alternate religious transnational networks" (2006, 483). These networks could speak to the particular and simultaneously engage the world.

NOTES

1. Although drawn from Aboriginal Australia, the term "songlines" has a strong resonance with the ideas in this chapter. Variously interpreted by different Aboriginal communities, this term is most often deployed to "refer to the musical expression of geographical movement associated with ancestral journeys across vast distances" (Toner 2007, 172). The physicality of the term, emphasizing every rock, tree, and water hole along the journey (Hayes 2007), combined with ancestral spirituality and eternal purpose, makes for a good fit with notions of global Christian music.

2. This research was kindly sponsored by the Department of Cultural History at the University of Turku.

3. Many thanks to research assistant Lauren Young for her work and engagement in the 2008 research project.

4. All live congregational albums feature extensive overdubbing and postproduction. The clarity and vibrancy for which Hillsong recordings have become renowned are simply not achievable in a purely live, large venue recording.

5. CCLI was initially established to assist churches and musicians with copyright licensing (including the collection and dispersal of funds). It now offers a range of services including video licenses, online subscription services for worship music, and an online television station that broadcasts worship music performances. See www.ccli.com for the full lists of top twenty-five songs from many countries around the world.

6. For more historical context on HMA and Hillsong Church, see Evans (2006).

7. Hillsong releases often perform extremely well in download sales, even in comparison to secular pop and rock releases. *Hillsong Live! This Is Our God* (2008) was the sixth most downloaded album across all genres on the first day of its digital release (see Spinhouse 2008). Hillsong United's album *Across the Earth: Tear Down the Walls* (2009) did even better, becoming the number one downloaded album on release in the United States and Australia.

8. For more on the notion of Hillsong as a brand, see Wagner (2014).

9. Unless otherwise stipulated, all quotes from Steve McPherson are taken from email communication with the author on June 25, 2009.

10. Unless otherwise stipulated, all quotes from Sarah Tiainen are taken from an interview with the author on June 12, 2009.

11. Before her official retirement from the church in 2010.

12. "John" preferred not to give his real name, which, I believe, speaks to some of the tension and nervousness that surrounded the launch of Hillsong Stockholm. During our interview in February 2009, it was clear that John was keen to take his place on the Hillsong team and reflect the ethos of his pastor and parent church. He did, however, have opinions about the music culture that he wanted to share and was trying to ensure that he did so in a way that honored his (new) church.

13. The history of the Vineyard movement in Finland is not well documented; however, Thomas Bossius documents the growth and dominance of the Vineyard movement in Sweden (2011, 56–61).

14. See "Finland in Facts" (2014) for full details.

15. See http://www.ccli.co.za/resources/top25/ for the full list.

16. Unless otherwise indicated, all quotes from Thanda Mthembu are taken from an email interview with the author on June 18, 2009, or personal communications with the author in June 2011.

17. While none of my field research consultants was able to recall a particular individual responsible for introducing Hillsong music, the most likely explanation involves a women's shelter in Durban run by Youth for Christ. The shelter, which mainly houses girls from KwaMashu, is staffed by short-term volunteers from around the world (particularly Australia and the United States) and South African counterparts (often from KwaMashu Zulu churches). It is probable that a volunteer brought along Hillsong CDs and introduced the music to his or her Zulu colleagues.

REFERENCES

Basden, Paul. 2004. *Exploring the Worship Spectrum: 6 Views*. Grand Rapids, Mich.: Zondervan.

Bossius, Thomas. 2011. "Shout to the Lord: Christian Worship Music as Popular Culture, Church Music, and Lifestyle." In *Religion and Popular Music in Europe: New Expressions of Sacred and Secular Identity*, edited by Thomas Bossius, Andreas Häger, and Keith Kahn-Harris, 51–70. New York: I.B. Tauris.

Butler, Melvin L. 2008. "The Weapons of Our Warfare: Music, Positionality, and Transcendence Among Haitian Pentecostals." *Caribbean Studies* 36 (2): 23–64.

Cameron, Ross. 2011. "The Hills Are Alive with the Sound of Music—and It's Uplifting." *Sydney Morning Herald*, July 7, 11.

Careless, S. 1999. "Former Pentecostal Leader Becomes Anglican." *Anglican Journal*, April.

Dowley, Timothy. 2011. *The Lion Companion to Christian Music*. London: Lion.

Evans, Mark. 2006. *Open Up the Doors: Music in the Modern Church*. London: Equinox.

Evans, Mark, and Denis Crowdy. 2005. "Wrangling the Figures: Marketing an Industry at the Margins." In *Markets and Margins: Australian Country Music*, vol. 3, edited by Mark Evans and Geoff Walden, 1–22. Gympie: AICM Press.

"Finland in Facts." 2014. This Is Finland. http://finland.fi/Public/default.aspx?contentid=160032&nodeid=44491&culture=en-US.

Hayes, Deborah. 2007. "Visions of the Great South Land in Peter Sculthorpe's Opera *Quiros.*" In *The Soundscapes of Australia: Music, Place, and Spirituality*, edited by Fiona Richards, 147–64. Aldershot: Ashgate.

So, Lap Yin. 2011. "How Song Language Difference Affects Musical Worship Experiences Among Chinese Christians in UK." Paper presented at Christian Congregational Music: Local and Global Perspectives, Ripon College Cuddesdon, September 1–3.

Lindenbaum, John. 2009. "The Production of Contemporary Christian Music: A Geographical Perspective." In *Sound, Society, and the Geography of Popular Music*, edited by Ola Johansson and Thomas Bell, 281–94. Burlington, Vt.: Ashgate.

Love, J. W., and Adrienne Kaeppler. 1998. *The Garland Encyclopedia of World Music: Australia and the Pacific Islands*. New York: Routledge.

Lynch, Gordon. 2006. "The Role of Popular Music in the Construction of Alternate Spiritual Identities and Ideologies." *Journal for the Scientific Study of Religion* 45 (4): 481–88.

Maddox, Marion. 2012. "'In the Goofy Parking Lot': Growth Churches as a Novel Religious Form for Late Capitalism." *Social Compass* 59 (2): 146–58.

Moberg, Marcus. 2011. "Christian Metal in Finland: Institutional Religion and Popular Music in the Midst of Religious Change." In *Religion and Popular Music in Europe: New Expressions of Sacred and Secular Identity*, edited by Thomas Bossius, Andreas Häger, and Keith Kahn-Harris, 31–50. New York: I.B. Tauris.

Riches, Tanya, and Tom Wagner. 2012. "The Evolution of Hillsong Music: From Australian Pentecostal Congregation into Global Brand." *Australian Journal of Communication* 39 (1): 17–36.

Robinson, Daniel. 2011. *Contemporary Worship Singers: Context, Culture, Environment, and Voice.* Ph.D. diss., Queensland Conservatorium, Griffith University.

Shelemay, Kay Kaufman. 1997. "The Ethnomusicologist, Ethnographic Method, and the Transmission of Tradition." In *Shadows in the Field: New Perspectives for Fieldwork in Ethnomusicology*, edited by Gregory F. Barz and Timothy J. Cooley, 189–204. New York: Oxford University Press.

Spinhouse. 2008. "Hillsong Shares Top 10 iTunes Albums Download Success with the Jonas Brothers, Miley Cyrus, Coldplay and More." Jesusfreakhideout.com, August 12. http://www.jesusfreakhideout.com/news/2008/08/12.HILLSONG%20SHARES %20TOP%2010%20iTUNES%20ALBUMS%20DOWNLOAD%20SUCCESS.asp.

Toner, Peter. 2007. "Sing a Country of the Mind: The Articulation of Place in Dhalwangu Song." In *The Soundscapes of Australia: Music, Place, and Spirituality*, edited by Fiona Richards, 165–84. Aldershot: Ashgate.

Wagner, Tom. 2014. "Branding, Music, and Religion: Standardization and Adaptation in the Experience of the 'Hillsong Sound.'" In *Religions as Brands: New Perspectives on the Marketization of Religion and Spirituality*, edited by Jean-Claude Usunier and Jörg Stolz, 59–73. Burlington, Vt.: Ashgate.

Webb, Michael. 2005. "Melanesia." In *The Continuum Encyclopedia of Popular Music of the World*, vol. 5, *Asia and Oceania*, edited by John Shepherd, David Horn, and Dave Laing, 289–92. London: Continuum.

Zahn, Heinrich. 1996. *Mission and Music: Jabêm Traditional Music and the Development of Lutheran Hymnody*. Boroko: Institute of Papua New Guinea Studies.

PART III

Media, Culture, and the Marketplace

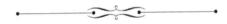

11

Charismatic Music and the Pentecostalization of Latin American Evangelicalism

Ryan R. Gladwin

In Argentine lore, dates such as May 18–25, 1810 (the May Revolution), October 17, 1945 (the demonstration for Perón's release from prison), and December 19–20, 2001 (*piquetero* and *cacerolazo* demonstrations against the government), are at the center of the national-mythic-celestial calendar, because they represent moments when *el pueblo* seemingly seized public space and time. For Latin American *evangélicos*, there are few such mythic moments in their collective history because they have long been a sector, in the words of José Míguez Bonino, condemned to gather members from "the loose dust on the surface of Latin American society" (1997, 53). However, September 11, 1999, finally marked one such prodigious moment, as between 150,000 and 400,000 evangelicals converged on the Obelisk in downtown Buenos Aires to the sounds of a two-hundred-instrument band and a large choir. El Obelisco, as the event came to be called, featured a central stage from which prayer and speeches were interspersed with songs. The event restated long-standing grievances over unequal legal recognition of religious rights and voiced prophetic critiques and concerns about national augmentation of poverty, unemployment, violence, and the disintegration of the family. It was a coming of age for evangelicals, a demonstration of social capital of seismic proportions. One national newspaper reported that a mini-earthquake was felt in the vicinity. While for some evangelicals the rumbling constituted a recapitulation of Acts 4:31—when early Christians felt the place in which they had gathered to pray start to shake—the more likely cause was the two hundred instruments, singers, and loudspeakers that shook the city with the sounds of Christian rock, anglicized cumbia, and *alabanza y adoración* (praise and worship),[1] all musical genres that form what I term "Latin American Charismatic Music" (LACM). However, perhaps it is best to interpret those urban rumblings as revelatory, as a seismic event that was in part the fruition of the moving beats and exponential proliferation of LACM.

This chapter will explore why it is not trifling that LACM accompanied the evangelical *pueblo* on that day. While a large body of work examines recent Latin American evangelicalism and its exponential growth, particularly through pentecostalism, there has been scant focus on the tunes and beats that have accompanied this expansion. Through the lens of Argentina, this chapter examines the significance of LACM in the formation of an influential "pentevangelical" culture. The first section will set the stage, contextualizing the conversation about LACM through an examination of its fruition amid the charismatic and neocharismatic growth and mobilization in Argentina in the 1980s and 1990s. Second, I will examine LACM as a constituent of the process of creation of a pan-pentevangelicalism, paying special attention to the instrumental and international figure of Marcos Witt as well as the Argentine Christian rock band RESCATE. Lastly, while recognizing that LACM represents a formidable attempt to produce a pentevangelical culture and to transform Latin America, I will raise some questions concerning the transformative possibilities of LACM and pentevangelicalism. Offering a fraternal theological critique of LACM and pentevangelical culture, I will argue that they have failed to form a worshipful culture that embodies Oscar Romero's declaration that "the glory of God is that the poor should live" (Trigo 1993, 299).

In Latin America, *evangélico* is a catchall term that, similar to the German *Evangelische* and the English *Protestant*, encompasses all types of Protestant groups and their different ideological stances—liberal, progressive, and conservative—and ecclesial traditions, including the many shades of Latin American pentecostalism.[2] In this chapter, I will use the terms "evangelical" and "evangelicalism" in this sense, unless otherwise noted. I use the acronym LACM in a broad sense to encompass praise and worship music focused on congregational and mass gatherings, as well as the numerous and varied styles of popular music for listening and dance (cumbia, salsa, merengue, reggaeton, rock, and so forth). When I use the term "pentecostalism" with a small "p," I am referring to the kaleidoscope of pentecostal ecclesial traditions, culture, and practices among classic Pentecostals, charismatics, and neocharismatics[3]—both those who self-identify as such and those who do not, but have pentecostal beliefs and practices. For example, Argentine neocharismatics do not typically self-identify as Pentecostals but rather as *evangélicos* or Christians.

Finally, I use the term "pentevangelical" to refer to a culture and practice that self-identifies as evangelical but demonstrates the direct influence of pentecostalism, in particular neocharismaticism.

Setting the Stage: LACM as Part of the Evangelical Surge

Pentecostalism arrived on the shores of Latin America long ago, and certain contexts with established evangelical populations, such as Argentina, proved resistant to this new Protestant cousin. This changed in Argentina during the infamous "lost decade" of the 1980s and the neoliberal boom of the 1990s. In Argentina, one can poignantly speak of at least three principal changes since the last and most heinous dictatorship (1976–83): profound socioeconomic structural changes under the guise of privatization and neoliberalism, a mutation of national political structures, and the formation of an exclusionary sociocultural context (Svampa 2005). The neoliberal boom, in which Argentina served as a trendsetter for Latin America, featured a plan of savage privatization and parallel openness to foreign economic and political influence (Brennan 1998, xii). This resulted in a sharp augmentation of poverty, a growing divide between the rich and the poor, and an influx of new religious groups as the religious market expanded (Wynarczyk 2009, 171–73). This period was marked by significant pentecostal growth, far outpacing decades of lackluster growth among classic Pentecostals, and a profound pentecostalization of evangelicalism as a whole.

While Tommy Hicks and Billy Graham generated mass gatherings in Argentina in 1954 and 1962, respectively, their efforts, as well as those of classic Pentecostalism and early evangelicalism, did not yield large-scale gains. It was only in the 1980s, with the rise of neocharismatics such as Omar Cabrera and Carlos Annacondia, that Argentine evangelicalism embraced the constellation of pentecostalism. A profound metamorphosis occurred in the formation of a parallel and associated pan-pentevangelical and supra-denominational culture (Wynarczyk 1989, 2009; Maróstica 1997, 1999, 2011). Annacondia, in particular, proved influential in preaching a gospel of power with the double message of repentance and liberation, as represented in the enduring theme "Jesus loves, saves, and heals you" (Algranti 2010, 79). Unlike evangelists of the past, Annacondia employed "power evangelism" (Annacondia 1998), a confrontational style of evangelism that used preaching and prayer as tools of spiritual warfare and liberation to confront and exorcise evil spirits. The flamboyant Annacondia would confront demonic powers in the opening prayer of his crusades by call-ing out, "¡Oíme bien, Satanás!" (Listen to me, Satan!).[4] Moreover, he effectively engaged local churches in the organization of his crusades, which produced a network through which to distribute a burgeoning pentevangelical culture, as well as generate growth among evangelicals (Maróstica 1997, 1999, 2011).

In the 1990s, the genus of pentecostalism was impressed even more firmly on evangelicalism with the neocharismatic *renovación* (renewal).[5] In 1992, Claudio Freidzon, pastor of the Assemblies of God church Rey de Reyes (King of Kings), made a trip to the United States to meet Benny Hinn after reading his books *Good Morning, Holy Spirit* and *The Anointing*. During this visit, Hinn prayed for Freidzon to receive *la unción* (the anointing), and Freid-zon subsequently brought this anointing to his church in Buenos Aires, from which it spread far and wide (Deiros 1998, 38; Holvast 2009, 60–61). While the anointing and renewal came well after the advent of neocharismaticism, nevertheless, as Hilario Wynarczyk has stated, it became "the most important cognitive area of neo-pentecostalism," incorporating prior existing practices (power evangelism, spiritual warfare/mapping, inner healing, liberation,[6] and the prosperity gospel) and becoming the functional power base upon which these practices operated (1997, 10).[7]

These tactical practices are rooted in a cosmology that views the physi-cal world as intimately intertwined with a contentious and dualistic spiritual reality divided between warring forces of good (God) and evil (the demonic). As Wilma Davies has commented, neocharismatics have "recreated a meta-narrative based around the cosmic story of Spiritual Battle" (2010, 211). For neocharismatics, the salvific message of Jesus Christ and the personal encoun-ter with God through the Holy Spirit save not only believers' souls from eter-nal damnation but also their bodies from sickness, disease, and poverty in the present (Yong 2010, 122–26, 258–63). While even classic Pentecostalism understood Jesus as savior and healer, neocharismatics have developed prac-tices that go beyond physical healing to include the spiritual, psychosomatic, and economic. Moreover, neocharismatics directly confront demonic spirits in order to bring healing and liberation; they understand themselves to be empowered through the Holy Spirit to confront and defeat the present powers of evil. Subsequently, neocharismatic practices frequently focus on proclaim-ing healing and blessings or breaking evil curses and exorcising evil spirits in the name of Jesus (Frigerio 1994, 11).

The rhythms and beats of LACM were not unconnected to these devel-opments. The preaching of influential evangelists, such as Annacondia, was always accompanied by music, and networks of local churches functioned to distribute songs and a particular style of worship, prayer, and preaching. Moreover, LACM proved to be a powerful conduit for the novice and confrontational evangelical culture of the 1990s. Freidzon's church, Rey de Reyes, proliferated the anointing and LACM, as its praise and worship band wrote and produced seven albums between 1997 and 2004 that became widespread within Argentine worship. LACM became part of the neocharismatic repertoire built upon the foundation of the anointing. "Anointed" praise and worship and rhythm-induced spiritual warfare served as evangelistic tools and begetters of a pan-pentevangelical culture and practice.

LACM and the Creation of Latin American Pan-pentevangelical Culture

The changes in the Latin American religious and social landscape in recent decades are as undeniable as the streets, city centers, and plazas that quake to the beats of LACM. A journalist noted that on the prodigious day of September 11, 1999, all in attendance appeared to sing a ballad asking God to "heal our nation" as if "they knew it by memory" (Reches and Iglesia 1999). The fact is that most probably did! Indeed, the planners of the event intentionally selected well-known songs and an all-encompassing theme: "Jesus by all and for all" (Proietti 2013). This is significant because it means that there was an existing, unbound evangelical songbook[8] from which to choose, which would not have been the case decades earlier.

In the 1960s and 1970s, change started with the development of *coritos*— short, repetitive, and easy-to-memorize songs that were typically written by Latin Americans and incorporated folkloric instruments, including guitars, tambourines, and drums (Palomino 2011, 19–26). Transmitted orally and not through notated scores, *coritos* began to displace the hymns from denominational hymnbooks that had been the mainstay among evangelicals since the nineteenth century. Whereas the hymnbook helped maintain a wall of separation between denominations, the *coritos* signaled a break with denominational musical traditions.

However, it was LACM that ultimately produced a common evangelical musical lexicon and form of praise and worship. Through radio, television, concerts, evangelistic gatherings, and musical production and marketing, evangelicals began to adopt more of the same beliefs and practices and to standardize the instrumental and stylistic repertoire in worship services (Palomino 2011, 31–32; Maróstica 2011). The proliferation of shared cultural practices, such as LACM, has fomented a genuine sense of unity. This shared pentevangelical culture has also helped make possible the repeated gathering of one hundred thousand or more—as in the first (1999) and second (2001) Obeliscos and the Luis Palau festivals of 2003 and 2008.

A prominent exemplar of LACM is Marcos Witt, an award-winning artist (five Latino Grammys won and more than eleven million records sold), megachurch pastor, and longtime influential leader in the development and diffusion of LACM (Deiros 1998, 42–43). The efforts of Witt and others have "made it possible that evangelical churches in the region sing the same songs, in the same musical scale and even with the same musical arrangements," effectively creating a "musical uniformity" (Palomino 2011, 22). The songs of the pioneer Witt became almost ubiquitous in evangelistic crusades, festivals, and churches in the 1990s and early 2000s. He has routinely led worship for the evangelist Luis Palau, an Argentine expatriate based in the United States, and performed throughout Latin America during the last three decades. Witt is the author of more than thirteen books, as well as the founder of a record label (CanZion Productions) and a praise and worship school (CanZion Institute), which comprises eighty sites in the United States, Latin America, and Europe.[9] His record label has its own website, Nuhbe, where people can purchase and download LACM,[10] and he has a significant social media presence, with almost six million followers on Facebook as of early 2015.

Witt's influence in Argentina has been, in the words of the president of ACIERA (Alianza Cristiana de Iglesias Evangélicas de la República Argentina), Rubén Proietti (2013), "tremendous . . . on the level of the growth of the church." Proietti also notes that, while Witt has long-standing ties with neo-charismatics,[11] his music and influence have extended broadly across all sectors of evangelicalism and even to Catholicism. He is arguably "Latin America's best-known worship leader" (Deiros 1998, 42), but he has also had a presence throughout Argentina through repeated performances and conferences in numerous cities. He led worship before forty-five thousand people in Buenos Aires in 1997 and was invited to lead worship at the second Obelisco on September 15, 2001, although he declined (Deiros 1998, 43; Wynarczyk 2009, 314–16). In 2006, he led worship at an ecumenical event organized by the Executive Commission of the Renewed Communion in the Holy Spirit of Evangelicals and Catholics, in which he shared the stage with the then archbishop of Buenos Aires and future Pope Francis, Jorge Bergoglio. He also founded his first praise and worship institute outside of Mexico in Buenos Aires in 2000 and wrote and produced the song "Argentina te bendigo" with this institute.

Witt's influence extends to the creation of the theology and practice of LACM. He is widely considered to be "the architect of the entire renovation of worship in Latin America," which entailed a change in both the evangelical hymnology and the format of worship services (Palomino 2011, 14, 31). Two of his books—*Adoremos* (1993) and *¿Qué hacemos con estos músicos?* (1995)—have been extremely popular and influential in the creation of LACM's theology of praise and worship. In *Adoremos*, Witt makes a clear distinction between *alabanza* (praise), celebration, and *adoración* (worship), the desire to be with God. While he advocates the exuberant celebration (*alabanza*/praise) of God through music, the central argument of the text is that celebration is not enough, because God desires *adoradores* (worshippers) (1993, 85). Using Old Testament imagery, Witt asserts that true worshippers are akin to priests in ancient Israel who sought to be with God in Zion and the Holy of Holies in the Temple. However, the modern temple, according to Witt, is the individual Christian believer, not an edifice, and praise and worship is led by anointed leaders who guide the masses into the presence of God—the Holy of Holies within each person. In *¿Qué hacemos con estos músicos?*, Witt instructs musicians on practical and professional issues such as playing quality music (1995, 55–58) and how to use money (101–17). However, the text's central concern is that musicians should be "psalmists" who worship God. Using the example of the religious cult under the Davidic kingship (38–47), Witt envisions musicians as full-time professional staff who function as priests, prophets, and servants for God's people (51–99, 120–61). Under the influence of Witt, the modus operandi of LACM has become that of a professional music team that acts as a priestly mediator to prepare and guide the people toward a personal encounter with God. Indeed, Witt is an archetypal leader because of his successful unification of the priestly model of the worship leader with the marketing model of the successful producer and businessman. In short, he helped prove that LACM can be popular and marketable.

Lastly, Witt has been influential in the proliferation of the marriage of LACM with neocharismatic practices, such as spiritual warfare. Borrowing again from the Old Testament, Witt teaches that music is used in the Scriptures for praise and worship as well as war (1993, 46–53; 1995, 139). For Witt, the music that accompanies church services and evangelistic crusades is not only praise and worship but also a weapon for battling the powers and principalities of evil. This "warrior worship" is a sacramental, grace-infused "weapon in the hand of God to make demons flee and liberate the captured" as well as a means to boldly declare blessings over the Latin American nations (1995, 65–68, 139). Traces of this confrontational style of worship appear in the aforementioned song "Argentina te bendigo" (Argentina I bless you) from the album *Otra generación*. The song's title and a repeated chorus declare blessings of "peace," "victory," "favor," and "joy" on the nation of Argentina "in the name of Jesus." The song also hints at the theme of confronting demons and liberating people from oppression with the lyric "we break curses."

Argentina te bendigo.	Argentina I bless you.
Con la paz del Señor	With the peace of the Lord
Te bendigo	I bless you
Con su luz y su amor	With his light and his love
Te bendigo	I bless you
Argentina te bendigo	Argentina I bless you
Te bendigo, te bendigo	I bless you, I bless you
En el nombre de Jesús	In the name of Jesus
Te bañamos con la luz de su gloria	We wash you with the light of his glory
Rompemos maldición	We break curses
Declaramos bendición y victoria	We declare blessing and victory
Recibe el favor	Receive the favor
Recibe el amor y el gozo del Señor.	Receive the love and the joy of the Lord
Argentina te bendigo.	Argentina I bless you.

While Witt has been extremely influential in the formation of the theology and practice of praise and worship music, LACM also encompasses a variety of styles of music for listening and dancing, such as cumbia, salsa, merengue, reggaeton, and rock. This branch of LACM has expanded through the radio, Internet, concerts, and evangelistic events, influencing the formation of an evangelical culture that actively engages mainstream musical genres while at the same time professing to be "countercultural" (Semán and Gallo 2008, 86; Jungblut 2007, 155–56). A poignant example is the hit Argentine rock band RESCATE, which has produced eight albums, filled soccer stadiums, toured in more than twenty-five countries, and played before Pope Benedict XVI at the twentieth World Youth Day in 2005. The name of the group is an acronym for Reyes al Servicio de Cristo ante Tiempos Extremos (Kings at the Service of Christ in Extreme Times) as well as a Spanish term used in youth culture to refer to a "rescue" from issues such as drug use and rebellion (Semán and Gallo 2008, 77). Ulises Miguel Eyherabide and his North American friend Jonathan Thompson founded the group in 1988, inspired by Christian rock bands such as Petra, White Heart, and the Newsboys. However, the group quickly developed a style akin to Argentine *rock nacional*, as exemplified by the bands Los Piojos and Divididos, which mix rock and folkloric tunes. RESCATE has also engaged mainstream youth and rock culture as a "countercultural" presence, appearing several times at the Pepsi Music Festival, the largest music festival in Argentina, and making a crossover from Christian rock to mainstream rock in 2004. Christian rock groups such as RESCATE have also served to "rescue" dance styles (such as *el pogo*)[12] and the rock and party (*fiesta*) scene and make them palatable for certain evangelical venues (Semán and Gallo 2008, 81–83, 85–86). Accordingly, the group has headlined with Luis Palau at his festivals and with fellow Argentine Dante Gebel in his Superclasicos de la Juventud (Youth Super Classics).[13] These events are not preaching venues where select songs serve as accompaniment, but a mix between a concert, a musical festival, and preaching, with a particular focus on attracting youth through a Christianized youth culture. While such festivals feature praise and worship tunes such as those popularized by Witt, the celebration of Christian folkloric, rock, and other music styles for listening and dancing sets them apart as youth festivals. Performances of groups such as RESCATE at these events represent an evangelical engagement of popular culture as well as the creation of a "Christianized" popular culture. In turn, this branch of LACM has been influential in forming a pentevangelical culture and practice intent on transforming Latin America.

LACM and Transformation

Once condemned to gather "the loose dust on the surface of Latin American society," Latin American evangelicals now constitute a significant minority who are no longer willing to be accepted as "second-class citizens." Indeed, Argentine evangelical leaders used these exact words in defending their right to hold El Obelisco to city government officials in 1999, after first being denied permission (Wynarczyk 2009, 301; Proietti 2013). This change in self-perception, coupled with the ability to engage in shared practices and repeated mass gatherings, has served to infuse evangelicals with confidence that they are active agents of transformation. However, the reality is much more complex.

This novel pentevangelicalism has proved adept at helping evangelicalism engage Latin American popular cultures and religion. It has been able to bridge the spiritual and physical, the premodern and postmodern, and the preindustrial and late capitalist. For example, neocharismaticism does not disdain the cosmology and practices of Catholic popular religion as superstition or magic but engages them through the lens of spiritual warfare. Likewise, the entrepreneurial know-how of businessmen turned preachers such as Annacondia and worship leaders turned record label owners such as Witt, linked with a cosmology that engages popular religion and culture, has given neocharismatics a clear competitive advantage in a context defined by neoliberalism, deregulation, and privatization (Chesnut 2003; Meyer 2008; Yong 2010, 19–38).

LACM is representative of this battery of practices of confrontation. Neocharismatics have embedded this confrontation in the warring task of musically led praise and worship. The focus is often on transforming geopolitical areas—the nations of Latin America. In Bolivia and across Latin America, preachers and worship leaders call out to God to *sanar la nación* (heal the nation) at the March for Jesus events, and, in Argentina, they sing songs declaring blessings over the nations, such as Witt's "Argentina te bendigo." These actions are more than mere symbolism, as they have fomented the emergence of new forms of religiopolitical structures and ecclesial polities that demonstrate a consolidation of social capital (Algranti 2010, 293–302; Petersen 2004, 2009; Wightman 2007, 245–52; Wynarczyk 2009, 296–325).[14]

The LACM styles for listening and dancing also engage with Latin American popular culture. This engagement has not occurred through confrontation but rather through selective interaction with Latin America's folkloric music traditions as well as youth cultures. Returning to the example of RESCATE, Christian rock has arisen from an open engagement with Latin rock, through the incorporation of music styles (such as *rock nacional*), dances (such as *el pogo*), and rock party venues. This incorporation represents a Christianizing of rock and youth culture, as it becomes a tool to spread Christian messages to non-Christian youth. It also represents the creation of a novel evangelical youth culture that understands itself as both a *fiesta* and a counterculture (Semán and Gallo 2008, 80–81). This desire to express a Christianity that fits in and yet is different is reflected in common slogans at rock venues and festivals—for instance, the "Christians are not boring" signs carried at March for Jesus events (Wightman 2007, 251).

While these creative interactions reflect the creation of a Latin American popular pentevangelical religion and culture, they also embody a confusing

cultural hybridity. First, LACM bears the indelible marks of a sustained relationship with North American cultural and economic influence. The diffusion
of LACM has been paved by Latin American worship leaders and organizations
who made it not only influential but also profitable. Marcos Witt again serves
as an apt example. Born in San Antonio, Texas, Witt was raised in Durango,
Mexico, as the son of Methodist missionaries. As mentioned above, he has
demonstrated his entrepreneurial skills and influence as an archetypal leader
through the development of his own record label, music institute, and influential books (Aguirra Arvizu 2009; Palomino 2011, 31, 36). However, his music
style demonstrates the unmistakable influence of North American music, as it
incorporates an adult contemporary pop style and the standardization of musical instruments—electric and acoustic guitars, drums, and digital pianos. The
same could be said for other worship leaders as well as rock groups such as
RESCATE, who developed as a result of the inspiration of North American
Christian rock. There also exist clear monetary ties to production and distribution studios and publishers based in the United States. Although Witt began in
Mexico, he has since moved to the United States to live and produce his albums,
and U.S. publishers (Thomas Nelson in Nashville and Casa Creación in Lake
Mary, Florida) have published the majority of his books. He is the cofounder of a
leadership school, Lidere, that utilizes and distributes the leadership teachings of
the North American pastor John Maxwell.[15] Similarly, RESCATE has attempted
to make the move to mainstream rock through the production of an album with
Sony Music. Thus, while LACM is not a direct North American importation,
it demonstrates strong North American economic and cultural influence.

Second, while pentevangelicalism engages popular culture, it has not clearly
developed a critique of the deep-seated social divisions that exist in Latin
America. The growth of pentevangelicalism and LACM was spurred by the
neoliberal turn of the 1980s and 1990s, which also resulted in an augmentation
of poverty and consolidation of power in the hands of the wealthy (Svampa
2005, 9–196). However, the songs of LACM have not actively engaged this
social reality or challenged neoliberal ideology and social structures. Indeed,
ideologically speaking, pentevangelicalism and LACM grew out of conservative Latin American evangelicalism and pentecostalism, which distanced
themselves in the 1960s from liberal and progressive evangelicals who engaged
with what Jürgen Moltmann has called "the other side of reconciliation": the
hope of justice, the humanization of humanity and society, and peace for all
creation (1967, 329).[16] The result is that pentevangelicalism espouses an engagement of popular culture (including Roman Catholic, folkloric, and youth

cultures), but it is not necessarily *popular*. Here I use that term—as Néstor Míguez, Joerg Rieger, and Jung Mo Sung have—to mean being representative of the poor and marginalized sectors of society by standing on the side of the margins against the centers of power and influence (N. Míguez, Rieger, and Sung 2009, 179; D. Míguez and Semán 2006, 24). While pentevangelicalism has occupied public space in the name of transformation, the songs of LACM have not tended to move beyond a generalized nationalism—for instance, "Argentina para Cristo"—or to engage the songs, stories, and struggles of *el pueblo*. Within the emerging pentevangelicalism, there have been occasional proclamations against corruption and injustice, such as during the first Obelisco, but these proclamations are significant precisely because they are unique.

Given LACM's ideological underpinnings, it is not surprising that there is not a clear engagement of *el popular* and issues of injustice in the songs of Witt as well as other big-name stars such as Jesús Adrián Romero and Alex Campos. Moreover, Witt's theology of praise and worship, which advocates for an anointed priestly and professional praise and worship team, represents a challenge to open engagement of those who are on the margins. For Witt, power and prosperity characterize those who are set apart as priests of worship. This division potentially creates a charismatic classism and clericalism that does not aid in breaking down the barriers between the rich and poor, but instead raises new ones. Finally, Witt advocates a marriage between worship and spiritual warfare that confronts demonic forces, such as popular Catholic saints, but does not adequately confront political and social structures that create and sustain poverty.

Similarly, there has been limited interaction with the themes of poverty and injustice in the LACM styles for listening and dancing.[17] This is surprising, given that genres such as reggaeton, *rock chabón*, and the folkloric traditions are noted for expressing social critiques (Semán, Vila, and Benedetti 2004). Groups such as RESCATE have undoubtedly influenced society by making evangelicalism more palatable to "mainstream" culture. For example, RESCATE won the inaugural Gardel Award, the most well-known music award in Argentina, in the newly created evangelical music category. However, it appears that RESCATE has ultimately been more instrumental in changing evangelical culture through the engagement of rock youth culture than in transforming rock youth culture itself (Semán and Gallo 2008, 76, 84–86). While evangelical rock groups such as RESCATE openly present themselves as "countercultural" and transformational, they have not developed songs that counter the unjust social structures of Latin America. Clearly, Latin

American societies are more open to evangelicals today, but this change has come through evangelicals assimilating into the mainstream culture, not by their standing against the oppressive centers of power and influence. It is hard to speak of LACM as *popular*, because the critiques of long-standing social ills such as poverty, racism, and class division are few and far between.

Conclusion

This chapter has demonstrated many ways in which LACM is used in formidable, innovative, and conscious attempts to form a pan-pentevangelical culture. Through its pervasive presence in evangelical congregational singing, mass events in public squares, and the profitable sounds of Argentine youth culture's music, it demonstrates a creative incorporation of diverse music styles and genres, powerful neocharismatic techniques and practices, a cosmology of spiritual conflict, and a theology of worship. Its participatory rhythms incorporate evangelical practices and culture and aid in their diffusion and systemization. However, the theology and mission of LACM have thus far failed to recognize the dialectical relationship between its success and neoliberal ideology and structure. Although the entrepreneurial skill of neocharismatics within LACM has clearly given them an advantage in the contemporary deregulated cultural market, entrepreneurial success is no guarantee of the pursuit of *justicia* (justice/righteousness). While LACM has been at the forefront of declaring God's desire to conquer Argentina and Latin America *para Cristo*, there has sadly been little critique of social injustices, poverty, and socioeconomic divisions. In this sense, LACM has failed to form a worshipful culture that embodies the proclamation of Oscar Romero that "the glory of God is that the poor should live" (*Gloria Dei vivens pauper*) (Trigo 1993, 299).

NOTES

1. All translations are mine unless otherwise noted.

2. In the English-speaking world, *evangélico* refers to a certain "type" of Protestantism. This is not the case in Latin America, where the term is most often used as a synonym for the lesser-used term "Protestant." However, there are many types of evangelicals, and not all are ideologically conservative, as it is often assumed. For example, since the 1960s, it has been possible to talk of at least three ideological perspectives: (1) ecumenical/liberal, (2) conservative, and (3) progressive. During the 1950s and 1960s, ecumenical/liberal evangelicals emerged through the formation of ecumenical organizations and the development of liberal theological perspectives that

intentionally engaged social reality. Rejecting what they saw as liberal and unbiblical theology that was focused on social activism instead of evangelism, conservative evangelicals formed their own separate ecumenical organizations, such as the Latin American Conference on Evangelism (CLADE) in 1969. Subsequently, another significant group emerged from within conservative evangelicalism that rejected both liberalism and conservatism and developed a progressive evangelical theology that was intentionally biblical and attentive to social reality. These progressive evangelicals formed the Latin American Evangelical Fraternity in 1970 and are recognized for their development of a theology of integral mission (Escobar 1995).

3. Here I borrow the threefold Pentecostal typology laid out in *The New International Dictionary of Pentecostal and Charismatic Movements* (Burgess 2002, xviii–xxi), but like Amos Yong (2005, 18–22), I use the terms "pentecostal" or "pentecostalism" with a small "p" to refer to the movement in general (that is, the conjunction of all three types of pentecostals) and "Pentecostal" or "Pentecostalism" with a big "P" to refer to classic Pentecostals. In Latin America, the term "neo-Pentecostal" is preferred to "neocharismatic," particularly among Argentine sociologists of religion, but I have chosen to use the term preferred in English for reasons of facility. For examples of Latin American scholarship on neo-Pentecostalism, see the work of Alejandro Frigerio (1994), Pablo Semán and Guadalupe Gallo (2008), Daniel Míguez and Pablo Semán (2006), Hilario Wynarczyk (1989, 1997, 2009), and Joaquín Algranti (2007, 2010).

4. Annacondia also wrote a book by this title (1997).

5. This is the common term used to describe the movement that began in 1992 and the churches and individuals who received the anointing.

6. This is a direct translation from the Spanish term *liberación*; it refers to spiritual deliverance.

7. Wynarczyk uses the term "neo-pentecostal" instead of "neocharismatic."

8. I speak metaphorically of an unbound songbook to refer to a conglomeration of well-known evangelical songs that were primarily transmitted orally and, unlike bound hymnals of the past, transcended denominational affiliation.

9. See http://www.canzion.com.

10. See http://www.nuhbe.com/en/.

11. Witt writes about his indebtedness to Annacondia and the influence of North American neocharismatic Peter Wagner (1995, 65). The promotional material for the CanZion Institute in Argentina refers to Annacondia and Freidzon (see http://www.institutocanzion.com/argentina/).

12. This is similar to the mosh dance that became popular in Anglophone alternative rock in the 1990s.

13. The term *superclasico* is borrowed from Argentine soccer and refers to the game between the two most popular club teams in the country.

14. One prominent and formal Argentine example is the Consejo Nacional Cristiano Evangélico, formed in 1996 in the wake of evangelical efforts for full freedom of religion during the constitutional reforms of 1994. It accounts for some twelve thousand churches among the various groupings of evangelicos and was instrumental in the organization of the first and second Obeliscos (Wynarczyk 2009, 296–325).

15. See http://www.lidere.org.

16. Neo-Pentecostalism represents an intensification of conservative evangelicalism's understanding of the Christian mission as the conversion of individuals through evangelism and church growth. Accordingly, it has shared conservatism's resistance to social activism and care for society and the creation.

17. One example is the song "Dale la mano" (Give a hand) from the album *Especie en peligro* (2003) by the reggaeton singer Funky. In the song, Funky exhorts others to "give a hand to the fallen, to the naked give a coat, to the hungry give food, and to the sad comfort," and he critiques those who "have not compassion."

REFERENCES

Aguirra Arvizu, Alejandrina. 2009. "El gran negocio de la música religiosa." *Contenido* 551:82–91.

Algranti, Joaquín. 2007. "La política en los márgenes: Estudio sobre los espacios de participación social en el neo-Pentecostalismo." *Caminhos, Golânia* 5 (2): 361–80.

———. 2010. *Política y religión en los márgenes: Nuevas formas de participación social de las mega-iglesias evangélicas en la Argentina*. Buenos Aires: Ciccus.

Annacondia, Carlos. 1997. *¡Oíme bien, Satanás!* Nashville: Grupo Nelson.

———. 1998. "Power Evangelism, Argentine Style." In *The Rising Revival: Firsthand Accounts of the Incredible Argentine Revival—and How It Can Spread Throughout the World*, edited by C. Peter Wagner and Pablo Deiros, 57–74. Ventura, Calif.: Renew Books.

Brennan, James P., ed. 1998. *Peronism and Argentina*. Wilmington, Del.: SR Books.

Burgess, Stanley M., ed. 2002. *The New International Dictionary of Pentecostal and Charismatic Movements*. Grand Rapids, Mich.: Zondervan.

Chesnut, R. Andrew. 2003. *Competitive Spirits: Latin America's New Religious Economy*. New York: Oxford University Press.

Davies, Wilma Wells. 2010. *The Embattled but Empowered Community—Comparing Understandings of Spiritual Power in Argentine Popular and Pentecostal Cosmologies*. Boston: Brill.

Deiros, Pablo. 1998. "The Roots and Fruits of the Argentine Revival." In *The Rising Revival: Firsthand Accounts of the Incredible Argentine Revival—and How It Can Spread Throughout the World*, edited by C. Peter Wagner and Pablo Deiros, 29–55. Ventura, Calif.: Renew Books.

Escobar, Samuel. 1995. "La fundación de la Fraternidad Teológica Latinoamericana: Breve ensayo histórico." In *25 años de teología evangélica latinoamericana*, edited by C. René Padilla, 7–25. Buenos Aires: FTL.

Frigerio, Alejandro. 1994. "Estudios recientes sobre el Pentecostalismo en el Cono Sur: Problemas y perspectivas." In *El Pentecostalismo en la Argentina*, edited by Alejandro Frigerio, 10–28. Buenos Aires: Centro Editor de América Latina.

Holvast, René. 2009. *Spiritual Mapping in the United States and Argentina, 1989–2005: A Geography of Fear*. Boston: Brill.

Jungblut, Airton. 2007. "A salvação pelo rock: Sobre a 'cena underground' dos jovens evangélicos no Brasil." *Religião e Sociedade* 27 (2): 144–62.

Maróstica, Matthew M. 1997. "Pentecostals and Politics: The Creation of the Evangelical Christian Movement in Argentina, 1983–1993." Ph.D. diss., University of California, Los Angeles.

———. 1999. "The Defeat of Denominational Culture in the Argentine Evangelical Movement." In *Latin American Religion in Motion*, edited by Christian Smith and Joshua Prokopy, 147–72. New York: Routledge.

———. 2011. "Learning from the Master: Carlos Annacondia and the Standardization of Pentecostal Practices in and beyond Argentina." In *Global Pentecostal and Charismatic Healing*, edited by Candy Gunther Brown, 207–30. New York: Oxford University Press.

Meyer, Birgit. 2008. "Commodities and the Power of Prayer: Pentecostal Attitudes Towards Consumption in Ghana." *Development and Change* 29 (4): 751–76.

Míguez, Daniel, and Pablo Semán. 2006. "Diversidad y recurrencia en las culturas populares actuales." In *Entre santos, cumbias y piquetes: Las culturas populares en la Argentina reciente*, edited by Daniel Míguez and Pablo Semán, 11–32. Buenos Aires: Biblos.

Míguez, Néstor, Joerg Rieger, and Jung Mo Sung. 2009. *Beyond the Spirit of Empire: Theology and Politics in a New Key*. London: SCM Press.

Míguez Bonino, José. 1997. *Faces of Latin American Protestantism: 1993 Carnahan Lectures*. Translated by Eugene L. Stockwell. Grand Rapids, Mich.: Eerdmans.

Moltmann, Jürgen. 1967. *Theology of Hope: On the Ground and the Implications of a Christian Eschatology*. London: SCM Press.

Palomino, Miguel A. 2011. *¿Qué pasó al culto en América Latina? La adoración en las iglesias evangélicas*. Lima: Ediciones Puma.

Petersen, Douglas. 2004. "Latin American Pentecostalism: Social Capital, Networks, and Politics." *Pneuma* 26 (2): 293–306.

———. 2009. "A Moral Imagination: Pentecostals and Social Concern in Latin America." In *The Spirit in the World: Emerging Pentecostal Theologies in the Global Context*, edited by Veli-Matti Kärkkäinen, 53–66. Grand Rapids, Mich.: Eerdmans.

Proietti, Rubén. 2013. Interview with the author. Buenos Aires, January 4.

Reches, Gabriel, and Mariana Iglesia. 1999. "Entre la música y los mensajes del los pastores: Una multitud de evangélicos llevó todo su fervor al Obelisco." *Clarín*, September 12. http://edant.clarin.com/diario/1999/09/12/e-04201d.htm.

Semán, Pablo, and Guadalupe Gallo. 2008. "Rescate y sus consquencias—Cultura y religion: Soló en singular." *Ciências Sociais e Religião* 10 (10): 73–94.

Semán, Pablo, Pablo Vila, and Cecelia Benedetti. 2004. "Neoliberalism and Rock in the Popular Sectors of Contemporary Argentina." In *Rockin' Las Américas: The Global Politics of Rock in Latin/o America*, edited by Deborah Pacini Hernandez, Héctor Fernández L'Hoeste, and Eric Zolov, 261–89. Pittsburgh: University of Pittsburgh Press.

Svampa, Maristella. 2005. *La sociedad excluyente: La Argentina bajo el signo del neoliberalismo*. Buenos Aires: Taurus.

Trigo, Pedro. 1993. "El futuro de la teología de liberación." In *Cambio social y pensamiento en América Latina*, edited by José Comblin, José I. González Faus, and Jon Sobrino, 297–317. Madrid: Editorial Trotta.

Wightman, Jill M. 2007. "Healing the Nation: Pentecostal Identity and Social Change in Bolivia." In *Conversion of a Continent: Contemporary Religious Change in Latin America*, edited by Timothy J. Steigenga and Edward L. Cleary, 239–55. New Brunswick: Rutgers University Press.

Witt, Marcos. 1993. *Adoremos*. Miami: Editorial Betania.

———. 1995. *¿Qué hacemos con estos músicos?* Miami: Editorial Betania.

Wynarczyk, Hilario. 1989. *Tres evangelistas carismáticos: Cabrera, Annacondia, y Giménez*. Buenos Aires: Prensa Ecuménica.

———. 1997. "El 'avivamiento' espiritual en la Argentina en perspectiva sociológica." *Boletín Teológico* 28 (68): 7–15.

———. 2009. *Ciudadanos de dos mundos: El movimiento evangélico en la vida pública Argentina 1980–2001*. Buenos Aires: UNSAM Edita.

Yong, Amos. 2005. *The Spirit Poured Out on All Flesh: Pentecostalism and the Possibility of Global Theology*. Grand Rapids, Mich.: Baker Academic.

———. 2010. *In the Days of Caesar: Pentecostalism and Political Theology*. Grand Rapids, Mich.: Eerdmans.

12

Blessed to Be a Blessing: The Prosperity Gospel of Worship Music Superstar Israel Houghton

Wen Reagan

No other music artist associated with the prosperity gospel—the proclamation that God gives health and wealth to those who have faith—has had the success and platform of Israel Houghton, worship leader[1] at Joel Osteen's Lakewood Church in Houston, Texas. His songs are sung in churches around the world, regardless of denomination or theological tradition. Since the release of his debut album in 1997, Houghton has won four Grammy Awards, six Dove Awards, and two Stellar Awards, rising to the top of the gospel and contemporary Christian music charts while collaborating with Christian musicians outside of the prosperity movement, including Chris Tomlin, TobyMac, Mary Mary, and Gungor.

Yet Joel Osteen's worship leader was not an outspoken ambassador for his pastor's school of theology. Houghton's most popular song, "Friend of God," made no explicit theological claim for prosperity, and in writing or interviews he was more likely to focus on his passion for worshipping Jesus than on the blessings of health and wealth that God provided. More than any other worship artist associated with the prosperity movement, Houghton garnered wide appeal *in spite of* his prosperity leanings. His popularity came not through trumpeting the prosperity gospel, but through his ability to transcend or translate its cultural, denominational, and theological borders. Thus, Rick Warren could denounce the prosperity gospel in *Time* magazine and yet regularly use Houghton's songs at his Saddleback Church (Van Biema and Chu 2006, 48).

My argument in this study, however, is that there is more prosperity gospel at work in Houghton's music and appeal than meets the eye (or the ear, as it were). Sometimes explicitly, but often indirectly, Houghton's prosperity theology informed his work and public image, whether it was in his testimony of God's empowering friendship, his fusion of musical styles, or the broadening of his lyrical focus toward social justice.

This study takes what the religious studies scholar Gordon Lynch calls an author-focused (or supply-side) approach (2005, 111–20). Instead of focusing on Israel Houghton's reception among American Christians, I focus on Houghton's biography, musical style, and lyrics. Though the author is but one figure involved in the production of cultural texts, Lynch notes that there is much to be gained by considering the author's vantage and role within his or her wider cultural context (120). While Lynch presents this approach as a prelude to a theological critique, I use it here as a parallel to a historiographical method of "snapshot biography," in which a biographical focus sheds light on larger social and historical forces. I consider how the unique context of an author of cultural texts illuminates a larger cultural world. By tracing how Houghton conceived of his own music, how he appropriated the theological and musical language available in his cultural repertoire, and how he then leveraged his own story, we gain insight into the intersection between the prosperity gospel and contemporary worship music. But this approach holds disadvantages: it offers no sustained analysis of how Christians have received or appropriated Houghton's music, of the collaborative nature of cultural text production, or of the fact that artists are not always aware of the potential meanings available in their work. As such, I supplement this author-focused approach by drawing on Gerardo Marti's sociological study of multicultural megachurches in order to consider, however briefly, the "demand side" of Houghton's music.

I start with Houghton's testimony—the narrative of his conversion and Christian journey—because it is an integral part of his appeal and because it traces the core of his prosperity theology. Houghton used his story not only to market the authenticity of his music and ministry but also to translate the prosperity gospel into a narrative of friendship and adoption. I then examine Houghton's music, which crossed genres, drew power from popular theories that undergirded the selection of worship music in churches, and went hand in hand with his own multiracial identity. In this, it both evoked and reinforced the multiracial character of prosperity culture. Finally, I consider Houghton's lyrical themes, which first coalesced around prosperity concepts of favor and increase but subsequently, as an outworking of his prosperity theology, focused on issues of social justice.

Before we turn to Houghton's story, however, we need to define the prosperity gospel. The prosperity gospel movement is a subculture within the nebulous

BLESSED TO BE A BLESSING

world of contemporary Pentecostalism and the charismatic movement. It does not stand as a monolithic doctrine or subculture but instead is a constellation of interrelated theologies revolving around the interchange between faith and prosperity, normally defined as health, wealth, and success. The prosperity gospel emerged as a fusion of what William James had called the "mind-cure movement" with the theology of the "deliverance evangelism" of postwar Pentecostalism. Certain late nineteenth- and early twentieth-century "positive thinking" philosophies—such as those of P. P. Quimby, Mary Baker Eddy, and Norman Vincent Peale—were fused with theologies that emphasized the immediate, contractual power of faith for healing, peddled by evangelists such as E. W. Kenyon, T. L. Osborn, and Thomas Wyatt.

This fusion appeared, perhaps most forcefully, in the ministry of mid-twentieth-century evangelist Kenneth E. Hagin, who sourced the potency of this healing faith in legal and scientific terms, calling it the "law of faith." Hagin's law of faith essentially declared that what believers asked for, God was obliged to give. As historian Kate Bowler explains, Hagin understood that Jesus's death transferred the legal rights to salvation, protection, and victory from Satan to believers, who then "became entitled to use God's power as their own." In a scientific sense, Hagin understood the law of faith as a "universal causal agent, a power that actualized events and objects in the real world" (Bowler 2013, 45). The power and efficacy of this spoken word—the *rhema*—was as reliable as the laws of physics. "Believe it in your heart; say it with your mouth," Hagin asserted. "That is the principle of faith. You can have what you say" (Hagin 1979, 17). Like gravity or electricity, faith was an invisible operator of cause and effect, blind to human opinions, but also able to bind God himself. While other ministers, such as Philadelphia's Reverend Thea Jones, preached the same thing, Hagin's "simpler, almost automated, law of faith" became the basis for the Word of Faith movement, undergirding most popular understandings of the prosperity gospel today (Bowler 2013, 46).

In the 1980s and 1990s, Hagin's theological legacy blossomed in global prosperity celebrities, including German evangelist Reinhard Bonnke, South African pastor Ray McCauley, and Singaporean pastor Joseph Prince. In America, Hagin's legacy lives on in Creflo Dollar, Joyce Meyer, Kenneth Copeland, his own son, Kenneth Hagin Jr., who now runs his father's ministry, and perhaps most visibly in Joel Osteen, pastor of Lakewood Church, America's largest megachurch.[2] As we will see, it was through Osteen that the prosperity gospel influenced Houghton's theology and lyrics. But first we turn to Houghton's story.

A Testimony of Blessing

When it came to Houghton's testimony, the beginning was essential.[3] In a June 2011 interview on TBN's *Praise the Lord*, after noting that there is "nothing accidental about our lives," Houghton confessed, "I spent a good portion of my life feeling . . . accidental" ("Israel Houghton on TBN" 2011). Born to a white mother and an absent black Jamaican father in Waterloo, Iowa, Israel Houghton came into the world as a shame to his mother's family. Pregnant at seventeen, Houghton's mother, Margaret, faced either losing a career as a concert pianist or giving in to family pressure to abort the baby and get on with life. She decided to keep the child and left for Oceanside, California (Houghton 2007, 115). Eight months pregnant, and with the threat of losing her child to the state because of drug use, Margaret was approached by a stranger on the street who proclaimed that Jesus loved her and that she was not forgotten. Houghton explained the religious epiphany that followed: "There was no organ playing, there was no 'heads bowed, eyes closed,' but literally she had her own altar call right on the street. And from that day did not touch another drug, from that day God just did miracle after miracle" ("Israel Houghton on TBN" 2011).

Though this was his mother's conversion story, it was also Houghton's creation narrative. Conceived, in his telling, as an interracial accident and almost aborted, Houghton understood his life as a miraculous intervention and one that necessitated giving glory back to the Creator. "Ever since I've known my story," he explained, "it changed the way I approached worshipping God. . . . The journey has been one really borne out of gratitude and out of a true heart for God and thanksgiving for what he's done" ("Israel Houghton // Interview" 2011).

After her conversion, Margaret met and married Pentecostal preacher Henry Houghton, and together they founded the Potter's House Christian Center in Santa Fe, New Mexico, where young Israel grew up. Reared as a preacher's kid in the Potter's House, Houghton came into constant contact with different cultures. As he put it, he "was the only black kid in a white family in a Hispanic church" (Cummings 2006). At age seven, the issue of race came to a boiling point when Houghton met his maternal grandfather for the first time, who rejected him in disgust (Watts and Blim n.d.).

Yet, as in his mother's story, suffering led to purpose for Houghton. After Psalm 139 convinced him that he was "fearfully and wonderfully made," he accepted his childhood agony as a source of empathy for "the pain that a lot of people feel." "I didn't just sneak into the earth," Houghton explained. "I was created for something great . . . [and] the more I share that with people who want to hear it, the better I feel about why I'm here" (Watts and Blim n.d.).

So while his racial identity brought confusion and suffering, Houghton renarrated his background as a blessing and a testimony that underlined God's love. He distilled his new identity as a child of God in his song "Identity" on his album *Live: A Deeper Level*: "You are my father / In you I find my identity / I can do all things / If you say I can / Show me I am free / Free to accomplish your plan for me."[4] Or consider the song "New Season" on his album by the same name: "The devil's time is up, no longer can he bother me / 'Cause the Creator of the universe He fathers me / If you don't know by now, you need to know it's jubilee / Where debts are canceled and your children walk in victory."[5] But to be a child of God was also to be a friend of God, as Houghton proclaimed in his song "Friend of God" on *Alive in South Africa*: "Is it true that you are thinking of me / How you love me, it's amazing / I am a friend of God . . . / He calls me friend."[6] He continued this theme in the song "Friend" on his album *Live from Another Level*: "There will never be a friend / As dear to me as You / Ev'ry time You call me friend / I receive Your healing."[7]

For Houghton, to be a friend of God, to be a son or daughter of God, was to be set free to worship God and to be open to God's blessings. Rejecting his existence as accidental meant accepting a great purpose for his life: "I have faith—a belief—that I was put on this earth, in this generation, to help change the world. Whatever the world looks like, whatever my part of the world is, I am here to help make a deep impact on it" (Houghton 2007, 60). Houghton's testimony contextualized not only his love for Jesus but also his rise to stardom. His story provided a theological rationale for his success. This was not simply the classic evangelical declaration that one was a sinner and only cleansed by Christ's blood. It was also a declaration that God had great plans for his children. As Houghton explained, his goal was "not just to get to heaven, but to truly build something lasting" (Watts and Blim n.d.).

This conviction—that as children and friends of God we are free to receive God's blessings and accomplish God's plans for us—was one of divine prosperity and sat at the heart of Houghton's testimony and music. Inspired by the logic of the prosperity gospel, identity for Houghton was inherently tied to the reception of God's blessing. And understanding God as a father and friend who had great plans for him both powered Houghton's testimony and explained his musical success.

A New Breed of Sound

Houghton's unique fusion of musical styles echoed the biracial identity fore-grounded in his testimony. His music resounded his journey of overcoming the negative alienation of his racial identity and transforming it to reflect the unity of all believers in the friendship of God. And though his musical style did not explicitly reflect a prosperity disposition, its combination of differ-ent musical genres, often associated with different ethnicities, reflected the emphasis on multiracial congregations and worship that emerged in prosper-ity culture in the 1980s and 1990s (Bowler 2013, 206). Even before Houghton made his way to Lakewood Church, his musical development reflected this multiracial emphasis.

Growing up as "the only black kid in a white family in a Hispanic church" meant that Houghton was attracted to artists who had a unique ability to cross genres and racial lines. Early on, he gravitated toward legendary black gospel artist Andraé Crouch, who was first popular among white college students in the early 1970s and only later developed an African American audience (Jen-kins 1990, 92).[8] Houghton was also influenced by Kent Henry and Ron Kenoly, two worship leaders who pioneered a fusion of "white" adult contemporary styles with black gospel forms.

In 1995, Houghton founded New Breed, a troupe of worship leaders who joined forces to tour and record live albums. New Breed members included Houston-based vocalist Jamil Freeman, Los Angeles songwriter Daniel John-son, and keyboardist Arthur Strong, among many others. There were also international members, such as Nigerian vocalist Olanrewaju Agbabiaka and South African vocalists Lois Du Plessis and Neville Diedericks. From the start, Houghton argued, New Breed was intended to break down the racial boundaries in worship music. He desired a team of "people of like spirit who [wanted] to see the cultures crossed, who [wanted] to see the barriers come down between" the races, a group that would bring "the sound of heaven to the earth" ("Israel Houghton Interview Hillsong Conference 2006" 2011). "New Breed is colorless," Houghton asserted. "It's this broad generation of people who just want God," instead of floundering on the racial and cultural differ-ences that plagued the church ("Israel Houghton Interview w/The Urban Post Worldwide" 2010). Though New Breed's members were dedicated to bridging the racial gulf in worship music, Houghton's assertion of colorlessness butted up against the fact that all publicity photos of the group featured an all-black cast, and only one touring member of New Breed, Ryan Edgar, was white.

Thus, while Houghton and his New Breed compatriots were genuinely interested in healing the racial divide in churches, their self-description was also part of what Jeremy Morris has called a "brand narrative"—the "collection of sounds, sights, reviews, concerts and merchandise that feed an artist's overall perception," as well as the marketing materials that shape the consumer experience (2005, 105–6). Houghton's brand was invested in the assertion of New Breed's colorless identity, and the narratives that he told had to reflect that, even when some of the visual marketing materials told a different story.

Still, Houghton's music was a mélange of pop, rock, gospel, and R&B styles that was difficult to place in one genre. "If you can categorize something," Houghton contended, "then you can cancel it at anytime" ("Israel Houghton Interview Hillsong Conference 2006" 2011). So New Breed deliberately fought categorization by infusing its music with different styles, rhythms, and melodic structures. This conviction to create "musical gumbo," as Houghton called it (Symmonds n.d.), was grounded in an eschatological vision of the eventual unity of God's people: "When we get to heaven, there's not going to be sections—'This is the black section of heaven. This is the white section of heaven. What kind of music do you like? Well, you're going to be over in that room.' I believe the Kingdom has a sound. I believe glory has a sound. So I want to be a part of doing it. I believe it's a very multi-cultural mix of sound and style and lyric and melody and everything else" (Watts and Blim n.d.).

Houghton's allegiance to multicultural forms made his music attractive to a wide audience of aspiring multiracial churches. As sociologist Gerardo Marti has shown, multiracial churches often attempted to structure worship music around what he labeled the "musical buffet" theory (2012, 34). This theory asserted that churches successfully built diverse congregations when they offered a "multicultural mix of sound," one that utilized different musical genres that appealed to different racial or ethnic demographics. Further, churches that adhered to the "musical buffet" theory often hired worship leaders who ascribed to a "pluralist philosophy" in developing their musical strategy. Pluralist worship leaders focused on creating ethnic diversity by cultivating musical variety. For pluralists, music was racialized and required "a buffet of racially specific styles to provide every group a source of musical resonance" (132–33).

The intentional blending of musical genres and styles put Houghton squarely in the pluralist and musical buffet camps. As Houghton asserted, his musical salad bowl was "not a white sound or black sound, [it was] a kingdom sound" (Houghton 2007, 158). And as his four Grammy Awards attest, this kingdom sound was immensely popular. According to Marti, this made sense, as the musical buffet theory has been "the most prominent and the most mentioned by church leaders who express any 'theory' at all," as well as popular among worship songwriters at large (2012, 34–35). For churches, worship leaders, and pastors around the country trying to develop ethnically and socioeconomically diverse congregations, Houghton's music stood out as a successful model and ambitious blueprint of what musical buffet and pluralist worship music could really be.

Yet the popularity of Houghton's music was not simply the result of its conformity to the musical buffet theory and a pluralist philosophy. Its instrumental scalability between guitar and piano and its stylistic mutability between black and white church music forms gave it broad appeal among black and white music leaders in large churches—churches that had the musical resources to pull off Houghton's sonic potpourri. At the same time, its blending of styles, backed by a theology of diversity that was inscribed in Houghton's biography, made his music appealing to churches seeking to create racially diverse congregations.

As a result, Houghton's music enticed multiethnic American megachurches. This was a sizeable crowd, as a 2005 Hartford Institute survey showed that 56 percent of megachurches were interested in becoming multiethnic in their congregational makeup, while one-fifth of megachurch attendees already belonged to a nonmajority ethnic group (Thumma, Travis, and Bird 2005). It made sense, then, that in 2001 Houghton ended up at Lakewood Church in Houston, Texas, one of the largest multiethnic megachurches in the country.

Houghton's role as a worship leader at Lakewood provided a suitable platform for his musical fusion of genres and styles. And this was not simply because it was a megachurch but also because it was a flagship church in the wider prosperity movement, which had continually transcended racial boundaries, attracting both blacks and whites to worship together at the feet of prosperity gurus such as Joel Osteen, Benny Hinn, Joyce Meyer, and Creflo Dollar. Lakewood's congregational diversity, backed by its message of prosperity that transcended race, found its soundtrack in Houghton's fusion of black and white church music forms.

From Blessed to Blessing

The same year that Houghton joined the staff at Lakewood Church, he released his second album, *New Season*, which featured songs proclaiming a gospel of prosperity, the declaration that God wants to bless his children with a new season of wealth, health, and abundance in this life, not just the next:

> It's a new season, it's a new day.
> A fresh anointing is flowing my way.
> It's a season of power (let the weak say I am strong)
> and prosperity (let the poor say I am rich).
> It's a new season coming to me.

As was common among prosperity teachers, Houghton focused on God's promises of prosperity and victory, even in the midst of difficult circumstances: "All that was stolen is returned to you a hundred fold / Tried in the fire but you're coming out gold" ("New Season").

This distinct recognition that one could move from darker days into the light of new blessing echoed Joel Osteen's own message of prosperity. Osteen's immense popularity was due to the broad appeal of his nonsectarian, positive message of hope and well-being. Historian Kate Bowler calls this "soft prosperity," and Osteen remains its lead ambassador. Osteen exchanged the hard causality between spoken word and reality (so often found in traditional prosperity teachings) for a soft causality that employed the language of popular psychology. Bowler argues that soft prosperity teachers such as Osteen tied psychological states to fiscal and personal success, asserting that a rightly ordered mind led to rightly ordered finances, health, and family. While the traditional prosperity mantra remained the same—change your words, change your life—for Osteen, the transformative power of positive declaration could be demonstrated psychologically, rather than simply via the supernatural forces of faith (2013, 125).

In his song "Your Latter Will Be Greater," Houghton fashioned Osteen's emphasis on positive declaration into lyrical form: "Your latter will be greater than your past / You will be blessed, more than you could ask / Despite all that has been done, the best is yet to come."[9] A maxim of the Lakewood pastor, "the best is yet to come" revealed Osteen's theological influence on Houghton, as Osteen frequently reminded believers that God would shower them with blessings in the future. But only if they would receive it. For Osteen, God's blessings could be limited by one's inability to imagine them, believe in them, and expect them. God "can do anything," Osteen asserted, "if you will simply stop limiting Him in your thinking." For Osteen, what one received was directly connected to how one believed and what one expected (Osteen 2004, 23, 22). In this mechanistic concept of blessing, God became a magical force to be called down from heaven and caged until the believer was willing to release him for blessing. Houghton narrated this mechanistic concept in his medley "Take the Limits Off / No Limits," sung from God's perspective:

> I'm not a man, I cannot lie
> I know the plans for your life
> I'm asking You to dream again, believe again
> And take the limits off of Me
> Take the limits off, take the limits off
> Release Me, to accomplish what I promised you[10]

Taking the limits off of God required belief—belief in a God who was ready to bless with abundance. But proper belief required a proper conception of God as a father who saw his children as "highly favored." This was the same conviction that powered Houghton's testimony, as the revolution in his thinking came when he embraced God as father and friend. Only then was Houghton able to conceive of his story as a journey of the "highly favored" of the Lord and thereby receive blessing.

Taking the limits off of God also required a proper self-image. For Osteen, the most powerful way to achieve this was through positive declaration: "As you speak affirmatively, you will develop a new image on the inside, and things will begin to change in your favor." Words built self-image for Osteen, for as they "permeate your heart and mind, and especially your subconscious mind, eventually they will begin to change the way you see yourself" (Osteen 2008, 97, 91). Houghton's popular song "Friend of God," though devoid of any explicit theological statements supporting the prosperity gospel, demonstrated this power of proclamation, as the assertion "I am a friend of God" was repeated thirty times. Yet this theme of friendship with God was not simply a declaration. It also became an effective intonation built on Osteen's conviction that to speak positively resulted in living positively. To declare that one was a friend of God was to *become* a friend of God.[11] Once one effected inward psychological and spiritual change by repeatedly singing "I am a friend of God," then one could truly understand oneself as a friend of God—and only then partake in the blessings that God granted to his favored children.

With the release of *Power of One* in 2009 and *Love God, Love People* in 2010, however, Houghton's lyrical focus moved from being blessed to becoming a blessing. In a 2009 interview with Beliefnet, Houghton explained that a new conviction inspired by God's words in the fifth chapter of Amos brought about this change: "It essentially says—I am totally paraphrasing right now in the sort of King James Brown version—I am tired of church as usual, I am tired of you guys getting together and singing a bunch of great songs and the fact that you haven't emphasized the poor, the widow, the orphan, the voiceless. . . . I am not even hearing your songs" ("Standing on 'The Power of One'" 2009). Houghton explained that the fifth chapter of Amos threatened his relationship with God. "[Are you] not even listening," he asked God, "to these songs that we wrote for you?" The answer back was no, as God told Houghton, "I want justice. . . . Take care of those that cannot take care of themselves, do that first, that's what being a Christian is about" (Symmonds n.d.). So, to restore friendship with God, Houghton turned his focus to justice.

This centrifugal change mirrored a larger trend toward social justice in American evangelicalism at the turn of the twenty-first century. Evangelical megachurch pastor Rick Warren led crusades against AIDS, Christian magazines such as *Relevant* attempted to educate their readership about "unjust war" and "creation care," and student worship conferences raised thousands for water wells in Africa. Evangelicals even began championing rock star Bono— who before had never been a "good" evangelical—as he proselytized for God and the global poor at concerts and National Prayer breakfasts (Sullivan 2010). Houghton's own message began to sound like Bono's as he sang the world to attention to the plight of the poor. Citing a line that Bono used at an NAACP awards show, Houghton sang that "God is with us when we are with them."[12] Like Bono, Houghton's message of love and solidarity brought him acclaim and record sales. But this emphasis on social justice also made his music more appealing to young American evangelicals who were drawn to the new crusade for social justice.

Though Houghton's move from blessedness to blessing—from an emphasis on being to agency—was influenced by forces outside of prosperity culture, it still reflected Osteen's logic. As Houghton explored the fruits of positive thinking according to Osteen's prosperity teachings, his focus had moved inward, and his introspection was grounded in a familial relationship with God. But once blessedness and subsequent calling were secured, he began to look outward. "It all begins with one, the power of one," Houghton crooned, explaining that if everyone took their beliefs and acted on them, together they could change the world.[13] He then summarized his conviction in "Love God, Love People": "I can't give it / Until I live it / Now that my eyes are open / Teach me how to love."[14] Now that his eyes were open to his true identity, Houghton was moved to action. Now that he was blessed, he could be a blessing.

Houghton's message remained tethered to the soft prosperity theology of Osteen in its combination of identity and action, in the connection between blessedness and blessing. Only from an identity grounded in God's love and favor came the desire to help and bless others. Yet, as evidenced in his post-2009 discography, Houghton's quest to change the world did not begin with economic redistribution or a Bono-like aid organization attempting to make structural change. Instead, it began with "the power of one" to change the way we view—and speak about—the world around us. And grounded in a prosperity logic, Houghton's lyrical declarations were not simply attempts to persuade his listeners to love and care for people. They were also *effective* declarations that worked an inward psychological change and asked God to give to the listener what God had promised: blessing, so that one could be a blessing.

Houghton expanded on this concept of blessing in his book *A Deeper Level*: "Why are we blessed? The reason we are blessed is to be a blessing. Maybe that is the only thing that needs to be adjusted. Maybe what needs clarification is not the blessing, but for whom the blessing is intended" (2007, 135). This combination of prosperity teaching with an outward focus had corollaries in the theological concept of stewardship, an older tradition with a rich heritage in North American Protestantism, in which disestablished religion required the laity to maintain buildings and pay clergy salaries (Johnson 2007, 71). And by combining prosperity teaching with an outward focus, Houghton's music became more palatable to anti–prosperity gospel American evangelicals, who nonetheless had often baptized the stewarding of prosperity for the sake of helping others.

While Houghton remained in conversation with the Word of Faith movement, his lyrics moved away from the narrower vocabulary of "favor" and "anointing" and embraced the wider, more generic language of American evangelicalism, the solidarity rhetoric of Bono, and the social justice emphasis of evangelical leaders such as Rick Warren. But this was not a new strategy. Time and again, American Christians exchanged limiting, confessionally specific doctrine for greater influence and acceptance in popular culture. As evangelicals sought a seat at the larger table of national culture, they in turn had to retool their rhetoric with nonsectarian language. This was true for Billy Graham and the neo-evangelicals in the 1940s and 1950s (Carpenter 1997, 241), just as it was for Joel Osteen as he built Lakewood. Likewise, Houghton's music transcended the borders of the prosperity movement because it came to transcend prosperity language. Like Billy Graham, Houghton discerned, appropriated, and adapted trends already in motion (Wacker 2014, 316). And by embracing these wider, nonsectarian impulses, Houghton, like Graham, transformed his prosperity theology in order to gain greater influence and acceptance in evangelical culture.

Conclusion

We began with a question: How did Houghton's music achieve such broad popularity among evangelical churches when the prosperity gospel was so maligned? At first glance, the answer is the simple one we just saw: Houghton diluted his prosperity theology with more generic evangelical language and a focus on social justice in order to increase his popularity. If we were to approach Houghton's lyrics alone as cultural texts, this is a logical conclusion. But when we consider the wider context afforded by an author-based approach—the ways in which Houghton integrated the prosperity gospel into his testimony, music, and lyrics, and, in essence, into his entire public persona and marketed musical package—we find a different story. Houghton's emphasis on the empowering friendship of God, his dedication to a multiracial musical style, his use of positive declaration and repetition, and his conviction that we are blessed in order to be a blessing not only made him attractive to evangelicals but also identified him as an innovative worship leader and theologian steeped in the prosperity tradition. Though at times indirect and even "soft" like his pastor's, Houghton's prosperity theology decidedly shaped his music. And though an overt prosperity gospel would have proved a liability among evangelicals, Houghton's soft prosperity bolstered his popularity. For churches looking for an answer to the problem of musical diversity in their congregations, for individuals moved by an inspiring role model who overcame adversity through the friendship of God, and for young believers who were more interested in the cause of social justice than in conservative evangelical social values, Houghton's music proved inspiring. For Houghton, of course, the reason was clear: it was blessed to be a blessing.

NOTES

1. For Houghton, as for many other professional Christian pop musicians, there is slippage between his role as "worship leader" and "Christian artist." While Houghton is a worship leader at Lakewood, he is also a recording artist for Integrity Media, and he splits his time between Lakewood and international touring and recording. Thus, his role at Lakewood is as much

about securing a mutual contract of celebrity visibility between himself and Osteen as it is about leading worship.

2. Joel Osteen's preaching does not embrace an explicit Pentecostal identity that highlights charismatic gifts, even though his father, John Osteen, founded Lakewood church after receiving the "baptism of the Holy Ghost." But Joel Osteen's debt to his father's Word of Faith theology, his emphasis on the accessible, miraculous power of verbal declarations, and his mother's healing ministry at Lakewood all point to the implicit Pentecostal heritage that is integral to Lakewood's identity. Similarly, Houghton's Pentecostal upbringing is not explicit in his music or public persona, but his Pentecostal sensibilities are implicit in his language, lyrics, and musical networks. In adapting and downplaying their inherited Pentecostalism, both Osteen and Houghton have extended their reach to wider audiences. For more on Osteen's and Lakewood's Pentecostal heritage, see Sinitiere (2012).

3. Houghton narrates his testimony in his book *A Deeper Level* and in several interviews: Watts and Blim (n.d.), "Israel Houghton // Interview" (2011), "Israel Houghton Interview Hillsong Conference 2006" (2011), "Israel Houghton on TBN" (2011), and Symmonds (n.d.).

4. "Identity." Words and music by Israel Houghton, Neville Diedericks. CCLI #5040153. ©2007 Integrity's Praise! Music (administered by EMI Christian Music Publishing).

5. "New Season." Words and music by Derick Thomas, Israel Houghton. CCLI #2927262. ©1997 Integrity's Praise! Music (administered by EMI Christian Music Publishing).

6. "Friend of God." Words and music by Israel Houghton, Michael Gungor. CCLI #3991651. ©2003 Integrity's Praise! Music (administered by EMI Christian Music Publishing).

7. "Friend." Words and music by Aaron Lindsey, Israel Houghton, Kevin Singleton, Meleasa Houghton. CCLI #4302816. ©2004 Integrity's Praise! Music (administered by EMI Christian Music Publishing).

8. Only when Crouch signed with Warner Brothers in 1979 did he begin marketing his music to black audiences.

9. "Your Latter Will Be Greater." Words and music by Derick Thomas, Israel Houghton. CCLI #3383908. ©2001 Integrity's Praise! Music (administered by EMI Christian Music Publishing).

10. "Take the Limits Off." Words and music by Aaron Lindsey, Israel Houghton. CCLI #4654210. ©2005 Sound Of The New Breed (administered by EMI Christian Music Publishing).

11. This has corollaries with J. L. Austin's performative utterance theory. Performative utterances, which Austin also labeled "illocutionary acts," were not simply sayings or descriptions but part of a performance of a certain action. See Austin (1975, 5).

12. "Love Rev." Words and music by Aaron Lindsey, Israel Houghton, Tommy Sims. CCLI #5763052. ©2010 Integrity's Praise! Music (administered by EMI Christian Music Publishing).

13. "The Power of One." Words and music by Israel Houghton, Ricardo Sanchez. CCLI #5348783. ©2009 Integrity's Praise! Music (administered by EMI Christian Music Publishing).

14. "Love God, Love People." Words and music by Aaron Lindsey, Israel Houghton, Tommy Sims. CCLI #5763021. ©2010 Integrity's Praise! Music (administered by EMI Christian Music Publishing).

REFERENCES

Austin, J. L. 1975. *How to Do Things with Words*. Edited by J. O. Urmson and Marina Sbisà. Cambridge: Harvard University Press.

Bowler, Kate. 2013. *Blessed: A History of the American Prosperity Gospel*. New York: Oxford University Press.

Carpenter, Joel A. 1997. *Revive Us Again: The Reawakening of American Fundamentalism*. New York: Oxford University Press.

Cummings, Tony. 2006. "Israel Houghton: The Pioneer Who Is an Advocate for Cross-cultural Worship." Cross Rhythms, April 26. http://www.crossrhythms.co.uk/articles/music/Israel_Houghton/21248/p1/.

Hagin, Kenneth E. 1979. *You Can Have What You Say!* Tulsa, Okla.: K. Hagin Ministries.

Houghton, Israel. 2007. *A Deeper Level*. New Kensington, Pa.: Whitaker House.

"Israel Houghton // Interview." 2011. YouTube video, 7:34. From an interview by Ben Prescott recorded at the 2011 Planetshakers Conference. Posted by planetshakerstv, May 4. http://www.youtube.com/watch?v=mQEWkdl-DbE.

"Israel Houghton Interview Hillsong Conference 2006." 2011. Youtube video, 5:54. From an interview by Nathan Tasker recorded at the 2006 Hillsong Conference. Posted by vickiereddy, August 15. http://www.youtube.com/watch?v=IalXGFKsCYw.

"Israel Houghton Interview w/The Urban Post Worldwide (Part 1)." 2010. Youtube video, 6:16. From an interview by Niele Anderson. Posted by urbanpostworldwide, February 24. http://www.youtube.com/watch?v=Byl4IVNfogo.

"Israel Houghton on TBN June3–2011 Interview and Testimony." 2011. YouTube video, 14:40. From an interview by Matt Crouch. Posted by skymegatoronto, June 7. http://www.youtube.com/watch?v=zbBTW5T8ses. Originally aired June 3, 2011, on *Praise the Lord*, Trinity Broadcasting Network, Costa Mesa, Calif.

Jenkins, Keith Bernard. 1990. *The Rhetoric of Gospel Song: A Content Analysis of the Lyrics of Andrae Crouch*. Ph.D. diss., Florida State University.

Johnson, Kelly S. 2007. *The Fear of Beggars: Stewardship and Poverty in Christian Ethics*. Grand Rapids, Mich.: Eerdmans.

Lynch, Gordon. 2005. *Understanding Theology and Popular Culture*. Malden, Mass.: Blackwell.

Morris, Jeremy. 2005. "Making the Brand: Exploring the Role of Branding in Popular Music." M.A. thesis, Ryerson University.

Marti, Gerardo. 2012. *Worship Across the Racial Divide: Religious Music and the Multiracial Congregation*. New York: Oxford University Press.

Osteen, Joel. 2004. *Your Best Life Now: 7 Steps to Living at Your Full Potential*. New York: Warner Books.

———. 2008. *Daily Readings from "Become a Better You": 90 Devotions for Improving Your Life Every Day*. New York: Free Press.

Sinitiere, Phillip Luke. 2012. "Preaching the Good News Glad: Joel Osteen's Tel-e-vangelism." In *Global and Local Televangelism*, edited by Pradip Ninan Thomas and Philip Lee, 87–107. New York: Palgrave Macmillan.

Sullivan, Amy. 2010. "Young Evangelicals: Expanding Their Mission." *Time*, June 1. http://www.time.com/time/nation/article/0,8599,1992463,00.html.

Symmonds, Nicole S. n.d. "Standing on 'The Power of One.'" Beliefnet. http://www.beliefnet.com/Entertainment/Music/Christian-Music/2009/Israel-Houghton-Interview.aspx.

Thumma, Scott, Dave Travis, and Warren Bird. 2005. "Megachurches Today 2005 Summary of Research Findings." Hartford Institute for Religion Research. http://www.hirr.hartsem.edu/megachurch/megastoday2005_summaryreport.html.

Van Biema, David, and Jeff Chu. 2006. "Does God Want You to be Rich?" *Time*, September 18, 48–58.

Wacker, Grant. 2014. *Billy Graham and the Shaping of Modern America*. Cambridge: Belknap Press of Harvard University Press.

Watts, Kristi, and Julie Blim. n.d. "Israel Houghton: An Intimate Portrait of Worship." CBN. http://www.cbn.com/cbnmusic/Interviews/700club_IsraelHoughton_041205.aspx.

13

Music, Culture Industry, and the Shaping of Charismatic Worship: An Autobiographical/Conversational Engagement

Dave Perkins

Introduction

The aim of this chapter is to explore subtle but nevertheless weighty shifts in power and influence that are by-products of the commoditization of worship music and may be impacting both the tone of charismatic worship and perceptions of what musical worship is and should be. Central to this discussion is the idea that culture industry,[1] with its power to manufacture demand for its products and to elevate particular models of musical expression over others through promotion and marketing, has a homogenizing or flattening effect on a music culture that was born in spontaneity and with a diversity of approaches.

My Point of View

The mid-1980s was a heady time in Nashville, Tennessee, for anyone who worshipped in a charismatic congregation and was also involved with the contemporary Christian music (CCM) industry.[2] At Nashville's Belmont Church, an air of expectancy was particularly present. By 1985, Belmont was well on its way to completing a remarkable metamorphosis from a Church of Christ congregation that eschewed instrumental music into a thoroughgoing Spirit-filled, charismatic congregation that provided a spiritual and musical home to a number of key CCM artists, including Amy Grant and Michael W. Smith.

Belmont had been my church home since 1976, and I shared the congregation's developing sense of destiny, the feeling that we were flowing with the sea change in Christian worship arts that was taking place in England, California, and elsewhere. We believed that Belmont had a role to play in the charismatic revival that would renew Christian thought and practice around the world.

It was clear to many of us that Belmont's contribution to the renaissance in worship arts and to what we thought of then as the redemption of popular culture would, in significant part, come through the music makers and Christian music industry leaders nurtured at Belmont. Not only was I a member of the Belmont congregation during this period, but it was then that my professional activities shifted away from the world of mainstream popular music toward the energized and emerging CCM scene. I am sure that Belmont's valorization of its Christian music artists had an effect on my thinking. Belmont's influence aside, however, the idea that there was a context in which I could make music with a high level of pop authenticity, but which would also allow me to include reflections on my spiritual life, was an enticement. And, as a more material lure, sales numbers for CCM seemed to confirm that the efforts to make a place in the popular arts for Christian sensibilities were succeeding. CCM artists such as Amy Grant were beginning to break into the worlds of pop music radio and press, albeit with a sort of grudging critical acceptance. The idea that Christian music would find success in the marketplace of pop culture was important to our Nashville community. It was also important to many other evangelical-minded Christians at that time who were exploring ways of dealing with the bifurcation of identity between spiritual and cultural citizenship through purposeful cultural activism.

From its start, my experience with CCM was a theological and cultural minefield. I struggled with how to connect my interpretation of Jesus's words regarding money with the commodification of faith as I was encountering it in the CCM industry. Almost simultaneous with my earliest involvement in CCM, I found myself participating in a recurring conversation among artists and individuals in the industry about whether Christian music artists should see their endeavors through the lens of business or ministry. Some of us struggled with the question more than others. For us, the worlds of moneymaking and spiritual devotion were like opposing magnetic poles. Unlike some of our friends and associates in the CCM industry, we were unable to make the poles mutually attractive. The "elephant in the room"—the shaping of faith, testimony, and ritual for commercial return—was a nearly constant, although often unspoken, presence in conversations and meetings. I grappled with a disquieting sense that something was at stake—at least for me. That disquiet became more profound as praise and worship (P&W), the music that had recently redefined my own worship life, became the industry's focus.

One aspect of my struggle—one that continues to complicate my attempts to understand Christian culture industry—was the difficulty of separating the people involved from the activities and effects of industry. Several close friends and others whom I esteem help make the world of Christian products and celebrity go around. I struggle with how to problematize the effects of the industry on churches and individuals, as I will do here, while knowing many of the people involved to be good, caring, and well intentioned. I carry that tension into this discussion.

It is to my benefit in this matter, however, that the fragmentation of the music industry as a result of digital technology and the Internet has opened up a sight line through which we can find perspective on where the real power governing the production and consumption of cultural goods lies. It is not solely in the will of individuals and companies but in a will that human beings have set loose in the cultural machinery—one that, as described by cultural theorists including Baudrillard (1994), Debord (1994), and Barthes (1977), now has a self-sustaining logic that seems natural to us. In that light, this chapter is not a critique of the Christian music industry except to the extent to which it molds itself or is molded by those culture-shaping forces that run through all culture industries and media and have become taken for granted in the culture of consumption.

It may be the case that the most significant product of culture industry is the lens through which we view the cultural landscape. The self-sustaining ways and means of the culture industry are to a large extent now invisible to us. They are woven into the fabric of everyday life. Through electronic media and mass communications, we daily come under the influence of ideologically charged cultural powers (Hardt 2004, 133–39; Adorno 2000). We have come to see the ubiquity of culture industry as natural. Many of the old cultural divides, such as between religion and pop culture, are, for better or worse, ruptured. We are, therefore, not surprised when we see (if we do) culture industry at work in our activities of worship. The already blurred line between sanctuary and marketplace is growing increasingly indistinct in subtle increments.

Worship Music as a General Market Commodity

My interest in the ways in which religion and business accommodate each other for the accomplishment of their individual goals sharpened in 2001.

It came unexpectedly with the experience of seeing *Shout to the Lord*, volume 1 of *Songs 4 Worship*—the first Time Life compilation of worship songs—advertised on cable television. I was taken aback by this ad. Missing in my reaction was the celebration anticipated in the CCM era, with its hope that one day we would see evangelical Christian cultural artifacts get equal time and evenhanded treatment in electronic media. Several months after the launch of the Time Life advertising campaign, a record label marketing person described it to me as a great success on business and spiritual levels.[3] The ad did not register with me as a win, however. My impression was that this was an occasion in which competing for attention in commodity culture had exacted a price that was not reducible to money. For me, the images of congregations with eyes closed, hands raised, and rapt expressions were sullied, as the sights and sounds of devoted worship in these ads were sandwiched between less noble images used to sell everything from car insurance to lingerie.

In hindsight, I know that my reaction to the Time Life ads was layered with complexities. At play was my internal conflict over the commoditization of faith. Again, it seemed to me that there was something at stake. Perhaps my experiences working within the culture industry had sensitized me to the whims of the marketplace and the ephemeral nature of its trends and products. Perhaps I was feeling protective of the important concepts on which Christian products are based—afraid that somehow those ideas would suffer by the falling out of fashion that is the fate of most pop culture products. I suspect that the most powerful dynamic at work was my affection for the new music of worship. Singing the new songs with fellow worshippers was powerful. It constituted a healing sonic experience that was, on the one hand, familiar and contiguous to my life outside the church and, on the other hand, a remove from the ever-present, unwanted noise of that life.

Over time, my questions regarding the industrialization of worship music became an academic interest. It was then that I turned to friends and associates at Belmont and beyond with whom I shared worship and music industry life to seek their observations and opinions on the commoditization of worship and its possible outcomes.

Conversations on the Business of Worship

In numerous conversations and interviews with individuals who are or were active both in worship leadership and in the culture industry, I heard viewpoints on the worship music industry at every point on the scale between enthusiastic support and vitriolic disparagement.[4] Where my conversation partners questioned the industrialization[5] of musical worship, there was often a point of friction between belief and business. They exhibited a split loyalty, a contested allegiance to two ideas: first, that certain areas of spiritual life should not be subjected unshielded to the whims of popular culture, and, second, that the industry can serve consumers in multiple ways, such as through the provision of a portable worship experience in the form of CDs and DVDs.

Most of my conversation partners have learned to live with their feelings of friction. A strong sense of calling attenuates the perceived downsides of commoditizing worship music and experience. Yet aspects of the industry that seem negative but elude easy appraisal continue to trouble them. As one conversation partner, a worship music writer and performer said, "It's my job and I love it. But, as a Christian, I have to say that there is something askew there."[6] To these individuals' credit, a mission of facilitating true worship maintains a secure place in their motivations and self-understanding as professional worship music makers. However, some of them are also savvy observers and analysts of cultural and religious phenomena.

As an executive at EMI Christian Records, Lynn Nichols was instrumental in giving worship music its current commercial weight. When Nichols went to work for EMI in the early 1990s, "Christian entertainment music," as he refers to CCM, was faltering in its market share. One musical trend was coming to a close; another was being kindled in local churches. Having a long personal history in charismatic worship, Nichols responded with enthusiasm when he witnessed the modern rock worship band Delirious? performing at a youth event in England. What he found in England was a band and a worship music scene that espoused purposes that aligned with his own desire to produce cutting-edge music for contemporary worshippers. Nichols was one of the people who shaped the sound, the look, and ultimately public perceptions of P&W. He was also a consumer, someone looking for music that would inspire and lift his own worship experiences.

Nichols's religious and musical sensibilities were shaped in and by the Jesus Movement of the late 1960s and early 1970s. It was there, he says, that he experienced "the move of the Spirit that spawned many unconventional churches and birthed a new music." As a young musician and a young Christian, Nichols was enthralled by the free and unpredictable musical worship he encountered in a New York charismatic community. He loved the songs. They were, to him, "now" and "relevant to the times and culture—unshackled from the stoic hymns of the past." "Eventually," Nichols explains, "the few Christian music companies that existed at that time seized this new marketing opportunity to sell to the youth market and the newly converted hippies." This was, as Nichols now sees it, the beginning of a process of commercialization wherein a musical experience that was once "fresh, honest, and inspired became stale."

Arguing from the viewpoint of a professional music producer, Nichols says that the culture industry's propensity to standardize products has a homogenizing effect.

NICHOLS: I think what [bothers] me most is that the music is turning into a very contrived, very derivative, very copycat kind of sound. So, there's not much freedom. It's become very restricted in how it's composed, how it's presented, how it's supposed to sound. This is largely for commercial reasons. I understand [why] because I've been in the commercial music business. But that doesn't make me like it. I don't like it in the pop music business either.

According to Nichols, recordings are sounding more and more alike, and the churches that use the songs are beginning to look and sound more and more alike. Homogenization, he suggests, is present at the point of consumption as well as the point of production—in the songwriting, the recording aesthetics, and, consequently, the performance of the songs at the local level. Whereas P&W was born in churches with independent spirits, each with its own nuanced ways of doing musical worship, there is now an "industry standard" by which many churches measure their worship arts.

NICHOLS: You program these [worship songs] on radio, and get them to top ten or number one positions, and a lot of Christian people drive around and listen to Christian radio because, to them, it's a positive reinforcement. They're not necessarily listening to it to hear the coolest new song or to find out where music is going. They want support in their beliefs. Most of these radio stations see themselves as purveyors of [that]: "We're feeding people, encouraging people, nourishing people, creating a safe family place." [However], what you start doing—and it's much like the film industry—you start telling people what is good and what they need.
PERKINS: The industry tells them?
NICHOLS: The industry does. You know, it happens in films. In both industries, you have people telling you what you need to have. That [happens] on pop radio. And that same equation moves over to Christian radio. After a while [people say], "Yeah, this is good." Repetition—which is going to motivate the purchase—has

an effect. Those people begin to think, "This is what worship music is. This is what it sounds like." And then they go to church, and almost every church that's a bigger church and that is evangelical is going to have a fairly competent worship band and they are singing these songs—just like they are heard on the CDs. The arrangements are going to be the same. You hear those songs and a lot of songs like them. The way this is impacting Christian culture is that [consumers] now embrace this as "This is worship." [This phenomenon] is not unique. The commercial market does this too. TV does. Magazines tell you when you open the page, "You have to look like this." It's the same selling methods really. There is no difference. So, they [industry] are creating their own Christian pop culture.

Speaking with Nichols, I get the impression that the most precious thing about his early charismatic experiences was his sense that the Holy Spirit was immediately present as an animating force within the congregation's performance of music. Nichols confides that this quality of worship is becoming harder for him to find. He sees this missing quality of worship as a casualty of the commoditization of the music. The homogenizing effects of industrialization have promoted predictability and compromised, for him, a clear sense of the leading of the Holy Spirit. It may be that Nichols knows too much about how songs and recordings are crafted to produce desired emotional responses. Nevertheless, the kind of spontaneity he finds becoming scarce is a deeply felt issue for him. Nichols reflects on how the industry is altering the qualities of P&W that attracted him early on:

NICHOLS: Another observation on worship bands generally—and I know there are exceptions—but, for the most part, it is a preprogrammed idea of worship. So, often there is no leeway to expound or let the Holy Spirit lead you. Now, not in every case, but more and more it's become . . .
PERKINS: It's a set liturgy?
NICHOLS: That's right. It's set. There's a set *list*! [*laughs*] Now, I'm not saying that people don't stray from it. But, for the most part, it is set. And, in a lot of churches, it's also the [radio or CCLI[7]] hit list. And it's a cover band, because you're covering [popular] worship songs.

Here, Nichols speaks from the perspective of a music maker. In addition to his other capabilities, he is an excellent guitarist with considerable experience as an improvisational player. He has come to see improvisational music making and charismatic worship in the same light. Nichols believes that whether an individual musician, band, or congregation is performing music, it is the Holy Spirit's active leadership that makes of the performance a transcendent experience. Hence, he complains that there is a lost opportunity when a worship band performs a well-known song exactly like the recorded version. By not making room for the Spirit's creative input in their individual and group performance, the performers miss an opportunity to participate in and experience inspired worship.

I asked Nichols whether it is enough that written into the arrangement of many worship songs is an opening for Spirit-led inspiration—where, in a sense, a place has been set at the musical table by the songwriter and record producer for the Holy Spirit.

PERKINS: There seems to be a linear quality to the arrangement and construction of worship songs, which allows for spatial shifts in the song to accommodate spoken or other sung things. In that sense, there is room in the songs [for spontaneity]. But you're saying that in the service itself there is no room?
NICHOLS: Well, there tends not to be. In my church, on occasion, there will be something where the song kind of ends or breaks down, and somebody is strumming something and somebody might talk . . . or, read a Scripture, or say something that's on their heart. But the thing that I noticed with some of these real worship leaders and worship writers when I went to England and, also, when I was part of a church in upstate New York in the '70s, there was an awful lot of spontaneity, which was *really* great! What I notice with my Delirious? friends and a lot of these English guys is when they're up there leading worship, it's much more likely to take a U-turn musically. It wasn't on that level. It was . . . venturing out into something where we don't know where we're going. We're following our nose, our antenna.

What Nichols saw in the Jesus Movement and again in England in the early 1990s was a scene unaffected by the conditions that, in Nichols's purview, now drive, shape, and restrict the sound and functional possibilities of worship music. Registering his belief that spontaneity was becoming more rare in charismatic worship, Nichols described these early worship scenes:

NICHOLS: Almost always, [the songs spontaneously] went someplace else. And that whole movement was about that. They would sing a song and maybe jump off here and do another thing. But, in order to make the music commercial, palatable, you have to get it down to a certain time—which is understandable if you're going to put it on a CD. Unless it's a live worship album, you have to edit it down. And if you're going to get it on the radio, it has to have a formula. So, this [then] goes into the church and makes the worship band be a little less spontaneous, more programmed—a little less open to having the freedom to [say], "We're going someplace else with this, and the Lord is saying this to us." PERKINS: Wasn't that actually the hook for all of this in the beginning? NICHOLS: Exactly right! That was what people were responding to—that God was on the move and you could feel it. Because people who feel that anointing, feel God moving, are touched and move into a different place. Maybe it opens up something for them and speaks to them in a different way. I feel like a lot of that is being limited by the commercialization factor. Because it was [once] the hook, as you said. That was why people went there. It wasn't "We're going to sing three hymns and then we're done."

When asked whether spontaneity could be "manufactured," Nichols responded that many churches include preprogrammed, rather than Spirit-inspired, "spontaneous" moments that are experienced as arising naturally by worshippers who have never "tasted" the real thing.

Nichols then raised the idea that, in the context of worship and perhaps beyond, music is a living metaphor for spiritual life. He sees music as the medium by which worshippers explore the inexhaustible possibilities of interaction with the divine. For Nichols, musical worship is an adventure. Moreover, it is an Abrahamic[8] adventure wherein worshippers respond to a call to seek God by moving into unmapped territories—as Nichols says, "to venture out," to "move into a different place." Behind Nichols's remarks is the suggestion that any adventure that proceeds according to a script is no longer truly an adventure and its rewards are diminished. Commercial worship music no longer holds surprises for Nichols. He knows the map. He helped draw it. From his perspective, it is troubling to think that worshippers are unaware or unconcerned that they are following a script. If I hear Nichols and some of my other interviewees correctly, to rediscover the spiritual adventure of musical worship is a necessary mission for worship leaders and congregations.

Worship Music and Radio

While radio has suffered since the ascension of the Internet and lost its pride of place in terms of where consumers hear new music, Nichols says that it

remains an important influence on how particular kinds of music get produced. Despite the diminishment of radio's effectiveness in selling music,
record companies continue the ingrained practice of standardizing their
recordings for radio. Radio playability lives on as a benchmark for establishing
when a recording is ready for the marketplace. Playability typically involves
sonic refinement, a relatively short playing time, and stylistic conformity to
a program's play list. Nichols suggests that tailoring worship music to radio's
sensibilities contributes to the homogenizing effect.

So, too, does John Styll, a former CEO of the Gospel Music Association.
Styll reports that, through extensive market research over time, adult contemporary Christian radio has learned that its target listener is "a woman, age
approximately thirty-four, mother of two, and driving an SUV or minivan."[9]
This representative listener/buyer is affectionately referred to by the industry
as Becky. New worship music coming across the desks of music directors at
adult contemporary Christian stations meets a litmus test: Will Becky like it?
As it turns out, Becky is favorable to P&W because its content is exclusive—
distinctly Christian. She can listen to it with her children present and not just
feel safe in terms of what they might hear; she believes that the clear messages
in the songs will have a positive, constructive effect on their lives.

Nevertheless, it is likely that Becky grew up listening to the hits of pop radio.
There is an expectation on her part as to what sounds good. P&W must please
Becky musically—in songwriting, performance, and production—or she will
lose interest, despite the Christian lyrics. Becky makes consumer decisions
through an inherited set of quality control filters. She expects her Christian
songs to sound as pleasing as pop songs. Moreover, Becky may get great satis-
faction from participating in a congregational performance of a ten-minute,
quasi-improvisational P&W song on Sunday morning, but her attention will
not hold for that length of time for a radio song. Hence, Becky is implicated
with regard to the mutation of P&W music from the free-form, led-by-the-
Spirit experience in the sanctuary described by Nichols and others to the world
of the four-minute recording and radio hit. In the quest for radio playability,
the Christian culture industry effectively puts Becky's face on every future
worshipper who will experience a particular worship song, which arrives in
their sanctuary off the rack and ready-made . . . for Becky.

One radio programmer[10] contends that making P&W viable for radio play
is merely a process of distillation, of compressing the salient moments and
effectual characteristics of P&W into the much shorter radio format and giving the recording a slicker production for radio playability. Nichols and Styll

see the matter from another perspective. They maintain that the processes of industrialization are depreciating the expressive range and spirit of P&W that was and continues to be formative for them. Nichols argues that the adaptation of P&W music to radio standards undercuts the music's best qualities—the adventurous attributes, spontaneity, and variety of expression that made it attractive to him in the first place.

Quantity Versus Quality

Culture industry sustains and reproduces itself through a persistent procession of new commodities, material and otherwise. Like other culture industries, the worship industry generates a constant flow of new product. Belmont Church worship leader Rob Frazier[11] acknowledges that keeping pace with the quantity of songs promoted to worshippers through the Internet, radio, magazines, and other media is difficult. The quantitative force of new music coming into churches affects what happens on Sunday morning. Frazier says that it is difficult for him, as a worship leader, to consider using even a small portion of the new songs produced regularly by publishers and record labels. Keeping pace with the industry's output is also difficult for his congregation. Frazier and his Belmont Church associates must make adjustments to maintain continuity in the face of the pressing flow of new songs.

FRAZIER: We are encouraged by the worship department to think in terms of continuity. We're actually forbidden to bring more than two new songs any given week. And I won't even do *that*. One new song is as much as I'll ever do because it takes a long time for people to learn it. The first time through, people are just staring at you. [We] have to remember that we're not dealing with a room full of musicians. And we try to make sure to do something, at least one or two songs, from the last week, just to keep a level of continuity. Because people do complain: "Oh man, all these new songs—I can't learn 'em . . . !" Here's something you hear: "I can't worship with all these new songs." What they mean is they're taking time away from their experience of God, as they understand it, to learn a new song—which is hard.
PERKINS: They have to think too much?
FRAZIER: Think too much, right. So, it's important to do some very familiar songs that people really know.

One explanation for the pressure to keep pace felt by Frazier and other worship leaders is that it is not just songs, styles, and sounds that are being mass imported into worship, but also pop culture's logic of music consumption. In the general marketplace, an underlying doctrine of disposability makes the continuous procession of music product normative. In worship, however, disposability and manufactured need are dynamics that test how effectively music serves the deepest and oldest intentions of worship. The idea that songs, which have attained sacred status, should be displaced to make way for the latest variations—and at the design of an outside entity or process—can be troubling to invested congregations. The fact that songs can remain on the CCLI chart much longer than do songs on pop charts may indicate that worshipping communities remain interested in a musical canon. Should that be true, the pop culture logic of consumption and the unrelenting flow of new songs may, at some point, cause resistance to the worship industry.

Songwriter and musician Phil Madeira[12] suggests that the industrialized flow of new product contributes to a glut of poorly written songs. Just like the pop music industry, the worship industry works to keep consumers interested by creating new variations of its product. In the continual push to increase sales, the industry produces more and more music, which inevitably results in music that lacks imagination and craftsmanship. Several of my conversation partners—fine songwriters themselves—deliver sharp critiques of some worship music. Madeira sees poor songwriting and uninspired performance as an industry by-product, but even more than that, as a stain on the word "Christian." He pushes back against the powerful marketing machinery that links the foundational concepts of Christianity and Christian identity with popular arts that he considers substandard and, in his opinion, drag the word "Christian" down.

MADEIRA: I am up there playing [for worship]. But why am I there? Sometimes I'm just rolling my eyes at the music.
PERKINS: What makes you roll your eyes?
MADEIRA: Oh, just what I consider as a craftsman to be a bad song. It's really not my place, in that moment, to be rolling my eyes. But I am. I'm sort of detached. What is interesting to me is the shift—the evangelical scene seems to be, and I'm not sure ["evangelical" is] even the right word . . . but that group of people that embrace the P&W thing—I mean, it all seems like one big conglomerate package of "This is who a Christian is, this is what a Christian looks

like, this is what a Christian eats, this is what he likes, this is what he doesn't do, this is how he votes." So, a person like me is eventually going to say, "I don't actually fit here. I believe so much of what they believe, but, in terms of the outward expression, it's not working for me." So, I am going to be naturally critical, for better or worse, of the whole program—of the Christian books, of the Christian music. Why would anyone ever put the word "Christian" in front of *this* if they wanted it to be meaningful?

Madeira's observations extend beyond his musical tastes. They reflect his concern that worship itself is being commercialized. For Madeira, narrowing the representational field of who and what qualifies as Christian is one of the ways he sees culture industry shaping perceptions of worship. With that flattening of diversity, the future of the kind of democratized worship and range of approaches that birthed P&W and attracted many of my conversation partners seems, to them, questionable. Nichols contends that most consumers are content with things as they are. He places some responsibility, however, on the music makers themselves to guide the trends of the worship industry.

NICHOLS: We humans tend to gravitate to a form. It's safe, familiar, and comforting. God, on the other hand, cannot be boxed in, nor can he be contained. By the way, he owns music. He created it. It is up to those of us who have been given the [musical] gift to listen and pay attention to which way the wind blows.

The Global and the Local

Considering the question of how best to produce an effective ethos of worship, several of my conversation partners made a distinction between the role of culture industry and that of churches, or, said more simply, between the global and local production of worship. Frazier commented on the authority of culture industry's media powers and how easily it can eclipse the value of locally imagined worship arts. Expressing a desire to see worship music maintain its vitality and elude the fate of all commercial trends—obsolescence—Nichols stresses that churches must explore their own creative resources. One of Belmont's first worship leaders, Wayne Berry,[13] takes the idea a step further by arguing that such an exploration is, itself, an act of worship. To carefully and gratefully see what congregational gifts are lying dormant, to inquire and find what has already been provided, is a foundational practice in the establishment of a congregation's worship life. In separate conversations, industry-affiliated worship leaders Rick Cua and Stu G shared this perspective:[14] the industry has a singular ability to serve and connect individuals and churches world-wide with state-of-the-art expressions of worship, but the local parsing and adaptation of the numerous choices that industry makes available is critically important. For an observer like Nichols, this accentuation of the role of the local is not a product of sentimental attachment to the good old days of con-temporary worship but an informed realization that the locus of the music and the movement's vitality, its hope for the future, are where they have always been—with local worshipping communities and their music makers who cre-ate songs in context, songs born out of the worship of real people in unique social-spiritual relationships, songs that immediately represent the devotional and prophetic voice of the community.

Conclusion

Belmont Church and similar churches that developed a strong P&W culture became locations of a significant shift in the relationship between church and culture at large. That change is most clearly expressed in a still-developing partnership between churches and culture industry, wherein churches seek fresh ways to live out the dual citizenships of culture and religion, to build membership and community, to substantiate the relevance of Christian wor-ship to contemporary culture, and to effectively utilize mechanisms of com-munication for the purpose of spreading the Gospel message. One result is that churches have gone into business with business in a way that connects worship and the cultural marketplace more directly than ever before. While music and religion have long shared space and purpose in the sanctuary, the industrialization of P&W introduces the question of whether the marketplace has joined the intimate relationship between worship and music in a ménages à trois, the unraveling of which, even if desired, may now prove difficult (Per-kins 2011, 2, 188).

Of concern in this chapter is the question of how and to what extent culture industry shapes worship music and ultimately the worship activities of the people who use it. Several of my conversation partners observed homogeniza-tion, an expanding sameness and loss of expressive diversity, resulting from the standardization of worship music as product. Many of my interviewees asserted that the current industry standard for how worship sounds and looks has, in one way or another, diverged from what initially drew them to charismatic worship and its progressive music culture. As culture makers, these individuals understand that things change. Yet they grapple with shifts that undermine what are, to them, foundational characteristics of the worship they value.

NOTES

1. My definition of culture industry is similar to that of Horkheimer and Adorno: "the constellation of entertainment businesses that produce film, television, radio, magazines, and popular music—all phenomena created by mass technology in which the lines between art, advertising, and propaganda blur" (Leitch 2001, 1220). I would update this to include all Internet-related content and its cultural effects.

2. For overviews of CCM, see Alfonso (2002), Howard and Streck (1999), and Cusic (2002).

3. See PR Newswire (2001).

4. The interviews featured here are a representative sample from a larger group conducted as fieldwork for my doctoral dissertation at Vanderbilt University (Perkins 2011). For that project, I interviewed, formally and informally, more than one hundred individuals. With the individuals named in this chapter, I revisited and, where necessary, updated those interviews.

5. As it appears here, the term "industrialization" is informed by Adorno's nuanced explanation: "The expression 'industry' is not to be taken literally. It refers to the standardization of the thing itself" (2000, 233).

6. Name withheld by request.

7. Christian Copyright Licensing International.

8. See Genesis 12:1–8.

9. From a special lecture at Vanderbilt University on September 23, 2008.

10. Name withheld by request.

11. Frazier, an award-winning CCM songwriter and recording artist, is now a worship pastor and musician at Belmont.

12. As a session musician, Madeira performed on numerous CCM and P&W recordings. Christian and country music artists have recorded his songs. In 2012, he released a critically acclaimed alternative worship album entitled *Mercyland: Hymns for the Rest of Us*.

13. Berry leads worship in Smyrna, Tennessee, at Springhouse Worship and Arts Center.

14. Rick Cua was a respected CCM artist with multiple albums released by Refuge, Reunion, and Sparrow Records. As an executive with the EMI Christian publishing team, he played an important role in the success of Worship Together. Cua participated in worship leadership at Belmont Church and is now a worship leader and pastor at Grace Community Church in Leipers Fork, Tennessee. Stu G (Stuart David Garrard) was a founding member of Delirious? He continues to write and produce new worship music as a member of One Sonic Society.

REFERENCES

Adorno, Theodor. 1991. *The Culture Industry: Selected Essays on Mass Culture.* Edited by J. M. Bernstein. London: Routledge.

————. 2000. "Culture Industry Reconsidered." In *The Adorno Reader*, edited by Brian O'Connor, 230–38. Malden, Mass.: Blackwell.

Alfonso, Barry. 2002. *The Billboard Guide to Contemporary Christian Music*. New York: Billboard Books.

Barthes, Roland. 1977. *Image, Music, Text*. Edited and translated by Stephen Heath. New York: Hill and Wang, 1977.

Baudrillard, Jean. 1994. *Simulacra and Simulation*. Translated by Sheila Faria Glaser. Ann Arbor: University of Michigan Press.

Bourdieu, Pierre. 1993. *The Field of Cultural Production: Essays on Art and Literature*. Translated by Randal Johnson. New York: Columbia University Press.

Burgess, Stanley. 2010. "Charismatic and Pentecostal Movements: Their History and Theology." In *The Cambridge Dictionary of Christianity*, edited by Daniel Patte, 186–88. New York: Cambridge University Press.

Cusic, Don. 2002. *The Sound of Light: A History of Gospel and Christian Music*. Milwaukee: Hal Leonard.

Debord, Guy. 1994. *The Society of the Spectacle*. Translated by Donald Nicholson-Smith. New York: Zone Books.

Firat, A. Fuat, and Nikhilesh Dholakia. 1998. *Consuming People: From Political Economy to Theaters of Consumption*. New York: Routledge.

Hardt, Hanno. 2004. *Myths for the Masses*. Malden, Mass.: Blackwell.

Horkheimer, Max, and Theodor W. Adorno. (1944) 2002. *Dialectic of Enlightenment: Philosophical Fragments*. Edited by Gunzelin Schmid Noerr. Translated by Edmund Jephcott. Stanford: Stanford University Press.

Howard, Jay R., and John M. Streck. 1999. *Apostles of Rock: The Splintered World of Contemporary Christian Music*. Lexington: University Press of Kentucky.

Kopytoff, Igor. 1986. "The Cultural Biography of Things: Commoditization as Process." In *The Social Life of Things: Commodities in Cultural Perspective*, edited by Arjun Appadurai, 64–91. Cambridge: Cambridge University Press.

Leitch, Vincent B. 2001. "Max Horkheimer and Theodor W. Adorno." In *The Norton Anthology of Theory and Criticism*, edited by Vincent B. Leitch, 1110–27. New York: W. W. Norton.

Lury, Celia. 1996. *Consumer Culture*. New Brunswick: Rutgers University Press.

Miller, Daniel A. 1998. *A Theory of Shopping*. Ithaca: Cornell University Press.

————. 2005. *Materiality*. Edited by Daniel Miller. Durham: Duke University Press.

Miller, Vincent J. 2005. *Consuming Religion: Christian Faith and Practice in a Consumer Culture*. New York: Continuum.

Perkins, David Horace. 2003. "Spiritual Aphrodisiac: Praise and Worship Music and the Re-enchantment of Western Culture." Paper presented at the annual meeting of the American Academy of Religion, Atlanta, November 22–25.

————. 2004. "Selling the Sacred: Contemporary Christian Worship Music as General Market Commodity." Paper presented at the annual meeting of the American Academy of Religion, San Antonio, November 20–23. Presented again in 2005 at the annual meeting of the Society for Ethnomusicology, Atlanta, November 17–20, and at the Forum on Music and Christian Scholarship, Princeton University, February 19.

————. 2005. "The Last Cathedral: Simmel, Sacred Music, and the Marketplace." Paper presented at the conference Culture and Modernity: Georg Simmel in Context, Harvard University, April 16–17, and at the annual meeting of the American Academy of Religion, Philadelphia, November 19–22.

————. 2010. "Praise and Worship." In *The Cambridge Dictionary of Christianity*, edited by Daniel Patte, 1000–1001. New York: Cambridge University Press.

———. 2011. "Selling the Sacred: Praise and Worship Music in the Sanctuary and Market-place." Ph.D. diss., Vanderbilt University.

PR Newswire. 2001. "Launch of *Songs 4 Worship* Proves to Be Largest Direct Response Television Launch in History of Time Life Music and Integrity Music." February 12. Available from the Free Library at http://www.thefreelibrary.com/Launch+of+Songs +4+Worship+Proves+to+Be+Largest+Direct+Response... -a070354468.

Simmel, Georg. 2004. *The Philosophy of Money*. Edited by David Frisby. Translated by Tom Bottomore and David Frisby. New York: Routledge.

Slater, Don. 1997. *Consumer Culture and Modernity*. Oxford: Polity Press.

14

We Can't Go Back: Liturgies of Worship and Consumer Culture at One African American Church

Will Boone

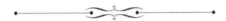

Since the year 2000, the increasingly intertwined relationship between consumer culture and pentecostal[1] practice has become a major topic for scholars of pentecostalism. Scholars' recognition of the influence exerted by the post–World War II rise of gospels of prosperity and the concomitant flourishing of the industry of Christian "lifestyle" products—recordings, books, videos, conference tours, and so on—has led them to see the necessity of a critical engagement with the economics of pentecostal-charismatic practice.[2] This essay argues for increased scholarly attention to be given to the ways in which local believers themselves respond to the influx of consumer culture into their belief communities. Because these responses are often embedded in nonlinguistic and extralinguistic practices such as music making and dance, analysis requires methods that can attend to the shades of signification that emerge from such embodied practices. In particular, I make the case for the value of an ethnographically informed theology and a theologically informed ethnography in studies of the intersection of consumer culture and pentecostal practice.

My ethnomusicological research has shown how some believers use worship not simply as a liturgical activity but as a way of grappling with the challenges and circumstances of their lives (Boone 2013). Believers might critique the influx of a consumerist ethos into the church for the same reason that they might embrace it—as part of a process of working to find hope, affirm life, and empower their communities. They critically engage the religious resources available to them—commercial gospel music or Word of Faith doctrines, for example—as they seek the guidance of the Spirit's signs and wonders. While the current chapter draws on the insights of Christian philosopher James

K. A. Smith as a way to guide its (ethno)musicological analysis of one musical occasion in a local congregation, I hope readers get the sense that the symbiosis between theology and ethnography that I advocate can feasibly take root in several different disciplines and draw on a range of methodologies. The last section of the essay highlights penetrating work from different disciplines—anthropology, sociology, and theology—that shows the theological agency of believers in local pentecostal communities who are grappling with the influx of consumer culture. At Faith Assembly Christian Center, an African American pentecostal church in Durham, North Carolina, where I have conducted research for the past several years, the intertwining of consumer culture and worship practice is perhaps most evident through the church's use of commercial recordings from the gospel music industry.[3] These recordings, which constitute the majority of Faith Assembly's repertoire, reach churchgoers primarily through radio, television, and the Internet, mass-mediated modes of dissemination in which these products are marketed not simply as musical recordings but as "worship experiences."[4] Recordings thus offer churchgoers two kinds of value. On the one hand, recordings have market value, in part because they ostensibly *capture* a genuine spiritual encounter. On the other hand, recordings have value because they participate in encounters that edify and empower the local community. In the first instance, the balance of agency tips toward producers; in the second instance, toward consumers.

This chapter explores one moment of a worship service in September 2012. This was a time when church members were grappling with the imminent death of their pastor. A group of six of the oldest women in the church performed a choreographed dance to a contemporary popular recording entitled "I Won't Go Back" (McDowell 2011). The song's verse/pre-chorus/chorus form, and its use of an extremely common four-chord harmonic progression in the chorus, makes it similar to dozens of other mid-tempo worship "anthems." Its marketers have used sophisticated techniques to sell it as an authentic, yet nondescript and widely accessible, "live worship experience." In short, the recording embodies many of the homogenizing forces at the heart of consumer culture. But rather than being rendered inarticulate by these forces, Faith Assembly used the recording as a medium through which the congregation could be highly articulate in a locally relevant way, transforming a product of consumer culture into a facilitator of a richly textured, community-situated experience.

I have two interrelated goals in exploring this moment. First, I want to examine how a recording such as "I Won't Go Back" can play a key role in facilitating a nuanced kind of communication that is especially important in the lives of pentecostal believers. In Faith Assembly's theological world, it is imperative that believers express an absolute faith in divine healing. They embrace the idea that they should "speak faith" and never "speak doubt." But given the prognosis for their pastor, members of the community had to grapple with the inevitability of his death, even if the ways in which they could speak about it were extremely restricted. The dance to "I Won't Go Back" created a situation in which those present did not have to do any actual speaking. A different level of exchange was allowed to emerge whereby the community could communicate about the unspeakable.

Second, my examination of this moment at Faith Assembly points toward the idea that significant theological content is embedded in nonlinguistic and extralinguistic practices such as dance. Revealing and better understanding this content will, I believe, necessitate an increased dialogue between ethnographers and theologians. There has been a notable turn toward issues of practice and embodiment in recent pentecostal scholarship. James K. A. Smith states that "a pentecostal worldview is *first* embedded in a constellation of spiritual practices that carry within them an implicit understanding. Pentecostal worship performs the faith" (2010, 30–31). If we accept this statement, then it is a short step to recognizing the value of ethnography to pentecostal theology. Using ethnographic methods to attend to what pentecostal believers *do* can provide insights that analyzing propositional statements of doctrine or belief cannot. At the same time, those trained in ethnography can turn toward theology to be able to better articulate the significance of the practices they observe in the field.[5] Together we can navigate a careful course that works to unpack the extreme complexities that arise at the intersection of pentecostal-charismatic practice and consumer culture.

Popular Religious Music and Cultural Liturgies

The notion of cultural liturgies as articulated by James K. A. Smith provides a useful framework for the discussion that follows. In his book *Desiring the Kingdom*, Smith defines liturgies as "ritual practices that function as pedagogies of ultimate desire" (2009, 87). Liturgies, he says, can include a large range of sacred or secular practices—everything from congregational singing to watching television to attending a university. But what makes a liturgy a liturgy for Smith is that it never merely *informs* us, but holistically forms us. Liturgies act on our minds, bodies, and hearts to "inculcate" within us particular "visions of the good life"—visions of what it "looks like for us to flourish and live well" (86, 53).

Most of Faith Assembly's members first encounter the music that they use in church not in the act of worship but through their participation in cultural liturgies such as watching Christian television or listening to FM gospel radio. In addition to music, these liturgies include a barrage of images, sounds, and advertisements, all of which suggest a particular vision of human flourishing. Images on television show gospel artists who are youthful, sexy, and every bit as glamorous as their secular counterparts. And the advertisements on gospel radio suggest that *you*, the listener, can be like that, too. All you need are these weight loss pills, varicose vein treatments, testosterone supplements, easy cash fast(!), a new car financed *without* a credit check, and a fifty-dollar ticket to the next "empowerment conference."[6] The liturgies of contemporary black gospel music television and radio work to form people according to the idea that human flourishing can easily be bought. Marketers have even worked to commodify the very idea of worship experience so that Christians formed along the contours of these cultural liturgies might recognize that, too, as an element of the good life that is available for purchase.

Consider the contemporary gospel album *Arise* (2011) by highly successful black Christian artist William McDowell. Not only is the album subtitled *The Live Worship Experience*, but its promoters released a series of relatively low-production promotional videos in which the artist speaks intimately to his potential audience. McDowell claims that the live album was the result of unmediated spiritual inspiration and that it is, in fact, a pure representation of the worship experience shared by the musicians and audience on the night that the recording was made. McDowell appears to look the viewer straight in the eyes as he says, "I only believe in writing songs when God is speaking. Therefore, out of this time, I believe that the Lord is saying something powerful to us as a church and as a people. . . . It is my desire that you would enter into the worship experience that we had that night. We didn't cut it. You will hear it the way it is from start to finish. That's how it was that night. I want to invite you on a journey called *Arise*. Come go with me" ("William McDowell" 2012). The way in which this album is marketed—as a "worship experience"—is an example of a phenomenon much discussed by a long line of Marx-inspired cultural commentators: in advanced capitalist societies, the very things that seem to most resist commodification—such as spiritual experience, the "aura" of an artwork, or anti-capitalist sentiment itself—are transformed into things that can be bought and sold.[7]

But if the marketing of worship experience is part of one kind of cultural liturgy, Smith claims that Christian worship among local communities potentially represents another kind of liturgy that forms worshippers to desire a different vision of human flourishing. Local worship, in other words, can have the power to form believers against the grain of the liturgies offered by consumer culture. What happened at Faith Assembly Christian Center on September 23, 2012, provides an example of one of these formative experiences. Interestingly, however, this locally specific worship experience was built on the foundation of a commodified "worship experience" in the form of a popular recording. This presents a complex situation that is worth exploring in depth.

I must preface this exploration by stating that my involvement with Faith Assembly dates back to 2002, when I began playing electric guitar in the church's band. Initially, I was a complete outsider—a non-pentecostal and the only white attendee. By 2010, however, when I officially began field research for my dissertation, I was very much ensconced in the community. Thus, my work inevitably reflects the fact that my roles as researcher and community member at Faith Assembly are thoroughly intertwined. The field reflection that follows is written from my vantage point in the band pit at the front of the sanctuary, from which I face the congregation.

September Dancing at Faith Assembly Christian Center

September 23, 2012. It was a rainy Sunday morning. All of us at Faith Assembly Christian Center were still reeling from the news that Bishop Leroy McKenzie had announced two weeks prior. He reported that he had been diagnosed with stage-four cancer and that the doctors had said all they could do was "help him be comfortable."

McKenzie was the church's founder, head pastor, and patriarch. Most of the one hundred or so regular attendees at the church considered him not only their pastor but a personal friend. Several church members saw him as a father figure and regularly referred to him as "my spiritual father," "like a father to me," or even "the father I never had."

On this Sunday, Bishop McKenzie, enfeebled and unable to preach, sat in an upholstered chair in the back of the sanctuary while his wife, Pastor Mary McKenzie, presided over the service. By the time the praise team—the small group of singers who lead the musical selections in each worship service—completed its second song, the atmosphere in the church was like static electricity.[8] The congregation crackled with bursts of tongues speech and cries of "hallelujah!" One woman lay prostrate by the wall at the far side of the sanctuary; another knelt at the altar.

Pastor Mary McKenzie tried to move the service forward but seemed powerless against the experiential tide. For several minutes, she simply stood in front of the congregation, her silent presence embodying the ineffability of the moment. Finally, Pastor McKenzie reined in the flood of feeling and welcomed to the front of the church a group called the Women of Faith, to "come bless us in dance."

Six of the "church mothers," each of them old enough to receive Social Security, stood in front of the congregation dressed in black and adorned with brightly colored sashes. They were still for a long moment while the sound man fumbled with the recording. As the congregation waited, reverberant spasms of emotional overflow moved across the church body like waves. Finally, the recording came on, playing at the extreme volume that is normal at Faith Assembly. The disembodied recorded voices of a group of singers filled the sanctuary with the words "I've been changed, healed, freed, delivered / I've found joy, peace, grace, and favor."

From my place in the band pit, I looked out over the congregation. Many church members hugged or placed arms around one another's shoulders. People were crying, singing together, and shouting out encouragements for the dancers. The church mothers' movements were far from agile, but there was a tremendous openness and magnanimity in them. Their moving bodies seemed to communicate deep wisdom as they danced before the congregation. These were the oldest members of the church, taking the helm for a moment, leading worship, becoming the unifying focal point. It was as if they were using dance to show the younger members how to live in the face of death. When the recording's anthemic chorus arrived, each woman lip-synced along: "I won't go back / can't go back / to the way it used to be / for your presence came and changed me."

"I Won't Go Back" expresses one of the most common sentiments at Faith Assembly and in popular gospel music in general: a dedication to forward momentum. Though churchgoers and recording artists often say that this is about rebirth and the cleansing resurrection of Christ, an insatiable desire for the new is also the engine that drives the liturgies of consumer culture. And standing as a vague signifier of the type in which commodified culture trades, the fist-pumping mid-tempo declaration "I won't go back" might apply to an individual's decision about a new hairstyle or pair of shoes just as easily as it could to an individual's decision to follow Jesus.

But in the instance I have just described, the lyric was potentially imbued with a much more specific meaning for the Faith Assembly community, particularly because this meaning was being channeled through the bodies of the church mothers. These older women seemed to be drawing on their personal wells of experience and speaking to the congregation about the inevitability of loss and how the living must continue living. They seemed to be speaking about the perpetual ebb and flow of joy and suffering and the unyielding insistence of time.[9]

The congregation sang along while the mothers danced, and the words "I can't go back to the way it used to be, for your presence came and changed me" could have just as easily been directed to Bishop McKenzie as to God. In fact, later in the same service, all of the dozen or so graduates of Faith Assembly Academy, the K–12 school run by the church, took turns speaking to Bishop McKenzie in front of the congregation. Several of them actually employed language similar to the song's lyrics, saying that his "presence in their lives" had "changed them for the better."

If the liturgies of consumerism form us to race headlong toward the next new thing rather than face the harsh realities of the present—if they form us to desire neatly packaged bits of captured experience over and above the unforgiving complexities of lived experience—then what happened at Faith Assembly in September 2012 pushed forcefully against the grain of these liturgies. The church mothers were dancing openly about death, preparing the community for the loss of its leader. The church was practicing a vision of human flourishing that was not glamorous in the way of the gospel stars on television; it was not characterized by easy fixes or tidy answers. As the church members participated together in the mothers' dance, they were not ignoring hardship but working together to find empowerment, consolation, and possibly even joy in the face of hardship. What emerged during the church mothers' dance was not the kind of nebulous and undemanding transcendence offered by marketers of "worship," but a thickly textured affirmation of life, community, and belief.

Of course, this was not necessarily explicit. It is primarily an interpretive move on my part to claim that the "church mothers were dancing openly about death." At the time, none of the church members specifically said anything to that effect. In fact, such a statement would not have been acceptable given the constraints of belief and practice at Faith Assembly. Belief in divine healing is a crucial part of church members' theology, as it is for most pentecostals. In addition, the idea of "positive confession"—a practice whereby believers speak *only* about positive outcomes as a way of making spiritual blessings manifest in the natural realm (Harrison 2005, 10–11)—resonates strongly at Faith Assembly. Although the church is nowhere near as strict and methodical about this practice as the "hard prosperity" ministries that brought it to prominence in the second half of the twentieth century (Bowler 2010, 114–20), Faith Assembly's leaders frequently emphasize the importance of thinking positively and "speaking faith." They make it clear that any words expressing doubt in God's omnipotence are not welcome. When Faith Assembly's members spoke about Bishop McKenzie after his diagnosis, they often said that they were "expecting a miracle" or "believing God for healing." I never heard anyone at the church explicitly acknowledge that McKenzie's death was a possibility.

But despite this emphasis on positive speaking, words never tell the whole story for African American pentecostals. Their communicative world is filled with complex webs of signifying sound, sight, motion, and touch, including melodies, moans, glossolalia, gestures, dance, hugging, and laying on of hands. Through these communicative webs, nuanced "conversations" unfold before and beyond the words that people speak. The church mothers' dance was one of these conversations. And in this instance, the commercial recording was a key facilitator of the conversation. While it played, it took over the role of "positive confessor." The disembodied voices on the recording declared, "I've been changed, healed, delivered." Those present became free to bodily express their own complex and various interpretations of what that meant to them. The church mothers led with their choreographed movements while some in the congregation cried, some leaped with joy, some hugged, and some simply stood motionless. But all of these embodied interpretations emerged within the context of a worship service where Bishop McKenzie's physically weak presence contrasted sharply with the vitality with which he had filled that same sanctuary for many years. In this context, the recording opened a space where church members could communicate a range of thoughts and feelings that they were not necessarily free to express in words.

While the products of consumer culture are often critiqued for the homogenizing force they exert, in a situation like this one, a commercial recording can allow for the expression and coexistence of complex and heterogeneous meanings. Rather than suppressing local agency, the recording provided a foundation on which community members could express nuanced responses to an emotionally trying local situation.

But even if the church mothers' dance to "I Won't Go Back" represented a powerful moment of community edification at Faith Assembly, on a broad scale this affective moment does very little to slow the steady creep of consumerism into pentecostalism. The potential negative consequences of this influx are amplified in the African American community, where, because of centuries of discrimination, many individuals lack financial safety nets in the form of accumulated wealth or savings (Oliver 2006; Conley 2010). In the contemporary moment, as many African Americans are plagued by debt, practices that embrace and encourage consumerism are potentially threatening to the socioeconomic health of individuals and communities.[10] Clearly, the issues that arise at the meeting place of Christian practice and consumer culture are extremely complex, and answers are not easy. Theologian Vincent Miller suggests that an ethnographically informed theology may be one of the best ways to move forward through this thorny terrain. He writes that the theological questions posed by consumer culture "are very difficult to answer. They require methods beyond the training of most theologians, and the subtleties involved make them resistant to quantitative social-science methods. . . . [They call] for something akin to the immersive methods of ethnography, whereby the anthropologist spends extended time with members of a culture, attending to the implicit logics of their practices and the texture of their daily lives" (2004, 227). In the concluding section of this essay, I want to consider Miller's suggestion in a bit more detail, thinking about how ethnography and theology might work together in studies of pentecostal practice.[11]

Scholarship and the Negotiation of Pentecostal Practice and Consumer Culture

Pastor and theologian Cheryl Sanders concludes a 2011 article on African American "pentecostal ethics and the prosperity gospel" with a call for "serious prophetic engagement of consumerism, conservatism, and TV studio multiculturalism by men and women who truly understand what it means to be 'in the world but not of it'" (151). Sanders's challenge seems to be directed toward church leaders, but it is my contention that such engagement is already being enacted by those in the pews. Of course, the ability of these believers to combat problems such as social injustice and systemic inequality on a national stage is limited, as most of them lack the privileges necessary to gain access to the gatekeepers of power, including corporate executives, policy makers, and those ensconced in ivory towers. Nevertheless, their words and actions are transformative in their own local communities.

Thus, I claim that the scholarly conversation about pentecostal practice and consumer culture can benefit from serious and sustained attention to the agency of local believers. Three examples of recent scholarship suggest the extent to which the practices of pentecostal-charismatic believers represent a critical engagement with, rather than a simple acceptance of, doctrines, beliefs, and theologies. Anthropologist and professor of African American studies and religion Marla Frederick-McGlathery worked with women in rural North Carolina for whom televangelism plays a major part in religious life. She explains how these women construct "alternative and contextualized readings of religious television that allow them to dissent from the politically conservative messages of televangelists while adopting the more biblically conservative tenets of evangelical Christianity" (2006, 287). Her conclusions focus on political rather than economic interpretations, but one can easily imagine how "alternative and contextualized readings" could be applied to the logic of consumerism just as they are to the logic of political conservatism.

Sociologist Milmon Harrison's research concerns believers in prosperity-embracing Word of Faith churches. Based on extensive interviews, Harrison shows how these believers construct and adopt strategies for negotiating the doctrinal demands of church membership (2005, 107–30). Through "filtering" and "venting networks," members continually question and critically engage with the expressed doctrines and beliefs of their leaders. Theologian Jonathan Walton uses the metaphor of jazz improvisation—which he borrows from Harvey Cox, his colleague at the Harvard Divinity School—in a recent essay about how attendees at Kenneth and Gloria Copeland's Southwest Believers' Convention negotiate the doctrines of Word of Faith theology (2012, 109). Drawing from interviews and conversations with conference goers, Walton concludes that "the Word of Faith movement offers a theological chord structure from which persons can theologically riff and spiritually improvise" (128).

Each of these examples suggests that the theologies that pentecostal-charismatic believers actually *live* emerge out of pragmatic concerns at least to the same extent that they reflect or enact specific beliefs and doctrines. On a micro-level, believers are already responding to the influx of consumer culture in incredibly nuanced and, to echo Cheryl Sanders, "prophetically engaged" ways—that is, ways that pragmatically address the concerns and needs of their communities. Importantly, these responses are often nonlinguistic and extralinguistic, unfolding in dance or music making. It seems to me that theological accounts of the intersections of consumer culture and pentecostal practice have much to gain from taking seriously the ways in which local worship "performs the faith" (Smith 2010, 31).

Working toward this scholarly goal will require a more ethnographically informed theology and a more theologically informed ethnography. Jonathan Walton's essay provides a good example of the kind of nuanced insight that can be facilitated by a theologian's use of ethnographic methods, but even his careful analysis rests primarily on propositional statements made by believers. What kind of theological insights will be revealed when ethnographic methods are used to seek meanings that emerge before and beyond words, in dance, music, and the heterogeneous webs of utterance that characterize pentecostal worship?

This essay has tried to ever so slightly begin to address that question within the frame of the meeting place between consumer culture and worship practice. In discussing a dance to a popular commercial gospel recording choreographed by the church mothers at Faith Assembly, I have shown how a moment of church members coming together in a local worship context can be read as an implicit critique of the ethos of consumer culture that has infiltrated African American pentecostalism. I argue, however, that this "critique" is best understood as a secondary dimension of the more pressing pragmatic work that had to be accomplished by this dance. Facing the death of their pastor, Faith Assembly's members needed to come together in such a way that could not be facilitated simply by a popular song or the doctrine of "positive confession." Led by the church mothers, they performed an in-the-moment theology that empowered them as a community of worshippers facing the imminence of deep loss and difficult transition. How might we describe the dimensions of such a theology so that it resonates beyond the boundaries of this single community? How might we articulate the significance of such moments of local practice for pentecostal theology more broadly? These are the kinds of questions that my training as a musicologist and ethnographer leaves me unprepared to answer satisfactorily. But I believe that they are fruitful questions that can be addressed through an increased dialogue between ethnographers and theologians.

The conversation about the challenging issues that arise at the intersection of pentecostal practice and consumer culture will, I believe, benefit greatly from works of theologically informed ethnography and ethnographically informed theology that value inside-out perspectives. I borrow this spatial metaphor from the folklorist Henry Glassie, who wrote in his 1982 book *Passing the*

Time in Ballymenone, "The way to study people is not from the top down or the bottom up, but from the inside out, from the place where people are articulate to the place where they are not, from the place where they are in control of their destinies to the place where they are not" (1982, 86). Working from this model, we can attend to local specificities, the richness of particulars, and community-situated experiences that will deepen our understanding of how believers are acted upon by forces of consumerism and how they exert agency amid those forces. We have a lot to learn from the myriad ways in which pentecostals across the world use the things around them—commodified or otherwise—to help affirm life and belief, even in their darkest hours.

NOTES

1. Small-*p* "pentecostal" is not meant to connote a particular denominational affiliation but instead refers to "the diversity of pentecostal/charismatic theologies while at the same time recognizing important family resemblances and shared sensibilities." See Smith (2010, xvii). Theologians such as Douglas Jacobsen and Amos Yong employ this usage as well.

2. Perhaps the most thorough of this kind of engagement is Yong's *In the Days of Caesar* (2010, esp. chap. 7). See also Attanasi and Yong (2012). A few examples of recent scholarship dealing with these issues specifically as they pertain to African Americans include Walton (2009); the special thematic issue of *Pneuma: The Journal for the Society of Pentecostal Studies*, vol. 33, no. 2 (2011); Alexander (2011, esp. chap. 9); and several of the essays in Yong and Alexander (2011).

3. There are two main ways in which recordings make their way into services at Faith Assembly: (1) the church performs its own versions of the songs on the recordings, and (2) the recordings are played over the sound system (usually as an accompaniment for dance).

4. A few recent examples from artists whose music is widely known among the African American communities with which I work are *Bishop Leonard Scott Presents: My Worship Experience* (Tyscott Records, 2010), Kathy Taylor's *Live: The Worship Experience* (Tyscot Records, 2009), and Marvin Winans's *The Praise and Worship Experience* (MLW Productions, 2012).

5. There is a growing body of theologically informed ethnomusicology (for example, Dueck 2011; Engelhardt 2009; and Ingalls 2011). There is also a body of ethnographic literature that attends closely to local pentecostal practice and thus articulates (at least implicitly) locally enacted theologies (for example, Hinson 2000 and Lawless 1988). With regard to African American pentecostalism and consumer culture, however, the extant research exists, for the most part, in two distinct strands. One the one hand, there is the theological work exemplified by Walton (2009) that explores popular and consumer culture in contemporary African American Christianity but does not engage deeply with the experiential and communicative dimensions of worship. On the other hand, there is the ethnographic work exemplified by Hinson (2000) and Nelson (2005) that explores the experiential and communicative dimensions of worship but does not engage deeply with popular and consumer culture. The present chapter claims that scholarship on African American pentecostalism and consumer culture could benefit from increased dialogue between these bodies of work.

6. I have regularly heard advertisements for each of these products on The Light 103.9, the North Carolina–based FM radio instantiation of the urban media corporation Radio One.

7. For a recent discussion of this phenomenon from a theological perspective, see Miller (2004).

8. By using this metaphor, I consciously invoke Cheryl Sanders's insightful discussion of the dialectic between static and kinetic energy in "Holiness-Pentecostal" worship. See Sanders (1996, 59–63).

9. The fact that this communication came from the church mothers is crucial to the significance of this moment. Among African American pentecostals, church mothers have long occupied a place of "tremendous power and authority." In her history of women's role in the Church of God in Christ, Anthea Butler writes, "Perhaps it seems strange to attribute much power to the church mothers. . . . [They] are not those who we normally think of as policy makers or theologians. Look closer. Church mothers are the women who recall the history of their churches, who chastise the pastor when he has interpreted the scriptures incorrectly, and who set the cultural and behavioral patterns for their congregations" (2007, 2). See also Hardy (2011).

10. DeForest Soaries Jr., a prominent New Jersey–based African American pastor, states in the recent CNN documentary *Almighty Debt*, "There is no question to me that debt is a bigger problem than racism [in the African American community]." For a clip containing this quotation, see Lieber (2010).

11. The combining of theology and ethnography is not a novel idea. Robert Orsi stands out as one scholar who has both incorporated ethnography into studies of religion and called for more similar studies (see esp. Orsi 2005). Eerdmans's new Series in Ecclesiology and Ethnography provides recent examples of this kind of work and discussions of how such work might be best conducted (see Ward 2012 and Scharen 2012). Unfortunately—and surprisingly, given the centrality of embodiment and performance to pentecostal practice—very little of this recent scholarship engages specifically with pentecostalism.

REFERENCES

Alexander, Estrelda Y. 2011. *Black Fire: One Hundred Years of African American Pentecostalism*. Downers Grove, Ill.: InterVarsity Press.

Attanasi, Katherine, and Amos Yong, eds. 2012. *Pentecostalism and Prosperity: The Socioeconomics of the Global Charismatic Movement*. New York: Palgrave Macmillan.

Boone, Will. 2013. "Hearing Faith: Musical Practice and Spirit-Filled Worship in a Contemporary African American Church." Ph.D. diss., University of North Carolina, Chapel Hill.

Bowler, Catherine. 2010. "Blessed: A History of the American Prosperity Gospel." Ph.D. diss., Duke University.

Butler, Anthea. 2007. *Women in the Church of God in Christ: Making a Sanctified World*. Chapel Hill: University of North Carolina Press.

Conley, Dalton. 2010. *Being Black, Living in the Red: Race, Wealth, and Social Policy in America*. Berkeley: University of California Press.

Dueck, Jonathan. 2011. "Binding and Loosing in Song: Conflict, Identity, and Canadian Mennonite Music." *Ethnomusicology* 55 (2): 229–54.

Engelhardt, Jeffers. 2009. "Right Singing in Estonian Orthodox Christianity: A Study of Music, Theology, and Religious Ideology." *Ethnomusicology* 53 (1): 32–57.

Frederick-McGlathery, Marla. 2006. "'But, It's *Bible*': African American Women and Television Preachers." In *Women and Religion in the African Diaspora: Knowledge, Power, and Performance*, edited by R. Marie Griffin and Barbara Dianne Savage, 266–91. Baltimore: Johns Hopkins University Press.

Glassie, Henry. 1982. *Passing the Time in Ballymenone: Culture and History of an Ulster Community*. Philadelphia: University of Pennsylvania Press.

Hardy, Clarence E., III. 2011. "Church Mothers and Pentecostals in the Modern Age." In *Afro-Pentecostalism: Black Pentecostal and Charismatic Christianity in History and Culture*, edited by Amos Yong and Estrelda Y. Alexander, 83–93. New York: New York University Press.

Harrison, Milmon F. 2005. *Righteous Riches: The Word of Faith Movement in Contemporary African American Religion*. New York: Oxford University Press.

Hinson, Glenn. 2000. *Fire in My Bones: Transcendence and the Holy Spirit in African American Gospel*. Philadelphia: University of Pennsylvania Press.

Ingalls, Monique. 2011. "Singing Heaven Down to Earth: Spiritual Journeys, Eschatological Sounds, and Community Formation in Evangelical Conference Worship." *Ethnomusicology* 55 (2): 255–79.

Jakes, T. D. 2008. *Reposition Yourself: Living Life Without Limits*. New York: Simon and Schuster.

Lawless, Elaine. 1988. *God's Peculiar People: Women's Voices and Folk Tradition in a Pentecostal Church*. Lexington: University Press of Kentucky.

Lieber, Ron. 2010. "Debt's Threat to Black Families." *Bucks* (blog), *New York Times*, October 21. http://bucks.blogs.nytimes.com/2010/10/21/debts-threat-to-black-families/.

McDowell, William. 2011. "I Won't Go Back." On *Arise: The Live Worship Experience*. Light Records / eOne Entertainment. Compact disc.

Miller, Vincent J. 2004. *Consuming Religion: Christian Faith and Practice in a Consumer Culture*. New York: Continuum.

Nelson, Timothy. 2005. *Every Time I Feel the Spirit: Religious Experience and Ritual in an African American Church*. New York: New York University Press.

Oliver, Melvin L. 2006. *Black Wealth, White Wealth: A New Perspective on Racial Inequality*. New York: Routledge.

Orsi, Robert. 2005. *Between Heaven and Earth: The Religious Worlds People Make and the Scholars Who Study Them*. Princeton: Princeton University Press.

Sanders, Cheryl J. 1996. *Saints in Exile: The Holiness-Pentecostal Experience in African American Religion and Culture*. New York: Oxford University Press.

———. 2011. "Pentecostal Ethics and the Prosperity Gospel: Is There a Prophet in the House?" In *Afro-Pentecostalism: Black Pentecostal and Charismatic Christianity in History and Culture*, edited by Amos Yong and Estrelda Y. Alexander, 141–52. New York: New York University Press.

Scharen, Christian B. 2012. *Explorations in Ecclesiology and Ethnography*. Grand Rapids, Mich.: Eerdmans.

Smith, James K. A. 2009. *Desiring the Kingdom: Worship, Worldview, and Cultural Formation*. Grand Rapids, Mich.: Baker Academic.

———. 2010. *Thinking in Tongues: Pentecostal Contributions to Christian Philosophy*. Grand Rapids, Mich.: Eerdmans.

Walton, Jonathan L. 2009. *Watch This! The Ethics and Aesthetics of Black Televangelism*. New York: New York University Press.

———. 2012. "Stop Worrying and Start Sowing! A Phenomenological Account of the Ethics of 'Divine Investment.'" In *Pentecostalism and Prosperity: The Socio-economics of the*

Global Charismatic Movement, edited by Katherine Attanasi and Amos Yong, 107–29. New York: Palgrave Macmillan.

Ward, Pete, ed. 2012. *Perspectives on Ecclesiology and Ethnography.* Grand Rapids, Mich.: Eerdmans.

"William McDowell—Track by Track—'I Won't Go Back.'" 2012. YouTube video, 2:44. Posted by Entertainment One Nashville, February 10. http://www.youtube.com /watch?v=1Wky4_TrMjo&feature=relmfu.

Yong, Amos. 2010. *In the Days of Caesar: Pentecostalism and Political Theology.* Grand Rapids, Mich.: Eerdmans.

Yong, Amos, and Estrelda Y. Alexander, eds. 2011. *Afro-Pentecostalism: Black Pentecostal and Charismatic Christianity in History and Culture.* New York: New York University Press.

15

Gospel Funk: Pentecostalism, Music, and Popular Culture in Rio de Janeiro

Martijn Oosterbaan

About sixty teenagers in the small church on the periphery of Rio de Janeiro go wild when Adriano climbs the stage. Adriano—lead singer of the group Adriano Gospel Funk—greets the audience and cheerfully introduces the three male dancers who accompany him. As DJ Irmã Vitória (Sister Victory) throws the first beats at the crowd, the uniformed dancers start moving energetically and the audience swiftly follows their lead. The music of Adriano Gospel Funk is clearly very familiar to the adolescent girls and boys gathered here tonight; they sing along with the chorus of each song and display their best dance moves.[1] After Adriano has entertained the adolescents, the pastor of the church asks them to sit down so that he can deliver a sermon. The sudden change of vibe signals that this is not a regular *baile funk* (funk party) but a *culto de mocidade* (youth service). As the pastor turns the lights back on and starts to preach, the teenagers calm down, and when I follow Adriano to the back of the church, all of them are sitting in their chairs, listening attentively to the pastor's voice.

As multiple authors have argued, Pentecostal movements have been highly successful in spreading a relatively coherent religious form across the world, and nearly all scholars interested in Pentecostalism confirm that music is an essential element of the appeal of Pentecostalism (Cox [1995] 2001; Hackett 1998; Miller and Yamamori 2007; Meyer 2010). In the contemporary Brazilian context, music is the cultural form par excellence through which Pentecostal messages are spread. Successful Pentecostal radio and television programs, magazines, and Internet sites are often related to the Brazilian gospel music industry (Mendonça 2008, 229).[2] Somewhat different than the term itself might suggest, the Brazilian use of "gospel" generally refers to the entire spectrum of contemporary Christian music (CCM) in Brazil. Though, in theory, Brazilian gospel music may include a wide variety of (global) music styles, in practice, discussions about the divine status of certain music recordings and performances revolve around differences between styles. For example, whereas nowadays one may often hear gospel music with Afro-Brazilian samba rhythms, for a long time Pentecostal adherents agreed that gospel music styles could range from slow ballads (*baladas românticos*) to up-tempo rock and pop songs but should not include Afro-Brazilian styles of music. Many Pentecostal adherents considered these typical Brazilian styles to be pagan or demonic. Now, most Afro-Brazilian styles are accepted in evangelical circles as legitimate forms of gospel music, just as hard rock gospel and hip-hop gospel have also become more accepted in Brazil.[3]

As many anthropologists and (ethno)musicologists have acknowledged, music genres can be powerful mediators of group identity and collective emotion (Keil and Feld 1994; Frith 1996; Maffesoli 1996; Stokes 1997; Turino 2008). In earlier work, I have discussed the important role of gospel music in the reproduction of collective evangelical identity in the *favelas* (slums) of Rio de Janeiro, and I have argued that the transmission of gospel music is experienced as the circulation of the redemptive powers of the Holy Spirit (Oosterbaan 2008, 2009). Though connections between music genres and social identities can be found in many societies, for Pentecostal adherents in the favelas, music is particularly potent. For these Christians, music is one of the most valuable ways of transmitting the Lord's power, because the densely populated favelas, with their porous houses, allow amplified sounds to traverse space relatively unhindered.

Eight years after my first fieldwork period in 2003, a remarkable shift had occurred in the field of Pentecostalism and popular music in Rio de Janeiro. Whereas in 2003 I did not hear anyone play gospel funk, in 2011 the popularity of this music style was undeniable. Gospel funk MCs performed at gospel dance parties throughout the city, and many Pentecostal adolescents carried gospel funk MP3s on their phones or MP3 players.[4]

The popularity of gospel funk is noteworthy because its music style—generally known as *carioca funk*—is closely associated with what most evangelicals consider to be the gloomy and immoral sides of favela life. For almost two decades, carioca funk has been the most popular dance music in the favelas of Rio de Janeiro. Carioca funk—also known as *baile funk*—is a Brazilian form of electronic dance music that became enormously popular in the public parties in Rio's favelas in the 1990s. Carioca funk derives its name from funk parties (*bailes funk*) that originally featured music similar to North American funk and later incorporated music influenced by Miami bass, a North American hip-hop/dance style developed in the 1980s and 1990s.

Carioca funk, with its thumping beats and explicit lyrics, rapidly replaced samba as the most popular music of the favela youth (Sansone 2001). In the present day (2012), bailes funk generally take place on public squares in the favelas and are one of the few affordable festivities for favela residents. Whereas, definitively, not all carioca funk is related to crime and violence, the sound of one particular form of carioca funk—*funk proibidão* (very forbidden funk)—became closely connected to Rio's drug gangs. In the past twenty years, many favelas have come under the rule of gangs that sell cocaine and marijuana from within the favelas and regularly enforce their control with violence. As Paul Sneed (2007) most insightfully describes it, funk proibidão is part of an ideological arena in which competing powers—gangs and state forces—attempt to convince residents of the legitimacy of their rule. Funk proibidão lyrics remind favela residents that traffickers control the means of violence in the favela, even as these traffickers attempt to convey that they are loyal to "the favela community."

As I have demonstrated in earlier work, Pentecostal adherents in the favelas of Rio de Janeiro regularly described carioca funk as the quintessential "music of the world," in opposition to gospel music, the "music of God" (Oosterbaan 2008, 2009). Carioca funk features explicit lyrics and is generally accompanied by erotic dance moves. Furthermore, evangelical inhabitants view the public consumption of drugs and alcohol during the bailes funk as deeply immoral. The rise of gospel funk therefore begs for a deeper explanation that clarifies how the shift I described above could occur.

Based on an analysis of gospel funk and interviews with gospel funk artists, I argue that the growing acceptance of gospel funk among Pentecostal adherents in Rio de Janeiro depends on a cultural reworking of the music (and its performance) with the help of evangelical rhetoric and style. To understand how gospel funk has been made acceptable, it is important to remember the insightful work of Jay Howard and John Streck, who have analyzed the incorporation of popular music styles in CCM in the United States. According to Howard and Streck, genres should not be conceived as static forms but rather as temporary expressions of an ongoing process that involves negotiations between artists, producers, critics, and audiences and is ultimately about the reproduction of community. In the same vein as CCM, Brazilian gospel can be conceived as a "splintered" art world "characterized by distinct and occasionally competing rationales for the forms that are created" (1999, 13). However, understanding the transformation of the boundaries of Brazilian gospel requires an understanding of the ways in which Brazilian music styles are connected to Brazilian social life.[5]

In contrast to a common approach that analyzes evangelical genre change solely in terms of market dynamics, I argue that the acceptance of gospel funk rests on religious and ethical considerations that should not be dismissed as superficial. One of the important motivations for artists is the profound wish to reach out to favela youth by way of gospel funk in order to save them from the perils of favela life. While market forces surely play an important part in the reproduction and appeal of gospel funk, it makes little sense to reduce deeply felt religious and ethical considerations to market forces, not in the least because evangelical producers and consumers are at times very critical of those forces themselves.

Controversies concerning music styles in Brazilian evangelical circles tell us much about what Timothy Rommen (2007) has described as the "ethics of style." As Rommen demonstrates, evangelicals in Trinidad experience music style as closely connected to the habits and customs of particular groups. Consequently, the introduction of new gospel styles generates an array of ethical discussions about the lifestyles of others and the boundaries of the religious community. Rommen's analysis of the interplay among music style, religious community, and ethics connects well with Birgit Meyer's (2009, 2010) conception of religious mediations in terms of "sensational forms." According to Meyer, sensational forms, which can be defined as "relatively fixed authorized modes of invoking and organizing access to the transcendental" (2009, 13), induce particular bodily sensations that bind practitioners with the divine and with one another. Meyer highlights the fact that sensational forms are not opposed to ethical norms. Aesthetic style structures religious experience and simultaneously clothes it as legitimate. The works of Rommen and Meyer point to the importance of form in religious worship and clarify why stylistic alterations can be experienced as extremely troublesome.

As I will show, gospel funk artists are aware that their music is controversial and that some people dismiss their use of carioca funk music as immoral. In order to make it morally and spiritually appropriate for their audiences to enjoy their music, gospel funk artists employ several strategies to sever the close links between the music form (style) and the (lifestyles of the) groups associated with it. Before exploring the incorporation of carioca funk in more detail, I will briefly describe some of the particularities of Brazilian Pentecostalism.

Pentecostalism in Brazil

Coinciding with Brazil's return to democracy in the late 1980s, Pentecostal churches expanded rapidly while the number of adherents of the Roman Catholic Church declined. The growth of evangelical churches in Brazil largely corresponds to the success of evangelicalism in the rest of Latin America and in most other parts of the world. In Latin America, evangelical groups have grown substantially since the 1980s (Boudewijnse, Droogers, and Kamsteeg 1998; Garrard-Burnett and Stoll 1993), and in various parts of Africa, Pentecostalism has become one of the most popular forms of Christianity (Meyer 2004). Indeed, as several authors have noted, the spread of evangelical Christianity runs markedly parallel to other well-known forms of cultural globalization (Coleman 2000; Csordas 2009; Droogers 2001; Martin 2002; Poewe 1994; Robbins 2004).

The Brazilian census of 2010 showed that 22 percent of the population described itself as *evangélico* (evangelical), a rise of approximately 61 percent in ten years.[6] In Brazil, the term *evangélicos* is used to denote the broader collection of Protestant Christians in Brazil.[7] Nevertheless, the majority of Brazil's 42.3 million evangélicos can be identified as Pentecostal, and much of so-called evangelical popular culture is produced and consumed in Pentecostal circles. Interestingly, the evangelical denomination that displays the biggest rise in affiliates (from 8.4 to 12.3 million in ten years) is, according to the 2010 census, the Assembléia de Deus (Assemblies of God), one of the oldest Pentecostal denominations in Brazil.[8]

The popularity of Pentecostal churches in Brazil should be understood in light of relative poverty and violence on the peripheries of Brazilian cities (Antoniazzi 1994; Lehmann 1996; Montes 1998) and the Pentecostal appropriation of modern mass media (Birman and Lehmann 1999; Corten 2001; Novaes 2002; Oro 2003). The transnational neo-Pentecostal Igreja Universal do Reino de Deus (Universal Church of the Kingdom of God), in particular, has become known for its use of communication networks. Over the last twenty-five years, this denomination has obtained one of the six national public television broadcast networks (Rede Record), mounted a professional website, and started its own publishing house and record company. It publishes the weekly newspaper *Folha Universal*, and it owns several radio stations.

Older Pentecostal denominations, such as the Assembléia de Deus, have also become much more visible and audible in the public domain, but the fragmented nature of many of them has thus far impeded the construction of a centralized media empire like that of the Igreja Universal. In line with a general increase in public presence, many of the Pentecostal churches have broken with their reluctance to interfere with "worldly politics" (Freston 2004; Oro 2003), and the Brazilian elections of the last fifteen years have demonstrated that their electoral base was quite solid. In their broadcasts and journals, Pentecostal politicians offer utopian visions of a better society, based on Christian moral values. They propose concrete practices such as church services, collective prayers, and the exorcism of evil spirits, which, according to adherents, counter the socioeconomic and personal problems of Brazilian citizens (Birman 2006).

Music, Pentecostalism, and the Market

In the United States and increasingly in Brazil, Christian music has become part of an industry with large revenues. In Brazil, it is no longer necessary to go to an evangelical shop to purchase gospel records, because they are on sale in large record stores all over the country. Moreover, the popularity of gospel music has recently prompted major record companies such as Sony Music and Som Livre (founded by Rede Globo) to contract Brazilian gospel singers for the first time in the history of these corporations.[9] Though most Brazilian gospel music can be categorized as pop rock songs or pop ballads, in the past decade, more evangelical performers have begun to adopt other music styles, such as reggae, *forró,* and hip-hop.

Several scholars analyze this recent expansion of gospel music in Brazil in terms of capitalist market dynamics and modern media culture, which slowly obfuscate stylistic borders between Christian and non-Christian music (see, for instance, Mendonça 2008). According to these scholars, the evangelical norm that a Christian song can be recognized by its Christian lyrics allows for an unprecedented incorporation of music styles. Clear lyrical distinctions remain between Christian music and "music of the world," even as their music styles begin to overlap.

Arguing along these lines, Magali Cunha writes that the "gospel explosion" in Brazil demonstrates how Brazilian evangelical culture has tried to come to terms with modernity without losing its traditional religious character, in keeping with its church-world / sacred-profane dualism; its individualistic, anti-ecumenical, and anti-intellectual tendencies; and its demonization of indigenous Brazilian and African culture (2007, 206). In addition, Cunha argues that the growth of gospel music in Brazil is possible because (1) it both fuses with *and* opposes other popular music styles; (2) market forces and mentalities support the inclusion of new genres in Brazilian gospel; and (3) borders between Christian and other popular forms are eroding. While I think that Cunha's points are compelling, she regards the incorporation of new styles first and foremost as expressions of the expansion of globalized capitalism and thus leaves very little space to understand religious transformations as more than reflections of market forces.

Against such a perspective, one could argue that worldwide religious transformations are much more ambiguous and involve much more than the breaching of fortifications that hinder the free circulation of commodities. First, Christianity and "the market" profoundly influence each other, as Laurence Moore (1994) has shown. Second, as Jean Comaroff has recently argued, "many of the features of contemporary Pentecostalism are in fact new and . . . share attributes with other revitalized faiths beyond the Christian fold. Moreover, . . . these developments are not merely endorsements or 'reflections' of free-market forms: they are reciprocally entailed with economic forces in the thoroughgoing structural reorganization I have identified in the current moment" (2010, 32). Under such reorganizations, Comaroff identifies the erosion of the institutional forms of liberal democracy and the growing tension between mobile capital and the nation-state.

Third, Pentecostalism itself harbors critiques of certain aspects of (economic) globalization. Fierce debates take place among evangelicals in Rio de Janeiro about the current changes in the gospel industry, and some of my Pentecostal informants (adamant gospel funk fans) criticized artists who seemed to have accepted Jesus only because the *gospel* market was booming. To picture Pentecostal adherents as people who naively follow the logic of the market deprives them of much of their agency and ethical judgment.[10]

Fourth, not all popular gospel music has the same status. While someday gospel funk may be considered uncontroversial, during my research it was still considered problematic by some. Though very popular, gospel funk is mostly presented as *estratégia* (strategy)—music made to attract teenagers who would otherwise opt for the worldly equivalent of the style. It is risky to reason that so-called strategic gospel music styles will necessarily possess the same meaning or acquire the same status as other gospel music styles. In the social worlds of Brazilian Pentecostals, these styles are employed and evaluated differently.[11] From a theoretical perspective, we should be wary of teleological arguments about the power of the market to eventually include all genres as equally fit for religious experience, because they obscure the power struggles that are taking place and the open-endedness of their outcome.

Reworking Carioca Funk

Not long after attending the youth service where Adriano performed, I visited a Gospel Fest Jovem (Youth Gospel Party) in the *complexo do Maré*, a conjunction of favelas in the northern zone of Rio de Janeiro. After passing an armed teenager who kept track of the movement in the favela, I reached the former factory that now served as a building for community festivities. As announced, the main performers at the Gospel Fest Jovem were Adriano Gospel Funk and LC Satrianny, both gospel funk artists with increasing fame in Rio de Janeiro.

The evangelical adoption of carioca funk music started with the Grupo Yehoshua in the early 1990s (Pinheiro 1998). During my research among adherents of Pentecostal churches in 2002 and 2003, I did not encounter a single adolescent who listened to gospel funk. Conversely, during my research in 2011, many teenagers expressed their liking for gospel funk, and many of my informants, including several artists, agreed that it was Adriano Gospel Funk who paved the way for the broadened possibilities of performing and listening to gospel funk in Rio de Janeiro.

Adriano Gospel Funk

Adriano, born and raised in a small municipality on the border of the city of Rio de Janeiro, started making gospel funk in 2003. Although Adriano is a member of the Igreja do Nazareno (Church of the Nazarene), an evangelical church that does not define itself as Pentecostal,[12] he frequently performs at Pentecostal churches and venues.[13] More importantly, he is very popular among adolescent members of Pentecostal churches in Rio de Janeiro. As he explained during an interview with me, it was incredibly hard to convince people that his music was appropriate for worship during the first years of his career. People wrote him disapproving emails in which they accused him of making "music of the flesh" and urged him to convert. According to Adriano, people gradually began to accept him because they saw the fruits of his work. More and more teenagers claimed to have accepted Jesus or returned to the church after hearing Adriano's music; this, according to Adriano, is the irrefutable sign that the Lord has blessed his endeavor to use funk.

Interestingly, arguments against the use of carioca funk also provide Adriano and his gospel funk colleagues with a powerful counterargument. Carioca funk is the most popular music among the favela youth, and many Pentecostal favela residents understand funk parties to be dangerous forms of entertainment that lead adolescents down demonic trails. According to Adriano, his gospel funk gives teenagers a chance to participate in the popular culture of the favela without risk and with the prospect of eventually choosing the right path over the many seductions and dangers that favela life offers.

In making gospel funk, Adriano is propelled by a genuine desire to reach people who have been brought up with carioca funk music by "speaking their language"; he wishes to use the very kind of music that will potentially lead them astray to save them. However, as Adriano himself indicated, some evangélicos were particularly wary about his attempts to use carioca funk, because it obfuscates the difference between genuine "music of God" and "music of the world." In response, Adriano explained that a number of crucial elements need to be safeguarded to distinguish gospel funk from ordinary carioca funk and to make sure that the music can perform its spiritual function to heal and save people.

First, the lyrics should, beyond a doubt, communicate that a song is Christian. Weaving biblical phrases into the text and explicitly invoking the Lord's name is customary, but gospel lyrics also regularly remind listeners to be watchful for demonic seduction and to critically evaluate the people, practices, and things they encounter. Take, for example, the sixth track, "Chuta que é laço" (Kick that which ties you down), on Adriano's CD of the same name:

Conte de um até três	Count from one to three
Antes de partir pro abraço	Before starting to embrace
Se não for benção de Deus	If it is not blessed by God
Sai correndo que é laço	Get away from that which ties you down
A embalagem é bonita mas tenho que analisar	The wrapping is beautiful but I have to analyze
Se for de Deus eu abraço	If it is of God I embrace [it]
Se não for chuta que é laço	But if it is not, kick that which ties you down
Chuta, chuta, chuta que é laço (4×)	Kick it, kick it, kick that which ties you down (4×)

Strikingly, Adriano's gospel funk song communicates the very same message that many evangelicals voiced in opposition to funk music. Many evangelicals regard funk as a suspicious style on account of its links to funk proibidão, the bailes funk, and the perceived immoral behavior of audiences. As a consequence, critics of gospel funk doubt that the carioca funk style can be used for worship. "Chuta que é laço" cleverly responds to this critique by incorporating it in a gospel funk song. The lyrics of "Chuta que é laço" are not only definitively Christian but also comment on evangelical discussions about the relation between form and content. Adriano attempts to sever the existing relation by stressing that one should not be seduced by the "wrapping" but rather analyze whether God has blessed the content.

Second, Adriano believes that the performer of the music should clearly be a person of God. Since the sacred condition of gospel music is partly dependent on the sanctified status of its performer(s), gospel artists do their best to demonstrate that they have accepted Jesus as savior. They generally preach against immoral behavior and take care not to display or encourage illicit sexual behavior, or to consume alcohol and drugs. It is also important that pastors and religious leaders authorize gospel funk artists as legitimate. Indeed, the pastor of the Church of the Nazarene gave Adriano his blessing to pursue a gospel funk career.

Last, the consecrated condition of gospel is also dependent on extramusical behavior during shows and performances. Specifically in relation to funk music, this concerns the erotic nature of dancing. Bailes funk, funk lyrics, and representations of carioca funk are riddled with sexual connotations, sexual movements, and erotic encounters. Therefore, as Adriano and members of his crew told me, they all remain very alert during gospel performances to prevent audience members from dancing erotically. In the words of Adriano,

> This month I was singing in a club, and during my performance, I saw a girl dancing with her hands on her knees [that is, wiggling her bottom provocatively]. In such a case, I stop singing, ask for attention, and while mimicking the movements of that person, I ask "Do you worship the Lord in this way?" I say it with a smile but then I explain, "Your body is the temple of the Holy Spirit, so worship the Lord with your best dance." Generally, people understand it and start to dance differently. . . . My crew has the authority to approach people who dance like that. To tap them on the back and tell them, "You are exaggerating [*exagerando*]." When people continue, they are asked to leave the event. What would

happen if someone would pick up a girl while I am singing and take her to a motel to do all kinds of things . . . lead her to perdition? It would be my responsibility. . . . Clearly, we have to earn something, but we also have to watch the salvation of the people.[14]

As the last sentence indicates, Adriano is well aware of the tensions between the desire to earn income and his moral responsibilities as a gospel artist. Moreover, as we will see below, Adriano's considerations resonate with the ideas and practices of other gospel funk artists.

LC Satrianny

LC Satrianny, who also performed at the Gospel Fest Jovem, was born and raised in the complexo do Maré and is a member of the Igreja Ministério Vida Plena (Ministry of Full Life Church), part of the denomination Assembléia de Deus. In contrast to Adriano, Satrianny had built a modest career as carioca funk artist before turning to gospel funk in 2007. Satrianny subsequently presented himself as "ex–MC Furacão 2000." (Furacão 2000 is one of the most popular organizations that produce bailes funk in Rio de Janeiro. To perform at Furacão 2000 events generally means that one has made it in the world of funk.) In Brazil, one regularly encounters gospel artists known as *ex-pagodeiros* (former *pagode* singers) or *ex-funkeiros* (former funk artists), who are presented in popular media as formerly belonging to "the world." While one might at first assume that such explicit display of one's worldly past would hinder full acceptance as a consecrated artist, these labels generally serve the purpose of demonstrating the unlimited powers of the Lord to save people who were once in the hands of the devil (Oosterbaan 2009).

In keeping with the desire to maintain clear demarcations between funk artists *do mundo* (of the world) and gospel funk artists, Satrianny changed his artist name from MC Satrianny to LC Satrianny. As he put it, "I was *mestre de cerimônia* [master of ceremonies], but now I am *levita de cristo* [Levite, gospel musician]."[15] In addition to modifying their names, converted gospel artists commonly transform older songs into gospel songs by changing the lyrics. Satrianny, for example, took a song that he had performed during his Furacão 2000 period and rewrote it as the song "Quem vai pra gloria" (Who aspires to glory). As he explained, with these alterations he transformed a "malediction [*maldição*] into a blessing [*bença*]."

According to Satrianny, it is very important to make gospel funk because favela teenagers adore funk music and want to dance. Evangelical teenagers should also have this opportunity. Satrianny contends that this should not be regarded as the corrosion of Christian values; rather, it is possible to *modernizar sem se mundanizar* (modernize without becoming worldly), to have *liberdade não libertinagem* (liberty but no licentiousness). Moreover, "funk is an evangelical strategy. Funk is bait to fish for the youth who are lost in the world, to get them in here [the church]. The teenagers come to dance, but in the middle of the baile you stop to address them, urge them to drink some water, and listen to the words of the pastor present."

Similar to Adriano, Satrianny emphasizes that the difference between funk of "the world" and gospel funk is evident in the way that adolescents dance, and he considers it his responsibility to scrutinize the events at which he performs. He regularly surveys the dance moves of his audiences. But, in his opinion, people generally do not need much correction; girls do not rapidly lower their bottoms to the ground while dancing, primarily because his lyrics do not call for this kind of erotic behavior.

Interestingly, some of Satrianny's lyrics remain close to the "classical" content of funk songs. Funk proibidão songs regularly feature references to gangs (*bondes*) that control particular favelas or areas (see Sneed 2007). Satrianny's lyrics, in turn, make reference to the power of the Lord, using slang ordinarily reserved for funk proibidão. Take, for instance, the following song written by Satrianny, entitled "Comboio chapa crente":

Vem com o bonde abençoado	Come with the blessed gang
Aumenta o som do radio	Raise the volume of the radio
Arrasta a mesa e o sofá	Move the table and the couch
Que o comboio chapa crente	The blazing gang of believers
Já ta entrando no ar	Is entering the air
Jesus Cristo no controle	Jesus Christ in control
Aqui é só unção	Here is it only anointment
Vem comigo nessa onda	Come with me on this wave
Pra curtir o nosso som	To enjoy our sound

As the lyrics show, Satrianny uses typical funk proibidão references to bondes that control favelas. Yet, instead of referring to drugs traffickers, Satrianny heralds a bonde of blessed people who work in the service of Jesus Christ.

The title of the track is a play on words, incorporating typical Rio de Janeiro slang. In general, people use the term *chapa quente* to describe a favela with many violent confrontations. *Comboio chapa crente*, which can be translated as "blazing gang of believers,"[16] hints at the courage and strength of evangelicals who operate in the favelas of Rio de Janeiro and save teenagers who might otherwise be seduced to follow the road to perdition.

Conclusion

In general, gospel singers and musicians who wish to incorporate new styles attempt to sever the rigid connections between the music form (style) and the (lifestyles of the) groups associated with it in order to make it spiritually appropriate for them and their audiences. In the case of carioca funk, such incorporation is complicated because of its association with funk proibidão, the erotic dance of bailes funk, and the perils of favela life. However, according to gospel funk artists, the incorporation of carioca funk is desirable and justifiable because it lures teenagers away from the perceived dangers of the bailes funk. As I have shown, gospel funk performers attempt to rework the music by including critiques of worldly phenomena in their gospel funk lyrics or by replacing the common reverence for gangs in funk proibidão with admiration for a *bonde abençoado* (blessed gang). In addition, gospel funk artists consider it their responsibility to safeguard the boundaries between ordinary carioca funk and gospel funk by inspecting dance moves during gospel parties. How Brazilian gospel funk artists critique and rework carioca funk bears many resemblances to how Trinidadian gospel dance hall artists use lyrics to "warn against the very issues that so concern church leaders" (Rommen 2007, 112).

Gospel funk performers do not regard their work as facile or uncontroversial. They are aware that some people suspect that religious conversions are the outcome of a growing gospel market and understand that their reputation as gospel performers stands or falls with their moral posture. In general, discourse about which gospel styles are appropriate also involves discussions of fame and money. Gospel singers who are suspected of performing for money instead of genuinely worshipping God run the risk of criticism specifically when they continue to produce the "worldly" style of music they did in the past. Gospel funk artists do not operate outside of capitalist modes of production and late modern forms of consumption; nevertheless, as I have argued, the gospel funk artists whom I interviewed in Rio de Janeiro are driven by a profound desire to reach and convert teenagers. They are bound by ethical norms and motivated by religious dreams that cannot be wholly reduced to the logic of globalized capitalism. Whereas Adriano does not deny that he likes to earn a living through his performances, it would be far too crude to insist that the rise of gospel funk is primarily an expression of the global reign of free market forces.

NOTES

1. To listen to one of the popular tracks that Adriano performed that night, "Chuta que é laço" (Kick that which ties you down), see "Adriano Gospel Funk (xuta q e laço)" (2008). I will discuss the contents of this track later on in this chapter.

2. See, for example, the website of the popular gospel radio station Radio 93, based in Rio de Janeiro and part of the company MK: http://www.radio93.com.br.

3. For a quick overview of some of the popular gospel artists and gospel music styles of Brazil, see, for example, the website of Gmúsica: http://musica.gospelmais.com.br.

4. Several examples of gospel funk music, including the songs of LC Satrianny, an artist whose work I discuss in this chapter, can be found on the website of Batidão Gospel: O Batidão do Crente (Gospel Beat: The Beat of the Believer). See http://www.batidaogospel.com.

5. Of course, ethnomusicologists made this argument some time ago (Merriam 1964; Blacking 1987).

6. According to the Instituto Brasileiro de Geografia e Estatística (Brazilian Institute of Geography and Statistics), http://www.ibge.gov.br/home/presidencia/noticias/noticia _visualiza.php?id_noticia=2170&id_pagina=1.

7. Evangélicos often define themselves as a unified group; the process of unity has been supported by political transformations and the consumption of "evangelical" products across denominations.

8. See the tables on the Instituto Brasileiro de Geografia e Estatística's web page "Censo Demográfico 2010: Características gerais da população, religião e pessoas com deficiência," at http://www.ibge.gov.br/home/estatistica/populacao/censo2010/caracteristicas_religiao _deficiencia/caracteristicas_religiao_deficiencia_tab_pdf.shtm. See also *Folha de São Paulo* (2012).

9. In 2012, Sony Music contracted the popular gospel singer Irmão Lázaro, originally part of the well-known Afro-Brazilian percussion group Olodum. See his page on Sony Music Gospel's website: http://www.gospelsonymusic.com.br/artist/lázaro. In January 2014, for the first time, Som Livre contracted a well-known Brazilian Pentecostal singer, Andrea Fontes, formerly contracted by the record company MK Music (Chagas 2014). For a sample of her work at MK Music, see http://www.andreafontes.com.br.

10. Ironically, evangelical informants in Rio de Janeiro claimed that Sony and Globo are interested in gospel music because, contrary to so-called secular music, only a small portion of evangelical music is copied and sold illegally or freely downloaded (*pirateria*). See also the popular magazine *Veja* (Levino 2011).

11. For a detailed example of the variety of meanings attributed to different gospel music styles, see the work of Timothy Rommen (2007).

12. Originally, the Church of the Nazarene was known as the Pentecostal Church of the Nazarene. It changed its name, among other reasons, to distinguish itself from churches where glossalalia is practiced, which the doctrine of the Church of the Nazarene opposes.

13. For instance, Adriano performed at the anniversary party for the well-known Rio de Janeiro pastor Marcos Pereira of the Igreja Assembléia de Deus dos Últimos Dias in 2010.
14. Personal interview with Adriano, March 25, 2011 (translation mine).
15. All quotations are from a personal interview with LC Satrianny, March 25, 2011 (translation mine).
16. The title *levita* is derived from the Bible and refers to the descendants of Levi (the Levites), who became responsible for the music in the Temple.
17. *Crente*, which literally means "believer," is a common term for evangelicals in Brazil.

REFERENCES

"Adriano Gospel Funk (xuta q e laço)." 2008. YouTube video, 3:06. Posted by raeleejuuh, May 18. http://www.youtube.com/watch?v=KormZVnIoeg.
Antoniazzi, Alberto. 1994. "A Igreja Católica face a expansão do Pentecostalismo." In *Nem anjos nem demonios*, edited by Alberto Antoniazzi, 17–23. Petrópolis: Editora Vozes.
Birman, Patricia. 2006. "Future in the Mirror: The Media, Evangelicals, and Politics in Rio de Janeiro." In *Religion, Media, and the Public Sphere*, edited by Birgit Meyer and Annelies Moors, 52–72. Bloomington: Indiana University Press.
Birman, Patricia, and David Lehmann. 1999. "Religion and the Media in a Battle for Ideological Hegemony: The Universal Church of the Kingdom of God and TV Globo in Brazil." *Bulletin of Latin American Research* 18 (2): 145–64.
Blacking, John. 1987. *"A Commonsense View of All Music": Reflections on Percy Grainger's Contribution to Ethnomusicology and Music Education*. Cambridge: Cambridge University Press.
Boudewijnse, Barbera, André Droogers, and Frans Kamsteeg, eds. 1998. *More than Opium: An Anthropological Approach to Latin American and Caribbean Pentecostal Praxis*. Lanham, Md.: Scarecrow Press.
Chagas, Tiago. 2014. "Andrea Fontes assina contrato com a Som Livre e se torna primeira cantora pentecostal da história da gravadora." Gmúsica, January 16. http://musica .gospelmais.com.br/andrea-fontes-assina-som-livre-primeira-pentecostal-gravadora -27296.html.
Coleman, Simon. 2000. *The Globalisation of Charismatic Christianity: Spreading the Gospel of Prosperity*. Cambridge: Cambridge University Press.
Comaroff, Jean. 2010. "The Politics of Conviction: Faith on the Neo-liberal Frontier." In *Contemporary Religiosities: Emergent Socialities and the Post–Nation State*, edited by Bruce Kapferer, Kari Telle, and Annelin Eriksen, 17–38. Oxford: Berghahn Books.
Corten, André. 2001. "Transnationalised Religious Needs and Political Delegitimisation in Latin America." In *Between Babel and Pentecost: Transnational Pentecostalism in Africa and Latin America*, edited by André Corten and Ruth Marshall-Fratani, 106–23. Bloomington: Indiana University Press.
Cox, Harvey. (1995) 2001. *Fire from Heaven: The Rise of Pentecostal Spirituality and the Reshaping of Religion in the Twenty-First Century*. Cambridge, Mass.: Da Capo Press.
Csordas, Thomas J. 2009. "Introduction: Modalities of Transnational Transcendence." In *Transnational Transcendence: Essays on Religion and Globalization*, edited by Thomas J. Csordas, 1–29. Berkeley: University of California Press.
Cunha, Magali do Nascimento. 2007. *A explosão gospel: Um olhar das ciências humanas sobre o cenário evangélico no Brasil*. Rio de Janeiro: Mauad.

Droogers, André. 2001. "Globalisation and Pentecostal Success." In *Between Babel and Pentecost: Transnational Pentecostalism in Africa and Latin America*, edited by André Corten and Ruth Marshall-Fratani, 41–61. Bloomington: Indiana University Press.

Folha de São Paulo. 2012. "Assembleia de Deus atrai 3,9 milhões de novos evangélicos." June 30. http://www1.folha.uol.com.br/fsp/poder/51844-assembleia-de-deus-atrai-39-milhoes-de-novos-evangelicos.shtml.

Freston, Paul. 2004. "Evangelical Protestantism and Democratization in Contemporary Latin America and Asia." *Democratization* 11 (4): 21–41.

Frith, Simon. 1996. "Music and Identity." In *Questions of Cultural Identity*, edited by Stuart Hall and Paul du Gay, 108–27. London: Sage.

Garrard-Burnett, Virginia, and David Stoll, eds. 1993. *Rethinking Protestantism in Latin America*. Philadelphia: Temple University Press.

Hackett, Rosalind I. J. 1998. "Charismatic/Pentecostal Appropriation of Media Technologies in Nigeria and Ghana." *Journal of Religion in Africa* 28 (3): 258–77.

Howard, Jay R., and John M. Streck. 1999. *Apostles of Rock: The Splintered World of Contemporary Christian Music*. Lexington: University Press of Kentucky.

Keil, Charles, and Steven Feld. 1994. *Music Grooves: Essays and Dialogues*. Chicago: University of Chicago Press.

Lehmann, David. 1996. *Struggle for the Spirit: Religious Transformation and Popular Culture in Brazil and Latin America*. Cambridge: Polity Press.

Levino, Rodrigo. 2011. "Música gospel: Trinados, fé e dinheiro." *Veja*, November 11. http://www.veja.abril.com.br/noticia/entretenimento/musica-gospel-trinados-fe-e-dinheiro.

Maffesoli, Michel. 1996. *The Contemplation of the World: Figures of Community Style*. Minneapolis: University of Minnesota Press.

Martin, David. 2002. *Pentecostalism: The World Their Parish*. Malden, Mass.: Blackwell.

Mendonça, Joêzer de Souza. 2008. "O Evangelho segundo o Gospel: Mídia, música pop e Neopentecostalismo." *Revista do Conservatório de Música da UFPel* 1:220–49.

Merriam, Alan P. 1964. *The Anthropology of Music*. Evanston: Northwestern University Press.

Meyer, Birgit. 2004. "Christianity in Africa: From African Independent to Pentecostal-Charismatic Churches." *Annual Review of Anthropology* 33:447–74.

———. 2009. "Introduction: From Imagined Communities to Aesthetic Formations: Religious Mediations, Sensational Forms, and Styles of Bonding." In *Aesthetic Formations: Media, Religion, and the Senses*, edited by Birgit Meyer, 1–28. New York: Palgrave MacMillan.

———. 2010. "Pentecostalism and Globalization." In *Studying Global Pentecostalism: Theories and Methods*, edited by Allan Anderson, Michael Bergunder, André Droogers, and Cornelis van der Laan, 113–30. Berkeley: University of California Press.

Miller, Donald E., and Tetsunao Yamamori. 2007. *Global Pentecostalism: The New Face of Christian Social Engagement*. Berkeley: University of California Press.

Montes, Maria L. 1998. "As figuras do sagrado: Entre o público e o privado." In *História da vida privada no Brasil*, vol. 4, edited by Lilia Moritz Schwarcz, 63–171. São Paulo: Companhia das Letras.

Moore, R. Laurence. 1994. *Selling God: American Religion in the Marketplace of Culture*. New York: Oxford University Press.

Novaes, Regina R. 2002. "Crenças religiosas e convicções politicas: Fronteiras e passagens." In *Política e cultura: Século XXI*, edited by L. C. Fridman, 63–98. Rio de Janeiro: Relume Dumará.

Oosterbaan, Martijn. 2008. "Spiritual Attunement: Pentecostal Radio in the Soundscape of a Favela in Rio de Janeiro." *Social Text* 26 (3): 123–45.

———. 2009. "Sonic Supremacy: Sound, Space, and the Politics of Presence in a Favela in Rio de Janeiro." *Critique of Anthropology* 29 (1): 81–104.

Oro, Ari Pedro. 2003. "A política da Igreja Universal e seus reflexos nos campos religioso e político Brasileiros." *Revista Brasileira de Ciências Sociais* 18 (53): 53–69.

Pinheiro, Márcia Leitão. 1998. "O proselitismo evangélico: Musicalidade e imagem." *Cadernos de Antropologia e Imagem* 7 (2): 57–67.

Poewe, Karla, ed. 1994. *Charismatic Christianity as a Global Culture.* Columbia: University of South Carolina Press.

Robbins, Joel. 2004. "The Globalization of Pentecostal and Charismatic Christianity." *Annual Review of Anthropology* 33:117–43.

Rommen, Timothy. 2007. *"Mek Some Noise": Gospel Music and the Ethics of Style in Trinidad.* Berkeley: University of California Press.

Sansone, Livio. 2001. "Não-trabalho, consumo e identidade negra: Uma comparação entre Rio e Salvador." In *Raça como retórica*, edited by Yvonne Maggie and Claudia Barcellos Rezende, 155–83. Rio de Janeiro: Civilização Brasileira.

Sneed, Paul. 2007. "Bandidos de Cristo: Representations of the Power of Criminal Factions in Rio's Proibidão Funk." *Revista de Música Latinoamericana* 28 (2): 220–41.

Stokes, Martin. 1997. "Introduction: Ethnicity, Identity, and Music." In *Ethnicity, Identity, and Music: The Musical Construction of Place*, edited by Martin Stokes, 1–28. Oxford: Berg.

Turino, Thomas. 2008. *Music as Social Life: The Politics of Participation.* Chicago: University of Chicago Press.

Conclusion

Improvisation, Indigenization, and Inspiration: Theological Reflections on the Sound and Spirit of Global Renewal

Amos Yong

The preceding pages have opened windows onto the music and worship of the global pentecostal and charismatic renewal. More empirically oriented readers have had the benefit of case studies and ethnographies of praise and worship and of music production practices, while the more conceptually inclined have been able to appreciate how these concrete analyses illuminate existing theoretical models, even as they generate alternative ways of thinking about the interface of musicology and pentecostal studies, both broadly considered. Musicologists and ethnomusicologists can see how the study of global renewal extends contemporary discussion and debates in their disciplines, just as scholars of pentecostal studies have been treated to the kind of substantial musicological investigations of these movements in a global context that build on other, more preliminary discussions.

In these concluding pages, I reflect as one trained in theological studies about the relationship between pentecostal and charismatic musicking—using Christopher Small's term (as mediated through Jean Kidula's chapter) to include the whole process of making and performing music and praise and worship—and pentecostal and charismatic theologizing. By the latter, I am referring not primarily to the more specialized academic field of pentecostal and charismatic theology that has recently been emerging (although I am not excluding this either), but to the broad scope of popular and implicit pentecostal and charismatic belief making, doctrinal formation, and theological construction in general.[1] The question I want to circle around is how pentecostal/charismatic musicking influences pentecostal/charismatic—or renewal (the all-encompassing term in what follows)—theologizing and vice versa. While the correlations cannot be tightly construed—after all, neither musicking nor theologizing is a mathematical science—I think that we can observe at least seven lines of resonance.

The first concerns what theological discourse calls the gospel-culture interface. If, in the theological world, there are multiple possibilities for interacting with culture,[2] we see this also in the global renewal movement's encounter with various musical cultures in local contexts. What we observe is that there is not one dominant approach across the board. Rejectionists such as the Diné Oodláni do not completely sever themselves from their past, even as redemptionists such as the Aboriginal pentecostals do not completely salvage all of theirs.[3] And the whole spectrum is occupied when we factor in how renewalists around the world are navigating how gospel worship intersects with cultural markets. Perhaps those who are engaging distinct local environments can be more contextually engaged (such as gospel funk artists Adriano and LC Satrianny in Rio de Janeiro) and those with more regional presence can develop a broader repertoire (such as Oro gospelers in Papua New Guinea); meanwhile, those with wider mass appeal (such as worship leader celebrities Israel Houghton and Marcos Witt) must have an arguably more generic gospel sound and message. Notice, then, that there is not one normative mode in and through which renewalists are engaging musical culture. Local agency and individual creativity play unpredictable roles here, as do globalization and market forces. If the classical renewalist instinct to make a break with the (cultural) past persists in some environments, one wonders when this set of sensibilities will seek to make such a break with the (global neoliberal economic) present. If the latter is particularly challenging for numerous reasons (many enumerated above), so also, upon closer examination, is the former. The tensions derive from the fact that Christians are "in the world," although their orientation is toward the coming reign of God. Theologically, then, this translates into the reality that there have been multiple modalities of gospel-culture interface, and these have to be discerned on a case-by-case basis. What works or is defensible (theologically and culturally) in one context may not be so in another, and even what works or is defensible in one situation at one time may be less viable in the same place at another time.

A second arena of resonance concerns the oral character of renewal spirituality, about which much has been noted in the preceding pages. This is most evident in its activity of musicking, understood broadly in this concluding chapter. Songwriting in particular and musicking more generally involve creativity, spontaneity, and contemporaneity, classic features of oral traditions. The theological tradition, of course, especially in the West, has become more textually oriented and even founded. Part of the reason for this has had to do with the perennial tension between charisma and institution, between prophet and priest. Renewal movements have had long histories of being marginalized from the institutional centers of Christendom because the charismatic claims of such "peoples of the Spirit" (Burgess 2011) have threatened the hierarchicalism and authoritarianism of the institutionalized church. Yet the history of song, music, and worship in the Western church is also one of ambivalence: on the one hand, the liturgy has been clearly distinguished from the church's dogmatic traditions; on the other hand, in some streams, it is arguable that the church has always sung its theological commitments and that the church's hymns are sometimes a more reliable indicator of what it believes than its confessions. My claim is that contemporary global renewal invites fresh reconsideration of the oral character of Christian belief and even confession. Rather than perceiving, from the perspective of the theological dogmatic tradition, that renewal churches are weak on doctrine or theology (in many cases because they lack confessional documents or creedal statements), perhaps we will find that the beliefs of these churches are emerging in their singing, praising, and worshipping, all vital aspects of their ecclesial and personal lives (see Boone 1996 and Mills 1998). In this case, the gap between liturgy and theology (or doctrine) is smaller than it may appear.[4]

A third resonating theme connects the affective and embodied character of renewal music and worship with contemporary theological developments. Undeniably, the growth of renewal Christianity around the world is related in part to how its oral spirituality embraces the emotional and kinesthetic dimensions of the Christian life. The expressive, intense, and participatory nature of pentecostal singing, dancing, and worshipping attracts many into its ranks, as several of the ethnographies in this volume depict (cf. Ma 2007). Theologians are gradually noticing that theological activity, once thought to be primarily if not predominantly cerebral, is also an embodied activity. This is related to the recognition not only that thinking itself is emotionally charged but that such is fundamental to human cognition. If the Western philosophical tradition since Plato has elevated the domain of abstract thought, the masses have always presumed that the body, the affections, and the emotions are part and parcel of human discursive activity. The chapters in this book thus reopen old questions about the embodied, affective, and emotional character of theological method. How do lying down and "soaking" impact our theologizing? How do chanting and gospel funk shape our attitudes toward and ideas about God? How is the digitization of the worship experience appropriated differently depending on the aesthetics of space—from storefronts and outdoor rallies to production studios and megachurches—and what are its attendant theological implications? Here, the geographies of sound and singing come to the fore, demanding a further account of how theologizing emerges from what people do (see Daniels 2008). And if music and worship are as central to human activity and meaning making as this volume suggests (and as many of us as readers can attest), then why has not more consideration been given among renewal theologians to the resonances between musical and worship styles and theological methodologies?

The preceding leads to a fourth line of inquiry regarding the interface between what might loosely be called matters of form (or style) and matters of function. Renewal orality and embodiment facilitate certain feelings or affects. Theologically, as Webb's chapter in this volume suggests, such affections can be understood eschatologically, signifying what Stephen Land (1993) calls the renewalist "passion for the kingdom." Yet part of the concern, as many other contributors to this book document, is the therapeutic existentialism symptomatic across large swaths of contemporary global renewal Christianity. What is disconcerting is how the repetitive, expressive, and popular style of much of renewal praise and worship not only revises (if not dismisses) traditional liturgies but caters almost only, and sometimes solely, to the affective domain. In the worst-case scenario, this means that contemporary renewal praise and worship are addressing human feelings but not the realities that are causing feelings in need of therapeutic attention (see Brandner 2011, 23). The result, combined with the eschatological sensibilities central to many renewal groups and churches, is (as noted by Gladwin) a kind of debilitating otherworldliness that disempowers Christian engagement with the present world and its challenges. Theologically, we now circle back to the more traditional concern enunciated a few paragraphs above: that the orality of the masses fosters a feelgood individualism that can derail, rather than foster, substantive theological reflection. The challenge, then, is how to nurture the affectively renewing and healing aspects of praise and worship without becoming theologically stale, vulnerable, or superficial. The renewalist response has been to continue the former (since it brings people into the church) but separate it from the more evangelical forms of theological and doctrinal sources, which are then adapted for renewal churches. Oftentimes, however, there is too much of a disconnect between evangelical cognitivism and intellectualism, which then leads to a dualism between renewal liturgy and (so-called) renewal theology. The way forward is to theologize through renewal music and worship both in order to critique their theologically debilitating and deficient aspects and to weave these into the heart of renewal theology so that there may be a seamlessness in how the movement sings and thinks (also the goal of Orthodox churches). On the musical front, we ought not minimize the work of those—such as pentecostal practitioners from the Great Southland—who are exemplary in showing how renewal sensibilities are not devoid of social implications.

Fifth, the global nature of contemporary renewal Christianity means that its musicking and theologizing are very diverse. Such diversity pertains not only at the level of individual performances but also at congregational levels. Yet our various congregational analyses register denominational and traditional differences. Pentecostal and charismatic renewal cuts across all ecclesial lines, so that its music reflects such diversity. However, as the chapters of this volume also show, neither congregations nor even denominations or whole churches are static (much less, of course, musical traditions—see, for example, Stowe 2011). The "bapticostalizing" of Faithful Central and the trans-, inter-, multi-, and non-denominationalizing of Hillsong are cases in point. In other cases, such as Nairobi Pentecostal Church, we see transitions at each of these levels, given the particular dynamic intersections navigated (colonial to postcolonial, classical mission church to indigenous valuation, pentecostalizing/charisma- tizing to globalizing trends, and so forth). The point is that just as there is not one musical style across the global renewal movement, neither should we expect one theological genre, form, or confession. Going even further, if the diversity of musicking is embraced, why not the diversity of theologizing? But, of course, such diversification can never be for its own sake, at least theolog- ically. The many tongues on the day of Pentecost each in its own way gave testimony to "God's deeds of power" (Acts 2:11, NRSV; see Yong 2005, chap. 4). Musicking and theologizing pluralism, then, is redemptive only when it gives such glory ultimately to God. This does not mean that it might not be contested as new forms and expressions emerge. It does mean that such evangelical and ecumenical diversity has theological limits set according to what the tradition believes to be God's revelation in Christ.

Having just championed the diversifying effects of musicking-theologizing resonance, I now turn to address another, countering trend. Contemporary globalization foregrounds this sixth set of resonances. The Reformation "priesthood of all believers" rendered a more democratic ecclesial space, one less demarcated by lines separating priests from laity. The renewal "prophethood of all believers" (Stronstad 1999)[5] promises an even more egalitarian and participatory field of operation, where anyone, anywhere, anytime—whether male or female, younger or older, rich or poor (cf. Acts 2:17–18)—can be a conduit for the charismatic gifts of the Holy Spirit. Translated onto a musical register, the Spirit's gifts can now be recognized as inspiring singers, songwriters, and musicians, alongside pastors, teachers, and evangelists. But of course the question persists: if all are equally and so inspired, then in effect none are. Mass mediatization may mean many things, but it does subject music to aesthetic criteria, perhaps alongside more theologically robust criteria: people vote on their "praise and worship" by downloading music, buying CDs, and attending concerts, and this may or may not be connected to their theological sensibilities, much less commitments (of which they may have none!). In this case, what the Spirit seems to be inspiring is not so much that each person in the image of God responds musically out of the depths of his or her historical, social, and culturally particular situation, but rather the creation of a globally marketable set of products, with the result that local languages, cultures, and traditions are now homogenized in global commerce. Theologically, my concern is that whereas the pentecostal and charismatic renewal of the early to mid-twentieth century promised a resurgence of the vernacular—in that people could praise and worship in their own languages and hence also theologize therein (see Sanneh 1989)—contemporary global renewal networks are transitioning us into a "global" cultural form and style (see Poewe 1994) that sometimes seems to have little room for and other times leaves behind altogether local dynamics and contributions. Renewal Christianity, and renewal music and worship, seemingly sits at an ambiguous crossroads. On the one hand, its aesthetics of style expects the ongoing diversification of renewal musical (and by extension theological) modes of creativity, production, and performance (used here descriptively rather than evaluatively). On the other hand, globalization trends suggest a reverse homogenization of musical (and by implication theological) repertoires. We observe these pressures in transnational developments such as Hillsong and Latin American evangelical-charismatic music (see Evans's and Gladwin's chapters above); hopefully, these will be productive tensions rather than incapacitating ones, both for music and worship and for theological reflection and work (Lanser 2008).

Last but not least, it almost goes without saying that music is a dynamic human, sociocultural, and historical construct, but I want to say this because of its theological and perhaps dogmatic implications. Human beings expect that the activity of musicking has a creative edge. While there still exists a kind of elitism in the discipline of musicology and the field of church music scholarship that privileges canonical traditions and in that sense defends a conservative approach even to musicking (as I am using it), contemporary musical culture within which renewal Christianity finds itself immersed rewards the imaginative, innovative, and forward-looking thrusts of musicking. Theology, on the other hand, has almost always been instinctively conservative. This is in part because even the Christian Scriptures urge attentiveness to and contention "for the faith that was once for all entrusted to the saints" (Jude 3, NRSV), and in part because of the processes of institutionalization following the growth of the church. This means, then, that the Christian tradition will always be suspicious of those who claim to be at the vanguard of a new theological discovery. Charismatic prophetism has certainly included its share of such pronouncements over the centuries, which explains why renewalists have always been on the margins rather than at the center of ecclesial history, as noted above. But if musicking makes room for, if not also prioritizes, this dynamic process, then why not theologizing? If musicking involves ongoing improvisation, then why not theologizing (Crawford 2013)? This is not an argument for anything goes; it is to point out the resonances between what people (renewalists in this case) do as musickers and as theologians. Renewalists thus often find themselves of two minds: a musical set of dispositions that is more future oriented and a theological mindset that is more conservative in nature. I would like to think that the parallels between musicking and theologizing invite not the abandonment of the past but its retrieval, reappropriation, and even renewal. If that is the case, then the past is not just restored (as if its former glory can be merely brought forward to the present) but redeemed: its failures and achievements are preserved and yet adapted for contemporary (and eschatological) purposes. This was how the day of Pentecost redeemed the many languages of Babel; it may also be how the ongoing and eschatological work of the Spirit redeems the many musics and theologies in anticipation of the coming reign of God.

None of these ruminations says much about what such a renewed theological imagination would look, sound, or feel like. We certainly can and should talk more about the content of a musically informed renewal theology. The theme of prosperity certainly needs to be attended to in the short and long term, especially given its central role in the global renewal movement (see Attanasi and Yong 2012). The crucial interconnections between the music industry and the church are a part of this discussion, as are the consumerist habits that many renewalists have been socialized into and have internalized. These motifs, touched on in many pages of this book, are nicely contrasted with the somber moods of the first two chapters. The healing power of a non-triumphalist liturgy such as soaking and the enabling role of lament (in the face of unanswered prayers) have been registered, even as their important functions need to be further explicated in renewal theological discourse.[6] All of these themes and many others broached in the pages of this volume beg for theological elucidation.

My focus in these concluding moments, however, has been on the resonances between musicking and theologizing, in particular the implications of how renewalists "do" praise and worship and how they might also "do" theology. I confess that these reflect my own interests as a pentecostal theologian concerned about methodological issues in the contemporary theological enterprise. I am convinced that part of the explanatory power of contemporary renewal lies in its musicking practices. If that is the case, then I want to urge theologians to pay more attention to what happens in the musicking process so that they may be able to think through the theological enterprise in similar fashion. I would particularly admonish renewal theologians not to merely borrow the theological repertoires of nonrenewal churches and traditions. While such cross-fertilization of theological reflection is important and necessary in the present ecumenical climate, uncritical adoption of the offerings of others risks undermining the vitality of renewal spirituality and practice. Instead, renewalists ought to think through their theological commitments from out of the depth of their liturgical, and musical, sensibilities so that there is greater congruence between the potency of their musicking and that of their beliefs. If and when this happens, renewalism will be known not only because of its spirituality (and musicking) but also because of its theology. That itself will signal the convergence of hearts and heads, of practices and beliefs, and a renewed global Christianity.[7]

NOTES

1. The questions related to theological methodology—the formal term in the theological guild for what I am here calling "theologizing"—are legion. For a substantive treatment, see Yong (2002).

2. H. R. Niebuhr's classic model (1951), one among many, suggests five possibilities: Christ against culture (breaking with the past); Christ of culture (embracing a form of cultural

Christianity); Christ above culture (wherein culture is fulfilled by Christ); Christ and culture in paradox (featuring persistent struggle between the two); and Christ transforming culture (Christ renewing culture). Not all of these are of equal value, at least not in the same sense in the same place and time; thus, evangelicals, as well as renewalists, debate the issues. One might be tempted to suggest how each of these categories is reflected in Christian music, but space constraints prohibit such elaboration.

3. Similar sophistication would be needed to describe what is happening in African pentecostal churches, which are making a break with the past and yet indigenizing their musical practices simultaneously. See Kalu (2010).

4. This would be a staple of Orthodox churches, whose liturgy is inseparable from their theology. However, Orthodoxy is just as much in need of renewal as other Christian traditions (see Nassif, forthcoming), and this itself may destabilize Orthodox theology more than even its practitioners would care to admit.

5. In fact, popular music, while awash in commercialism, can also function prophetically and redemptively, as Don Compier (2013, ch. 3) shows; see also Saliers (2007, chap. 5).

6. One might even say that the practice of soaking reflects a form of "soft lament" that waits on God to heal painful histories and experiences. Thanks to Austin Jacobs, an Evangel University (Springfield, Missouri) student, who coined this term in response to my discussion of this issue at a lecture on November 1, 2012.

7. Thanks to Dr. Michael Kolstad at Evangel University for an invitation to speak about aspects of this chapter at the university on November 1, 2012, a lecture from which the chapter's broad contours emerged.

REFERENCES

Attanasi, Katherine, and Amos Yong, eds. 2012. *Pentecostalism and Prosperity: The Socio-economics of the Global Charismatic Movement.* New York: Palgrave Macmillan.
Boone, R. Jerome. 1996. "Community and Worship: The Key Components of Pentecostal Christian Formation." *Journal of Pentecostal Theology* 8:129–42.
Brandner, Tobias. 2011. "Premillennial and Countercultural Faith and Its Production and Reception in the Chinese Context." *Asian Journal of Pentecostal Studies* 14 (1): 3–26.
Burgess, Stanley M. 2011. *Christian Peoples of the Spirit: A Documentary History of Pentecostal Spirituality from the Early Church to the Present.* New York: New York University Press.
Compier, Don. 2013. *Listening to Popular Music: Christian Explorations of Daily Living.* Minneapolis: Fortress Press.
Crawford, Nathan. 2013. *Theology as Improvisation: A Study in the Musical Nature of Theological Thinking.* Boston: Brill.
Daniels, David D., III. 2008. "'Gotta Moan Sometime': A Sonic Exploration of Earwitnesses to Early Pentecostal Sound in North America." *Pneuma* 30 (1): 5–32.
Kalu, Ogbu U. 2010. "Holy Praiseco: Negotiating Sacred and Popular Music and Dance in African Pentecostalism." *Pneuma* 32 (1): 16–40.
Land, Stephen J. 1993. *Pentecostal Spirituality: A Passion for the Kingdom.* Sheffield: Sheffield Academic Press.
Lanser, Alma. 2008. "Rap and Roots: Youth and Music in Immigrant Churches." In *A Moving God: Immigrant Churches in the Netherlands,* edited by Methteld Jansen and Hijme Stoffels, 159–75. Berlin: LIT.
Ma, Wonsuk. 2007. "Pentecostal Worship." *Asian Journal of Pentecostal Studies* 10 (1): 136–52.

Mills, Robert A. 1998. "Musical Prayers: Reflections on the African Roots of Pentecostal Music." *Journal of Pentecostal Theology* 6 (12): 109–26.

Nassif, Bradley. Forthcoming. "Religious Affections in the Byzantine Liturgy of St. John Chrysostom." In *The Spirit, Affectivity, and the Christian Tradition*, edited by Dale Coulter and Amos Yong. Notre Dame: University of Notre Dame Press.

Poewe, Karla, ed. 1994. *Charismatic Christianity as a Global Culture*. Charleston: University of South Carolina Press.

Saliers, Don E. 2007. *Music and Theology*. Nashville: Abingdon Press.

Sanneh, Lamin O. 1989. *Translating the Message: The Missionary Impact on Culture*. Maryknoll, N.Y.: Orbis Books.

Stowe, David W. 2011. *No Sympathy for the Devil: Christian Pop Music and the Transformation of American Evangelicalism*. Chapel Hill: University of North Carolina Press.

Stronstad, Roger. 1999. *The Prophethood of All Believers: A Study in Luke's Charismatic Theology*. Sheffield: Sheffield Academic Press.

Yong, Amos. 2002. *Spirit-Word-Community: Theological Hermeneutics in Trinitarian Perspective*. Burlington, Vt.: Ashgate.

———. 2005. *The Spirit Poured Out on All Flesh: Pentecostalism and the Possibility of Global Theology*. Grand Rapids, Mich.: Baker Academic.

CONTRIBUTORS

Peter Althouse (Ph.D. University of St. Michael's College at the University of Toronto) is Professor of Religion and Theology at Southeastern University in Florida. Publications include *Catch the Fire: Soaking Prayer and Charismatic Renewal* (Northern Illinois University Press); *Spirit of the Last Days: Pentecostal Eschatology in Conversation with Jürgen Moltmann* (T&T Clark); *The Ideological Development of "Power" in Early American Pentecostalism* (Edwin Mellen Press); *Winds from the North: Canadian Contributions to the Pentecostal Movement* (Brill); and *Perspectives in Pentecostal Eschatologies* (Pickwick Press).

Will Boone (Ph.D. University of North Carolina at Chapel Hill) is an ethnomusicologist who researches sound and dance in African American pentecostal worship. His work appears in the volume *Christian Congregational Music: Performance, Identity, and Experience* (Ashgate, 2013) and in several entries in the *Grove Dictionary of American Music* (2nd ed.).

Mark Evans (Ph.D. Macquarie University) is Head of the School of Communication at the University of Technology, Sydney. He previously served as Head of Media, Music, Communication, and Cultural Studies at Macquarie University from 2008–14. He is the coeditor of *Perfect Beat: The Pacific Journal of Research into Contemporary Music and Popular Culture* and author of the book *Open Up the Doors: Music in the Modern Church* (Equinox, 2006).

Ryan R. Gladwin (Ph.D. University of Edinburgh) is Assistant Professor of Christian Social Ministry at Palm Beach Atlantic University. He has published work and presented papers on social ethics, practical theology, pentecostalism, and Latin American and Latino/a theology and religion. He is currently working on a monograph on Latin American ecclesiology and social ethics.

Monique M. Ingalls (Ph.D. University of Pennsylvania) is Assistant Professor of Church Music at Baylor University. Published in the fields of ethnomusicology, media studies, hymnology, and religious studies, she is coeditor of *Christian Congregational Music: Performance, Identity, and Experience* (Ashgate, 2013). She is also cofounder of the Christian Congregational Music: Local and Global Perspectives conference and its affiliated Congregational Music Studies Network.

Birgitta J. Johnson (Ph.D. UCLA) is Assistant Professor of Ethnomusicology at the University of South Carolina. Her primary areas of research are African American music and music of the African diaspora in relation to the African musical continuum, musical change, identity, converging movements, and shared traditions. She is currently writing a book manuscript based on her ethnographic research of music, tradition, and contemporary liturgical worship trends entitled "Worship Waves, Navigating Identities: Music in the Black Church at the Turn of the Twenty-First Century."

Jean Ngoya Kidula (Ph.D. UCLA) is Associate Professor of Music (Ethnomusicology) at the University of Georgia in Athens, Georgia. Her publications include articles on Kenyan ritual and religious folk and popular music, and on musicians in the African Academy. She has also written on gospel music in North America and Africa. She is a coauthor of *Music in the Life of the African Church* (2008). Her latest monograph, *Music in Kenyan Christianity: Logooli Religious Song* (2013), has won the 2014 Kwabena Nketia Book Prize from the African Music Section of the Society for Ethnomusicology.

Miranda Klaver (Ph.D. Vrije Universiteit [VU] Amsterdam) is Assistant Professor of Religion and Media at the VU University Amsterdam. Trained as an anthropologist and theologian, she has published on Dutch evangelicalism and pentecostalism. Her research focuses on the interaction between transnational evangelical/pentecostal movements and Dutch Protestantism, and on the rise of transnational evangelical/pentecostal churches in global cities.

Andrew Mall (Ph.D. University of Chicago) is Visiting Assistant Academic Specialist in the Department of Music at Northeastern University in Boston. His research focuses on underground popular music and the contemporary Christian music recording industry. He has presented several papers at annual meetings of the Society for Ethnomusicology (SEM) and the International Association for the Study of Popular Music, U.S. Branch (IASPM-US) and is a contributor to the *Continuum Encyclopedia of Popular Music of the World* and the *Canterbury Dictionary of Hymnology*.

Kimberly Jenkins Marshall (Ph.D. Indiana University) is Assistant Professor of Anthropology at the University of Oklahoma. Blending approaches drawn from anthropology, ethnomusicology, and folklore studies, she researches the proliferation of pentecostalism in Native North America, specifically as it gains voice in expressive form at Navajo-led tent revivals. Her manuscript "Oodláni Resonance" is based on extensive ethnographic work with a Navajo-speaking, Navajo-led independent pentecostal church located in northwestern New Mexico and is currently under contract with the University of Nebraska Press.

Andrew M. McCoy (Ph.D. University of St. Andrews) is Director of the Center for Ministry Studies and Assistant Professor of Ministry Studies at Hope College in Holland, Michigan. He has also previously served as a scholar-in-residence with the Calvin Institute of Christian Worship at Calvin College in Grand Rapids, Michigan. He is currently researching the relationship between congregational worship practices and vocational discernment.

Martijn Oosterbaan (Ph.D. University of Amsterdam) is Associate Professor of Cultural Anthropology at Utrecht University. He has published on pentecostalism and media in Brazil and Europe. His research focuses on religious transformations in Brazil as a result of the widespread use of mass media and on Brazilian migration to Europe in relation to transnationalism, religion, and (new) media. Currently, he is codirecting a research program on the "popular culture of illegality," which focuses on the music, representation, and material culture of criminal organizations in Latin America; he is also codirecting a research program on women's soccer in the Netherlands. In both programs, Oosterbaan investigates contemporary intersections of religion and bodily culture.

Dave Perkins (Ph.D. Vanderbilt University) is Associate Director of the Religion in the Arts and Contemporary Culture Program in the Divinity School at Vanderbilt University. He began his scholarly career after a twenty-five-year career in the music industry. As a guitarist for hire, Perkins has built relationships through recording and live performance with many iconic American performers. He had a long tenure in the contemporary Christian music industry, where, as a songwriter, his songs were recorded by many notable artists and, as a record producer and session musician, he participated on numerous significant albums.

Wen Reagan is a Ph.D. candidate and James B. Duke Fellow at Duke University. He is currently writing a dissertation on the cultural history of contemporary worship music in America. Reagan also serves as the worship director at

Christ Community Church in Chapel Hill, North Carolina, and as an artist for Cardiphonia, a collaboration of songwriters committed to revitalizing traditional hymnody in new musical settings for the benefit of the church.

Tanya Riches holds an M.Phil. from Australian Catholic University and is currently pursuing a Ph.D. at Fuller Theological Seminary in Pasadena, California. The author of worship songs including "Jesus, What a Beautiful Name," she has led worship internationally, releasing her first solo worship album, *Grace*, in 2012. She is originally from Australia's Hillsong Church, where she directed choir and sang, as well as administrated Hillsong's youth band, United Live, from 1996 to 2003.

Michael Webb (Ph.D. Wesleyan University) is an ethnomusicologist and Senior Lecturer and Chair of the Music Education Unit in the Sydney Conservatorium of Music at the University of Sydney. Webb is a coauthor of the 2011 volume *Music in Pacific Island Cultures*, part of Oxford University Press's Global Music Series, and is currently completing a book on music and colonial culture, from 1875 to 1975, in the port town of Rabaul, Papua New Guinea. Since 2008, his research has concentrated on historical and contemporary aspects of Christian hymnody in urban Papua New Guinea and rural Vanuatu. He is also currently working on a film documenting a gospel hymn and indigenous dance tradition in the Maskelyne Islands, Vanuatu.

Michael Wilkinson (Ph.D. University of Ottawa) is Professor of Sociology at Trinity Western University in British Columbia. His publications include *The Spirit Said Go: Pentecostal Immigrants in Canada* (Peter Lang); *Canadian Pentecostalism: Transition and Transformation* (McGill-Queen's University Press); *Winds from the North: Canadian Contributions to the Pentecostal Movement* (Brill); *A Liberating Spirit: Pentecostals and Social Action in North America* (Pickwick Press); *Global Pentecostal Movements: Migration, Mission, and Public Religion* (Brill); and *Catch the Fire: Soaking Prayer and Charismatic Renewal* (Northern Illinois University Press).

Amos Yong (Ph.D. Boston University) is Professor of Theology and Mission and Director of the Center for Missiological Research at Fuller Theological Seminary in Pasadena, California. He is the author or editor of more than two dozen volumes, many of them on pentecostal-charismatic Christianity.

INDEX

Typeset by
CLICK! PUBLISHING SERVICES

Printed and bound by
SHERIDAN BOOKS

Composed in
MINION AND WHITNEY

Printed on
NATURES NATURAL

Printed in the USA
CPSIA information can be obtained
at www.ICGtesting.com
LVHW091726030724
784591LV00002BA/118

9 780271 066639